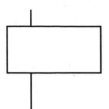

Becoming a teacher

Third edition

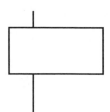

Becoming a teacher

Issues in secondary teaching

Third edition

Edited by
Justin Dillon and Meg Maguire

Open University Press

Open University Press
McGraw-Hill Education
McGraw-Hill House
Shoppenhangers Road
Maidenhead
Berkshire
England
SL6 2QL

email: enquiries@openup.co.uk
world wide web: www.openup.co.uk

and Two Penn Plaza, New York, NY 10121–2289, USA

First published 2007

A catalogue record of this book is available from the British Library

ISBN-10: 0 335 22144 0 (pb)   0 335 22145 9 (hb)
ISBN-13: 978 0 335 22144 8 (pb)   978 0 335 22145 5 (hb)

Library of Congress Cataloging-in-Publication Data
CIP data applied for

Typeset by RefineCatch Limited, Bungay, Suffolk
Printed in Poland OZ Graf S.A.
www.polskabook.pl

The *McGraw·Hill* Companies

To the memory of Rod Watson (1947–2007).
Our colleague and friend.

Contents

Notes on contributors

Chris Abbott taught in primary, secondary and special schools for 16 years before joining King's College London in 1994, and has taught on the English and ICT PGCE as well as developing Masters modules on information and communications technology (ICT), literacy and the Internet. His recent publications include *ICT: Changing Education* (2000), *Symbols Now* (2000), *SEN and the Internet: Issues for Inclusive Education* (2002) and *Symbols, Literacy and Social Justice* (2006). His research interests focus on ICT, literacy and inclusion, and he has led a series of projects on the use of symbols for communication and literacy.

Philip Adey taught science in a school in Barbados for some years before becoming involved in curriculum development and teacher education programmes in the Anglophone West Indies. This led to his questioning the nature of difficulty in science concepts, and a PhD on cognitive development in the Caribbean, which he pursued while working in the Concepts in Secondary Mathematics and Science Concepts Project at Chelsea College. After a spell with the British Council in Indonesia, he returned to Chelsea/King's College to work with Michael Shayer on CASE (Cognitive Acceleration through Science Education). This eventually required significant attention to the question of how teachers might effectively be helped to develop their practice. Adey is now Emeritus (that is, retired) Professor of Science, Cognition, and Education at King's.

Louise Archer is a reader in education policy at King's. Her research interests include issues of identity and inequality in relation to 'race'/ethnicity, social class and gender. Her publications include *Race, Masculinity and Schooling* (Open University Press, 2003), *Higher Education and Social Class* (with Alistair Ross and Merryn Hutchings, Routledge, 2003) and *Understanding Minority Ethnic Achievement* (with Becky Francis, Routledge, 2006).

Paul Black is Professor Emeritus of Science Education at King's. He was Chair of the Government's Task Group on Assessment and Testing in 1987–1988 and Deputy Chairman of the National Curriculum Council from 1989 to 1991. In the last few years, he has contributed to the work at King's on assessment for learning. This work has involved both research studies and development work with schools. The published reports, notably *Working Inside the Black Box* and *Assessment for Learning; Putting it into Practice*, have been widely read and have influenced practice in many schools.

Margaret Brown is a professor of mathematics education at King's. She has directed more than 25 research studies in the learning, teaching and assessment of mathematics, across all levels and ages. Before that she was a teacher in primary and secondary schools, and involved in teacher education. She has been a member of several government committees, chair of the Joint Mathematical Council, President of BERA, and currently chairs the education sub-panel for the 2008 RAE.

Ann-Marie Brandom taught religious education for ten years before joining King's in 1998. She is subject director for the RE PGCE course and teaches on the Masters course. Her research interests include assessment for learning. She was part of the King's research team involved with the education department in Jersey and has led a number of INSET courses on AfL. She co-edited the book, *Learning to Teach Religious Education in the Secondary School* (2000).

Jeremy Burke taught mathematics in London comprehensive schools for 17 years, including being a head of department and then a senior manager. At King's, he has had responsibilities for the PGCE in Mathematics, the MA course in 'Policy and the Mathematics Curriculum' and is currently programme director of the PGCE. His research interests are in the sociology of mathematics education, technology, pedagogy and pedagogic relations. He has published on teaching mathematics and the use of technology in education.

Simon Coffey taught languages for many years, both in the UK and abroad, before joining King's where he now teaches on the PGCE in modern foreign languages and is programme director for the BA/BSc with Education degrees. Simon is also involved in delivering the PGCE Professional Studies programme and is particularly interested in issues relating to pastoral care in schools. Other research interests include language learning and teaching methodology, internationalism and inclusive pedagogies. He has recently worked on projects researching citizenship education, primary–secondary transition and learner identities. Simon is co-author (with Jane Jones) of *Modern Foreign Languages: A Guide for Teachers* (2006).

Alan Cribb joined King's in 1990 having previously worked for the Centre for Social Ethics and Policy and the Department of Epidemiology and Social Oncology, University of Manchester. His research interests include moral and political philosophy and applied ethics. His most recent book is *Health and the Good Society: Setting Healthcare Ethics in Social Context* (2005), published by Oxford University Press.

Justin Dillon taught in London schools for ten years before joining King's in 1989. Since then he has been deputy director of the PGCE and science co-ordinator. He is currently subject director for chemistry and Professional

Studies co-ordinator. He has research interests in professional development and learning inside and outside the classroom. He has co-authored a range of edited collections including *Learning to Teach Science* (1995), *Becoming a Teacher* (1995, 2001 and 2007) and *The Re-emergence of Values in the Science Curriculum* (2007). He is an editor of the *International Journal of Science Education* and Chair of the London Wildlife Trust.

Peter Duncan is programme director for the postgraduate programmes in Health Promotion and Health and Society at King's. His research interests include health education and health promotion theory and practice, and the ethics of public health policy and interventions. He is the author of *Critical Perspectives on Health* (Palgrave Macmillan, 2007) and (with Alan Cribb) *Health Promotion and Professional Ethics* (Blackwell, 2002).

Brenda Gay has taught in both the independent and maintained sectors. She was headmistress of a girls' independent school and has worked in teacher education and educational research. She has recently retired as senior lecturer in classics education at King's where she was also subject director for the PGCE in Classics and taught on undergraduate and Masters programmes. Brenda has published in a wide range of areas, including religion in the independent school, spirituality, accountability, the management of conflict in the classroom and classics teaching and learning as part of global communication.

Sharon Gewirtz is a professor of education at King's. Her books include *Markets, Choice and Equity in Education* (with Stephen Ball and Richard Bowe, Open University Press 1995), *New Managerialism, New Welfare?* (with John Clarke and Eugene McLaughlin, 2000) and *The Managerial School: Post-welfarism and Social Justice in Education* (2001).

Roxy Harris is a senior lecturer at King's. He has worked extensively with teachers on questions of language and education. He has a particular interest in the relationships between language, power, ethnicity and culture, and has researched and published on these issues, including *My Personal Language History* (1988), *Language and Power* (1990) and *New Ethnicities and Language Use* (2006).

Christine Harrison is a lecturer at King's College London where she works on the PGCE and Masters courses. Chris was co-director of the influential King's-Medway-Oxfordshire Formative Assessment-Project and has advised government on the implementation of assessment for learning in England, Scotland and Jersey. Chris continues to research in the area of assessment and currently leads the Assessment for Learning research group with Paul Black.

John Head is a former secondary schoolteacher who has worked in the UK and the USA. His current research interests, as a visiting senior lecturer at King's, encompass psychology applied to issues of adolescence such as identity development and gender differences.

Jeremy Hodgen taught mathematics in primary and secondary schools before joining King's where he teaches on the PGCE, MA and doctoral programmes. His research interests include assessment, learning and teaching in mathematics education. He is co-author (with Dylan Wiliam) of *Mathematics Inside the Black Box* (2006).

Jill Hohenstein is a lecturer in the psychology of education at King's. Her primary area of expertise is in children's cognitive development in relation to their language environments, particularly in informal contexts. She has studied learning in the UK, the US and in Mexico, with speakers of English and Spanish.

Jane Jones taught for many years in primary and secondary schools in London and Kent. Her last school post was senior teacher responsible for profiling and assessment in a large comprehensive school in Wandsworth. Her research interests include school leadership and governance, counselling in schools, citizenship education and all aspects of language learning. She is responsible for modern foreign languages teacher education at King's and is a member of the Assessment for Learning Group. She directs the UK aspects of several EU-funded research projects.

Heather King joined King's in 2002 having previously worked as an education officer in a number of museums and international development agencies for nine years. She directed a five-year research project which examined learning in informal environments and the relationships between informal science institutions and schools. She is now evaluating the Permanent European Resource Centre for Informal Learning (PENCIL).

Constant Leung taught in schools and worked as advisory teacher and manager in local education authorities for 15 years. His research interests include curriculum development and language policy. He joined King's in 1999 and is active in promoting continuous professional development for teachers working with linguistically diverse students. He has published extensively on language education issues both nationally and internationally. His recent publications include *Reconfiguring Europe – The Contribution of Applied Linguistics* (co-edited with Jennifer Jenkins, 2006). He was appointed Professor of Educational Linguistics in 2005.

Meg Maguire taught for many years in London schools, including a spell as a headteacher. She has a long-standing interest in the life and work of school-teachers, teacher education and with the challenges of inner-city schooling. Her publications include, *Choice, Pathways and Transitions Post-16* (with Stephen Ball and Sheila Macrae, 2000) and *The Urban Primary School* (with Tim Wooldridge and Simon Pratt-Adams, 2006).

Alex Manning taught science in inner London schools for six years. She joined King's in 2003, and now co-ordinates the physics PGCE, in addition to being the deputy course director for the PGCE. Alex's research interests are initial teacher education, urban science education and teacher career trajectories.

Bethan Marshall taught English, media and drama for nine years in London comprehensives before taking up her current post at King's. She combined this job for five years with that of English adviser working in both the secondary and primary phases. She has written and commented extensively on English teaching and its assessment in academic journals and the media as well as in her book *English Teachers – The Unofficial Guide* (2003). She is also a member of the King's team working on formative assessment and was a co-author of their book *Assessment for Learning: Putting it into Practice* (2003).

Mike Poole taught physics and religious education for 14 years at Forest Hill School in London. He then spent three years preparing and broadcasting radio programmes on science and religion, and teaching part-time at King's, before becoming a full-time lecturer in science education. Currently Visiting Research Fellow in science and religion, he was presented in 1998 with an international award from the Templeton Foundation for quality and excellence in teaching science and religion. He has written a number of books, as well as some 70 papers and articles, on issues of science and religion, their relevance for science teachers, religious education specialists and for general readership.

Ian Stevenson taught mathematics and IT in London schools for ten years. He joined King's in 2004 after working at the London Institute of Education and the University of Leeds. His research interests include the design and evaluation of educational software, computer-based modelling, and learning non-euclidean geometry. He directed a project for Becta on 'ICT and Measures of Attainment', and co-directed the EU project 'Collaborative and Network Distributed Learning Environments' on sharing and reusing courseware using the Internet. Currently, he teaches on the ICT and mathematics PGCE courses at King's.

Dylan Wiliam taught in inner London for seven years before joining Chelsea College in 1984. The college later merged with King's where Dylan worked until 2003. During his time at King's, he ran the mathematics PGCE, spent four years as Head of School, and two years as Assistant Principal. In 2003, he moved to the USA, to work as Senior Research Director at the Educational Testing Service, and in 2006 he returned to the UK to take up the post of Deputy Director of the Institute of Education. His current main research interest is teacher professional development, with a particular focus on the use of assessment *for* learning.

Chris Winch taught in primary schools in Yorkshire for 11 years. He is currently Professor of Educational Philosophy and Policy at King's. His main research is in the areas of philosophy of education and vocational education. One of his current interests is in the nature of teaching as a profession. He is author of, among other books, *Philosophy and Educational Policy: a Critical Introduction* (2004), with John Gingell.

Andrew Wright is a lecturer in religious and theological education and co-ordinator of the Centre for Theology, Religions and Culture at King's. Before entering higher education, he was a secondary religious education teacher. He has taught extensively on PGCE and MA programmes, and now works mainly with doctoral students. He is the author of *Spiritual Pedagogy* (1998), *Spirituality and Education* (2000), *Religion, Education and Post-modernism* (2004), and co-editor, with Ann-Marie Brandom, of *Learning to Teach Religious Education in the Secondary School* (2000). He has just completed a book on truth in religious education. His research interests focus on the development of religious literacy.

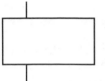

Foreword to the third edition

I am delighted to have been asked to write a foreword to the third edition of this best-selling book.

How well we cope in life, either as individuals or as nations, depends essentially on our knowledge, skills, creativity and attitudes. Teachers are critical in helping us to develop each of these qualities. So, ultimately, our future depends on the expertise and commitment of teachers.

This clearly puts a premium on producing the best possible teachers, through the highest quality of education and training. We need to prepare teachers not only to fit well into the way schools currently operate, but also to have the ability to adjust to future change. Indeed, our aims should encompass more than this: new teachers should be competent initiators of change, able to critique current practice and to plan and undertake innovation.

Even within the limitations of current practices, teaching is a skilled profession. It requires not just the expertise to respond to routine classroom situations, but a deployment of a wide variety of skills in order to deal with any specific problems that may arise. What is the best way of presenting this material so that it will engage this class? Why does this student find it difficult to learn this and what can I do about it? What would be a fair and appropriate way to assess understanding of these ideas? Which of these on-line resources is appropriate?

To be able to solve such problems, teachers need to develop their knowledge on several fronts: first, of their subject areas; second, of how students learn, or fail to learn, and why they develop specific attitudes and behaviours; and, third, of the most effective ways of teaching, both at the general level and at the level of the specific concept or skill, including available teaching resources.

Teachers need to be able to deal not only with issues that arise in their classrooms, but also those that confront departments, schools or colleges as a whole. Decisions need to be made on what curriculum to offer, what methods of assessment and recording of progress to use, how to group pupils, how best to deploy resources of people and money, and a wide range of other such issues.

In the past these decisions were often based on personal prejudices of either teachers or those who advised them. As chair of the 2008 Research Assessment Sub-Panel for Education, I am only too aware of the fact that more and more research is becoming available to inform the decisions that teachers make both individually and collaboratively. Some research studies are small in scope. But when taken together with other national and international research, reliable evidence can often be accumulated to indicate which strategies are likely to be the most effective in which circumstances.

It is therefore extremely important that new teachers – and indeed more experienced teachers too – are acquainted with the most recent research findings, just as it is important that doctors keep up with medical research in their fields. In the same way as patients are entitled to the best-informed medical practice, our students in schools and colleges are entitled to the best-informed teachers and teaching that we can provide.

This book aims to introduce new teachers to issues they will encounter in their professional lives, and to present summaries of research findings in these fields. The contributors are my colleagues in the Department of Education and Professional Studies at King's College London. They are well placed to report the issues, combining expertise as leading researchers, continuing close contact with teachers and classrooms, and successful experience in teacher education.

I commend the book to both intending and existing teachers. I am sure that it will interest, stimulate and inform and thus be instrumental in serving the aim we are all striving to achieve – improving the quality of education provided to all our students.

Margaret Brown
Professor of Mathematics Education
King's College London

Introduction

Justin Dillon and Meg Maguire

If you are learning how to be a teacher, this book has been written for you. It has been written by a group of people who have two things in common. The first is that they have devoted most of their lives to education – teaching, researching or both. The second is that they have all worked in the Department of Education at King's College London. This unique and powerful combination has resulted in what you hold in your hands – thoughts, ideas, words, questions, answers, wit and wisdom.

Some time ago, a visit from Her Majesty's Inspectorate encouraged us to look critically at the amount of reading that King's students did during their PGCE year. For many reasons, including accessibility of libraries, the cost of books, and funding, the amount of reading that students did was much less than we thought appropriate. Looking around we could not find a textbook that addressed the issues that we knew concerned our students. So we wrote one ourselves – for internal consumption. It proved to be popular so, with the help of Open University Press, we produced, in 1997, a more polished version. The first edition proved to be popular too, and had to be reprinted. However, education changes rapidly and books date – even if many ideas remain valid over decades. We decided that a second edition could and should be written. The second edition was first published in 2001 and it has been even more successful than the first edition. Now, six years on, it is time for another edition.

This edition contains 28 chapters, two more than the second edition and five more than the first edition. There are new chapters on education for sustainability, school effectiveness and improvement, and education policy. There are 11 new contributors and many new ideas and issues. However, the overall philosophy of the book remains unchanged. This is not a 'tips for teachers' book, although some chapters do focus on technical issues. Each chapter is designed to give you some background in terms of, say, the historical context and to illuminate the key issues that you will be faced with every day. Some of the chapters should enable you to make sense of what goes on in school and should help you to gain an overview of a particular topic. The authors have tried to give you evidence to support points of view – there is too much unsubstantiated opinion in education, which has affected teachers and children detrimentally for too many years. This book will give you some evidence from the literature to back up, or maybe to challenge, your own opinions and experience.

Much of teaching relies on confidence. You need to be confident in your knowledge of your subject. Your students need to be confident in you as a teacher. Confidence can develop through experience and through feedback from other people. This book is designed to help you to become more confident in your understanding of what learning to teach involves. There will be much in this book that you have not thought of before – things that you disagree with or things that you feel are obvious. It is designed to be dipped into rather than read from beginning to end and, we hope, will point you in the direction of further reading.

How to use the book

Each chapter is designed to be read on its own although you will find recurrent themes. If you are doing an essay on a topic such as learning or special educational needs, or you feel that there are areas of education about which you know very little, then you can use the chapters here as starting points. Some of the chapters are linked in terms of content, so if you are interested in learning, you will find that the chapters on adolescence, differentiation and assessment for learning are interrelated. Indeed, the complexity of education is what makes it such an interesting area to work in.

The book is divided into four major sections. We have called Part 1, *First thoughts*, because it sets the scene – addressing some fundamental areas of concern for a new teacher.

Part 2, *Policy, society and schooling*, provides a grounding in the broader context in which education sits. As well as looking at the historical roots of the problems facing teachers and learners, particularly in the inner city, this part provides a vision of alternative and possible futures.

In the classroom, most of your concerns will be more immediate than those outlined above and Part 3, *Teaching and learning*, is a collection of interrelated articles addressing issues such as classroom management, adolescence and assessment for learning. In each chapter you will find practical advice based on sound theoretical understandings as well as some key issues to consider.

Part 4, *Across the curriculum*, appears daunting. The responsibilities of teachers beyond that of subject specialist have grown steadily over the years. The authors of the chapters in this part provide information about roles and responsibilities in areas including personal, social and health education, information technology, literacy and citizenship. As well as looking at how the form tutor's role is changing in school, the section contains a chapter that examines continuing professional development.

Some thanks

As well as our fellow authors and the team at Open University Press, other people have contributed to the production of this edition of *Becoming a Teacher*. We would like to thank Ellen McCallie, Richard Maloney, Laurie Smith and Blaine Stothard for their critical friendship, for reading and commenting from their positions as experienced educators and colleagues. Special thanks to Chris Winch for his mentoring of a less-experienced colleague.

And finally

In putting together this book we have tried to emphasize the three Rs: reading, reflection and research. Effective teachers are able to learn from their experiences, reflecting on both positive and negative feedback. The best teachers are often those who not only learn from their experience but also learn from the experiences of others. Reading offers access to the wisdom of others as well as providing tools to interpret your own experiences. We have encouraged the authors contributing to this book to provide evidence from research to justify the points that they make. We encourage you to reflect on that evidence and on the related issues discussed in this book during the process of becoming a teacher. Over to you.

Part 1 | First thoughts

Developing as a beginning teacher

Justin Dillon and Meg Maguire

If you are engaged in a course of teacher training you face what may be the most challenging period of your life. But take heart – the stimulation and the enjoyment of working with learners can be immense. Looks on faces, words of thanks, the physical excitement that young people are able to generate come frequently enough to justify the effort.

Most of your own experience of education will probably have been spent sitting down, facing the front being directed by an older person. Your teacher training will involve a series of rapid dislocations; some of the time you will be the teacher and some of the time you will be a learner. It is not a dichotomous situation though – you will be learning and teaching simultaneously.

As a teacher you will develop in many obvious and subtle ways. Many of these changes will be in response to other people or to external circumstances. If you are the same after you have read this book as you were when you started then we have failed as authors and educators. Take change out of education and there is not much left. You might find yourself getting up much earlier than was previously the case or you might find, as we did, that we became more patient. In the years to come, you will know more, be more skilled than is the case now, and your values will be tried and tested. You will indeed make mistakes, some minor and instantly forgettable and possibly some ground-opening horrors that will come back to haunt you for years on end. Through all this experience you will grow older, wiser, calmer and so on. It is on this growth that this chapter focuses.

What sort of teacher are you going to be? At the moment your model may be based on teachers that you have had or, possibly, based on the teachers you wished that you had had. This is common in new teachers and, on occasion, you might find yourself saying and doing things that your teachers said and did to you. Your first concern may well be with the behaviour of your students and there will be times, usually just before a lesson, when you look back at your decision to become a teacher and think, 'Why did I do that?' As you become more confident and more competent at teaching your concern will shift from behaviour to learning (see Chapter 13 for a discussion of theories of learning). The two are intrinsically linked. It is difficult for students to learn if they are not working in a well-managed environment and if they feel they are learning something worthwhile they are more likely to respond to being managed (see Chapter 14 for a discussion of classroom management).

Learning to teach involves a range of practical skills and, as one of our former colleagues has written, 'a subtle appreciation of when and how to apply them' (Claxton 1990: 16).

> Whether you like it or not, how you teach and how you learn to teach are bound up with your own personality, philosophy and values. Somewhere inside there is a set of personal standards – whether tacit or articulated, ill-informed or carefully thought out – that determine what shocks you, interests you or angers you about schools, and that serve as the benchmarks which you will use to guide and evaluate your progress as a teacher.
>
> (Claxton 1990: 18)

Training to become a teacher can therefore be a challenging as well as a frustrating business. A lot of ground is covered in a short time and this can result in feelings of stress and anxiety (Troman 2000, Bubb and Earley 2004). Your undergraduate learning experience may have focused on a formalized acquisition of content. In seminars you may well have looked at prepared papers or had content-driven academic debates. While these forms of learning feature in current teacher training, and while there is a necessary emphasis on classroom techniques and skills, learning to teach is fundamentally a personal challenge where practical, personal and emotional attributes are just as salient as intellectual capacities. The PGCE provides a vocational training built around a demanding and challenging induction into the teaching profession – the whole progress is better conceptualized as teacher development (See Chapter 8 for a discussion of the processes of teacher development). As John Head, one of the authors of this volume, once wrote: 'The PGCE is a complex and unique part of becoming a teacher' (Head *et al.* 1996: 83).

Many secondary trainee teachers (but not all) come into teaching as mature students, with a rich and broad experience of working in a variety of settings. Taylor, in a small-scale study of participants on teaching taster courses found high levels of commitment among the potential trainees (Taylor 2006). Ninety-seven per cent of her respondents rated their commitment to teaching as high. Teachers, particularly aspiring teachers, can be a hugely committed group. Some trainee teachers are parents and have direct experience of their own children's schooling. Sometimes in the light of these experiences, teaching can seem to be a common-sense affair – all about conveying some useful and hopefully interesting aspects in a lively manner which motivates young people to succeed. For people who think this way, becoming a teacher can sometimes explode any 'simple' model of teaching and learning. Teaching children who are less motivated than ourselves or who do not seem like the children we know, can present practical and personal difficulties where we may 'blame' the children instead of our own inexperience. However, it can also make for a stimulating and rewarding work setting.

Teacher qualities

At the heart of this book is a concern with becoming a teacher. Teachers are in an extremely privileged position; educating other people's children is a critical and influential task in any society. But this job is made more complex in times of acute social, economic and political change. One way in which to approach becoming a contemporary teacher is from the trainee perspective – hinted at above. Another way might be to ask what is involved in teaching and what might we, as a society, want to prioritize at particular moments in time? Do we want compliant pupils who can apply what they have learned? Do we want problem solvers and flexible learners? Do we want specialists or generalists? Are there any common strands that are recognizable as key components of a good teacher? In what follows we will consider four main themes through which we hope to raise questions about the central qualities involved in being and becoming a teacher: classroom management, the wider role of the teacher, professional and personal qualities.

Classroom management

As Jeremy Burke discusses in Chapter 14, there are some well known key aspects that are fundamental to good teaching. Good classroom management and organization, the capability to teach effectively in a mixed 'ability' classroom (and are not all classrooms mixed ability, however they are arranged?), good knowledge of subject and subject application, assessment, record keeping and all the other criteria listed by the government are important. But what is important to recognize is that all of these variables depend on the degree to which a teacher can maintain a positive and open climate in the classroom. The research into classroom life demonstrates that teachers and school students are in constant negotiation over boundaries, relationships, curriculum content, sequencing and pacing (Beynon 1985; Delamont 1990; Mackay 2006). This finding means that there are not simple codes or regimes which have a totality of application: it does not mean that new teachers cannot be helped with these issues either, but these are not just aspects of performance that are incrementally added to the teaching repertoire. They require a different type of learning and a different type of understanding.

We all know that the very best teaching depends on sensitive communication. We all know very well-qualified people who really understand their subject but cannot help others into it in a user-friendly manner. It is not only important to be able to help our students understand by clear and effective communication modes; it is important that teachers listen, observe and become sensitive to the children and 'where they are at' in relation to their understanding. Teachers need to be able to listen to and 'read' their students. This ability takes time and practice to refine, and even for the most experienced of teachers, it sometimes goes wrong. Dealing with adolescent people is not always straightforward or predictable as John Head discusses in Chapter 12. Sometimes it is the unrecognized forms of communication – non-verbal expressions or aspects of body language that need consideration (Neill 1991; Wooton 1993; Robson 1997). At other times there is the basic issue of respect for persons, sometimes ignored when dealing with youngsters. Thus, 'every job that requires significant interaction with other people (such as teaching) is an emotional practice' (Hargreaves 1999: 8).

Trainee teachers frequently worry about 'control' and eagerly seek out strategies to help them in their school experience settings. Experienced teachers know only too well that controlling – or creating a climate to allow learning to happen – is intimately bound up with a knowledge of the children. Trainee teachers are placed in a novel situation of attempting to manipulate the atmosphere in large grouped settings. This is an unusual skill to develop and is not the same as managing adults in a workplace setting. It takes time and personal investment in good relationships with school students and it would be unrealistic for new teachers to achieve this overnight. All this suggests that 'control' is more related to relationships than external strategies or mechanistic skills.

The wider role of the secondary school teacher

Teaching in contemporary schools involves building relationships with many different students with a variety of backgrounds, needs, expectations, motivations and aspirations. It is not possible to help children learn effectively unless you have some knowledge and insight into their concerns. The pastoral role of a teacher is related to the widest aims of teaching (see Chapter 27 for a discussion of a teacher's pastoral role). The National Curriculum places a statutory responsibility upon schools to promote 'the spiritual, moral, cultural, mental and physical development' of the school students. This means being interested in the children, getting to know them, feeling comfortable about discussing issues related to their learning and perhaps advising them in certain ways. The revised National Curriculum, launched in 2000, introduced the theme of citizenship in order to address important matters which had perhaps become marginal to the work of schools (see Chapter 21 on citizenship). At particular times issues related to health, sexuality, substance abuse, and so on, become salient in the classroom, and society expects schools to address and educate around these concerns. Teachers need to know what they can do, as well as what they cannot, in this context (see Chapter 23 on 'The importance of teachers and schools in health promotion').

From this pastoral role comes an obvious extension – working with parents. In the current policy setting, this aspect of the role of the teacher has significance for the maintenance of a healthy developing school (Gewirtz *et al.* 1995; Crozier and Reay 2005; Rudney 2005). Communicating clearly and professionally with parents is a core attribute for effective teaching; it is recognized that parents and schools working together provides a continuity and coherence for the school student and is critical for achievement (Vincent 1996; Reay 2001).

Professional qualities

It is often the case that new teachers need to be oriented to the fact that becoming a teacher means entering into membership of a particular community (see Chapter 2 for a full discussion of what 'being a teacher' might mean). You will be a member of a school staff, involved in a profession that needs to hold debates within itself and you will have to participate in these debates. You need to keep up with your subject(s) and you should be encouraged to join a relevant subject association or phase-specific group. Essentially teachers need a feeling of responsibility and control over their work. They need to participate in decision making and indeed hopefully will develop over time to take a lead in this process. The General Teaching Council (established in 2000) has a role to play in this development. Other professional qualities which we believe are required are related to the structural elements of the job. Teachers need to be on the inside of professional concerns and issues related to their salary, pay structure and conditions of service as well as issues of professionalism (see Furlong *et al.* 2000).

Another important dimension to all this development is the capacity to relate with colleagues and to work collaboratively. Teachers need the confidence to challenge assumptions about their work and the way in which it proceeds. They need to be in a position where not only can they work with colleagues but they are able collectively as a staff, as well as individuals, to ask fundamental questions about what they are doing (Adey *et al.* 2004). Is it worthwhile? It is this capacity that is characteristic of a professional teacher as opposed to a 'deliverer' of a curriculum devised elsewhere.

Personal qualities

Typically, new teachers experienced their school days as well-behaved and well-motivated students. Their role model of what it is to be a teacher may well have been constructed from this experience. For intending teachers who may have experienced selective schooling and may have been in top sets, the challenges of working with different types of students may be initially daunting. Children who have come to a recognition that school has little to offer them, that school only confirms in them a sense of failure and of 'being stupid' are going to be harder to reach and harder to teach, something that we have known about for many years (see, for example, Hargreaves 1982). In some of our schools, beginning teachers may well meet many different types of children from the sort of children that they were – restless, unable to concentrate, demotivated or perhaps with some particular learning difficulty. They will also meet students who are assertive, who demand respect and who will not be passive recipients of teachers' knowledge. Students will challenge what they perceive to be unfair or unjust in a way that might sometimes be constructed as provocative.

Beginning teachers will discover that they need lots of different responses – different ways of being with children in the school setting. They will need to experiment with different strategies. They will need to develop a flexible and adaptive repertoire of teaching. They will need to see themselves as learners throughout their lives and see this as a challenge and an opportunity, not a threat. At the heart of these personal qualities for teachers and student teachers must be the capacity to see their professional life as one of continual growth and development (Forde *et al.* 2006). For new teachers what is required is a state of adaptability, an experimental attitude, a capacity to recognize that they are going through a period of 'transitional incompetence', perhaps learning to tolerate their own fallibility and accepting that they can make mistakes as part of this process of becoming a teacher.

Working with others

Throughout your teacher training you are going to be working closely with more experienced, wiser people. You will be constructing new ways of working with people and new identities for yourself (but see Atkinson 2004 for some caveats about reflection). Teachers can be seen as autonomous beings working in a collegial environment. However, as Clement and Vandenberghe (2000) point out, there are tensions between autonomy and collegiality: 'Simply put: in order to collaborate adequately, teachers need to work alone sometimes, and, vice versa, in order to work autonomously adequately, teachers need to collaborate sometimes ... (Clement and Vandenberghe (2000: 85). The problem that you might face is that you will be forced to work alone when sometimes you would like to be more collaborative and vice versa! Trying to manage others' expectations of your needs when you are not clear what your own needs are, is a complex and challenging business.

In recent years, teachers have been encouraged to take a much greater role in the development of beginning teachers than was the case in the past (see Boyd (2002) for a critique of a school's involvement in initial teacher education). You will normally be allocated a mentor in each school in which you are placed. It has to be said that it is not easy being a mentor and good mentors are not as common as we might like to think. We know less about mentor development than we do about most other areas of teacher development in the UK, but we do know some things. In the US, Stanulis and Russell describe three themes that are key to effective mentoring: trust and communication; jumping in as a tool for learning to teach (that is rather than sitting at the back marking or taking notes all lesson); and conversation (between mentors and university tutors) as a tool for learning about mentoring (Stanulis and Russell, 2000: 69). Effective, regular, planned and sympathetic communication between you and your mentor are quintessential to your success as a beginning teacher and will go a long way to making you feel needed, valued and supported, oh, and happy.

Researchers are beginning to try out a range of strategies designed to improve the impact of mentors on teachers' practices. For example, Williams and Watson (2004) describe an initiative in which participants on a university pre-service course in teaching English to speakers of other languages were given feedback on their lessons about 20 hours after the lesson ended rather than immediately. The quality of reflection of those students was noticeably greater than that of trainees who were given immediate feedback. Somewhat more disturbing is the finding of Edwards and Protheroe that: 'Student teachers' learning is heavily situated and that students are not acquiring ways of interpreting learners that are easily transferable, but they are learning about curriculum delivery' (Edwards and Protheroe 2003: 227).

The implication of this study is that what you might learn about pupils in one school with one mentor and one set of colleagues might not be transferable to other situations. This finding is something to be aware of when you are discussing your experiences with other colleagues.

Concluding comments

The teacher is the ultimate key to educational change and school improvement. The restructuring of schools, the composition of national and provincial curricula, the development of benchmark assessments – all these things are of little value if they do not take the teacher into account. Teachers do not merely deliver the curriculum. They develop, define it and reinterpret it too. It is what teachers think, what teachers believe and what teachers do at the level of the classroom that ultimately shapes the kind of learning that young people experience.

For some reformers, improving teaching is mainly a matter of developing better teaching methods or of improving instruction. For them, training teachers in new classroom management skills, in active learning, personalized learning, one-to-one counselling and the like are the main priorities. These things are important, but we are also increasingly coming to understand that developing teachers and improving their teaching involves more than giving them new tricks. Teachers need to be creative and imaginative in their work; they need to be able to use 'intuitive, rational and reflective thinking' as well as having the 'confidence to take risks in learning and a sense of cognitive self-efficacy in a range of learning contexts' (Eraut 2000: 267).

Teachers teach in the way they do not just because of the skills they have or have not learned. The ways they teach are also grounded in their backgrounds, their biographies, in the kind of teachers they have become. Their careers – their hopes and dreams, their opportunities and aspirations, or the frustration of these things – are also important for teachers' commitment, enthusiasm and morale. So too are relationships with their colleagues, either in supportive communities, or as individuals working in isolation, with the insecurities that this sometimes brings.

As we are coming to understand these wider aspects of teaching and teacher development we are also beginning to understand that much more than pedagogy, instruction or teaching method is at stake. Teacher development, teachers' careers, teachers' relations with their colleagues, the conditions of status, reward and leadership under which they work – all these affect the quality of what they do in the classroom.

(Hargreaves and Fullan 1992: ix)

For those of you who are reading this and who are in the process of becoming a teacher there is one more fundamental issue which has to be addressed. There is a distinction between being a good teacher and someone who helps school students become good learners: those whom Claxton (1990) calls mentors. Claxton has set up a simple model to illustrate his point. He talks about the traditional 'good teacher' as someone who tells things clearly, points out the key features, and maximizes the training procedures through which pupils 'perform smoothly and successfully in situations – like most exams – that ask them to apply familiar operations to familiar content' (Claxton 1990: 154). One consequence can be the development of an unimaginative and inflexible learner:

Good pupils often perform well and look good but at the expense of precisely those qualities that distinguish good learners: resourcefulness, persistence and creativity. And it is just this kind of quality that mentors care about. Their main concern is to equip their pupils with the ability to be intelligent in the face of change.

(Claxton 1990: 154)

Becoming a teacher is not just a matter of training in basic skills and classroom procedures, essential as these all are as a starting place. It is also a matter of choice and of various personal and professional decisions, judgement and even intuitions (Atkinson and Claxton 2000). That is why teaching is such a tantalizing, challenging and rewarding occupation.

References

Adey, P., Hewitt, G., Hewitt, J. and Landau, N. (2004) *The Professional Development of Teachers: Practice and Theory.* Dordrecht: Kluwer Academic.

Atkinson, D. (2004) Theorising how students teachers form their identities in initial teacher education, *British Educational Research Journal*, 30(3): 379–94.

Atkinson, T. and Claxton, G. (eds) (2000) *The Intuitive Practitioner. On the Value of Not Always Knowing What One is Doing.* Buckingham: Open University Press.

Beynon, J. (1985) *Initial Encounters in the Secondary School: Sussing, Typing and Coping.* London: Falmer Press.

Boyd, P. (2002) Rose-tinted reflection? The benefits for teachers of initial teacher education in secondary schools, *Journal of In-service Education*, 28(2): 203–17.

Bubb, S. and Earley, P. (2004) *Managing Teacher Workload: Work-life Balance and Well-being.* London: Paul Chapman.

Claxton, G. (1990) *Teaching to Learn. A Direction for Education.* London: Cassell.

Clement, M. and Vandenberghe, R. (2000) Teachers' professional development: a solitary or collegial (ad)venture? *Teaching and Teacher Education*, 16: 81–101.

Crozier, G. and Reay, D. (eds) (2005) *Activating Participation: Parents and Teachers Working Towards Partnership*. Stoke-on-Trent: Trentham Books.

Delamont, S. (1990) *Interaction in the Classroom*. London: Routledge.

Edwards, A. and Protheroe, L. (2003) Learning to see in classrooms: what are student teachers learning about teaching and learning while learning to teach in schools? *British Educational Research Journal*, 29(2): 227–42.

Eraut, M. (2000) The intuitive practitioner: a critical overview, in T. Atkinson and G. Claxton (eds) *The Intuitive Practitioner. On the Value of Not Always Knowing What One is Doing*. Buckingham: Open University Press.

Forde, C., McMahon, M., McPhee, A.D. and Patrick, F. (2006) *Professional Development, Reflection and Enquiry*. London: Paul Chapman.

Furlong, J., Barton, L., Miles, S. *et al.* (2000) *Teacher Education in Transition. Reforming Professionalism?* Buckingham: Open University Press.

Gewirtz, S., Ball, S.J. and Bowe, R. (1995) *Markets, Choice and Equity in Education*. Buckingham: Open University Press.

Hargreaves, A. (1999) Classrooms, colleagues, communities and change: the sociology of teaching at the turn of the century. Keynote address given at 50th Anniversary of the Japanese Society of Sociology of Education, Tokyo, August.

Hargreaves, A. and Fullan, M.G. (eds) (1992) *Understanding Teacher Development*. London: Cassell.

Hargreaves, D.H. (1982) *The Challenge for the Comprehensive School: Culture, Curriculum and Community*. London: Routledge & Kegan Paul.

Head, J., Hill, F. and Maguire, M. (1996) Stress and the postgraduate secondary trainee teacher: a British case study, *Journal of Education for Teaching*, 22(1): 71–84.

Mackay, T. (2006) *The West Dunbartonshire Literacy Initiative: The Design, Implementation and Evaluation of an Intervention Strategy to Raise Achievement and Eradicate Illiteracy. Phase 1 Research Report*. Dunbarton: West Dunbartonshire Council.

Neill, S. (1991) *Classroom Nonverbal Communication*. London: Routledge.

Reay, D. (2001) Parents and schooling, in J. Dillon and M. Maguire (eds) *Becoming a Teacher. Issues in Secondary Teaching* (2nd edn). Buckingham: Open University Press.

Robson, P. (1997) *Body Language*. London: Franklin Watts.

Rudney, G. (2005) *Every Teacher's Guide to Working with Parents*. Thousand Oaks: Corwin Press.

Stanulis, R.N. and Russell, D. (2000) 'Jumping in': trust and communication in mentoring student teachers, *Teaching and Teacher Education*, 16: 65–80.

Taylor, A. (2006) Perceptions of prospective entrants to teacher education, *Teaching and Teacher Education*, 22: 451–64.

Troman, G. (2000) Teacher stress in the low-trust society. Conference paper, Annual Meeting of the American Education Research Association, New Orleans, April.

Vincent, C. (1996) *Parents and Teachers: Power and Participation*. London: Falmer Press.

Williams, M. and Watson, A. (2004) Post-lesson debriefing: delayed or immediate? An investigation of student teacher talk, *Journal of Education for Teaching*, 30(2): 85–96.

Wootton, M.J. (1993) *Not Using Your Voice: Non-Verbal Communication Skills in Teaching*. Upminster: Nightingale Teaching Consultancy.

Further reading

Bennett, H. (2006) *The Trainee Teacher's Survival Guide*. London: Continuum.

Borich, G.D. (1995) *Becoming a Teacher. An Inquiring Dialogue for the Beginning Teacher*. London: Falmer Press.

Hargreaves, A. (1999) The psychic rewards (and annoyances) of classroom teaching, in M. Hammersley (ed.) *Researching School Experience. Ethnographic Studies of Teaching and Learning*. London: Falmer Press.

2	# On being a teacher

Chris Winch

Introduction

This chapter will try to answer the question 'When you become a teacher, what exactly is it that you become?' The issue of occupational identity has always worried teachers, as it is bound up with their standing with the public, with other professions and with the state and politicians. It is a question endlessly chewed over by academics who have come up with various accounts of what it is to be a teacher. All of these accounts contain some problems. In this chapter I will review the various possibilities and then take a look at what the government thinks of the issue, sketching out some possibilities for the future development of teachers' occupational identity.

A brief historical survey

In the period from the 1960s until 1988, teachers enjoyed a historically unprecedented degree of autonomy within the educational system. This was particularly true of primary teachers, as we shall shortly see. However, this was not always the case; in particular, the Revised Code of Inspection that existed from the 1860s until 1898 provided for the regular inspection of teachers with a view to determining their pay scales according to the results of a test conducted by one of Her Majesty's Inspectors. The work of teachers was, therefore, under scrutiny from headteachers and government officials and there was little room for professional independence or initiative. The Revised Code 'payment by results' system testifies to the lowly status and low trust accorded to teachers at this period and echoes

Adam Smith's views in his *Wealth of Nations* of 1776, where he argues that there should be a discretionary element in the pay of state-funded teachers otherwise the schoolmaster 'would soon learn to neglect his business' (Smith 1776, BkV, p.785).

By the 1960s great changes had occurred. The 1944 Education Act had provided for curricular control by Local Education Authorities (LEAs), which in practice few, if any, exercised with any degree of vigour. The 11-plus selection exam for the grammar schools imposed a *de facto* curriculum on those classes that were specially prepared in order to pass this exam. However, given the unwillingness or inability of headteachers to exercise control of the curriculum within their schools, inevitably much of the power to do this passed to the classroom teacher within the constraints imposed by the 11-plus. The demise of the 11-plus led to a further weakening in curricular control and to a period, after the passing of the Plowden Report of 1967, that explicitly sanctioned experimentation within the classroom and even questioned the pre-eminence of the traditional aim of primary education in terms of grounding in the basics (see Alexander 1984, Ch.1). In this period teachers were allowed to experiment, not only with curricula and pedagogy, but also with what they considered to be the aims of primary education (see Mortimore *et al.* 1988 for evidence of this process). The picture was somewhat different in secondary schools. Those 80 per cent of children who were not in grammar schools attended secondary schools in which, by and large, they did not prepare for any public examinations (Taylor 1963). Furthermore, the schools were given considerable latitude within their non-academic brief to innovate, which many did. The rise of the comprehensive school, and the advent of the CSE examination altered the situation somewhat, but still gave schools considerable freedom to innovate if they so wished.

This 'golden age' of teacher autonomy came to an abrupt end in 1988. A unitary exam for nearly all 16 year olds, the GCSE, came into being. But much more important, the Education Reform Act of 1988 set in place a universal statutory curriculum and scheme of summative assessment to which all schools and teachers in England and Wales had to conform. At a stroke, teachers' *de facto* ability to set their aims, their curricula and their assessment procedures, came to a halt. Primary and secondary teachers had, henceforth, to work to guidelines as to what they should teach and they also had to teach in such a way that children were adequately prepared to take the Key Stage Assessments at age 7, 11, 14 and 16 on which schools were, to a large extent, to be judged by the government and the public. However, teachers and their representatives were able to affect the construction of the National Curriculum (see Cox (1991) for an account of what happened to the English curriculum and Graham 1993, for a more general account). There was a degree of scope for interpretation of the requirements of the curriculum in terms of construction of schemes of work and lesson plans, and teachers were free to teach in a way that conformed to their professional judgement.

By 1992, however, further legislation ushered in mandatory regular formal inspections of schools according to a comprehensive set of criteria published in an inspection handbook. Individual teachers were to be judged on their performance in the classroom and the results of inspections for schools were to be published. In practice therefore, the formative assessment and pedagogical methods of teachers were to be subject to scrutiny and potential sanction. Finally, in 1997, the advent of the National Literacy and National Numeracy Strategies brought state control of pedagogical methods onto the agenda, through detailed prescription of methods to be employed in English and Mathematics for one hour each day, both in the primary and secondary school. In nine years, therefore, teachers had apparently moved from a position of unparalleled autonomy to one of unparalleled control by the state. Did this signify, as many have argued, the demise of teachers as *professionals* and their emergence as low level *technicians*, putting into effect recipes written by state agencies and policed by agents of the state? The position is actually much more complicated and interesting than this stark judgement suggests, but in order to see this, it is first necessary to understand what could be meant by such a claim that teachers were *deprofessionalized*, or even *proletarianized*, that is, reduced to the status of unskilled workers.

What is a professional?

For many years it was common for teachers to be described as 'professionals' and for them to describe themselves as such. At first sight, such a description suggests that they are of the same kind as doctors, lawyers and clergymen. However, the standard account of a professional found in the textbooks of sociologists of work casts some doubt on that claim. Professionals are supposed to have access to specialized, abstract and difficult-to-acquire knowledge, which they put into practice in the course of their work. Their ability to put this esoteric knowledge into practice constitutes, arguably, the core of their expertise and hence of their professional status (Eraut 1994). It justifies the public trust reposed in them, their ability to regulate their own affairs and their ability to control entry into the profession through the possession of a licence to practise guaranteed by the state, usually through a legislative instrument. It is sometimes also argued that the professions, unlike other occupations, are uniquely concerned with human well-being through their attention to fundamental human needs of health, justice, spiritual salvation, learning and moral development. (This has been powerfully argued, for instance by David Carr – see Carr 1999 and 2000, for example.)

However, these accounts of what it is to be a professional pose difficulties for anyone who wishes to call teachers a professional group in any straight-forward sense. In the first place, it is not clear what teachers' esoteric professional knowledge actually is. One answer would be that it is *subject knowledge*, the material that they teach. However, this attribute would not normally serve to distinguish teachers from other individuals, who are not teachers, who have also acquired such knowledge through pursuing a university degree. Perhaps it lies in their ability to put this knowledge into practice, in the way in which a surgeon puts knowledge of anatomy, physiology and biochemistry into practice in diagnosis and in the operating theatre, or a lawyer who puts knowledge of the law into practical effect in the courtroom. The surgeon requires, in addition to the ability to make on the spot medical judgements, manipulative and managerial abilities. The lawyer has to deploy forensic and rhetorical powers to win cases. Such knowledge involves the practical interpretation of their theoretical knowledge in context in such a way as to achieve the desired result. In this sense, these professionals conform to the Aristotelian notion of a technician, by employing reason to achieve a given end. In their case, the reason involves interpreting a body of theoretical knowledge to meet the needs of the particular patient or client in the particular operating theatre or courtroom. Based on this analogy, teachers have to deploy their subject knowledge in the same way, interpreting the subject matter in such a way that children learn it effectively. If this story is true, then teachers are a kind of *high-level* technician, like a surgeon or a lawyer. Just as lawyers and doctors do not individually determine the aims of health care or justice (although they may have a say in determining them), so teachers do not determine the aims of education, nor what should be taught, but possess expertise in the pedagogic methods of transforming subject knowledge into a form suitable for pupils to acquire. It might be added that surgeons and doctors do not determine their own 'curriculum' either, in the sense that the knowledge that they deploy is framed by scientists and legislators rather than by doctors and lawyers themselves (although, again, they may contribute). In some cases, even the 'pedagogy' of doctors is prescribed (certain surgical techniques and drugs rather than others are recommended, and the effectiveness of the doctor or surgeon is to some extent judged on whether or not they deploy such techniques). The puzzle about teachers is this: if teachers insist on calling themselves professionals, then why do they often complain when their work is brought into greater likeness with other occupations whose professional status is unquestioned, by endowing them with a body of theory to inform their practice?

Part of the answer undoubtedly lies in the fact that teachers do not control their own affairs in the way that these other professions do. They do not control a licence to practise and their power to influence the curriculum, pedagogic methods, assessment procedures, as well as their power to discipline their own membership is very limited and, in the latter case, shared with government within the General Teaching Council (GTC). Furthermore, there is a high level of turnover in teaching, many teachers leave after a few years' practice and teaching enjoys one of the highest levels of casualization of any occupation (see Gallie *et al.* 1998). In terms of social status, therefore, it is in a weak position compared to other professions.

But many would also maintain that the description of teachers' professional knowledge given above is seriously incomplete. Some maintain that the ethical role of teachers as guardians of human well-being puts them in a pre-eminent position regarding determination of the aims of education, as well as curriculum and pedagogy, even though it is arguable that other interests in society have some role in determining these things (see Carr 1999 for a discussion that tends along these lines). But even if we were to allow that to be unrealistic, a very powerful school of thought maintains that teachers have, or should have, the knowledge of *how children learn* and it is this knowledge, above all, that is the mark of their professional expertise (see Wood 1988; Donaldson 1992 for the problematic nature of this claim). At its most extreme this view is encapsulated in the old *cri de guerre* of the 'progressive' teacher: 'we teach children not subjects'. This view is extreme as it discounts the significance of subject knowledge as something to be imparted to children and, by implication, discounts the need for teachers to have it as well. However, there is a broad consensus among teachers that they do have expertise on how children learn and that this constitutes a significant part, if not the core, of their occupational knowledge.

Before dealing with this issue, however, I want to question the claim that the professions have a unique stake in determining human welfare. It is undoubtedly true, as Carr maintains, that they deal in fundamental human goods (although some varieties of cosmetic surgery and legal claim-chasing may cast some doubt on certain cases), but it is also true that other occupations such as farming, plumbing, train driving and business activity are not only concerned with enhancing life, but also with ensuring it. Some occupations, such as nursing, are particularly concerned with *caring*, where the occupational expertise seems to be a single-minded concern with the physical welfare of a patient or client. But, significantly, such occupations are not classified as professions, but rather, at the most, as semi-professions (Etzioni 1969).

Professionals, craft workers and technicians

If teachers were professionals in the traditional sense, they would have at their disposal a body of applicable theoretical knowledge concerning how students learn, which they could deploy in appropriate conditions. Alternatively, and possibly in addition, they would possess a body of normative theory (theory that recommends or directs) concerning what should be taught, rather as lawyers and doctors have rules concerning how they should proceed. Commentators on the nature of professionalism, such as Freidson (1986), argue that the key quality of professionals is that they are technicians; that is, those whose work involves applying theoretical knowledge to practice. However, there has traditionally been considerable resistance to the view that applicable theory constitutes the professional knowledge of teachers. This is particularly evident with the case of the National Curriculum. When it was introduced in 1988, many teachers complained that they were reduced to technicians from their previous professional status. However, according to the analysis in some of the literature on professionalism, they were just gaining attributes of professionalism that they previously lacked (Freidson 1986).

How can this reaction be explained? The post 11-plus period had brought unparalleled autonomy to teachers. They were, in effect, responsible for their own curricula and even their own *aims* of education (Mortimore *et al.* 1988). These responsibilities were removed in 1988, so it is understandable that teachers thought that their professional autonomy had been radically diminished. That does not, however, explain their rejection of the 'technician' label, which, post 1988, seemed more applicable to them as professionals than before. Indeed, by being given a body of normative theory within which to work and within which to exercise their professional judgement, it could be said that they were losing an indeterminate status, exercising powers on behalf of society that they could not possibly exercise, and gaining the position of other professionals, as trusted interpreters of the aims and general direction of an important public service. Indeed, just as doctors and lawyers are thought to have an important, although not decisive, say in the nature and workings of the medical and legal systems, so teachers would now have an important, although not decisive, say in the nature and general direction of education. Their anomalous position would be removed and their professional status confirmed.

Why was this not the reaction of the majority of spokespeople for teachers? To understand this, we need to look at another influential account of the nature of teachers' knowledge. This account suggests that teachers are not technicians (the archetype of the technician, in the public mind, is the skilled industrial worker, who applies theory to practice, such as an engineer or electrician), but that they are more akin to the pre-industrial craft worker, such as the potter, the wheelwright or the agricultural labourer. Craft knowledge is implicit, informal and non-codifiable and it is manifested in practice rather than in any book of rules and principles. Craft workers learn their trade through *apprenticeship*, in which they acquire expertise through observation and gradually increasing their participation in the craft activity. As they do this, they learn the aims, ethos and ethics of the craft and can eventually pass them on to future generations. Craft work does not involve the application of theory to practice but the application of manual skills and situated judgement to the materials at hand, oriented to the particular purposes of clients (Sturt 1976). The craft worker's knowledge is, above all, of local needs and conditions, not about applying general principles to particular situations, nor about applying theory to practice. Thus, teachers learn their trade through practising it and they become masters of their craft through understanding the needs of the children that they teach and the communities that they serve. By understanding these needs they will devise aims and construct curricula that serve those needs. The craft conception of the teacher then includes the ability to devise aims and curricula, as well as pedagogies.

Seen in this light, it would not be surprising that a significant body of teachers would resist the removal of their control over aims and curricula and would see the role of the technician, albeit the 'professional' technician, as a demeaning one (but see Silcock 2002 for a more complex view). However, the craft conception of the work of teachers leads to a serious difficulty. A craft worker does not, on the whole, set the aims and general principles of the craft, these are handed down traditionally and only gradually modified over generations. Therefore the analogy between the teacher and the craft worker is a misleading one. And there is a further difficulty, for the craft knowledge of the craft worker is essentially non-academic and practical. If teachers are craft workers, their knowledge of what curriculum to follow and the principles of pedagogy to adopt are intuitive, rather than rational. But if this is the case, then in what sense can teachers claim a similar status to doctors, lawyers and clergy? Much of their professional knowledge is, as we have seen, applied theory and there seems to be no room for theory in the knowledge of teachers. How could they even be entitled to a professional training, let alone professional status, if their knowledge is craft knowledge?

And there is worse to follow. Suppose a craft teacher's 'knowledge' is not really knowledge at all, but prejudice picked up in the staffroom. Teachers might claim to 'know' that some kinds of children are less able than others, that you can't teach reading using phonics, etc. Others again might deny these very propositions. What is the basis for such knowledge claims? It won't do to say 'intuition' or 'experience' because these are not justifications for action, but rather a claim to authority which is itself questionable. If the much-prized professional knowledge of teachers turns out to be, on inspection, prejudice, then it is a poor substitute for the 'technical' knowledge of other professions. But if, on the other hand, there is no knowledge for teachers that is analogous to the surgeon's knowledge of biochemistry or the lawyer's of civil or criminal law, then how can they avoid being an occupation whose much-vaunted professional expertise is a kind of folk wisdom of dubious provenance? There is some evidence, unfortunately, that teachers have, at least until the recent past, seen themselves as belonging to such an occupation (see Alexander 1984, Chapter 2, for some of the evidence). Hoyle (1974) suggested that a majority of teachers saw themselves as what he called 'restricted professionals' or workers who have no interest in theoretical knowledge and whose practice is based on experience and intuition, rather like that of a traditional craft worker. But unlike a craft worker, the supposed knowledge is not of the behaviour of wood, stone or clay, but of the actions, beliefs and attitudes of people.

However, the knowledge of the traditional craft worker is, in a sense, self-validating. A potter who does not intuitively understand the properties of clay will not be able to successfully make pots and this will become rapidly apparent. It is not so clear that one could easily detect the lack of knowledge of the teacher. Children who do not learn what an observer thinks that they should learn do not necessarily count against this. A teacher might plausibly say that their aims for education were the development of an integrated personality, not someone able to read and write; as, for example, Rousseau appears to have thought. A teacher might also say that one should not aim too high in teaching some children, as high expectations are not appropriate for some kinds of children (see comments in Alexander 1984; Thrupp 1999). It is not a simple matter to distinguish the good from the bad teacher merely on the basis of one's own view of what education should be, if others do not share that view.

Some of these problems are solved by the existence of a national curriculum, which works to a set of aims and indicates, in broad terms, what should be taught. Teachers can then be judged against the extent to which they meet those aims and successfully reach the aims of the relevant sections of the national curriculum. However, this does not solve the difficulty concerning the *empirical* part of a teacher's knowledge, or the knowledge of how children learn and the best way to teach them that is supposed to constitute part of the core of a teacher's knowledge. We cannot depend on staffroom prejudices, but what if we have no reliable empirical theory to go on either?

Do we have research-based knowledge of teaching and learning?

At first sight, this seems a strange question to ask. After all, tens, if not hundreds of millions of pounds must be spent every year on educational research across the developed world. Surely that expenditure cannot be in vain? The problem is, though, that we do not really know. Much work that was, at one time, thought to be highly significant is now thought to be compromised and may be of little or no value. In their day, theories such as various forms of developmental stages, intelligence, verbal deficit and psycholinguistic theory have all enjoyed periods of prestige and influence and have then declined in the face of damaging counter-evidence. This is not the only educational research of course, much work consists of smaller-scale studies of specific aspects of teaching and learning or how particular schools function. But this more context-specific research poses its own problems, for how does one draw more general lessons from it? Research in education is always under attack, on the one hand, from those who denounce the general and overarching theories inferred from the small empirical base on which some large theoretical claims are made, on the other hand, from those who claim that small-scale, context-dependent studies, whatever their virtues, cannot be generalized to larger subjects. This seems to be such a problem that there is an influential body of thought that doubts that empirical educational research does have, or even could have, any practical value (see Barrow in Barrow and Foreman-Peck 2005, for example).

The problem seems to be that, despite the huge amount of money and effort spent on it, we do not really have a clear enough picture of what is and is not reliable in educational research. Furthermore, very often interpretations differ as to what the available evidence tells us, and it is all too tempting for academics to discount research whose results they don't like and to praise research whose results they do. We are still a long way from getting a clear view of what we do know and what we don't, and hence are still a long way from having a reliable knowledge of the theory underpinning successful pedagogies that could form the basis for teacher education.

However, it also seems that we have little choice but to develop such a knowledge base successfully, for the alternatives are not very appetising. If teacher knowledge is a kind of craft knowledge, like that of a potter or a wheelwright, then it should best be imparted within schools rather than in academic settings, just as one should learn to be a potter in a potter's workshop and a wheelwright in a wheelwright's shop. But if this 'knowledge' is, in reality, nothing more than prejudice or unjustified belief which may well be false, then it cannot be a good idea to rely on schools alone to educate future generations of teachers. Since it is not possible to rely on knowledge claims that may often be little more than prejudice, one cannot dispense with research, both conceptual and empirical. However, the amount and quality of research currently available may not be sufficient to sustain the professional education of teachers and, even if it does exist, may not be universally accepted by all those involved in the education of teachers.

It does seem, therefore, that in the absence of credible empirical knowledge about teaching and learning, the professional knowledge of teachers might largely rest with their subject knowledge and their ability to put that subject knowledge into practice in designing syllabuses, schemes of work and lessons. This ability is sometimes known as professional curricular knowledge and is, arguably, the core competence of teachers. In-depth knowledge of the subject allows a teacher to make necessary and appropriate decisions concerning *what* to teach and *how* to teach it. Clearly, a necessary condition of having this ability is good subject knowledge. However, it is also important to know how that knowledge is selected and presented to students and, above all, what are the most effective ways of teaching it. Professional curricular knowledge therefore seems to span both the subject and the professional knowledge of teachers and to constitute the core of their expertise, particularly in secondary education.[1]

At the secondary level, most teachers are involved in teaching subjects and are expected to develop syllabuses and lessons that effectively enable students to learn in those subjects. Teachers' expertise in knowing how students learn is, therefore, to a large extent bound up with their professional curricular knowledge. There are good reasons, however, for thinking that such knowledge is simply a *knack* of applying subject knowledge, which can be gained with some experience in the classroom. There is, for example, a large amount of research within particular subjects that claims to provide teachers with vital know-how concerning the best methods for teaching particular subjects and even claiming authority on the sequencing of subject matter. If this research is reliable, then the problem for secondary teachers in particular is that of understanding and applying that relevant research in their daily practice. But if it is not, then professional curricular knowledge has to be acquired through experience and through working with experienced teachers. One of the pressing problems for teachers concerning professional curricular knowledge is that, especially in some subject areas, it is highly contested. This is not merely because different researchers disagree about findings, but also because they often start from different and contested philosophical assumptions about the nature of the subject knowledge and its acquisition in their subject areas. See, for example, the debate between Wally Suchting and Ernst von Glasersfeld about science education (von Glasersfeld 1989; Suchting 1992). Nor is this problem confined to secondary education. Consider the debates about, for example, the teaching of writing and reading in primary education that have raged over the years.

If this is true then it leaves teaching in a position unlike that of other professions, in that knowledge of how to carry out relevant professional tasks is, on the one hand, based on research and, in a lot of cases, hotly contested, or on the other, not dependent on research or theory, but on having mastered the informal rules of successful practice. One should distinguish between two claims here. One is that there *could* be no research-based empirical theory concerning how one should teach, a position that seems to be adopted by some influential commentators such as Carr and

---

[1] In some respects the issues for primary educators are different. For example, the knowledge of applied linguistics necessary to be an accomplished curriculum leader in English in the primary school is imparted to pupils as skill and understanding in reading and writing rather than as factual information. Which is not to say, of course, that subject knowledge is nothing more than facts – it also concerns methods of enquiry and verification (see Hirst 1974).

Barrow. In this account, we should not wait upon good educational research to guide the practice of teachers because, by its nature, educational knowledge is not of the kind that could be yielded in this way, any more than the practice of a nineteenth-century wheelwright was dependent on theoretical knowledge of botany, economics and psychology.

Another, more optimistic, view is that educational research has not *sufficiently developed* to a point at which it can form the basis for teachers' practice. Even in those cases where knowledge obtained is reasonably reliable, it has not always been incorporated into practice. A greater effort needs to be made to evaluate extant research and to disseminate that which has been validated according to rigorous procedures and which has been replicated in a wide variety of practically relevant situations. It is, after all, most unlikely that there could be *no* knowledge of how children best learn and of how to teach them. One argument, found in Barrow (1984), is that teachers should never act on generalizations since all findings are only valid in the situations in which they have been obtained. Unfortunately, this claim is self-refuting as it is the kind of generalization it is meant to deny. If Barrow is right, then the generalization that one should not act on generalizations means that there is at least one generalization that one should act on, namely his own. And if that is so, why not on others?

Educational research sceptics hardly ever deny that there are educational facts, just that there are general educational facts (for example, Barrow in Barrow and Foreman-Peck 2005). They believe that some schools are more effective than other schools and that some methods of teaching reading are better than others, but claim that research cannot reveal these facts. However, they and others like them act as if they do know some particular educational facts: they send their children to some schools rather than others in the belief that such schools are more effective, they make judgements about the quality of teachers, of certain kinds of lessons, about the efficacy of methods of teaching reading and so on. How do they do it? According to Barrow and Foreman-Peck (2005: 29):

> More often than not educational truths, however, will be revealed rather by a combination of reasoning, reflection and informal experience. So, this is not a counsel of despair. It is an argument to the effect that we need to emphasise other things in educational research than empirical inquiry on the model of the natural sciences.

But we have seen that this really will not do. Common sense may be nothing more than prejudice and different people may lay claim to different versions of common sense. For example it may be the case that the choice is based on the social class composition of the children in the school (Ball 2003). As Phillips (2005: 591) points out, what seems obvious may only become so after research has confirmed it.

> Consider the classic question of whether it promotes learning better to distribute practice examples on a new mathematics skill over time, or mass the practice following the teaching of the skill. *After the research has been done*, it might seem intuitively obvious that massing the practice until mastery is achieved is the more effective, but would we have made this choice beforehand? (And be alert here, for I might

be playing a prank! Maybe the research shows that massed practice is *less* effective!) My point is that intuitions are unreliable here, and certainly do not substitute for careful research![2]

It does rather look as if carrying out good, reliable educational research is unavoidable if we wish to improve the work of teachers. In the past we have, maybe, been too hasty in expecting quick results and broad conclusions from small amounts of evidence. In the meantime, however, we have to make do with what we have.

The government's views of teacher knowledge

Past and present governments appear to tackle this tricky subject non-specifically. Generally speaking, standards for classroom teachers suggest that there is knowledge about learning and that even Newly Qualified Teachers (NQTs) should possess it. Thus, teachers should: 'understand how the progress and well-being of learners are affected by a range of influences and use this knowledge to inform their own teaching' (Training and Development Agency for Schools 2006a: 8).

The fact that the standards are described in behavioural terms is slightly confusing. The phrase 'this knowledge' does not refer back to any knowledge previously described in the document, but does imply that it exists. However, this may not be the case and then there would not be anything to draw on. But it is not clear upon whom teachers are supposed to rely when obtaining this knowledge. Despite the fondness of governments over the last two decades for basing a lot of initial teacher education in schools, they seem to realize that one could not reliably expect that teachers possess that knowledge. The very fact that the 1997–2001 government thought it necessary to introduce national literacy and numeracy strategies, which subsequent governments have continued, suggests that they do not believe that the knowledge of practising teachers is sufficient for two central parts of the National Curriculum. The government at the time of writing (like its last five predecessors) also regards university departments of education with some suspicion, suspecting that they are not really committed to evidence-informed practice. To some extent the problem can be alleviated by the kind of evaluation of research undertaken by organizations such as the EPPI (Evidence for Policy and Practice Information and Co-ordinating Centre) centre for the evaluation of educational research, which attempts to pull together and draw general lessons from a review of all the relevant, good quality research on a particular topic (see the comments of Hegarty 2000 on the knowledge base). However, both the conduct and the interpretation of meta reviews, which would form the basis for evidence-informed research, requires specialist skills and must, therefore, be done by qualified specialists. Carrying out,

---

[2] By 'massing the practice' Phillips means to give the pupils a lot of practical examples to do, immediately or shortly after explanation of, for example, a new mathematical operation.

understanding and interpreting research is the key expertise of the professional, qualified researcher and is not something that teachers can be expected to do as part of their normal professional duties. If such skills were taught either as part of their initial academic education or their professional education, then arguably at least some of the profession would be in a position to take on such a role. But such expertise is not available through initial teacher education, nor is it available to serving teachers except through high-level and specialized qualifications such as the EdD, MPhil and PhD.

If that is the case, then how will teachers obtain such knowledge in a form useful to them in their professional practice? Research findings could indeed be taught to them as part of their initial teacher education, if there was a consensus on what research should underlie practice. But, as we have seen, there is not. So should the government decide, in conjunction with centres like EPPI, about what research is useable by teachers, rather in the way that the National Institute for Clinical Excellence evaluates and rules which drugs should be prescribed to patients in the NHS? In such a case, the situation would be that those methods deemed to work will be put onto the syllabus of BA Education and PGCE courses and then taught as prescriptions for practice to intending teachers.

However, the equivocal way in which such knowledge is described in the draft standards makes it unclear whether it is believed that there is such knowledge. Standards are defined *behaviourally*. Teachers' understandings of factors influencing learning are manifested in the way that they use that knowledge. There are no academic components to teachers' qualifications structures. Even though a teacher may have a qualification at NQF 7 (Masters level) as a newly qualified teacher, neither academic subject knowledge nor research-based curricular or pedagogic knowledge is required in the qualification, provided competence specifications are met. Contrast the qualification framework for secondary teachers in France, which is based largely on subject knowledge and which has a higher tier qualification (the Aggrégation) for those who have excellent subject knowledge. The qualification for headship in England, NPQH, a qualification for the most senior kind of teacher, is not accredited at level 7 and needs further academic work by the student before it can be upgraded to a level 7 qualification by a university. The provenance of the knowledge that teachers at all levels are supposed to have is far from clear: is it staffroom 'common sense' or rigorously filtered research findings, critically interrogated academic research or an amalgam of all these things? It does not look as if the last feature is what the writers of the standards have in mind, since a specifically academic component is missing from the specification of levels of expertise, apart from that already present within initial qualifications. There is, for example, no evidence from the standards document that Masters level qualifications are needed to move up the promotional scales, even though they are now the level at which many NQTs are qualified. Professional standards for NQTs do not require the ability to put theoretical knowledge into practice, as we have seen. Indeed, this would be difficult given the importance that the government attaches to school-based routes to qualified teacher status (QTS). Currently there are *five* distinct routes to qualified teacher status that are work rather than college-based. One of these, the Registered Teacher Programme, takes candidates with qualifications at NQF level 4 or above and works as follows:

> Once on the programme your training will be tailored to your own individual needs and lead to qualified teacher status (QTS). Your training provider will also work with a local higher education institution to ensure that you receive suitable training to extend your subject knowledge to degree level.

> (TDA 2006)

It appears that in this programme, the professional knowledge and professional curricular knowledge will be developed entirely within the school, while the higher education institution has the job of bringing academic subject qualifications up to level 5 or 6 (honours degree level is not specified; this would be NQF level 6). All these considerations incline one to think that the current government standards would not make teachers professionals in the sense described above. They would tend, rather, to make them a kind of technician, but not the kind who uses their knowledge base to inform professional judgement, but one who uses recipes given by someone else to carry out practice; in other words, a low-level technician rather than a technician in the professional sense. With some routes, such as the Registered Teacher Programme, the preferred model seems to be craft knowledge developed in the workplace under the tutelage of experienced practitioners. Of course, it might still be the case that applying one's subject knowledge to the creation of syllabuses, schemes of work and lesson plans within the framework of the National Curriculum would require professional judgement based on subject knowledge. Here, perhaps, the claim that teachers have been reduced to 'mere' technicians, that is, recipe followers in all areas of the curriculum, would be least convincing, despite the frequent claims that this is what the National Curriculum has done (see Silcock 2002 for teachers' reactions). However, the overall picture is one of a series of governments over the last 20 years that are not particularly interested in teachers building up a rigorous knowledge base in partnership with academic and research institutions with which to inform their professional practice, but are rather interested in craft knowledge and/or technical recipes as the preferred model of professional knowledge.

Concluding comments

One can conclude, therefore, that the enhancement of teachers' professional status does, to a considerable extent, rest on the development of such a knowledge base. This is most likely to occur if two things happen. First, all teachers undertake a programme that qualifies them to Masters level as an initial qualification, which includes a critical training in understanding and evaluating educational research and theory; second that teachers themselves are stakeholders in the development of such theory, testing, commenting on and participating in the generation of findings relevant to classroom practice (Winch 2004).

References

Alexander, R. (1984) *Primary Teaching*. London: Holt.

Ball, S. J. (2003) *Class Strategies and the Education Market. The Middle Classes and Social Advantage*. London: Routledge

Barrow, R. (1984) *Giving Teaching Back to Teachers*. Brighton: Harvester.

Barrow, R. and Foreman-Peck, L. (2005) *Is Educational Research Any Use?* London: Philosophy of Education Society.

Carr, D. (1999) Professional education and professional ethics, *Journal of Applied Philosophy*, 16(1): 33–46.

Carr, D. (2000) *Professionalism and Ethics in Teaching*. London: Routledge.

Cox, B. (1991) *Cox on Cox*. London: Hodder & Stoughton.

Donaldson, M. (1992) *Human Minds*. London: Allen Lane.

Eraut, M. (1994) *Developing Professional Knowledge and Competence*. Brighton: Falmer.

Etzioni, A. (ed.) (1969) *The Semi-Professions and their Organization: Teachers, Nurses and Social Workers*. London: Collier-Macmillan.

Freidson, E. (1986) *Professional Powers: A Study of the Institutionalization of Formal Knowledge*. Chicago: University of Chicago Press.

Hegarty S. (2000) *Characterising the Knowledge Base in Education*. http://www.oecd.org/dataoecd/18/22/1855192.pdf.

Hirst, P. H. (1974) *Knowledge and the Curriculum*. London: Routledge.

Hoyle, E. (1974) Professionality, professionalism and control in teaching, *London Education Review*, 3(2): 15–17.

Gallie, D., White, M., Yuan, C. and Tomlinson, M. (1998) *Restructuring the Employment Relationship*. Oxford: Clarendon Press.

Graham, D. (1993) *A Lesson For Us All: The Making of the National Curriculum*. London: Routledge.

Mortimore, P., Sammons, P., Stoll, D., Lewis, D. and Ecob, J. R. (1988) *School Matters: The Junior Years*. Wells: Open Books.

Phillips, D. (2005) The contested nature of empirical educational research, and why philosophy of education offers so little help, *Journal of Philosophy of Education* 39(4): 577–97.

Silcock, P. (2002) Under construction or facing demolition? Contrasting views on English teacher professionalism across a professional association, *Teacher Education*, 6(2): 137–55.

Smith, A. [1776] (1981) *The Wealth of Nations*. Indianapolis: Liberty Press.

Sturt, G. (1976) *The Wheelwright's Shop*. Cambridge: Cambridge University Press.

Suchting, W. (1992) Constructivism deconstructed, *Science and Education*, 1(3): 223–54.

Taylor, W. (1963) *The Secondary Modern School*. London: Faber & Faber.

Thrupp, M. (1999) *Schools Making a Difference – Let's be Realistic!* Buckingham: Open University Press.

Training and Development Agency for Schools (TDA) (2006) Registered Teacher Programme. http://www.tda.gov.uk/Home/Recruit/thetrainingprocess/typesofcourse/rtp.aspx, accessed 21.01.07.

Von Glaserfeld, E. (1989) Cognition, construction of knowledge, and teaching, *Synthese*, 80(1): 121–40.

Winch, C. (2004) What do teachers need to know about teaching? *British Journal of Educational Studies*, 52(2): 180–96.

Wood, D. (1988) *How Children Think and Learn*. Oxford: Blackwell.

Part 2 | Policy, society and schooling

3	**Education policy and schooling**

Meg Maguire and Justin Dillon

Introduction

All aspects of learning to teach and teaching are controlled, explicitly and implicitly, by policy. Sometimes these policies appear to be driven by coherent and interrelated strategies for reform; at other times, education policy making seems to be chaotic; little more than a set of ad hoc responses to social dilemmas and public concerns. Until the late 1980s, 'you would have been hard-pressed to find many educationalists who thought that their world extended much beyond that of the classroom or their institutions' (Bottery 2000: 1). Since the late 1980s, the educational policy climate and its impact on schooling has reversed this situation. Education policy making has been appropriated by the central state in its determination to control, manage and transform society and, in particular, reform and drive education provision. The role of the school, and indeed the local authority, is subordinated to and by national policy imperatives. Currently, in the UK, as elsewhere, the role and work of schools and teachers are heavily prescribed by central government. What is being demanded of schools and their role in national prosperity and cultural cohesion is encoded in a litany of policy statements, documents and legislation. In consequence, schools and teachers have to be familiar with, and able to implement, policies that are planned for them by others and they are held accountable for this task.

In this chapter, we are taking 'policy' to refer to the plans for education developed by politicians and their advisers. However, with Jones (2003: 1), we recognize that any policy agenda is informed by the wider social context – 'social and cultural, economic and political' – and this includes global trends and pressures. Thus, macro factors will influence policy debates and policy responses, as we shall see. In such a short piece of writing, it is impossible to provide a detailed account of specific pieces of policy reform or pedagogical policies such as personalized learning or behaviour management, important though these undoubtedly are. Rather, what we want to do is provide an overview of educational reconstruction and reform through exploring four key policy imperatives. These are: the insertion of market forces as a lever for reform and change; the rise of managerialism in education; the pursuit of raising standards; and the policies of privatization. This approach represents an attempt to group and classify a wide range of policies that are, in practice, interrelated and interwoven. There is a very large literature in each individual policy arena, and so all we are able to do here is provide an overview of the sorts of debates, ideas and policies that currently shape education provision.

Before we attempt this, there are three key points that need to be addressed. First, at the heart of all social policy is a tension between what should be taken to be a public or a private responsibility and this conflict is reflected in education provision as in other aspects of social welfare policy. This tension continues to generate 'a process which is never settled and always evolving' (Drakeford 2000: 183). Thus, debates continue about what the state can and should be providing in a time when there seems to be an aversion to raising taxes. There are conflicts between freeing up individuals to make their own decisions and make their own choices, set alongside calls for the state to take further responsibility and control. There are highly contested struggles over who is best placed to provide welfare services such as education and health. New Labour has attempted to resolve this conflict by calling for more 'partnerships' and co-operation between public and private providers in welfare provision (Cardini 2006). Its current policy position is that what counts is what is provided. Who (and for what reason) provides the service is just not important.

Second, in this chapter we are tracing what we see as the dominant policy agenda that currently circumscribes the work of schools and teachers. Thus, we do not intend to explore current legislative intentions and specific outcomes such as trust schools, in any great depth. Our intention is to provide some indication of the fundamentals of policy intentions. But, in saying this, it is important to appreciate that there are other overlapping and sometimes conflicting policy agendas. For example, New Labour has a stated commitment towards social inclusion and a desire to reach out to constituencies that have historically been less well served by education provision (Whitty 2002). However, these inclusive policies are sometimes less influential than other more 'noisy' interventions. In policy terms, different policies co-exist and sometimes contradict one another. Schools may have to make careful, and sometimes painful, decisions about where their policy priorities lie. In the need to survive, they may sometimes feel pressed into particular ways that do some violence to their integrity, culture, ethos and social circumstances too.

Third, in this chapter we are going to speak in the main about English policy making. The UK is made up of four educational 'departments' that share some common features as well as many points of difference. In terms of educational policy making, however, England has been the most 'radical' in terms of its policy agenda (Jones 2003) and serves as a good example of 'change forces with a vengeance' (Fullan 2003). As Jones explains, there are similarities such as class inequality and limited social mobility, similar forms of qualifications and low levels of post-16 participation, but there are differences too in the four settings. Relations between teachers, parents and local governments vary and 'on such key themes of current policy as selection and social inclusion there are strong differences of inflection, in which much is at stake' (Jones 2003: 3).

Markets – choice, competition and diversity

In the UK, the state did not take on the responsibility for providing free universal secondary schooling until relatively recently in 1944. What it then provided was differentiated and related to selection based on deterministic concepts of 'ability'. It was argued that 'ability' could be measured and therefore used to justify different sorts of (unequal) provision (Hattersley 2004). 'This notion has cast a long and pernicious shadow over the education of less privileged groups throughout the twentieth century' (Tomlinson 2005: 16). What was being argued for in principle and policy, however, was a collective responsibility for the education of all children, organized and provided by the local educational state, regardless of capacity to pay and free to children and their families at the point of use. Gradually, in many areas, provision in secondary schools became comprehensivized. Secondary schools educated a more diverse intake under the same roof, if not always in the same classroom (see Chapter 16). The comprehensive school was seen as more inclusive and capable of challenging the debilitating and wasteful outcomes of early selection that had, not surprisingly, favoured children from more advantaged backgrounds. It was argued that non-selection, mixed ability teaching and a more child-responsive approach to pedagogy would produce a more equal society where the talents of all could flourish. Almost as soon as the new comprehensive policies were being put into practice, they were being challenged. It is not possible here to do justice to the attack on policies of comprehensivization (see Tomlinson 2005) but, essentially, they related to allegations about reduced standards, calls for more selection, claims that 'clever' children were not being challenged and a demonization of so-called permissive classroom teaching.

In terms of global pressures and influences for reforming state education, all these debates took place in a period of international economic recession and high unemployment and so it was relatively easy to argue that schools were not meeting the needs of employers or the labour market. It was also argued that in an ever-increasing global market place, typified by the free flow of goods, services, knowledge and labour, the capacity of nation-states to remain competitive and viable in the internationalized market place depended on the capacity of their educational system to respond positively to a globalizing economy (Olssen et al. 2004). Although aspects of the globalization thesis have been critiqued as overly deterministic and the role of the nation-state is seen as still wielding power, nevertheless the economic and labour-market arguments for an education policy that recognizes the global imperative are still very influential in the UK (Ball 1998).

The major response to these perceived problems of falling standards and a lack of labour market-responsiveness in education provision was to argue for the insertion of market forces into social welfare policy and practice. Social welfarism, it was alleged, was failing to deliver what was needed. Uneconomic, inefficient and poorly controlled education provision was not responsive to individual or societal needs. It was argued that a market-led approach was the best way to solve problems and provide any social welfare provision. 'The forces of the market will out, the good will survive, the weak will go to the wall, and everyone will be better off than before' (Gewirtz et al. 1995: 1). The Conservatives were elected into power from 1979–1997 and during this extended period set up a 'whole paraphernalia of a market system' (Gewirtz et al. 1995:1). To some extent, there has always been a market in education. Parents have always seen some schools as 'better' than others and some parents have done their best to ensure that their children were able to access the more 'successful' schools in their area. In terms of education policy, however, 'the market solution represents a paradigm shift in the economics of education policy and indeed of social policy generally' (Gewirtz et al. 1995: 2).

What was argued was that the market provided the best policy solution to any social policy question. Although the state would still be responsible for providing education, parents would be able to express a choice of school for their child. This choice would drive provision. Schools would be funded in terms of their student numbers. Popular schools (with high standards) would grow and less popular (bad) schools would either reform themselves or close. In terms of market forces, this process would mean that competition would drive provision. And in order for competition to thrive, the consumer (parent) would need to be able to make their selection based on some knowledge of the success, or otherwise, of the schools under consideration. Schools would need to provide an education that responded to the needs of a globalizing market to ensure that the UK was economically successful. Simultaneously, in a market economy, there would need to be a diversity of provision – choosing between identical goods is not a choice.

From the 1980s onwards, educational provision in the UK was restructured to incorporate a neo-liberal approach towards policy and practice. In education, a quasi-market form was inserted. As Gewirtz et al. (1995: 2) explain:

> The education market (like all markets) is intended to be driven by self-interest: first, the self-interest of parents, as consumers, choosing schools that will provide maximum advantage to their children; second, the self-interest of schools or their senior managers, as producers, in making policy decisions that are based upon ensuring that their institutions thrive, or at least survive, in the marketplace . . . The result is meant to be competition, emulation and rivalry: survival can only be ensured by attracting consumers away from other schools.

The Education Reform Act (1988) introduced a national curriculum and national testing. The publication of league tables reflecting each secondary schools' success at GCSE was to be a lever for consumer choice, as well as a stick with which to berate 'failing' schools. Different types of schools were set up to promote diversity of choice in the education market place.

Although it is important to state that this policy intervention was and still is contested, nevertheless, in essence, marketization has continued to influence education policy and provision right up to the current time (Whitty 2002; Ball 2007). Through marketization, the public provision of education has once more become an individualized good, and a private responsibility, albeit still largely funded by the taxpayer. And although many researchers have demonstrated the way in which market choice privileges middle-class choosers (Ball 2003) and, rather than reducing inequality, market forces actually drive up the gap between the poor and the rich (Hill 2004), nevertheless, New Labour is still convinced of the power of market forces in driving their policy agenda, albeit with some differences (Fergusson 2000: 202).

Managerialism

One of these key differences lies in the way that New Labour has attempted to reduce some of the damage caused by the rampant neo-liberalism of the previous Conservative administrations. As Fergusson explains: 'In many ways, New Labour's education policies could be summarized as using broadly similar means to the New Right to achieve ostensibly different ends' (Fergusson 2000: 202). Fergusson suggests that New Labour's concern to improve schooling for those who have historically gained the least, connects with a more social democratic impulse. New Labour policy is now based on a belief that national prosperity cannot be left to the unpredictable forces of the international market place. Rather, the national state has a central role to play in ensuring that, through its educational system, it is producing the sorts of flexible, up-skilled workers that will be needed in the technologically rich twenty-first century. One imperative of this economistic intention is to ensure that everyone is included in this national project. Another is to ensure that no one involved in delivering this process is neglectful of their responsibilities.

The policy consequence of these imperatives is seen in managerialism. Managerialism is a response to the perceived failings of earlier forms of social welfare policy. At the heart of managerialism lies the desire to extract the 'methods' of the business environment and insert them into the public services. In this way, it is claimed that provisions such as health and education will become more efficient, effective and accountable. The focus in managerialism is with 'what works' to achieve ends that are determined at the centre and not on the ground. To achieve these (frequently economy-related) ends, there is an increasing need to educate and train more managers and to set and achieve clear sets of targets in order to raise standards, as well as ensuring that all individuals in the organization are working towards the same goals. Managerialism is a form of organizational, and individual, control. Those on the ground are charged with 'delivering' what others elsewhere have decided is best.

Managerialism is about asserting that particular problems exist which have to be addressed in certain ways. For example, it is alleged that there is a massive literacy problem as only about 80 per cent of children achieve level four at the end of Key Stage Two. This 'fact' has led to claims that many children cannot read rather than a discussion of what else could be the case – that some children are on the borderline; that some children develop a little later than others; that some children are making less progress because of the debilitating impact of childhood poverty, poor housing and other complex social and contextual reasons. Regardless of these possible explanations, or any others, all state schools are exhorted to adopt the national literacy strategy and to introduce 'ability' setting, if they have not already done so, and this in spite of much contradictory evidence (see Chapter 16). Schools have to deliver on national targets, they have to deliver on national strategies for raising standards and they are regularly assessed and inspected in order to assure that they are sticking to the script. Technical 'problems' in these new managerial times, such as inefficient teachers or schools that are not successful enough (the 'stuck' school for instance) will be subjected to further scrutiny and regulation. (It is not surprising that many of these sorts of schools are in less affluent areas.) In terms of attempting to 'control' the delivery side of education, central government has taken upon itself the responsibility for determining the curriculum and has set 'standards' for teacher education courses. (Imagine if central government were to determine, regulate and inspect the curriculum and its delivery for the professional training of other professional groups!)

As Clarke and Newman (1997: xii) claim, 'the "can do" culture of management has a strong preference for practical prescriptions over mere academic analysis'. Of course, with more analysis, some of the 'problems' to which managerialism is addressed, might be seen to be more related to broader social-contextual factors, rather than inefficiency or ineffective classroom teaching. Bottery has argued that a fundamental dilemma with managerialism is that if education policy making is being driven by economic imperatives (the need for international competitiveness or the production of a particular type of workforce), alternative questions such as where any emphasis should lie or issues to do with society as a whole can get sidelined (Bottery 2000: 61). In a situation where policy makers take the initiative based on assumptions of 'knowing best', there is a real danger of erosion in democratic forms of accountability and a reduction in active citizenship.

There are claims for the value of managerialism in terms of supporting effective practices and reducing wasteful inefficiencies, as well as some support for localized forms of managerialism that can potentially be more responsive to local issues. Nevertheless, there are criticisms of managerial assumptions and practices in education that are worth some consideration. Bottery (2000) argues that managerial approaches to problems identified elsewhere, which contain pre-packaged remedies that have to be complied with (and compliance is a key word in these managerial times), may sideline other alternatives for action. One example he offers is that in seeking to 'hit' short-term targets, the bigger aims might never be addressed. For example, some secondary schools, seeking to do well in the national league tables, ensured their success by producing new forms of assessment (GNVQs) that were equivalent to five GCSEs. This curriculum package was then sold on to other schools who were also able to raise their performance. Whether the students' attainment had actually been raised in numeracy and language, for instance, was not explored. The crucial league table target of five GCSEs had been achieved. Targets, testing, performance management techniques, inspection and reporting become 'a system for delivering government policy, not for discussion of what the aims of education might be; and when governmental policies are so clearly predicated upon economistic ends, managerialism is doubly controlling' (Bottery 2000: 79). In the longer term, it is argued that technicist managerial approaches, on their own, can generate feelings of lack of ownership and over-dependency on pre-packaged policies and curriculum strategies, perceptions that can negatively impact on school progression and effectiveness (Fullan 2003).

Standards

Our third key policy dimension is the concern about standards and the drive to raise attainment in schools. This strand of the current policy agenda is woven into and is a fundamental element of the marketization, managerialism and privatization that constitute the current policy ensemblage (Ball 1997). There are some questions in terms of the raising standards agenda that are sometimes less aired. For instance, is there a ceiling on what it is possible to attain? Is it really the case that standards are far too low? What do we really mean by 'standards' anyway? What about the evidence that suggests schools can only do so much to improve the situation; that the social milieu is equally if not more powerful in shaping attainment (Thrupp 2005). Be this as it may, the issue of standards is not going away and it is a subject that has powerful implications for parents, educationalists and policy makers. Policy making in the area of the 'raising standards' agenda is reflected in a massive industry of testing, measuring and assessment that sometimes seems to dominate the contemporary educational context. The outcome of this can sometimes mean that if an item cannot be tested or measured (such as being a caring member of the classroom), then it does not really count for much at all.

Nevertheless, for some time, our popular media (and some educational research) have been suggesting that educational standards are too low. No government can afford to ignore the potency of these claims. In consequence, all governments of all political persuasions have to be seen to pursue the raising standards agenda. No one can afford to be seen as complacent in this key area of educational policy and practice. However, what has happened is that for some time now, a popular but somewhat pernicious discourse of failure and fault-finding has crept into the standards debate. Even though research suggests that there has been a gradual improvement in children's attainments over time (DfES 2001), the popular view does not reflect these incremental gains. Indeed, every summer in the UK, we seem to face an impasse; if students' results go up, then it is because standards have fallen and the tests are too easy. If results go down, it is because standards of teaching are too low. A veritable Catch-22 situation.

In the face of this standards impasse, it is not surprising that national governments seize on the key discourses of the day and weave them into justifications for their own policies. It would be possible to find echoes of this concern about standards across all the New Labour policy texts but, here, examples from one must suffice:

> A generation ago, Britain tolerated an education system with a long tail of poor achievement because there was a plentiful supply of unskilled and semi-skilled jobs . . . Every child, whatever their circumstances, requires an education that equips them for work and enables them to succeed in the wider economy and in society.
>
> (DfES 2001: 5)

The White Paper, *Schools: Achieving Success* (DfES 2001) concentrates on the need for secondary schools to improve. The paper claims that 'while there are clear signs of progress, this has been neither rapid nor dramatic' (p. 5). 'All schools must deliver high minimum standards and constantly push up the ceiling on aspiration, ambition and achievement' (p. 16).

In a setting where the dominant discourse is of blame, fault-finding and a constant barrage of exhortations to schools to raise standards (would they really want to lower them?), it is not surprising that parents and the media exhibit concerns about attainment. It is not surprising either that secondary schools who are judged on their percentage of students who achieve five GCSEs at C grade or above are encouraged to look for ways to attain this target. For example, one tactic is to concentrate on students with predicted grades at the C/D border, rather than any other group, as moving students into a C from a D can significantly improve a schools' league table position. Moving from a B to an A has no statistical or league table significance at all (Gillborn and Youdell 2000). Another tactic might be to ensure that a secondary school recruited as many pro-school students as possible. Thus, the standards agenda might work in a slightly skewed manner and might, for example, disrupt alternative policies aimed at inclusion.

Policy initiatives do not always achieve what they set to accomplish. As Ball (1997) has argued, policies have unintended outcomes. A culture of blame and fault-finding might indeed be counterproductive. For example, Black and Atkin (1996: 199) argue that 'people are motivated when their accomplishments are recognised'. As they say:

> Building on existing strengths may serve to steal the wind of destructive reforms, those that follow one another at breakneck speed because priorities cannot be allowed to stand or new shortcomings are perceived every day. Such initiatives never recognise present merit and assume that everything is in steep decline [. . .] where the direction of policy is towards finding fault rather than finding virtue, it is difficult to move to a more evolutionary view of educational change, one that recognises that there is normally much of value in the existing system.
>
> (Black and Atkin 1996: 199)

We are not arguing for the status quo and we are certainly not suggesting that holding high aspirations for school students is unimportant or trivial. What we are suggesting is that in the standards policy agenda, constant fault-finding and a lack of sensitivity to the incremental gains that have occurred in children's learning can have some unintended outcomes. Children (and teachers) do not thrive in a setting where they are constantly berated or tested and found wanting. Teachers leave (the job) and children absent themselves from school.

So far, in this section, we have discussed student attainment as one major part of the standards agenda. The other lever for raising standards lies with improving and reforming the work of individual teachers and schools. As part of managerialist policies that inflect the standards 'crusade' (DfES 2001: 3), teachers' performance is measured through their target attainments, their students' examination results, their capacity to meet centrally imposed standards and a whole range of 'performance indicators and measurable outcomes' (Ball 1999: 20). In teacher training courses, pre-specified 'standards' have to be met. In the first year of teaching, these standards have to be consolidated. From then on, through devices such as appraisal for individuals, performance assessments as part of promotion, target setting for the whole school and other tactics of managerialism, teachers are cajoled to conform to a battery of measures and performance indicators (Mahony and Hextall 2000). One danger is that schools, needing to respond positively to these centrally determined targets, will strive to organize and present themselves in a way that is compliant, but which involves a great deal of 'fabrication' – manipulating their performance to tell a positive story (Ball 2001). As a corollary to this, other important policy issues, inclusion for instance, may well be sidelined and sacrificed to the more dominant policy agenda. In terms of curriculum and learning, in the literacy strategy, students may be encouraged to explore small pieces of text in order to consider grammatical construction but may rarely read a whole book for pleasure. As Bernstein has warned: 'the steps taken to measure and maintain performance, for the survival of the institution, is likely to facilitate a state-promoted instrumentality. The intrinsic value of knowledge may be eroded' (Bernstein 1996: 75, cited in Ball 1999: 20–21).

Privatization

Our final policy imperative, educational privatization, is also interwoven into and between all the policy shifts we have already discussed. Green (2005: 3) claims that 'using the private sector with the public sector in collaborative mode is the successor to marketisation'. We do not necessarily see privatization as a 'successor' policy – policy making is not linear, nor is it composed of single successor policies. Rather, educational policy making is a process of bringing together 'products of multiple (but circumscribed) influences and agendas' and they are always 'both contested and changing' (Ball 1993: 12). However, it is clear that beliefs about the potency of market forces to deliver the greatest good; the privileging of individualism through choice mechanisms and a fundamental trust in the power of business practices to best shape public sector provision contribute towards more forms of privatization in education as in other forms of social welfare provision.

In education, for some time now there has been a form of 'creeping privatisation' (Green 2005). Through the outsourcing of provisions which were historically managed by schools or local education authorities in a not-for-profit capacity, aspects such as school meals, school cleaning and perhaps more educationally significant matters such as inspection, staff development and headship appraisal, for example, have in many parts of the country have been taken over by private companies. Some of these companies are multinational concerns with interests in other countries. Other companies been formed by ex-public sector workers who have been able to use their expertise (and their commitment to the public sector, in some cases) to provide educational services such as supply teaching, appraisal and the whole-scale management and organization of local authorities (Ball 2007).

One concern is the degree to which these newly privatized services are not-for-profit or for-profit concerns. For example, it could be argued that CEA, which is a not-for-profit company, is only providing a service that would have been provided by advisers and/or the local authority that it has replaced. Through greater efficiencies and by concentrated attempts at effective management and support, CEA would claim to have replaced some 'failing' local authority providers with better support systems (see Ball 2007 for more discussion of the providers). Thus, there may well be real savings where money for education is not diverted from schooling to shareholders, for example. Other cases, and other companies, are earnestly profit-driven for that is their *raison-d'être*. Indeed, New Labour seems to believe that market forces and public–private partnerships will produce new money (not from direct taxes, which it wants to keep down) as well as enhanced levels of measurable effectiveness and improvements. The belief is that business acumen will be more effective, particularly in areas where education historically has not done well. Interestingly, there seems to be a refusal to recognize that businesses sometimes fail and are not always that successful. There seems also to be a failure to acknowledge the ineptitude of some business consultancy interventions into the public sector, for example, the Child Support Agency's work (Craig and Brooks 2006). Notwithstanding all this, New Labour has been, and continues to be, active in promoting a range of private financial initiatives in health and in education.

In order to get the rapid growth it wants in Private Financial Initiatives (PFIs), the government openly dangled before the city the prospect of huge sums of public money guaranteed in long-term contracts. The Chancellor, Gordon Brown, made a direct appeal to financiers four years ago. 'These are core services,' he said, 'which the government is statutorily bound to provide and for which demand is virtually insatiable. Your revenue stream is ultimately backed by the government. Where else can you get a long-term business opportunity like that?' (BBC File on 4, 4 July 2004, cited in Ball 2007: 162).

PFIs are based around companies borrowing money at much higher rates than the government would obtain from the money markets, and then, for example, building hospitals or schools with their loans. The company then receives a 'mortgage payment' from the state over an extended period. 'These partnerships challenge the traditional welfare model where funding, regulation and provision of public services were in the hands of the central state' (Cardini 2006: 14). This approach takes as 'axiomatic that, while public organisations were likely to fail, private firms delivered consistent success' (Crouch 2003: 38).

> The public sector gets the infrastructure it needs to deliver its services – be those for school children, older students or young or long-term unemployed jobseekers. The private sector gets the opportunity to enter into long-term contracts which are defined in terms of outputs, so maximising the scope for innovation, development and profit. These opportunities should not be neglected.
>
> (DfES 2006a)

The City Academy school movement is one high-profile and contentious example of a move towards privatization in education provision. The Academies Programme is designed to be independent of local government control, and thus, local forms of accountability as well. These new schools have private or voluntary (often from various Church groups) sponsors. The sponsors donate £2m towards the Academy and, in return, have control of staffing policies, the curriculum and the organization and management of the school. Academies are located in 'areas of disadvantage [. . .] Academies will break the cycle of underachievement in areas of social and economic deprivation' (DfES 2006b). Academies are funded at a much higher level than other state-maintained schools. They are frequently housed in purpose-built, state of the art accommodation. They are 'not bound by the National Curriculum' and are expected to 'adopt innovative approaches to the content and delivery of the curriculum' (DfES 2006b). Academies will be free from 'unnecessary bureaucracy' in order to 'maximise the freedoms and flexibilities available to them' (DfES 2006b).

> The involvement of sponsors in running Academies maximizes the benefits that can be derived from a partnership with business and other non-government partners. The different perspective that sponsors can bring to both the basic curriculum and curriculum extension and enrichment activities is key to the change in culture and attitude required to break the cycle of underachievement. Sponsors can give extra focus and sharpness to the management of Academies.
>
> (DfES 2006b)

Critics of the academies argue that these schools are perhaps a precursor of wider attempts at privatization (for example, trust schools) (Hatcher 2006). Academies weaken the capacity of local education authorities to plan and organize strategically in their areas. In exchange for £2m, sponsors are entrusted with a great many responsibilities, such as setting up the governing body and staff recruitment, without necessarily having an educational background. (One survey has indicated that much of this money has not actually been transferred into the system, Taylor and Evans 2006.) Flexibility in staffing might mean that unqualified people are employed to teach classes or that teachers are discouraged from joining professional associations or unions. Above all, the evidence that the Academy schools are successful in raising standards is slight. What evidence there is seems to indicate that the Academies that are 'improving' are perhaps 'changing their intake or are not even the most disadvantaged in the area' (Gorard 2005: 376).

Concluding comments

In this chapter, we have tried to provide an overview of the key imperatives that inform and constitute state-produced education policy. As we have argued at the start of this chapter, there was a time when education policy was perhaps more of a taken-for-granted but distant event that had little real bearing on the daily life and work of the school and the teacher. Even if this was ever so, this is no longer the case. While we have concentrated in this chapter on providing a description of contemporary policy shifts, two fundamental issues need to be repeated here. First, the tension between what is an individual responsibility and what is best left to the state to provide, in terms of meeting societal rather than individual needs, is a recurring debate. Second, while education policy and practice is being driven by the state, 'education policies are the focus of considerable controversy and overt public contestation' (Olssen *et al.* 2004: 2). Teachers and all those interested and involved in education provision need to have an awareness of current policy trends; the challenge is to shape these trends towards socially inclusive and progressive ends.

References

Ball, S. J. (1993) What is policy? Texts, trajectories and toolboxes, *Discourse*, 13(2): 10–17.

Ball, S. J. (1997) Policy sociology and critical social research: a personal view of recent education policy and policy research, *British Education Research Journal*, 23(3): 257–74.

Ball, S. J. (1998) Big policies/small world: an introduction to international perspectives in education policy, *Comparative Education*, 32(2): 119–30.

Ball, S. J. (1999) *Educational Reform and the Struggle for the Soul of the Teacher*, Lecture given to the Chinese University of Hong Kong, 27 November 1998.

Ball, S. J. (2001) Performativities and fabrications in the education ceremony: towards the performative society in D. Gleeson and C. Husbands (eds) *The Performing School: Managing, Teaching and Learning in a Performance Culture*. London: RoutledgeFalmer.

Ball, S. J. (2003) *Class Strategies and the Education Market. The Middle Classes and Social Advantage*. London: Routledge.

Ball, S. J. (2007) *Education plc: Private Sector Participation in Public Sector Education*. London: RoutledgeFalmer.

Black, P. and Atkin, M. (1996) *Changing the subject: Innovations in Science, Mathematics and Technology Education*. London: Routledge.

Bottery, M. (2000) *Education, Policy and Ethics*. London and New York: Continuum.

Cardini, A. (2006) An analysis of the rhetoric and practice of educational partnerships in the UK: an arena of complexities, tensions and power, *Journal of Education Policy*, 21(3): 392–413.

Clarke, J. and Newman, J. (1997) *The Managerial State: Power, Politics and Ideology in the Remaking of Social Welfare*. London: Sage.

Craig, D. and Brooks, R. (2006) *Plundering the Public Sector; How New Labour are Letting Consultants Run Off with £70bn of Our Money*. London: Constable and Robinson.

Crouch, C. (2003) *Commercialisation or Citizenship. Education Policy and the Future of Public Services*. London: Fabian Society.

Department for Education and Science (DfES) (2001) *Schools Achieving Success*, Cmd 5230. London: The Stationery Office.

Department for Education and Science (DfES) (2006a) DfES Public Private Partnership website. Accessed 14 May 2006. Available at www.dfes.gov.uk/ppppfi/business/p7/shtml.

Department for Education and Science (DfES) (2006b) DfES Academies website. Accessed 17 May 2006. Available at www.standards.dfes. gov.uk/academies.

Drakeford, M. (2000) *Privatisation and Social Policy*. Harlow Essex: Pearson Education Limited.

Fergusson, R. (2000) Modernizing Managerialism in Education, in J. Clarke, S. Gewirtz and E. McLaughlin (eds) *New Managerialism, New Welfare?* London and Thousand Oaks: Sage.

Fullan, M. (2003) *Change Forces with a Vengeance*. London and New York: Routledge/Falmer.

Gewirtz, S., Ball, S. J. and Bowe, R. (1995) *Markets, Choice and Equity in Education*. Buckingham: Open University Press.

Gillborn, D. and Youdell, D. (2000) *Rationing Education*. London: Routledge.

Gorard, S. (2005) Academies as the 'future of schooling': is this an evidence-based policy? *Journal of Education Policy*, 20(3): 369–78.

Green, C. (2005) *The Privatization of State Education: Public Partners, Private Dealings*. London: Routledge.

Hatcher, R. (2006) Privatisation and sponsorship: the re-agenting of the school system in England, *Journal of Education Policy*, 21(5): 599–619.

Hattersley, R. (2004) The case against selection, in M. Benn and C. Chitty (eds) *A Tribute to Caroline Benn*. London: Continuum.

Hill, J. (2004) *Inequality and the State*. Oxford: Oxford University Press.

Jones, K. (2003) *Education in Britain. 1944 to the Present*. Cambridge: Polity.

Mahony, P. and Hextall, I. (2000) *Reconstructing Teaching: Standards, Performance and Accountability*. London: RoutledgeFalmer.

Olssen, M., Codd, J. and O'Neill, A. M. (2004) *Education Policy. Globalisation, Citizenship and Democracy*. London and Thousand Oaks: Sage.

Taylor, M. and Evans, R. (2006) Sponsors fail to hand over academy cash, *Guardian*, 3 May, p 1.

Thrupp, M. (2005) *School Improvement: an Unofficial Approach*. London: Continuum.

Tomlinson, S. (2005) (2nd edn) *Education in a Post-welfare Society*. Maidenhead: Open University Press.

Whitty, G. (2002) *Making Sense of Education Policy*. London: Sage Publications.

Ideology, evidence and the raising of standards

Paul Black

Introduction

A teacher's classroom work is constrained by a framework of rules and beliefs about curriculum and assessment. In England and Wales that framework underwent a revolution when a national curriculum and assessment system was put in place, for the first time, by the Education Reform Act of 1988. This chapter is about that revolution, about its consequences, and about the broader lessons that can be learnt from it. The first section discusses the background – the ideas and beliefs that helped drive the development of the new policies. Subsequent sections will discuss the developments, first of the National Curriculum, and then of the assessment system (Chapter 17 deals with the more technical aspects of assessment).

Whilst some of what is described is now history, this is offered both to inform understanding of present systems in the light of their origins, and to aid reflection on obstacles to reform in the future. Many of the problems arise from the myriad pressures that bear on policy makers – pressures which will not go away. It is important, therefore, to understand these, but also to look beyond them. Thus a final section addresses fundamental purposes by returning to the themes of the first section, looking at beliefs and assumptions that stand in the way of a more coherent and effective approach to education policy.

Nostalgia, fear and myth

The world of politics is driven by a mixture of rationality, myth and expediency. In education, three powerful myths have driven political thinking and public opinion. This section examines those myths in turn.

The first is that standards have fallen. This myth, which has been a feature of public debate for well over a century, is not confirmed by any thorough review of evidence: policy is often driven by selective evidence and hearsay.

Between 1970–1971 and 1991–1992, the percentage of pupils obtaining no graded examination results as school leavers fell from 44 per cent to 6.2 per cent (due in part to the raising of the school leaving age from 15 to 16 so that all pupils were in school to take the age 16 examinations). The percentage of those leaving school before the age of 17 who gained five or more higher grades at GCSE (or the earlier equivalents) was about 7 per cent (DfE 1994) in 1970, whereas in the last few years it has been just over 50 per cent (DfES 2006). Despite year on year fluctuations, the trend for over 30 years has been of steady increase, which points to the enormous success of teachers in our comprehensive schools.

A second myth is that this 'fall in standards' has been due to the adoption of 'progressive' methods of teaching. Again this flies in the face of the evidence of Eric Bolton, former head of the national inspectorate, based on his experience of thousands of hours of observation by his staff:

> The evidence of inspection is that poor standards of learning are more commonly associated with over-direction by teachers, rather than with teachers opting out and allowing pupils to set the pace and style of learning.
>
> Far from having an education service full of trendy teachers led, willy-nilly, this way and that by experts and gurus (the 'Educational Mafia'), we have a teaching profession that is essentially cautious and conservative: a profession that is highly suspicious of claims from within or without its ranks that there is a particularly fool-proof way of doing things. Teachers are too close to the actual, day-to-day complexity of classrooms, and to the variability of people and pupils, to be anything else but pragmatic and commonsensical in their thinking and actions.
>
> (Bolton 1992: 16–19)

The third myth is that learning would be improved by a return to traditional methods. Here again the evidence contradicts the myth. Numerous research studies have shown the debilitating consequences of rule-bound traditional learning. The study of Nuthall and Alton-Lee (1995) on the methods pupils use to answer tests showed that long-term retention depends on the capacity to understand and so reconstruct procedures, and the work of Boaler (1997) showed that more open methods produce better attitudes and performance in mathematics than traditional methods (see also Chapter 16). There is also evidence which suggests that children learn more effectively if they are listened to and helped to understand by themselves (Weare 2005). An extensive survey of teaching methods in Chicago public schools showed that teachers who teach for understanding achieved higher results on the state's standardized tests than those who just 'teach to the tests' (Newmann *et al.* 2001). The results of such studies are entirely consistent with contemporary research on the ways that children learn (Pellegrino *et al.* 1999). Consider the following from a review of such work:

> Even comprehension of simple texts requires a process of inferring and thinking about what the text means. Children who are drilled in number facts, algorithms, decoding skills or vocabulary lists without developing a basic conceptual model or seeing the meaning of what they are doing have a very difficult time retaining information (because all the bits are disconnected) and are unable to apply what they have memorised (because it makes no sense).
>
> (Shepard 1992: 303)

This dominance of mythology is linked to neglect of research, or to selective use of research results, and a distrust of change. The following quotations help to explain this neglect (the first is about a former Conservative Minister – Sir Keith Joseph):

> Here Joseph shared a view common to all conservative educationists: that education had seen an unholy alliance of socialists, bureaucrats, planners and Directors of Education acting against the true interests and wishes of the nation's children and parents by their imposition on the schools of an ideology (equality of condition) based on utopian dreams of universal co-operation and brotherhood.
>
> (Knight 1990: 155)

> Tories really did seem to believe in the existence of left-wing, 'education establishment' conspiracies.
>
> (Lawton 1994: 145)

Such suspicion is shared by many in the other parties. Thus one can understand why research evidence is untrustworthy – those responsible for this evidence are part of the conspiracy.

After 1997, the Labour Government was only a little less suspicious of educational research, and its record of taking research findings seriously is a very uneven one. Indeed, there has hardly been any change since 1997 in another relevant policy, namely the application of the ideology of the marketplace to education. The application of a market model to education has been criticized by many, notably in the reports of the NCE (1995), in the analysis offered by Stephen Ball (Ball 1994: Chapter 7), and in a review of the effect of over a decade of parental choice of schools in Scotland: 'Parental choice has led to an inefficient use of resources, widening disparities between schools, increased social segregation and threats to equality of educational opportunity' (Adler 1993: 183).

A market implies consumer choice between expensive products of high quality and cheaper products of poorer quality, while demand is linked to willingness and ability to pay, not to need. The right-wing Hillgate Group has commented that 'Consumer sovereignty does not necessarily guarantee that values will be preserved' (McKenzie 1993). Keith Joseph believed in the 'blind, unplanned, uncoordinated wisdom of the market' (1976: 57), but it is clear that markets favour those who have the knowledge and the power to choose effectively – the children of the less well informed will suffer (Ball 2003).

There are other myths which are prevalent amongst politicians, some teachers and many of the general public. One is that selective education systems produce better pupil learning overall than comprehensive systems. The House of Commons Select Committee on Education and Skills conducted an investigation into this issue in 2003–2004. Their conclusion was: 'We have found no evidence that selection by ability or aptitude contributes to the overall improvement of educational standards' (Select Committee (2004) report (8) para. 258).

Another myth is that it is better, notably in mathematics, to use setting or streaming of classes rather than mixed ability classes. Reviews of research investigations in which the results of the two approaches are compared do not support this belief (Harlen and Malcolm, 1999 and, for mathematics, Burris *et al.* 2006).

Thus it seems that many changes, or refusals to change, in our education policy have been and still are based on a combination of nostalgia, folk wisdom, and fear of change, driven in some areas by an inappropriate market model for education. Such views are protected by a neglect of evidence, so that we do not learn from experience (Whitty 2002). Taken together, they constitute an eclectic ideology, one which seems to have remained powerful despite changes in the governing party.

The curriculum – pragmatic, traditional, unprincipled

The Education Reform Act 1988 devoted about three lines to the principles on which the curriculum should be based – it was to promote the spiritual, moral, cultural, mental and physical development of pupils. It then moved to list the ten subjects, which were thereby established as if they were self-evident 'goods'. Then, as the separate formulations for these subjects were developed, and have since been revised, there has been no attempt to check that they serve these principles either separately or in a mutually coherent way. Furthermore, these subjects, with the notable exception of design and technology, were the subjects which constituted my own grammar school education in the 1940s and 1950s. It is easy to expose the intellectual poverty of this way of specifying a national curriculum and its consequences (White 1990), but the specification survived the 1997 change in government and is enshrined without debate, as did much of the rest of the Conservative policy (see Tonlinson 2005, Chapter 5; Whitty 2002, Chapter 8).

Some other countries have policies in education that contrast sharply with England's (Scotland has always been different, and Wales and Northern Ireland having changed significantly since their regional powers gave them control over education) and do not share these weaknesses. In Finland, for example, a policy document on the framework for the curriculum (National Board 1994) discussed changes in social needs and values, and went on to emphasize that our new understanding of learning showed the need to emphasize 'the active role of the student as the organiser of his [sic] own structure of knowledge' and the need for 'organizing teaching into inter-curricular issues and subjects'.

The Norwegian Ministry document on the Core Curriculum (Royal Ministry 1994) was in chapters with titles as follows:

- The spiritual human being
- The creative human being
- The working human being
- The liberally educated human being
- The social human being
- The environmentally aware human being
- The integrated human being

Here we have governments who, in sharp contrast to our own approach since 1988, present to their country a deeply argued rationale for the aims of their curriculum.

Education policy has to confront concerns about the changing world of the child and the adolescent (see also Chapter 12 for a discussion of the pressures of adolescence). Changes in family stability and in the stability of employment, and the increasing power of the media, have meant that young people face an environment that is rich in information and vicarious experience, poor in first-hand experience, weaker than it ever was in emotional security and support, and overshadowed by the threat of unemployment (Beck 1992). Where the world of the child has been impoverished, the task of the school is both more complex and more vital. Yet it has to be carried out in a society where the authority of teachers, as with other professionals, is not taken for granted.

A nostalgia-driven return to traditional policies ignores such problems, and cannot provide for the contemporary needs of young people and of society. In 1995 a group of European industrialists stressed the importance of literacy, numeracy and of science and technology, but added to these critical thinking, decision making, the need to be able to learn new skills, the ability to work in groups, a willingness to take risks and exercise initiative, curiosity, and a sense of service to the community (ERT 1995). British employers see the same needs (Ball 1990: 103). More recent debates in the UK that have expressed similar concerns, some to do with basic literacy and numeracy skills, some with broader issues such as citizenship, and spiritual and moral education, are all evidence of the inadequacy of the 1988 formulations, which subsequent revisions have failed to redress.

National assessment – the rise and fall of the TGAT

In 1987 the Cabinet Minister then responsible for education, Kenneth Baker, invited me to chair the Task Group on Assessment and Testing (TGAT) to advise on assessment policy for the new National Curriculum. I accepted because my experience made me optimistic that valid, and therefore helpful, external national tests could be set up. I was also optimistic because government statements seemed to recognize the importance of teachers' own assessments in any national scheme (DES 1987: para. 29; 1988a: Appendix B). The task group members represented a wide range of interests and relevant experience. Five had been members of public examination boards – one as chairman, two had directed different subject areas of the government's Assessment of Performance Unit, one was director of the National Foundation for Educational Research, another the director of one of the leading agencies for post-16 vocational examinations, while two others were distinguished researchers in examining. The group also included the Chief Education Officer of one of the largest local authorities, a senior Her Majesty's Inspector (HMI) (the national inspectorate) and two headteachers, one secondary, one primary.

The TGAT proposals (DES 1988a, 1988b) emphasized the centrality of teachers' own assessments in promoting the day-to-day learning of pupils. They went on to recommend that national assessments should be based upon a combination of teachers' own assessments and the results of external tests, on the grounds that external tests helped establish common standards and criteria, but were of limited reliability and limited in the range of learning aims that they could validly test.

These proposals were at first accepted as government policy, and then abandoned one by one in the next few years (Black 1993, 1997). It was clear at an early stage that Baker's acceptance of the TGAT report might not have wholehearted support from his Prime Minister:

> The fact that it was then welcomed by the Labour Party, the National Union of Teachers and the *Times Educational Supplement* was enough to confirm for me that its approach was suspect. It proposed an elaborate and complex system of assessment – teacher dominated and uncosted. It adopted the 'diagnostic' view of tests, placed the emphasis on teachers doing their own assessment and was written in an impenetrable educationalist jargon.
>
> (Thatcher 1993: 594–5)

A more explicit rejection was delivered later by Thatcher's new Education Minister, Kenneth Clarke:

> The British pedagogue's hostility to written examinations of any kind can be taken to ludicrous extremes ... This remarkable national obsession lies behind the more vehement opposition to the recent introduction of 7-year-old testing. They were made a little too complicated and we have said we will simplify them ... The complications themselves were largely designed in the first place in an attempt to pacify opponents who feared above all else 'paper and pencil' tests.
>
> (Clarke 1991)

The TGAT argument, that priority should be given to supporting assessment by teachers, was accepted by Baker. However, the agencies responsible for developing the national assessment policy devoted hardly any of their time or resources to teachers' assessments – they concentrated on external testing (Daugherty 1995; Black 1997). This should not have been a surprise in view of earlier reversals. Consider for example Baker's statement in 1989:

> The balance – characteristic of most GCSE courses – between coursework and an externally set and marked terminal examination has worked well. I accept the Council's judgement that assessment by means of coursework is one of the examination's strengths.
>
> (Quoted in Daugherty 1995: 131)

In 1991 the Prime Minister, John Major, reversed this conclusion:

> It is clear that there is now far too much coursework, project work and
> teacher assessment in GCSE. The remedy surely lies in getting GCSE
> back to being an externally assessed exam which is predominantly
> written.
>
> (Quoted in Daugherty 1995: 137)

Government directives then, without either consultation or consideration
of evidence, reduced the coursework component of GCSE. At the time of
writing, the present (2006) government is proposing further reductions.

Underlying this flux of debate is a basic question – how can policy and
practice in testing and assessment raise the standards of pupil work in
schools? Many politicians have a simple answer to this question – set tests
and make schools accountable for them and improvements will follow
automatically. There is hardly any evidence to support this belief. Indeed,
such policies lead to a system where short, written, external tests dominate
the curriculum, tests which cannot reflect some of the important aims of
education. Yet the pressure on schools to do well in them means that they
distort and damage learning (Fairbrother *et al.* 1995; Gipps *et al.* 1995);
there is also evidence that while above average pupils have improved on
tests, the absolute standards of those well below the average have fallen
(Bell 1995), and that testing pressures have adverse effects on the anxiety
and motivation of many pupils (ARG, 2002). Furthermore, as schools concentrate on drilling pupils to do well in sets of short test items, they can
improve their scores on these particular tests, but do so by giving less attention to developing in pupils the skills needed to apply their learning to
complex and realistic tasks. Further distortion arises in two ways. One is
that some schools bend admission, or exclusion, practices to 'cherry-pick'
pupils whose results will may do them credit in the future (Gillborn and
Youdell 2000). The other is that some schools have been tempted to 'play
the system' by focusing attention on pupils close to the critical C/D borderline, to enhance the – reported – number who have attained above this, to
the neglect of any who are well below it.

To make matters worse, it is also clear that the results of short external
tests are bound to be of limited reliability. The evidence available (Gardner
and Cowan, 2005, Black and Wiliam 2006) indicates that if we had sound
data for the short national tests, or for GCSE, or for A levels, these would
all turn out to involve rather large margins of error. However, while these
tests are the basis on which teachers are to be judged and pupils' life
chances determined, such data are not available. Other countries have
accepted the limitations of external testing. In Sweden, national tests
calibrate schools but the results for individual pupils are left to teachers to
determine (Eckstein and Noah 1993). In the Australian state of Queensland,
external testing for pupils' certification was abandoned in 1982 and to date
there is no sign that they will ever be reintroduced (Cumming and Maxwell
2004).

Research evidence clearly indicates a quite different answer to the basic
question. Dramatic improvement in pupils' achievement can be made by
changes in the way that teachers use assessment to give feedback to guide
pupils' learning. The key to raising standards lies in supporting the work of

teachers in the classroom, not in attempting to control and harass them from the outside (Black and Wiliam 1998a, 1998b).

Other countries have realized this. In France, national testing has been deployed, not to blame teachers at the end of a teaching year, but to help them by providing diagnostic information about their new classes of pupils at the start of a school year (Black and Atkin 1996). The National Board of Education in Finland has written (1994: 29) that:

> The task of evaluation is to encourage all students – in a positive way – to set their own aims, to plan their work and to make independent choices. For this to take place, all students gradually need to learn to analyze their own studies and those of others through the use of self-evaluation and group evaluation. The ability to do that in the future means the ability to survive in a situation where there is more and more uncertainty and where the individual is subjected to all kinds of choices and sudden changes. Practical ideas about how to achieve such reform have been developed with teachers.
>
> (Black *et al.* 2002, 2003)

Can we find new directions?

My aim here is to discuss six issues that need to be confronted in any attempt to formulate a coherent policy for the improvement of education. The first is concerned with the process of change. An OECD review of 23 case studies, spread over 13 countries, which examined the progress of different educational innovations, revealed striking differences between the models of change that were adopted (Black and Atkin 1996). At one extreme there were top-down models in which central authority tells everyone what to do. Where this was done, either very little happened at classroom level, or teachers, being disoriented, delivered an impoverished interpretation of the intentions.

The opposite approach, which was to leave as much as possible in the hands of schools and of teachers, also had difficulties, for the process was slow and such delegation implied that only a very general framework could be prescribed. However, there are powerful arguments, of principle and from empirical evidence, that this is the most effective and acceptable strategy (Fullan 1991; Posch 1994). Where matters are interlinked in complex ways and where one has to be sensitive to the local context in which this complexity is situated, then only those who have freedom of manoeuvre can turn a good idea into a really effective innovation. This approach has been adopted in business and industry (Peters and Waterman 1982), where the response has been to move from long hierarchical chains to so-called 'flat' management structures. If new aims for education are to be achieved, we have to give teachers freedom to work out the best ways for their school:

> While the existence of central national and regional (local government) institutions is necessary to guarantee social equity in education and to supply guidelines and expertise, it is essential that educational

institutions at every level should have autonomy to implement the
changes they see as necessary.

(ERT 1995: 18)

The OECD study also concluded that worthwhile educational reform cannot happen quickly – it takes several years for the majority of teachers to
turn innovation plans into practice through changes in their classroom
work. This time scale is long compared with the interval between elections.
More alarmingly, it may be too long in relation to the pace at which our
society, and – therefore – at which its demands on education, are changing.

Teachers are the focus of my second issue. Where teachers have low
status, they become targets for blame, and are treated with remarkable
insensitivity:

We are struck by the extent to which German and French education
systems place responsibility on the shoulders of professional teachers.
It contrasts sharply with the mood of distrust of professionals which
has grown in this country in recent years, not without government
encouragement. This mood has been carried too far and must be
reversed.

(NCE 1993: 340)

Such treatment is not only unjust, it is also counter-productive, for in any
but the most narrow mechanical view of teaching, it must be recognized
that teachers are the sole and essential means to educational improvement.
If they do not share the aims of an innovation, it cannot happen effectively.

Furthermore, to define teachers as mere providers of the market goods
that the parent customers require is to misconstrue their fundamental role.
A former chair of the Headmasters' Conference, Father Dominic Milroy,
wrote:

They [parents] know that, for the child, the encounter with the teacher
is the first major step into outside society, the beginning of a long
journey towards adulthood, in which the role of the teacher is going
to be decisive . . . all education is an exercise in collaborative parenting,
in which the profession of teaching is seen as a complement to the
vocation of parenthood . . . Teachers are, therefore, not in the first
instance agents either of the National Curriculum Council (or whatever follows it) or of the state. They are bridges between individual
children and the culture to which they belong . . . This culture consists
partly of a heritage, which links them to the past, and partly of a range
of skills and opportunities, which links them to the future. The role of
the teachers is, in this respect, irreplaceable.

(Milroy 1992: 57–9)

This perspective replaces the notion of teachers as paid agents with a
concept of partnership in which the role of teachers is to take authority for
developing young adults. Indeed, parents give this authority to the school
and the teachers because they want their children to learn the many ideas
and skills that they cannot themselves give them, and society reinforces
this when it sets up a curriculum within which parents are not free to pick
and choose if their children go to schools funded by their taxes. The teacher

is a pivotal agent of change, sharing authority with parents for the development of children, and representing society as the agent to achieve nationally agreed aims for education.

A third issue is the need to clarify what society wants teachers to achieve, which is to say that we need a fresh consensus about the educational aims that society wants schools to pursue. This is lacking because of rapid social change, because our society is divided about its fundamental beliefs and values and because society has weakened in many ways the support given to the developing child outside school.

A national curriculum which stresses details of subjects, flimsily related to a few very broad aims, leaves schools in a very difficult position. It might make sense to give schools no direction at all. It might be better to set out for them the broad framework of aims that society wants them to achieve and leave them to find the detailed ways to achieve such aims. It surely makes no sense at all to specify the detailed ways but to leave them to decide the overall aims.

My fourth issue has already been discussed above. We need a new policy for assessment, one which will support the assessment aspect of teachers' work, which will have helpful rather than damaging effects on good teaching by assessing those aspects of learning that young people need to be effective in a changing society, and which will give information, to individuals and to the public, that is both relevant and trustworthy. This issue has been fully explored in a thorough review by the Assessment Reform Group (ARG, 2006).

The fifth issue is that we need to have a proper respect for evidence, which means that we have to be willing to review existing evidence, to monitor the progress of our educational changes and to research in depth some of the most important problems that this raises. This implies that the level of investment in research in education should be very sharply increased.

If we are to be able to work effectively at these five issues, I believe we shall need to take up a sixth, which is that we need to build up a much better public understanding of the complexities of teaching and learning. The public ought to be far better informed about educational issues than at present. Myths about our schools are too powerful and policy thinking about our education is too weak. There ought to be a sustained effort to help the public, and especially politicians and their policy advisers, to achieve a more realistic, and therefore more complex, understanding of the realities of schools, of classrooms, of testing and of educational change.

However, a list such as this does not do justice to the complexity of the relationship between educational policy and effective change. Such problems as striking the right balance between over-prescription and policy stagnation, and the need to achieve sustainable change that is relevant to the inevitable, increasingly rapid pace of social change, all call for a more subtle and comprehensive analysis, such as that attempted by Fullan (2003).

References

Adler, M. (1993) An alternative approach to parental choice, in *National Commission on Education, Briefings*. London: Heinemann.

Assessment Reform Group (ARG) (2002) *Testing, Motivation and Learning: a Report from the Assessment Reform Group*. Cambridge: University Faculty of Education.

Assessment Reform Group (ARG) (2006) *The Role of Teachers in the Assessment of Learning: a Report from the Assessment Reform Group*. London: Institute of Education.

Ball, S.J. (1990) *Politics and Policy Making in Education*. London: Routledge.

Ball, S.J. (1994) *Education Reform: A Critical and Post-structural Approach*. Buckingham: Open University Press.

Ball, S.J. (2003) *Class Strategies and the Education Market. The Middle Classes and Social Advantage*. London: Routledge.

Beck, U. (1992) *Risk Society: Towards a New Modernity*. Newbury Park, CA: Sage.

Bell, C. (1995) In a different league? *British Journal of Curriculum and Assessment*, 5(3): 32–3.

Black, P. (1993) The shifting scenery of the National Curriculum, in P. O'Hear and J. White (eds) *Assessing the National Curriculum*. London: Paul Chapman.

Black, P. (1997) Whatever Happened to TGAT? In C. Cullingford (ed.) *Assessment vs. Evaluation*. London: Cassell.

Black, P. and Atkin, J.M. (eds) (1996) *Changing the Subject*. Routledge: London.

Black, P., Harrison, C., Lee, C., Marshall, B. and Wiliam, D. (2002) *Working Inside the Black Box: Assessment for Learning in the Classroom*. London: NFERNelson.

Black, P., Harrison, C., Lee, C., Marshall, B. and Wiliam, D. (2003) *Assessment for Learning – putting it into practice*. Buckingham: Open University Press.

Black, P. and Wiliam, D. (1998a) Assessment and classroom learning, *Assessment in Education*, 5(1): 7–71.

Black, P. and Wiliam, D. (1998b) *Inside the Black Box: Raising Standards Through Classroom Assessment*. London: nferNelson.

Black, P. and Wiliam, D. (2006) The reliability of assessments, in J. Gardner (ed.) *Assessment and Learning*. London: Sage, pp. 214–39.

Boaler, J. (1997) *Experiencing School Mathematics: Teaching Styles, Sex and Setting*. Buckingham: Open University Press.

Bolton, E. (1992) The quality of teaching, in *Education – Putting the Record Straight*. Stafford: Network Press, pp. 13–19.

Burris, C.C., Heubert, J.P. and Levin, H.M. (2006) Accelerating mathematics achievement using heterogeneous grouping, *American Educational Research Journal*, 43(1): 105–36.

Clarke, K. (1991) Education in a classless society, 'The Westminster Lecture'. Given to the Tory Reform Group, June.

Cumming, J.J. and Maxwell, G.S. (2004) Assessment in Australian schools: current practice and trends, *Assessment in Education*, 11(1): 94–108.

Daugherty, R. (1995) *National Curriculum Assessment. A Review of Policy 1987–1994*. London: Falmer.

Department of Education and Science (DES) (1987) *The National Curriculum 5–16: A Consultation Document*. London: Department of Education and Science and the Welsh Office.

Department of Education and Science (DES) (1988a) *Task Group on Assessment and Testing. A Report*. London: Department of Education and Science and the Welsh Office.

Department of Education and Science (DES) (1988b) *Task Group on Assessment and Testing: Three Supplementary Reports*. London: Department of Education and Science and the Welsh Office.

Department for Education (DfE) (1994) *Educational Statistics for the United Kingdom*, Statistical Bulletin 1/94. London: DfE.

Department for Education and Skills (DfES) (2006) *Educational Statistics GCSE results 2004/5*, at http://www.dfes.gov.uk/rsgateway.

Eckstein, M.A. and Noah, H.J. (1993) *Secondary School Examinations: International Perspectives on Policy and Practice*. New Haven, CT: Yale University Press.

European Round Table of Industrialists (ERT) (1995) *Education for Europeans: Towards the Learning Society*. Brussels: ERT.

Fairbrother, R.W., Dillon, J. and Gill, P. (1995) Assessment at Key Stage 3: teachers' attitudes and practices, *British Journal of Curriculum and Assessment*, 5(3): 25–31, 46.

Fullan, M. (2003) *Change Forces with a Vengeance*. London: RoutledgeFalmer.

Fullan, M.G. with Stiegelbauer, S. (1991) *The New Meaning of Educational Change*. London: Cassell.

Gardner, J. and Cowan, P. (2005) The fallibility of high stakes '11-plus' testing in Northern Ireland, *Assessment in Education*, 12(2): 145–65.

Gillborn, D. and Youdell, D. (2000) *Rationing Education*. London: Routledge.

Gipps, C., Brown, M., McCallum, B. and McAlister, S. (1995) *Intuition or Evidence? Teachers and National Assessment of 7-year-olds*. Buckingham: Open University Press.

Harlen, W. and Malcolm, H. (1999) *Setting and streaming: a research review. SCRE research series no. 18*. Edinburgh: Scottish Council for Research in Education. Available for download at http://www.scre.ac.uk/pdf/setting.pdf.

Joseph. K. (1976) *Stranded in the Middle Ground*. London: Centre for Policy Studies.

Knight, C. (1990) *The Making of Tory Education Policy in Post-War Britain 1950–1986*. London: Falmer.

Lawton, D. (1994) *The Tory Mind on Education 1979–94*. London: Falmer.

McKenzie, J. (1993) *Education as a Political Issue*. Aldershot: Avebury.

Milroy, D. (1992) Teaching and learning: what a child expects from a good teacher, in various authors, *Education – Putting the Record Straight*. Stafford: Network Press.

National Board of Education (1994) *Framework for the Comprehensive School 1994*. Helsinki: Painatuskeskus (in English).

National Commission on Education (NCE) (1993) *Learning to Succeed: Report of the National Commission on Education*. London: Heinemann.

National Commission on Education (NCE) (1995) *Learning to Succeed. The Way Forward*. London: NCE.

Newmann, F.M., Bryk, A.S. and Nagaoka, J.K. (2001) *Authentic Intellectual Work and Standardized Tests: Conflict or Coexistence?* Chicago: Consortium on Chicago School Research. Available at http://www.consortium-chicago.org.

Nuthall, G. and Alton-Lee, A. (1995) Assessing classroom learning: how students use their knowledge and experience to answer classroom achievement test questions in science and social studies, *American Educational Research Journal*, 32(1): 185–223.

Pellegrino, J.W., Baxter, G.P. and Glaser, R. (1999) Addressing the 'two disciplines' problem: linking theories of cognition with assessment and instructional practice, *Review of Research in Education*, 24: 307–53.

Peters, T. and Waterman, R. (1982) *In Search of Excellence*. New York: Harper & Row.

Posch, P. (1994) Strategies for the implementation of technology education, in D. Layton (ed.) *Innovations in Science and Technology Education Vol. V*. Paris: UNESCO.

Royal Ministry of Church, Education and Research (1994) *Core Curriculum for Primary, Secondary and Adult Education in Norway*. Oslo: Akademika a/s (in English).

Select Committee (2004) *House of Commons Education and Skills Committee Secondary Education: Schools Admissions 4th Report Session 2003–2004 July 22nd 2004*. See Parliament website: http://www.publications.parliament.uk/pa/cm/cmeduski.htm.

Shepard, L.A. (1992) Commentary: what policy makers who mandate tests should know about the new psychology of intellectual ability and learning, in B.R. Gifford and M.C. O'Connor (eds) *Changing Assessments: Alternative Views of Aptitude, Achievement and Instruction*. Boston, MA: Kluwer.

Thatcher, M. (1993) *The Downing Street Years*. London: HarperCollins.

Tomlinson, S. (2005) (2nd edn) *Education in a Post-welfare Society*. Maidenhead: Open University Press, McGraw Hill.

Weare, K. (2005) *Improving Learning Through Emotional Literacy*. London: Paul Chapman.

White, J. (1990) *Education and the Good Life: Beyond the National Curriculum*. London: Kogan Page.

Whitty, G. (2002) *Making Sense of Education Policy*. London: Sage Publications.

| 5 | Values and schooling |

Alan Cribb and
Sharon Gewirtz

Introduction

In this chapter we explore some of the ways in which fundamental questions about values and schooling are currently 'asked' and 'answered'. We will argue that, in many respects, these questions are marginalized, or even buried, and that there is a widespread and understandable scepticism about them. We will also argue, however, that this scepticism is an important feature of what might be called 'the prevailing values climate' – a climate that has a neutral and common-sense face but that is by no means neutral.

Most of the chapter will be given over to sketching out some of the features of this value climate. The first part of this sketch covers features of the general philosophical and ethical context, particularly the role of value scepticism and value neutrality. The second part of the sketch focuses in on aspects of the current social and political context of English schooling, and the value shifts inherent in the reforms set in train by the Education Act of 1988 and built on by successive governments since then.

Parallel reforms to those made in England in 1988 were introduced in Wales, Scotland and Northern Ireland but in this chapter we are only referring to the situation in England. Such broad coverage as we provide here makes it impossible to cover issues in much depth, or to trace through all the themes or possible links between the features discussed. However, we hope that there are also advantages in working on a broad canvas. In particular, we hope to draw attention to a powerful compound of factors which serve to undermine the critical function of value debate.

What are schools for?

Virtually all questions about schooling are value questions – but some of these are fundamental in the sense that the answers we give to them determine our answers to the others. 'What are schools for?' is an example of one of the most fundamental value questions that needs to be asked. The issues raised by this question are the most far-reaching and arguably the most practical matters facing a prospective teacher. The way in which schools are organized, priority setting and the allocation of resources, the attitudes towards (and attention given to) different sorts of tasks, the general modes of behaviour, and the nature and quality of relationships will all be shaped by beliefs about the purpose of schooling. Mike Bottery makes this point nicely in his book, *The Ethics of Educational Management* (1992). He identifies a number of different philosophical perspectives on the ultimate purposes of education and argues that these produce very different relationships and approaches to management within schools. For example, the 'cultural transmission' perspective:

> values knowledge which is perceived as part of a country's cultural heritage. It sees the child as essentially a passive imbiber . . . Teachers, therefore, are seen as guardians, transmitters of appropriate values, and as headteachers will be transmitters, and supervisors of those below them who are also transmitting, the situation will be an essentially hierarchical one.
>
> (Bottery 1992: 12)

The 'child-centred' perspective, on the other hand:

> sees the curriculum as based on each individual child's experiences and interests, each of them being active, involved, unique constructors of their own reality . . . The teacher, in this situation, becomes a facilitator, a constructor of beneficial situations for the child, but in no way a transmitter . . . Hierarchy makes little sense, and one moves increasingly towards a model of democracy.
>
> (Bottery 1992: 13–14)

These are just examples. Others include what Bottery calls the 'social reconstruction' perspective, which 'sees schools as essentially concerned with pressing social issues which need to be resolved', and the 'gross national product' perspective, which 'values knowledge which is conducive to the furtherance of national economic well-being' (Bottery 1992: 12). Such approaches are not necessarily all mutually exclusive and can be interpreted and combined in various ways. This is exemplified in the Australian sociologist, R.W. Connell's seminal 1985 ethnographic study, *Teachers' Work*. Connell's teachers hold a range of views on the fundamental purposes of education, which is reflected in their different approaches to teaching.

Our purpose here has not been to answer the question 'What are schools for?' but merely to underline its fundamental nature for anyone pursuing a career in teaching. Although there is no doubt some wisdom, as well as a legal and moral obligation, in taking a lead from the policies and ethos generated by one's employing institution and one's colleagues, anyone who wants to make a contribution to the policy-making process operates, implicitly or explicitly, with a view of schooling. Even if a teacher were to retreat to a position of mere employee, virtually every practical decision they made, every conversation they had in the classroom or the corridor, would betray a personal conception of what schools are for.

Thus the challenge could be issued to everyone embarking on a career as a teacher – 'How will you affect the balance of the debate? What are your conceptions of the aims of education, and of schooling? What do you see as the role of schools in society?' Perhaps it would be foolish to start a career with a set of confident and dogmatic answers. Yet not to have any answers might be deemed professionally negligent.

It is not as simple as this, however. There is a whole array of factors that militate against individuals forming such a personal vision of the role of education. In fact, when it comes to answering questions about values and schooling there is a loosely related range of 'licensed avoidance tactics'. In answer to the question 'What are schools for?' you could say, in short, 'There are no right answers'; and/or 'There are different answers – and you have to be neutral between them' and/or 'You need to use a neutral mechanism to determine what people want from schools'. These avoidance tactics will be explored further in the sections that follow, but they all have the effect of marginalizing both value debate and teachers' own personal value positions.

Scepticism

It is easy to stress the practical importance of questions about values and schooling, but it is much more difficult to answer them. What is an individual teacher to do? What is the appropriate stance towards ethical and political issues? This is where scepticism enters the picture.

At base, scepticism is the view that knowledge of something – in this case ethical or political matters – is impossible, that there is no procedure for arriving at, or demonstrating, the truth or falsity, rightness or wrongness, of value claims. This is not the place to discuss the nature of scepticism in any depth, but perhaps it is worth mentioning that it is very difficult to argue convincingly against scepticism in any area of knowledge. However, for a number of reasons scepticism about value judgements is peculiarly pervasive in everyday culture. Indeed, the phrase 'It's a value judgement' is often treated as synonymous with expressions like 'It's just a personal opinion' or 'Who can say?'

The growth of value scepticism has been a long and complex process (MacIntyre 1985), but to a large extent it is the product of the modern fixation with certain models of knowledge, in particular models of rationality, observability and testability associated with the natural sciences which seek to separate out the 'hard' public realm from the 'soft' realm of personal beliefs and feelings, the 'objective' from the 'subjective', facts from values. In the twentieth century a number of philosophical theories were advanced to the effect that ethical judgements are nothing more than expressions of emotions, attitudes, or preferences. At one extreme these would entail that no ethical position is better grounded, or more warranted, than any other. Something very like this has also become a major current in common-sense thinking. If this were treated as the whole story, however, the implications would be drastic. There would be no basis on which to criticize any ethical or political position. Teachers would be on an equally strong footing whether they pulled their value judgements out of a hat or whether they deliberated carefully about them. Asking about the aims of schooling would be asking a question for which there were no right answers.

Although value scepticism is prevalent in theoretical and popular discourse, it is only part of the picture. Other aspects of everyday culture tell a different story. First, there are, of course, people who are comfortable maintaining that they do have good grounds, and justified beliefs, regarding their moral and political judgements, the most clear-cut, and most visible, being religious fundamentalists of one kind or another. Second, even people who dismiss the idea that they operate with defensible moral convictions tend to change their minds in practice if certain lines are crossed (for example, if their flatmate turns out to be a cannibal). Third, very many people take overt moral and political stances, and show conviction and commitment in the pursuit of these stances, and may simply leave the question of the epistemological status of these stances on one side (although, once again, in practice they will typically offer reasons and arguments in the defence of these stances). The powerful convictions surrounding conflicts around racism or animal welfare testify to the limits of scepticism in practice.

These two facts about current values talk – the widespread currency of scepticism and the vigorousness of moral challenge and argument – appear to be contradictory. However, they are probably better seen as two complementary facets of a new orthodoxy.

Neutrality

Whether or not ethical systems are rationally defensible, ethics does not require a rational foundation. All that is required is a shared tradition and framework of beliefs, feelings and habits. Within such a tradition there can be scope for rational debate and disagreement about principles and ideals, and how they should be interpreted and applied. The difficulty is to know what to do if the reality, or even the idea, of a shared tradition breaks down and is replaced by a situation of moral or value pluralism. In many respects value scepticism is a response to value pluralism. Ours is a society that is suspicious of the controlling use of ethical traditions and systems, one that contains people with different world views, that encompasses different cultures and traditions, and in which there is increasingly less consensus about the right starting point for debate.

In the context of pluralism, the combination of scepticism and conviction mentioned above appears more coherent, although this combination is perhaps better understood as a consequence of the 'privatization of morality' and as a weak version of moral relativism, which allows scope for value divergence between individuals and groups within society but which draws the line at stronger versions of relativism. (Stronger versions would accord equal status to outlooks which sought to destroy this equilibrium.) This combination is characteristic of what might be called a 'liberal ethic', which is arguably the dominant outlook in the contemporary values climate and the orthodoxy of value pluralism! A liberal ethic allows for alternative beliefs about 'what is good' to operate at the private level, or within relatively self-contained groups, while preserving a thin framework of public morality. The latter is necessary to protect the private sphere and to ensure that people rub along together satisfactorily (Mulhall and Swift 1993). The primary value in a liberal ethic is autonomy, and respect for autonomy. According to liberal political philosophy the role of the state is to be, as far as possible, neutral between competing conceptions of the good. Individual conceptions of the good are to be autonomously determined and pursued. We can have our personal value convictions providing we do not use the public realm to impose them on anyone else.

From this standpoint, developing and promoting the autonomy of young people becomes the central aim of education. The role of schools as public institutions is to introduce young people to the different perspectives that make up the pluralist culture and to support them in finding their own path through it and arriving at their own convictions. This approach is largely incompatible with the advocacy of any particular value position, and some might feel it should entail playing down the overt ethical and political dimensions of education.

The problem for this sort of liberalism is that, not only do public institutions tend not to be neutral in practice, but it is far from clear that neutrality is a possibility even in principle. This is particularly evident in the case of schools. In practice, a liberal ethos is overlaid with some favoured value system. The role of Christianity or particular attitudes towards sexuality will serve as examples. But how could a school be organized in such a way as not to favour certain world views? This may be a useful ideal for some purposes (up to a point it would serve to support a tolerant, respectful and inclusive ethos) but it is surely not a realizable one. One reason it is unrealizable is that a liberal ethos can conflict with some of the standpoints it might seek to embrace – for example, how could a school be neutral between sexual equality on the one hand and anti-homosexual beliefs on the other?

Scepticism and neutrality provide avoidance tactics for teachers who are asked to make value judgements about the purpose, content and organization of schooling. Indeed, there are good reasons for teachers to be cautious. It would seem arrogant to set oneself up as an authoritative arbiter of political and ethical matters. Surely it is necessary to recognize that there are very different beliefs about these matters, and there is a need to recognize this diversity, and to treat different views with respect? Perhaps those people who determine the organization and ethos of schools should try to steer a middle course, and to avoid extremes? Up to a point this attitude is plausible but it is also highly prone to exploitation. Forms of scepticism and neutrality serve as very fertile conditions for the spread of dominant norms and ideologies. Teachers who retreat behind them – as a way of avoiding engagement with challenging value questions – may be in an unwitting conspiracy with some strongly 'non-neutral' stances.

Effectiveness and efficiency

In the practical contexts of politics and policy making there is not very much talk about 'neutrality'; the idea is rarely advocated explicitly, but it is an important implicit dimension of real world politics. Some very sophisticated mechanisms exist to present value-laden positions as if they were value neutral. In fact, one aspect of the politics of policy making is to 'neutralize', and thereby help to legitimize, certain value judgements – to render ideology into common sense. A good example of this manoeuvre in recent UK politics has been the championing of the goals of effectiveness and efficiency in the reformed public sector.

It would be perverse not to be in favour of effective schools, or to favour wasteful schools. Here is a language that everyone can share, which – at least on the face of things – is outside of ethical and political ideology. However, in reality the use of these ideas within education policy has been part and parcel of the deliberate imposition of a specific ideological framework on schooling and the reinforcement and creation of specific value environments for schools. We will look at some features of this process in more detail below, but first we will briefly review the two main 'neutralizing mechanisms' of efficiency: utilitarianism and markets.

Utilitarianism

Faced with the task of evaluating social institutions, and given the diversity and contestability of possible criteria, there is a tendency to identify or stipulate some lowest common denominator to serve as the arbiter of success or effectiveness, and as the means of comparing performance over time or between institutions. These measures of output or performance indicators will need to be publicly observable and easily measurable. An efficient institution will be one that achieves the highest score of success at lowest cost. Of course this approach has the effect of replacing all of the complexity and value debate (about, for example, what schools are for) with whatever measure happens to be identified or stipulated. There will always be pressure to introduce more sophisticated and multidimensional criteria of success but equally inevitably there will always be countervailing pressures to simplify complex measures in order to provide definitive and decisive scores and comparisons. Throughout the remainder of this chapter we use 'utilitarianism' as shorthand for this concern with maximizing 'productivity' according to some relatively simple measures of success. It is this current of utilitarianism which, we argue, is built into specific educational policies. There are, of course, other conceptions of utilitarianism and other currents within the utilitarian tradition.

Markets

Resorting to 'markets' of one kind or another represents the other main mechanism for smoothing out value diversity and conflict. The market can be represented as a neutral mechanism for efficiently aggregating and responding to the variety of 'consumer' preferences – for providing what it is people actually want. The market, it is claimed, merely reflects preferences rather than imposing some external standard on institutions, which would also mean deliberately imposing a contestable value position on people who do not share it. It does not follow from the fact, however, that a market mechanism may be an effective way of circumventing open-ended value debate, that its effects are more defensible or acceptable, or that its consequences, because they are 'unplanned', amount any less to an imposition. War is another mechanism that serves to circumvent debate but it is common to resist the accompanying idea that 'might is right'.

Although they are only two threads of a complicated picture, utilitarian and market thinking are undoubtedly important currents in recent public and education policy. In some varieties they are in strong tension with one another, because utilitarianism tends towards simple specified yardsticks, whereas market ideology emphasizes process and diversity. They can be combined in various ways, however, and they are linked by a preoccupation with efficiency and the attempt to cut through the contestability of values. It is this combination that makes them – along with the language of 'standards' and 'effectiveness' – suitable vehicles to import a specific value climate under the guise of neutrality.

Reform in England since 1988

We now want to turn to more concrete matters and, in particular, to sketch the specific form in which utilitarian and market principles have been combined in the restructuring of the English education system since 1988. We will then look at some of the particular ways in which this restructuring has begun to generate a shift in the values climate of the English school system. In doing so, our aim is to use the concrete example of school reform in England to illustrate the general point that utilitarianism and markets represent key policy mechanisms for imposing, under the guise of neutrality, a particular set of values on schooling. We should say at once that the following account is only one interpretation of this specific values shift; our main intention is to draw attention to the process that is taking place. This is an important task, because in order for practising teachers to be reflexive about their own values they need to be aware of the ways in which these values, and the opportunities to act on them, are shaped and constrained by the values embedded within the structures of the school and the education system as a whole.

Those currently working within schools do not only suffer from living within a general philosophical climate that marginalizes value debate. They are also being bombarded with a particular genre of 'new managerialist' literature designed to help them 'improve' and be more 'efficient' and 'effective' (Thrupp and Willmott 2003). Most of this literature tends to neglect the social and value context of schooling, except in so far as it relates to the 'image' of the school in the education 'marketplace'. Some of it goes further and seeks positively to discourage school managers and teachers from concerning themselves with such things that are deemed to be beyond their control and an unnecessary distraction from the core tasks of being efficient and effective. However, the New Labour government first elected in 1997, unlike its Conservative predecessor, has at least explicitly addressed the fundamental issue of what values it wishes to promote in education. These were set out in the *Revised National Curriculum for England* (QCA/DfEE 1999) as follows:

> Foremost is a belief in education, at home and at school, as a route to the spiritual, moral, social, cultural, physical and mental development, and thus the well-being, of the individual. Education is also a route to equality of opportunity for all, a healthy and just democracy, a productive economy, and sustainable development. Education should reflect the enduring values that contribute to these ends. These include valuing ourselves, our families and other relationships, the wider groups to which we belong, the diversity in our society and the environment in which we live. Education should also reaffirm our commitment to the virtues of truth, justice, honesty, trust and a sense of duty.
>
> (QCA/DfEE 1999)

Thus for New Labour, education has a range of purposes, reflecting what Bottery (1992) has called the 'gross national product' perspective, alongside an environmentalist perspective and concerns more traditionally associated with liberal humanism, including equality of opportunity, democracy and valuing diversity. This liberal humanist perspective was also reflected in the decision to include citizenship as part of the statutory curriculum from 2002. The importance of collaboration between schools and between schools and other agencies concerned with the welfare of children and the importance of the inclusion of families deemed to be 'socially excluded' are other values emphasized in New Labour policies – for example, the Sure Start, Excellence in Cities and Every Child Matters initiatives.

New Labour education policies can, therefore, be differentiated in specific respects from the policies of the preceding Conservative governments. There are also some important continuities, however. There has, for example, been no increased level of public debate about what schools are for under New Labour, and the list of 'value outputs' in the revised National Curriculum has not been accompanied by any discussion of value issues relating to the processes or contexts of schooling. Moreover, New Labour has inherited, and in some respects reinforced, the four key mechanisms that the Conservatives had introduced to create a market in schooling. These mechanisms – choice, diversity, per capita funding and devolved management – were first introduced by the 1988 Education Reform Act (ERA).

In the rhetoric justifying the 1988 legislation, choice and freedom were presented both as good things in themselves and as mechanisms for raising standards. Standards would improve, it was suggested, because, within the market, 'good/strong' schools would thrive, while 'poor/weak' ones would go to the wall or have to improve. In this survival-of-the-fittest approach to educational provision, good schools and colleges are defined as those that are popular with consumers (parents and/or students), and poor schools as those that are unpopular. It is appropriate to note here that in the debate about choice in education at school level, it is the parents who are more often than not described as the consumers, not their children.

The market introduced by the Conservatives and retained by New Labour cannot be characterized as a free market, nor as a neutral mechanism of resource allocation, but is more accurately described as a form of what Hayek (1980) has termed 'ordered competition'. This is because in addition to the market mechanisms of choice, per capita funding and devolved management, mentioned above, the Conservatives also introduced – under the 1988 Act – a set of specific performance indicators based on a centrally prescribed National Curriculum and a system of national testing at four Key Stages. These components incorporate utilitarian aspects into the reforms.

The system of information established by the 1988 Act is constituted by published league tables of national test results based on the National Curriculum, as well as Ofsted inspection reports. This information is meant to enable consumers to compare the performance of schools and assist them in making their choices. The 1988 legislation was therefore designed to encourage schools to respond to consumer wishes, but at the same time the Government was trying to send very clear messages about what consumers should be looking for in a school. Under New Labour, these messages have arguably been articulated even more forcibly and extensively. For example, the Government has set up a website for parents which both promotes and provides information on school choice and includes links to the schools results tables and Ofsted reports (http://www.parentscentre.gov.uk/). In addition to an intensification of consumerist rhetoric, there has arguably also been an intensification of utilitarian currents through an increased emphasis on target setting and performance monitoring – and there are indications that, particularly with the introduction of performance-related pay in 2000, utilitarian discourses of efficiency and effectiveness have penetrated some teachers' professional identities, whilst prompting others to leave the profession (Mahony et al. 2004).

The ostensibly neutral formal arrangements identified in the preceding paragraphs – markets, national testing, the publication of test results and Ofsted inspection reports, and performance management – inevitably carry a set of beliefs about what schools are for and about how those involved in managing them should behave. For example, although on the surface the market reforms value freedom of choice, that value is compromised by an alternative set of values embedded within legislation. First, the introduction of markets means that the concept of neighbourhood schooling is devalued through the effective abolition of catchment areas. Neighbourhood schooling is based on the idea that children should go to their local school with other local children. Within the marketized system, however, it is assumed that consumers (or responsible ones at any rate) will only choose the local school if it performs well in the league tables. If sufficient parents in a neighbourhood choose not to send their children to a local school, then there is, in effect, no longer a neighbourhood school for other parents in that area to choose. This means that freedom of choice espoused by supporters of marketization does not necessarily include the choice of a neighbourhood school.

Second and relatedly, the emphasis within both the 1988 legislation and New Labour's reforms appear to us to be focused mainly upon the instrumental goals of education. More specifically, legislation is geared towards the improvement of 'standards' that are narrowly defined in terms of output: for example, test results, attendance levels and school-leaver destinations. The implication is that 'good' schools are those that perform well in league tables – either on the basis of their raw scores or their rates of improvement. The information required to be published is limited, and despite more recent adjustments to make the measures more representative of schools' 'added value', some important characteristics are ignored. For example, there is no requirement for schools to publish information on: the expressive, co-operative and community aspects of schooling, on levels of enjoyment, happiness, stimulation and challenge for teachers and students, on degrees of innovation and creativity in school approaches to teaching and learning, on the quality of special needs provision, on the pastoral, social and extra-curricular dimensions of schooling, nor on collaborative relationships within and between schools. Good attendance might be a reflection of these things, but then again it may well be a reflection of other factors, such as the kind of students who attend the institution.

Values drift

It can be argued that the overall effect of these arrangements for the control and management of schools is a process of values drift. This argument (set out in much greater length as part of research reported in Ball 1994, Gewirtz *et al.* 1995 and Gewirtz 2001) suggests that, in practice, the market constitutes an incentive structure that rewards schools for particular kinds of behaviour and values and penalizes them for others. The argued drift consists of a diminishing concern with need, equity, community and co-operation and an increasing concern with image, discipline, output measures, academic differentiation and competition. (Talk of 'a drift' is a simplification, and reflects a general tendency – the effects of which are partial and patchy – not a universal before-and-after switch!)

It is argued that values drift occurs in large measure because school managers perceive that their schools will be judged on the basis of their exam league-table performance. This leads them to implement policies that they feel will make their schools more attractive to children with a high measured 'ability'. Such students are likely to enhance the schools' league table performances at lowest cost. At the same time, many schools seem to be concerned not to attract too many students deemed to have learning, emotional or behavioural difficulties. Such students demand a high level of investment while producing little return in terms of exam league-table performance (Audit Commission 2002).

According to this interpretation, it appears that prospective students are effectively being divided into two categories by schools – those students whom they desire to attract and those whom they do not. The former category consists of children of a high measured 'ability', those who are perceived to be committed to education and those with supportive parents. A particularly desirable category of children are girls, who are perceived as behaviourally more amenable than boys and academically more highly achieving. The second category of consumers, the undesirables, consists of the less 'able', children with emotional problems or who are behaviourally disruptive, working-class children whose parents are viewed as not valuing education, who 'just' send their children to the school because it is local, and children with learning difficulties and other special needs (although there are some exceptions) who are expensive to educate and who threaten 'balanced' intakes. Schools with strong special needs departments need to be concerned about the image conveyed by strength in this area as well as by the financial consequences of having large numbers of children with learning difficulties (MacBeath et al. 2006). In addition, national statistics on exclusions suggest that Black Caribbean boys are at least covertly being assigned to the 'undesirables' category (Parsons et al. 2004).

Within some schools, resources appear to have shifted from students with special needs to students defined as being more able. In secondary schools, learning support departments have contracted and, given recent Government policies to remodel the school workforce, there is a risk that the specialist expertise of special needs teachers will be displaced by a reliance on less qualified teaching assistants (MacBeath et al. 2006). At the same time, through the Excellence in Cities programme, New Labour has introduced additional funding specifically targeted at students deemed to be 'gifted and talented'. These shifts in the balance of targeting affect all children and not just those deemed to be 'special' for one reason or another. Increasingly, schools have invested energy and resources on students judged to be at the threshold of achieving more than five A*–Cs or at least one A*–G at GCSE (the key indicators used to compile the exam league tables) (Gillborn and Youdell 1999).

Developments noted by other researchers lend support to the argument that values drift is a reality in English schools. For example, Woods (1993) in his study of 11 secondary schools in three LEAs pointed to 'indications . . . of senior staff in the case study schools giving emphasis to middle-class parental perspectives, by making changes which it is assumed will be attractive to them'. Among the changes the author noted were more attention to discipline, uniform, homework and examination policies. Two of his case study schools systematically identify the primary schools whose pupils go on to achieve the best GCSE results in order to target their promotional activity. Fitz et al. (1993) noted what they refer to as a 'reinvigorated traditionalism' in a number of the schools they studied:

> several had strengthened their dress codes and reinforced school uniform codes; others were giving increased emphasis to customary standards of pupil behaviour, including ways of approaching and

addressing teachers; while at least one had banned the use of 'biros' in favour of fountain pens.

(Fitz *et al.* 1993: 73)

Once again it is plausible that the 'reinvigorated traditionalism' that Fitz *et al.* describe represents efforts to make schools more attractive to middle-class students with good GCSE potential who will help to raise the league table position of the schools.

At the heart of the 'values drift' thesis is a concern that the fundamental value axis of English schooling is changing; that there is a gradual erosion of the principle 'that the education of all students is intrinsically of equal value' (Daunt 1975) which underpinned much educational thinking (if not always practice) in the pre-1988 'comprehensive era'. In opposition to this principle, it is argued, forms of marketization and utilitarianism work to promote the values of competitive individualism within the English school system.

It is important to note that the evidence upon which the values drift thesis was originally based was assembled before New Labour's coming to power in 1997. It still remains to be seen what the overall effects of New Labour's more complex policy mix will be, with its concurrent emphasis on markets and utilitarianism, on the one hand, and collaboration, inclusion and respect for democracy and diversity, on the other. Having acknowledged this uncertainty, however, there are a number of powerful indications which suggest that the balances in this policy mix will not substantially alter the relevance and validity of the values drift thesis (Gewirtz 2001; Wilson *et al.* 2006).

Concluding comments

Whether or not credence is given to the idea that the value climate of English schooling is fundamentally changing – moving away from an equal commitment to all – and whether or not the explanation set out in the values drift thesis is a sufficient one, significant changes have clearly taken place since 1988. Changes in the social and political context of schooling and in the control and management of schools have implications for conceptions of schooling: for what is possible, for what is deemed desirable, for whose voices are influential and so on. The way in which the question 'What are schools for?' is answered in practice inevitably changes over time, and the reforms that have been introduced since 1988 are only one – albeit significant – example of this process. Within individual schools the balance that is struck between different educational and schooling perspectives evolves through conflict and adjustment. In some settings aspects of child-centredness and 'social reconstruction' may well be losing out to a new emphasis on economic instrumentalism. In others, schools may be able to harness the more humanistic strands of New Labour's reforms to resist the pressures towards utilitarianism and competitive individualism. It is within the framework of these kinds of value conflicts that an individual teacher has to orient herself or himself both theoretically and practically.

We would argue that, faced with these fundamental questions about values and schooling, the role of professionals – individually and collectively – is not only to take up stances but also to enter into explicit value debate with one another and with the wider community. This debate about the purposes of schooling, and the respective merits of equality, freedom, and other basic principles, is both intellectually and emotionally challenging. There is an understandable temptation to take refuge in forms of scepticism and neutrality. But, as we hope to have illustrated, teachers contribute to changes in their values climate either self-consciously or by default.

References

Audit Commission (2002) *Special Educational Needs: a Mainstream Issue*. London: Audit Commission.

Ball, S.J. (1994) *Education Reform: A Critical and Post-Structural Approach*. Buckingham: Open University Press.

Bottery, M. (1992) *The Ethics of Educational Management*. London: Cassell.

Bourne, J., Bridges, L. and Searle, C. (1994) *Outcast England: How Schools Exclude Black Children*. London: Institute of Race Relations.

Connell, R.W. (1985) *Teachers' Work*. Sydney: George Allen & Unwin.

Daunt, P. (1975) *Comprehensive Values*. London: Heinemann.

Fitz, J., Halpin, D. and Power, S. (1993) *Education in the Market Place*. London: Kogan Page.

Gewirtz, S. (1996) Market discipline versus comprehensive education: a case study of a London comprehensive school struggling to survive in the education market place, in J. Ahier, B. Cosin and M. Hales (eds) *Diversity and Change: Education, Policy and Selection*. London: Routledge.

Gewirtz, S. (2001) *The Managerial School: Postwelfarism and Social Justice in Education*. London: Routledge.

Gewirtz, S., Ball, S.J. and Bowe, R. (1995) *Markets, Choice and Equity in Education*. Buckingham: Open University Press.

Gillborn, D. and Gipps, C. (1996) *Recent Research on the Achievements of Ethnic Minority Pupils*. London: HMSO.

Gillborn D., and Mirza H.S. (2000) *Educational Inequality: Mapping 'Race', Class and Gender: A Synthesis of Research Evidence*. HMI 232, Of, available at: www.ofsted.gov.uk.

Gillborn, D. and Youdell, D. (1999) *Rationing Education: Policy, Practice, Reform and Equity*. Buckingham: Open University Press.

Hayek, F. (1980) *Individualism and Economic Order*. Chicago, IL: University of Chicago Press.

MacBeath, J., Galton, M., Steward, S., MacBeath, A. and Page, C. (2006) *The Costs of Inclusion: a Report Commissioned by the NUT Concerning Inclusion in Schools*. Cambridge: University of Cambridge, Faculty of Education.

MacIntyre, M. (1985) *After Virtue: A Study in Moral Theory*. London: Duckworth.

Mahony P., Menter I. and Hextall I. (2004) The emotional impact of threshold assessment on teachers in England, *British Education Research Journal*, 30(3): 443–64.

Mulhall, S. and Swift, A. (1993) *Liberals and Communitarians*. Oxford: Blackwell.

Parsons, C., Godfrey, R., Annan, G., Cornwall, J., Dussart, M., Hepburn, S., Howlett, K. and Wennerstrom, V. (2004) *Minority Ethnic Exclusions and the Race Relations (Amendment) Act 2000. Research Report RR616*. London: HMSO.

QCA/DfEE (Qualifications and Curriculum Authority/Department for Education and Employment) (1999) *The Revised National Curriculum*. London: QCA.

Thrupp, M. and Willmott, R. (2003) *Education Management in Managerialist Times: Beyond the Textual Apologists*. Maidenhead: Open University Press.

Wilson, D., Croxson, B. and Atkinson, A. (2006) 'What gets measured gets done': headteachers' responses to the English secondary school performance management system, *Policy Studies*, 27(2): 153–71.

Woods, P. (1993) Responding to the consumer: parental choice and school effectiveness, *School Effectiveness and School Improvement*, 4(3): 205–29.

<table>
<tr><td>6</td></tr>
</table>

School effectiveness and improvement

Brenda Gay

Introduction

This chapter looks at research undertaken on school effectiveness and improvement and examines both the policies of successive governments and the initiatives taken by schools to further school improvement. Some policies have had far-reaching consequences for the ways schools are organized and managed, whilst others have focused on improving teacher effectiveness. In looking at school effectiveness and improvement, it is important to consider the values and assumptions behind both the research and the policies.

Changing perspectives on pupil achievement

The desire to see standards of education and pupil performance improving is driven by several concerns, such as individual fulfilment and social justice. For example, the role of education in serving the economy has been an issue for governments over the past two centuries. In the late nineteenth and early twentieth centuries, pupil success, or lack of it, was the basis upon which grants were awarded to schools from which teachers were paid – hence what became known as the notorious 'payment by results' system.

Different causal factors for student underachievement have been emphasized at various times. The dominant model in this country and the USA in the 1940s and 1950s focused on psychological determinants. Cyril Burt, among others, suggested that intelligence was an innate and relatively fixed quality and that tests could be devised to determine an individual's intelligence score. Under the tripartite system of secondary schooling introduced by the 1944 Education Act in this country (see Chapter 26), IQ tests formed the basis upon which pupils were allocated to either grammar, technical high or secondary modern schools (see Gay 2001: 89).

Research in the late 1950s put the emphasis on sociological determinants. The lack of confidence in schools' abilities to make a difference was highlighted in the USA by the Coleman Report (1966) which suggested that school differences only counted for a small percentage of difference in pupil attainment. The work of Christopher Jencks and his colleagues (1970) also suggested 'that the most important determinant of educational success was family background' (Jencks, cited by Silver 1994: 79). A plethora of studies in this country identified both material and non-material factors in the home which produced differential achievement and were largely linked to social class (Floud *et al.* 1957; Crowther 1959; Jackson and Marsden 1962; Robbins 1963; Plowden 1967; Bernstein 1970). Hargreaves (1967) and Lacey (1970) found differences between the quality of provision in grammar schools and secondary modern schools in terms of teacher qualifications, facilities and other resources, and that these differences were widest in schools serving less-advantaged communities.

In response to concerns raised by these studies and to questions about the validity of the 11-plus examination, the comprehensive system was introduced in this country in an attempt to provide greater equality of opportunity (see Chapter 26). At the same time, the Plowden Report (1967) drew attention to the impact of social disadvantage on educational opportunity and recommended that a new administrative principle, 'positive discrimination', should be exercised through the educational system to counteract the effect of a poor environment. As a result, areas of extreme deprivation were identified as educational priority areas; extra resources were allocated to them, including incentive payments to teachers. Whilst government policy was directed at the major reorganization of secondary education at a structural level, and the allocation of differential resources where need was greatest, attention was diverted from processes within schools to the inadequacy of the home or society that could lead to differential patterns of achievement.

School effectiveness research

In the late 1960s, the emphasis began to switch to factors within schools, as research emerged which indicated that processes within schools and teacher–pupil interactions could and did affect pupil performance. In the USA, Rosenthal and Jacobsen (1968) drew attention to what they termed a self-fulfilling prophecy, whereby teachers' expectations of their pupils' ability consciously or sub-consciously influenced their interactions, so that pupils performed in line with the teachers' expectations rather than with their measured ability levels. In this country Dale and Griffiths (1965), Lacey (1974) and Hargreaves *et al.* (1975), among others, drew attention to the part played by streaming in both establishing pupils' sense of identity and contributing to teachers' expectations and the subsequent effects on performance (see Chapter 16, 'Setting, streaming and mixed ability teaching'). Michael Power (1967) found significant differences in the delinquency rates in secondary schools in Tower Hamlets that could not be explained by pupils' social class background but which, Power suggested, might be to do with factors within the schools themselves.

The seminal study by Michael Rutter and his colleagues *Fifteen Thousand Hours* (Rutter *et al.* 1979) in 12 South London inner-city secondary schools with similar, predominantly working-class intakes, showed that the schools had different success rates when measured against a set of four outcomes – attendance, behaviour, examination success and delinquency. The research identified a number of school features and processes which accounted for the differences, including the degree of academic emphasis; teacher actions in lessons; the availability of rewards; and the extent to which pupils were able to take responsibility. The cumulative effect of these various social factors, 'school ethos', was considerably greater than the effect of any of the individual factors (Rutter *et al.* 1979: 179). At the same time, in the USA studies focused on schools which were known to be 'effective', 'specially effective' or 'exemplary' and identified some of their characteristics (see Silver 1994: 81 for details). 'The underlying question addressed by those interested in the idea of effective schools found increasing expression in the 1970s and had to do with differences between schools' (Silver 1994: 80). Thus the school effectiveness research movement gathered pace in the 1980s and 1990s, in this country and abroad, as a result of a change in perspective that recognized:

> that schools affect children, that there are observable regularities in the schools that 'add value' and that the task of educational policies is to improve all schools in general, and the more ineffective schools in particular, by the transmission of this knowledge to educational practitioners.
>
> (Reynolds *et al.* 2000: 3)

What makes an effective school?

In the late 1980s and 1990s, Peter Mortimore and his colleagues at the University of London Institute of Education undertook a considerable amount of work into school effectiveness. From their 1988 study of primary schools in London, which focused on pupil intakes, school environment and educational outcomes, they concluded that an effective school raised the performance of all pupils. They classified the contributory factors into four categories: at the school level, 'given' factors such as buildings, resources, intake; at the policy level, style of leadership, organization, staff, curriculum, relationships with parents; at the classroom level, 'given' factors such as class and pupil characteristics and policy (teachers' aims and strategies). They suggested that when each of these makes a positive contribution 'the result can be an increase in the school's effectiveness' (Mortimore *et al.* 1988, cited in Silver 1994: 93).

Sammons *et al.* (1997) pointed out that an issue raised by school effectiveness research in the 1990s was the use of raw data about pupils' academic achievements as a means of answering questions about a school's performance. They suggest a more meaningful measure for stimulating school self-evaluation and school improvement was the 'value-added' component, which they defined as 'an indication of the extent to which any given school has fostered the progress of *all* students in a range of subjects during a particular time period' (Sammons *et al.* 1997: 24). This ties in with Mortimer's definition of an effective school as one in which students progress further than might be expected from consideration of the school's intake (Mortimore 1991, cited by Sammons *et al.* 1997: 189). Sammons *et al.* suggested that to measure 'value added', accurate information is needed about prior attainment as well as information on pupils' backgrounds such as age, gender and entitlement to free school meals. They showed that league tables which used raw data may have led schools in educationally advantaged communities to become complacent, whilst schools in disadvantaged areas may have been adding greater value.

In 1994, the Head of Quality assurance at Ofsted commissioned the International School Effectiveness and Improvement Centre to conduct a review of school effectiveness research with particular regard to the key determinants of school effectiveness. Sammons, a member of the team, pointed out that, 'Although our primary focus is on the school effectiveness tradition, we have examined research in the related field of teacher effectiveness' (Sammons 1999: 186). Whilst she urged caution in interpreting findings concerning school effectiveness from studies in the early research that were based on small numbers of schools and interpreting correlations as causes, she concluded that the review made it possible to analyse 'key factors likely to be of relevance to practitioners and policy-makers concerned with school improvement and enhancing quality in education' (Sammons 1999: 187). Table 6.1 lists Sammons' 'Eleven key factors for effective schools'.

Leadership and school effectiveness

The quality of leadership emerged as a crucial factor in a school's success. Various studies have been made of the relative effectiveness of different leadership styles (Stoll and Fink 1996; Sergiovanni 2001; Harris and Lambert 2003; Harris *et al.* 2003). Summarizing research on leadership styles, Stoll and Fink compared several models. The structural functional or traditional rational model focuses on roles, role differentiation and hierarchical structure. The instructional model, according to Mortimore and his colleagues (1988), occurred when the headteacher was actively involved in the school's work and knowledgeable about what was going on in the classrooms, without exerting total control over the rest of the staff. Transactional leadership, the model dominant in the 1980s, contains an implicit leader–follower dichotomy in which leaders are superior to followers and followers depend on leaders. Transformational leadership, by contrast, focuses on the cultural context and requires an approach that transforms the feelings, attitudes and beliefs of followers. From their work with a hundred headteachers, Stoll and Fink (1996) derived a model of invitational leadership which is built on four premises – optimism, respect,

Table 6.1 Eleven key factors for effective schools (Sammons 1999: 195)

1. Professional leadership	Firm and purposeful A participative approach The leading professional
2. Shared vision and goals	Unity of purpose Consistency of purpose Collegiality and collaboration
3. A learning environment	An orderly atmosphere An attractive working environment
4. Concentration on teaching and learning	Maximization of learning time Academic emphasis Focus on achievement
5. Purposeful teaching	Efficient organization Clarity of purpose Structured lessons Adaptive practice
6. High expectations	High expectations all round Communicating expectations Providing intellectual challenge
7. Positive reinforcement	Clear and fair discipline Feedback
8. Monitoring progress	Monitoring pupil performance Evaluating pupil performance
9. Pupils' rights and responsibilities	Raising pupil self-esteem Positions of authority Control of work
10. Home–school partnership	Parental involvement in their children's learning
11. A learning organization	School-based staff development

trust, and integrity. This model synthesizes leadership models with the result that:

> through staff development activities, evolutionary planning and constant monitoring of the school's context, the invitational leader helps the school reinvent itself continually.
>
> (Stoll and Fink 1996: 116)

School improvement

It is against this research background that the policy initiatives of successive Labour and Conservative governments to improve schools will be examined.

From the 'Ruskin' Speech to the 1988 Education Reform Act

By the 1970s there was a concern that the school system was not providing value for money. The country was experiencing a period of economic stagnation; employers' complaints about the lack of basic numeracy skills among school leavers were reinforced by an Institute of Mathematics survey (Ollerenshaw 1978); standards of literacy were seen to be at best static if not actually falling (Bullock 1977); the freedom over the curriculum enjoyed by local education authorities (LEAs) and schools meant that a child's educational experience could vary considerably from one LEA to another, and from one school to another. In his speech at Ruskin College, Oxford, the Prime Minister at the time, James Callaghan, warned that schools and teachers were failing to deliver value for money and that education was not fulfilling its role as the producer of a workforce that would enable the country to compete on the international stage.

> We spend six billion pounds a year on education so there will be discussion [. . .] To the teachers I would say that you must satisfy parents and industry that what you are doing meets their requirements and the needs of their children.
>
> (Callaghan 1976)

Thus, school and teacher accountability came to the fore. Rather than it being centrally directed, the onus was on LEAs to develop mechanisms for making schools and individual teachers accountable. Some, for example, the Inner London Education Authorities and Oxfordshire, drew up comprehensive schemes that involved teachers and schools self-auditing and drawing up action plans (see Gay 1981 for details). However, because of the patchy response, by the time a Conservative government came to power in 1979, more radical action seemed needed. Thus began a move for more central government control over schools, including what had hitherto been regarded as the 'secret garden' – the curriculum, coupled with an emphasis on school effectiveness and improvement.

The Education Reform Act of 1988

An era of rapid education change was ushered in by the Education Reform Act of 1988. Among its provisions were the devolution of responsibilities to headteachers and governors that had hitherto belonged to LEAs; the introduction of a National Curriculum; the monitoring of performance and the annual publication of league tables based on pupils' results in the National Curriculum tests and public examinations; greater parental choice of school; and the provision of a greater variety of schools with different financial arrangements. Thus, at the same time as giving schools greater autonomy in some respects, in others the government took greater control and opened up the way for schools to become more publicly accountable.

The pressure for greater accountability arising from the 1988 Education Act led to demands for a more rigorous system of inspections. A system of inspection, Her Majesty's Inspectorate, had been in place since 1839 when the government first intervened in education with the award of government grants to the National Society and the British and Foreign Society. HMIs remit widened following the introduction of universal elementary education in 1870 and the development of secondary schools under the Education Act of 1902. During the period following the 1944 Education Act, HMI 'largely relinquished its inquisitorial role in favour of a more advisory one' (Wilcox and Gray 1996: 26), although it continued to inspect and publish reports on individual schools.

In 1990, the Office for Standards in Education (Ofsted) was set up as a non-ministerial government department, separate from the Department of Education and Employment, to monitor and report on schools, measuring them against a set of benchmarks. Its remit is to 'to improve standards of achievement and quality of education through regular, independent inspection, public reporting and informed independent advice' (www.ofsted.gov.uk). Initially a four-year cycle for inspecting every school in the country was introduced, but this has now been reduced to every six years for schools that are deemed to be doing well. Ofsted inspections began to be seen as punitive, particularly as their reports were used a basis for identifying 'failing' schools and for putting them into special measures, which will be discussed later (see also Chapter 8).

City Technology Colleges

A major policy shift in the 1980s was the encouragement of public–private partnerships to fund and manage public services. This process took several forms, such as contracting out of hitherto internally-managed services, the injection of money for capital projects or shifting the entire responsibility for providing and running a service for which the government paid. In 1987, the City Technology Colleges Trust was established as a public–private partnership, under whose aegis City Technology Colleges were set up. Behind this scheme lay the aims of creating more diversity in secondary education, producing a more technologically skilled work force and developing links with local industry. City Technology Colleges were intended to offer pupils of all abilities in urban areas the opportunity to study a curriculum geared to the world of work, with a focus on a particular specialist subject. The colleges enjoyed greater freedom compared with other schools in terms of management, pay structures and their curriculum. Private sector sponsors paid one-fifth of the initial and subsequent capital costs, the underlying assumption being that business involvement could do what the education service was failing to do, that is, ratchet up standards.

Policy initiatives of the Conservative government 1993–1997

Interest in the possible contribution that school effectiveness research could make to school improvement continued to grow in the 1990s.

Specialist Schools

Following on from the work of the City Technology Colleges Trust, the Specialist Schools Trust was set up in 1994. Whilst the City Technology Colleges were an attempt to raise standards in urban areas, Specialist Schools were to serve all parts of the country and existing schools were able to apply for specialist status in one of four curriculum areas – technology, arts, sports or languages. Whilst they had to teach the full National Curriculum, they were also to give special attention to their chosen subject area. The intention was for Specialist Schools to become local flagship schools, which would be better funded, with a distinctive character and better examination results. They were able to select up to 10 per cent of pupils on the basis of their aptitude in their specialism. Under this public–private partnership, the school was responsible for raising £50,000 from private sponsorship in order to qualify for the £100,000 government start-up grant.

'Naming and shaming' and 'special measures'

The commitment to raising standards in all schools resulted in 'one of the cruellest and most pointless policies developed in the wake of the Education Act 1993 – that of attacking so-called "failing schools"' (Tomlinson 2005: 79).

The 1993 Act allowed for special measures to be taken when a school was identified by an Ofsted inspection as failing against a set of criteria including poor standards of achievement, poor quality of education, demoralization of staff, high turnover and disruptive behaviour, truancy and high levels of racial tension.

Blame for a school's failings was laid firmly upon the head and teachers and overlooked the fact that many of these schools were serving disadvantaged communities and had a disproportionate number of disadvantaged pupils. The problems were, in some cases, compounded by the effects of greater parental choice which led successful schools to become oversubscribed and schools which were already facing challenging circumstances to take a greater number of underachieving pupils, pupils from difficult backgrounds or pupils for whom English was an additional language. Furthermore, the demoralizing effects of being put into special measures on staff, pupils and parents, which in turn led to falling rolls, were ignored.

Policy initiatives of the Labour governments: 1997–2006

Interest in the possible contribution of school effectiveness research to school improvement 'emerged as a particularly strong feature of government education policy since the 1997 election of a Labour administration' (Sammons 1999: 183). The New Labour government rapidly set out to fulfil its election promise that education was to be a high priority with a raft of policies that, in many ways, were a continuation or development of the policies of the previous Conservative governments. Two main reasons lay behind the importance attached to education; firstly, the 'over-riding imperative of Labour's political project is competitiveness in the global economy' (Hatcher 1998: 486) and secondly, the need to ensure equality of outcome:

> what is now needed is for educators in Britain to continue the creation of a technology of educational policy and practice that is so strong, so relentless and so powerful that it outweighs the effects of outside school influences and helps bring all schools to high standards of achievement, independently of their different backgrounds and starting points.
>
> (Reynolds 1997, cited by Hatcher 1998: 492)

Education Action Zones

The continued influence of private investment in education was seen in the creation, in 1998, of Education Action Zones (EAZs), whose aims were to raise standards in underperforming schools in areas with high levels of social disadvantage. EAZs were 'intended as test-beds for a new approach to improving education in socially disadvantaged areas which could then be generalised throughout the school system' (Hatcher 1998: 495). The zones comprised two or three secondary schools and their feeder primary schools. They were governed by action forums, composed of representatives from schools, parents, business interests and the LEA, and direct appointees of the Secretary of State. Government funding of £75,000 was allocated to each EAZ which, in turn, had to raise funding from the private sector. Because EAZs, by their very nature, were serving communities which had little experience of running their own affairs, they often failed to raise the necessary money from the private sector.

'Fresh Start' schools

The policy of naming and shaming failing schools was initially continued but was abandoned in 1998 when the 'Fresh Start' programme was introduced. An underlying premise of this programme was that failing schools have often lost their capacity to turn themselves around and therefore it was necessary to bring in external agencies. Failing schools were closed and subsequently reopened with a new name but on the same site, with new management and, often, new staff. The programme was extended in March 2000 when the then Education Secretary, David Blunkett, introduced a zero tolerance approach by threatening the closure of nearly 70 secondary schools with the lowest GCSE results in England unless at least 15 per cent of pupils achieved at least five good GCSE passes for three successive years. These schools would then be reopened under the fresh start scheme, costing around £1.5 million per school. The plan included appointing ten 'superheads' on salaries of £100,000.

Again, the blame for underachievement was placed on schools and teachers, and the characteristics of the schools' intakes were ignored. Not all 'Fresh Start' schools were successful and during the week that the extension of the programme was announced, the headteachers in three of the ten existing 'Fresh Start' schools resigned (see Tomlinson 2005 for a fuller discussion). Whilst the injection of funding and the initiatives undertaken by the 'superheads' initially led to a dramatic improvement, this was not always sustainable when the support was removed. The 'Fresh Start' scheme was abandoned in 2003.

The Excellence in Cities initiative

The policies of investment into areas of greatest urban need and public–private partnership were continued with the Excellence in Cities (EiC) programme which was launched in 1999, and extended during the following two years. Its aims were to raise standards in urban schools and to offer diversity of provision in order to meet the needs of all pupils within a framework of co-operation and partnership between schools. The DfES claims that the policy has been successful:

> [. . .] performance tables for the last four years show that on average, results in terms of five good GCSEs or equivalent rose faster in EiC schools than elsewhere. In 2002 and 2003 EiC Schools improved at twice the rate of non-EiC schools and in 2004 EiC schools improved by about four times the rate of non-EiC schools.
>
> (DfES 2006 standards site)

However, Her Majesty's Chief Inspector, David Bell (2003) argued that the EiC initiative had not raised standards noticeably but had provided a confidence boost for schools.

The expansion of the Specialist Schools initiative

The government expanded the number of Specialist Schools in a bid to provide greater choice and diversity. By 2005, the number of specialisms a school could offer had increased to ten – arts, business and enterprise, engineering, humanities, languages, mathematics and computing, music, science, sports and technology; and the number of these schools to two thousand. The intention is that by 2010, all schools will be Specialist Schools. The question arises as to how far the Specialist Schools have improved relative to other schools. Results from research undertaken by Jesson (2004) showed that whilst Specialist Schools ranked well in their specialism, they showed improvement across most disciplines, with improvement being most marked for pupils with average Key Stage 2 scores. As many specialist schools were in low socio-economic areas the better results were not the result of better intake. However, as Jesson pointed out, not all Specialist Schools showed improvement.

City Academies

In what was seen as a further admission by the Secretary of State for Education and Employment, David Blunkett, that the comprehensive system had failed to deliver 'what its advocates hoped for, never mind what we require for the 21st century' (*The Times* 2000), the City Academy policy was announced as 'a radical new approach to promote greater diversity and break the cycle of failing schools in inner cities' (*The Times* 2000) Again, the scheme implied distrust of the educational professionals as it aimed to involve private sector sponsors, such as businesses, individuals, churches and other faith groups or charities, which were required to contribute £2 million to the start-up costs, with a further £25 million provided from the DfEE. City Academies were to be located in areas of disadvantage, either to replace one or more existing schools that had already failed, or to be established where there was a need for additional school places. The Academies are able to select their intakes. Initially 17 Academies were set up, with proposals in 2005 to expand the number to 200. However, the desirability of extending the scheme was questioned by a Commons Select Committee on Education on the grounds that there was insufficient evidence of their success. Reporting this, *The Times* (2005) went on to list the failure of two Academies to improve. Using evidence of the drop in the numbers of children on free school meals attending Academies, the *Guardian* on 31 October suggested there was evidence that the Academies were skewing their intakes to improve results.

Teacher effectiveness

As well as policies to drive up standards, the government has also introduced measures to improve the quality of teachers from trainees through to heads.

Building leadership capacity for school improvement

All the research confirmed by HMI, and more recently Ofsted, suggests that leadership is the *key* factor in improvement and success in improvement and success (Brighouse and Woods 1999: 45). In 2000, in recognition of the importance of the role of leadership in driving forward school improvement, the government established the National College for School Leadership to provide professional support for teachers and other senior staff. The college emphasized the need for 'a clear national benchmark for entry to headship and clear national quality assurance' (DfEE 2000). A set of National Standards for headteachers was drawn up in 1999 and revised in 2004.

There is no denying that preparation and training for headteachers was much needed. However, the approach of the school leadership project is open to question. As with all attempts to measure the quality of teachers, the 'standards' for headteachers fall back on a narrow technicist rather than an holistic approach. Smith (2002) argues that the project is ethically flawed. Firstly, it fails to address the question of how far changes in an organization can be attributed to the actions of leaders or to other factors. Secondly, it conceives of education in reductionist terms of setting measurable targets for school improvement (Smith 2002: 22).

Initial teacher education and professional development

The government has sought to improve teacher effectiveness in a number of ways. A major focus has been on initial training and ongoing professional development, and a significant responsibility for this was given to the Teacher Training Agency (TTA) (now the Training and Development Agency for Schools (TDA)), which was set up in 1994. The agency's remit includes accrediting initial teacher training; allocating student numbers to providers; and improving the quality of initial teacher training courses. The TDA sets the standards which all trainees must meet in order to be awarded Qualified Teacher Status (QTS). The standards have been revised several times but, like the standards for headteachers, potentially reduce teaching to a set of competencies. The prescriptive nature of the standards and the requirements laid down for providers, means that control over the content and structure of initial teacher education has largely passed from institutions of higher education to a government agency.

The TTA emphasized the importance of ongoing professional development. In 1998 it introduced the Career Entry Profile which students graduating from PGCE courses are required to complete in order to identify strengths and priorities for future professional development during their first year of teaching. The following year, provision was made for a mandatory induction year. The latest revision of the standards, which will come into effect in 2007, lays out a set of standards for QTS, induction year teachers, classroom teachers, Advanced Skilled Teachers and Excellent Teachers. This is a further attempt to ensure continuous professional development (see Chapter 28). However, these standards are again based on a competency model rather than looking more broadly at the qualities that make a good teacher.

School-based initiatives for improvement

At the same time as responding to government initiatives and incorporating the National Curriculum and the National Strategy into their planning and teaching, schools themselves have developed a variety of strategies for self-improvement. Whilst it is not possible within the confines of this chapter to give a comprehensive account of the vast range of activities that are going on in individual schools, we can give some examples. As part of continuous professional development, teachers are undertaking peer observation of each other's lessons. Appraisal schemes linked to the school's development plan enable the appraisee to set targets which are then reviewed the following year. Joint departmental planning of schemes of work and lesson plans has become part of good practice in schools. This has a number of advantages including reducing disparity among teachers in lesson content; enabling the sharing of ideas and resources; and acting as a means of professional development.

Schools have been keen to provide additional support for pupils in a variety of ways in an attempt to drive up standards. In many schools, homework clubs are now a feature and provide a conducive atmosphere for pupils to do their homework, as well as enabling them to make use of school facilities, such as the library and ICT. Attention has been focused on ways of stretching the gifted and talented, including providing out-of-classroom activities, enrichment activities within lessons and accelerated classes in particular subjects. For example, one specialist science school in Hampshire selected pupils at the end of Year 7 to start a three-year GCSE course in double science in September 2006. They will take the GSCE examination at the end of Year 10 and the AS level in environmental science at the end of Year 11. Recognizing the link between nutrition and educational performance, some schools are encouraging healthy eating and provide drinking water coolers. Some schools, usually those serving less-advantaged communities, have set up breakfast clubs.

Critiques of research into school effectiveness and school improvement

Both school effectiveness research and policies directed towards school improvement have been criticized. Some critics see 'a tendency for school effectiveness research to be yoked into the service of conservative education policies' (Campbell *et al.* 2004). There is also a concern that school effectiveness research has tended to ignore social and economic factors. Using his research in New Zealand into the effects of the socio-economic status of schools on pupil outcomes, Thrupp (1999) argued that while the 'problem-solving approach in school improvement has a common-sense appeal it is full of holes. Why *should* we expect schools to hold all the answers to wider societal problems?' (Thrupp 1999: 57).

School effectiveness research can lead to an instrumental attitude towards education by reducing teaching and learning to a set of observable techniques. Campbell *et al.* (2004), critiquing research into teacher effectiveness, argue that:

> Teacher effectiveness research has tended to neglect the analysis of values in two senses: the general values associated with the processes of education and the more specific values underlying effective teaching.
>
> (Campbell *et al.* 2004: 452)

These values, they argue, include respect for pupils; the importance of establishing a good rapport; encouraging pupils to develop their own independent learning strategies; challenging accepted wisdom; and establishing a climate for inclusiveness.

Another criticism is that school improvement policies have not reduced inequality but have widened the gap between social classes. Ball (2000) argues that many of the school effectiveness initiatives 'indicate a willing-ness to make policies which reinforce and indeed enhance, the educational advantages of the middle-class' (Ball 2000: 7). He cites the reassertion of setting, which disadvantages working class and ethnic minority pupils and the creation of specialist schools, which recruit a smaller proportion of students entitled to free school meals. Ball adds:

> even more cynically it could be argued that the displacement of equity by standards as a presentational device, is itself a way of reassuring the middle classes that their privileges are safe in what is an increasing competitive and uncertain labour market.
>
> (Ball 2000: 7)

Likewise, the greater diversity of schools and various criteria for selection of pupils favours the middles classes who are more likely to be what Gewirtz (1995) has called 'skilled choosers'. Tomlinson points out that the result of New Labour's education strategy was that:

> a number of covert and overt selective policies, designed to ensure privileges for the middle and aspirant classes ensured that familial self-interest and scramble for good schools continues. School education continued to be a divisive rather than a cohesive force.
>
> (Tomlinson 2005: 114)

Concluding comments

Research into school effectiveness has shown that schools can and do make a difference. Recognizing this, successive governments, from 1976 onwards, have put into place policies directed at school improvement. However, there are several questions that we must ask. Are the criteria against which success is measured the right ones? Is an 'effective' school necessarily a good school? Is there a danger that the creation of different schools with different levels of funding will lead to an inequitable system? To what extent can schools really compensate for society?

References

Ball, S. (2000) Reading policy texts, *Education and Social Justice*, 3(1): 6–8.

Bell, D. (2003) Education Action Zones and Excellence in Cities, *Education Review*, 17(1): 10–15.

Bernstein, B. (1970) Education cannot compensate for society, *New Society*, February 26.

Bullock, G. (1977) *A Language for Life: A Report of The Central Advisory Council for Education for England*. London: HMSO.

Callaghan, J. (1976) Speech delivered at Ruskin College, Oxford, *The Times Educational Supplement*, October 22.

Campbell, R., Kyriakides, L., Muis, R. and Robinson, W. (2004) Effective teaching and values: some implications for research and teacher appraisal, *Oxford Review of Education*, 30(4): 451–65.

Coleman, J.S., Campbell, E., Hobson, C. *et al.* (1966) *Equality of Educational Opportunity*. Washington: US Government Printing Office.
Crowther, D. (1959) *Early Leaving: A Report of The Central Advisory Council for Education for England (The Crowther Report)*. London: HMSO.
Dale, R. and Griffiths, S. (1965) *Downstream*. London: Routledge & Kegan Paul.
Department for Education and Employment (2000) *National College for School Leadership – a Prospectus*. London: DfEE.
Department for Education and Skills (2006) City Academies. http//www// standards.dfes.gov.uk.
Floud, J., Halsey, A. and Martin, F. (1957) *Social Class and Educational Opportunity*. London: Heinemann.
Gay, B. (1981) Accountability in Education: a review of literature and research in the UK, *Westminster Studies in Education*, 4: 29–43.
Gay, B. (2001) Social justice in schools, in J. Dillon and M. Maguire (eds) *Becoming a Teacher: Issues in Secondary Teaching* (2nd edn). Buckingham: Open University Press.
Gewirtz, S., Ball, S. and Bowe, R. (1995) *Markets, Choice and Equity in Education*. Buckingham: Open University Press.
Guardian (2005) Are the city academies really helping the poorest children? *Guardian*, 31 October.
Hargreaves, D. (1967) *Social Relationships in a Secondary School*. London: Routledge & Kegan Paul.
Hargreaves, D., Hestor, D. and Mellor, F. (1975) *Deviance in Classrooms*. London: Routledge & Kegan Paul.
Harris, A., Hopkins, D., Hargreaves, A. *et al. (2003) Effective Leadership for School Improvement*. London: Routledge Falmer.
Harris, A. and Lambert, L. (2003) *Building Leadership Capacity for School Improvement*. Milton Keynes: Open University Press.
Hatcher, R. (1998) Labour, official school improvement and equality, *Journal of Education Policy*, 13(4): 485–99.
Jackson, B. and Marsden, D. (1962), *Education and the Working Class*. London: Routledge & Kegan Paul.
Jencks, C., Smith, M., Acland, H., Bane, M., Cohen, D., Ginits, H., Heyns, B. and Michelson, S. (1970). *Inequality: A Reassessment of the Effect of Family and Schooling in America*. New York: Basic Books.
Jesson, D. (2004) *Educational Outcomes and Value Added by Specialist Schools*. London: Specialist Schools Trust.
Lacey, C. (1970) *Hightown Grammar*. Manchester: Manchester University Press.
Lacey, C. (1974) De-streaming in a 'pressurized' academic environment, in J. Eggleston (ed.) *Contemporary Research in the Sociology of Education*. London: Routledge & Kegan Paul.
Mortimore, P. and Whitty, G. (1988) Can school improvement overcome the effects of disadvantage? In P. Mortimore (ed.) *The Road to Improvement: Reflections on School Effectiveness*. Lisse: Swets & Zeitlinger.
Ollerenshaw, K. (1978) *Accountability and the Curriculum, Memorial Lecture of the College of Preceptors*. London: Joseph Payne.
Power, M. J. (1967) Delinquent schools? *New Society*, July 22: 3–5.
Plowden, B. (1967) *Children and their Primary Schools: A Report of The Central Advisory Council for Education for England (The Plowden Report)*. London: HMSO.
Reynolds, D. and Teddlie, C. (2001) Reflections on the critics, and beyond them, *Journal of School Effectiveness and School Improvement*, 12(1): 99–113.
Reynolds, D. and Teddlie, C. with Creemers, B., Scheerens, J. and Townsend, T. (2000) An introduction to school effectiveness research, in C. Teddlie and D. Reynolds (eds) *International Handbook of School Effectiveness Research*. London and New York: Falmer.

Robbins, G. (1963) *Higher Education: A Report of The Central Advisory Council for Education England (The Robbins Report)*. London: HMSO.

Rosenthal, R. and Jacobsen, L. (1968) *Pygmalion in the Classroom*. New York: Holt, Rinehart & Wiston.

Rutter, M., Maughan, B., Mortimore, P. and Ouston, J. (1979) *Fifteen Thousand Hours*. London: Open Books.

Sammons, P. (1999) *School Effectiveness: Coming of Age in the Twenty-First Century*. Lisse: Swets & Zeitlinger.

Sammons, P., Thomas, S. and Mortimore, P. (1997) *Forging Links: Effective Schools and Effective Departments*. London: Paul Chapman Publishing.

Sergiovanni, T. (2001) *Leadership: What's in it for Schools?* London: Routledge

Silver, H. (1994) *Good Schools, Effective Schools*. London: Cassell.

Smith, M. (2002) The School Leadership Initiative: An ethically flawed project? *Journal of Philosophy of Education*, 36(1): 21–40.

Stoll, L. and Fink, L. (1996) *Changing our Schools*. Milton Keynes: Open University Press.

The Times (2000) Academies for all. *The Times*, 16 March.

The Times (2005) Welcome to the shame academy. *The Times*, 17 March.

Thrupp, M. (1999) *Schools Making a Difference: Let's be Realistic!* Buckingham: Open University Press.

Tomlinson, S. (2005) *Education in a Post-Welfare Society*. Buckingham: Open University Press.

Wilcox, B. and Gray, J. (1996) *Inspecting Schools: Holding Schools to Account and Helping Schools To Improve*. London: Taylor & Francis.

Reforming teachers and their work

Meg Maguire and Justin Dillon

Introduction

Ever since the state took over the responsibility for supplying teachers for schools in the nineteenth century, teachers and their work have been almost constantly subjected to criticism and reforms. Some of these criticisms have been driven by questions related to the curriculum or how to best educate intending teachers and prepare them for their demanding role in schools. Other critiques and reforms have been driven by pragmatism and expediency; here the almost constant dilemma of the supply of and demand for teachers has shaped the various ways that teachers have been trained/educated over time. Other concerns, such as the 'needs' of the economy and the 'needs' of society for high quality teachers to raise standards in schools, have also been reflected in various reforms of teachers and their work. Perhaps one of the most infamous reforms was the 'payment by results' policy of the nineteenth century, where teachers were paid in proportion to their students' capacity to respond to the oral questions of the annual inspection.

One of the dilemmas in all this teacher and teacher education reform activity is that, frequently, aspects of different attempts at change and improvement come into conflict with one another. Another dilemma is that sometimes, in fixing our view on the technicalities of the reform such as how to do it better or faster, we sideline and marginalize wider ethical questions such as what should be, or what ought to be, the role of the teacher in our society. For example, is teaching just a 'directed profession' (Bottery and Wright 2000) led by the demands of various governments where teachers are trained and prepared in the technicalities and delivery of what has been nationally mandated? Should teachers become 'agents of change' (Johnson and Hallgarten 2002) who take control of their professional destinies and influence policy in their area of expertise?

What we want to do in this chapter is to reflect on some of the current attempts to reform and restructure the role of teachers and the work that they do. In what follows, we want to explore some of the long-standing dilemmas that characterize the preparation, supply and work demands of teachers. In this short chapter, we will not be able to cover all the issues and complexities in these long-standing struggles and debates. However, through our focus on issues of teacher supply, retention and diversity in pre-service routes, we intend to unpick some of the central and enduring questions to do with what is entailed in being a teacher. For those of you who are in the process of becoming a teacher, this will be a fundamental, if sometimes unrecognized, question as you proceed in your professional development. Your responses to this question will shape your practice throughout your lives as teachers. However, before we start this discussion, we want to preface our chapter with a brief consideration of reforms and processes of reform in teacher education and the role of the teacher.

Reform and processes of reform

The work of teachers has always been subjected to criticism. If there are concerns about the attitudes and behaviours of young people, then teachers and teacher education have to respond to these concerns in some way. If there are societal 'needs' for greater literacy and numeracy skills in the workforce, then teachers and teacher education have to be reformed to respond to this call for change. If the economy 'demands' a different kind of workforce, then again education, and by implication, teacher education, has to be changed to meet this requirement. If teacher professionalism is seen to be in short supply, either that teachers are in some ways 'failing' in their work, or that they are not accountable enough to various stakeholders in society, then additional changes and reforms are called for.

> People are always wanting teachers to change. Rarely has this been more true than in recent years. These times of global competitiveness, like all moments of economic crisis, are producing immense moral panics about how we are preparing the generations of the future in our respective nations.
>
> (Hargreaves 1994: 5 cited in Furlong *et al.* 2000:1)

No one would challenge the desire and intention to improve schooling. Indeed, in many respects, the liberal history of state-maintained educational provision has been one of increased supply, enhanced access to higher education, albeit class-based, and all round increases in levels of literacy and numeracy (see Chapter 4 and also Chapter 20). Thus, there has always been a school reform movement of some description. More recently, since the late 1980s or so, a formalized movement of school improvement and effectiveness has grown up, concerned to identify processes that facilitate and inhibit educational change (for discussion of this, see Thrupp 2001). Common sense tells us that there will always be a sound case for improving educational provision.

'Education influences and reflects the values of society, and the kind of society we want to be' (DfEE/QCA 2000: 100). However, society has changed since the late 1980s. For example, technological changes and globalizing economies have resulted in changes in work and in leisure. It is axiomatic that education needs to be proactive in responding to the challenges these sorts of changes represent. Reforming education is an international phenomenon, and, as elsewhere, the impulse for change in the UK has been driven by a desire to overcome some of the key social, cultural and economic dilemmas that have faced the state. These are: the need to reduce public spending, make schooling more responsive to the needs of industry and restore public confidence in state schooling. The attempts to manage these problems have been seen in the almost constant stream of initiatives that have flowed from Conservative and Labour governments alike.

There are some points of tension in any demands for reform. First, it depends on where the call for reform originates. Calls for reform will come from a number of different sources and exert different requirements for compliance. Some demands may come from within the profession itself, for example, for better work-life balance. These sorts of demands may not always be fully responded to because of lack of resources. Other reforms may come from within individual schools and classrooms. Earlier reforming attempts to work in a more student-centred manner, for example, are evidence of this order of reform. Reforms may come from the local or national state and may be mandated. Indeed, at certain points in time, the reforms that are imposed by governments or their agencies may be the only reforms that are recognized as legitimate (Bates 2004). In a complex and demanding occupation such as teaching, the only time that is available may have to be spent concentrating on these mandated reforms. As we have already said, reforms may also be enacted in response to perceptions held in the wider society, for example, moral panics about 'standards' or behaviour.

Many attempts at reforming teachers and their work will be enacted simultaneously, for example remodelling the workforce and the raising standards agenda in England. There may be conflicts and contradictions between different aspects of policy reform. Simply providing a policy response towards a problem, such as teacher shortages for instance, might not always have the desired effect, as we shall see later on in this chapter. What will almost certainly emerge will be another policy problem. It is also important to remember that teachers will always have some capacity to question and criticize reform attempts (Sachs 2003). There may be a tension between what they think is in the best interests of their students set against what is mandated by national legislation (Arrowsmith 2006: 1).

Teacher supply

Any attempt to improve, refine and reform the work of the classroom teacher is usually a two-stepped process. While some aspects of policy reforms concentrate on the classroom in an attempt to change the practices of in-service teachers, other initiatives will focus on the pre-service teacher, the teacher in training. If changes are to be effective, then it is axiomatic that change at the source has to occur. In many ways, change at the source (teacher education) is much easier to manage and control through manipulating the education, training and competencies (or standards) required of beginning teachers. However, in the real world context, the capacity to reform at pre-service or in-service may be hampered by the need to recruit and retain enough teachers. Thus, policies of reforming and restructuring teachers and teacher education are enacted alongside other policies that attempt to recruit and retain. This competing tension can produce unexpected consequences.

In England, and elsewhere, many of the recent reforms in teacher education have been designed, it has been argued, 'by concerns to bring teacher education under tighter control of state elites and by desires to prepare teachers differently so that schools will function more effectively in preparing more productive workers' (Ginsberg and Lindsay 1995: 6). Bates (2004) believes that the rhetoric of many governments in this policy area is laced with references to 'competition', 'best practice', and 'quality assurance', 'compliance' and the 'new economies'. Reform and improvement is set within this dominant agenda.

> The need to raise standards of education for all young people is almost universally recognised. This is partly a matter of economics. The British economy, and indeed the wider European economy, would appear to depend on having a well-educated, adaptable, continuously learning work-force which is able to generate and implement innovation.
>
> (Barber 1995: 189)

However, any attempt to control and manage teachers and their work has to accommodate itself to tensions around the issue of supply and demand. For instance, if controls became so great, that professional autonomy were to be completely eroded, then the sorts of people coming forward to teach might not be the critical, reflexive, inspirational and ethical people that some of us would want to have in our classrooms working with our children (Campbell 2003). Put more bluntly, many talented people would potentially not regard teaching as an occupation that was challenging, if there were no scope for their interpretation and inventions and creativity. But there is another set of tensions; if teaching is such a demanding, intensive, complex job that requires extremely long hours with extra work undertaken at home over the weekends, many individuals would simply not be capable of this and many would not want to stay in such an occupation for very long. So, any reforms of teaching have to bear these facts in mind. Additionally, a period of changing demographics exerts complex pressures in terms of more or less need for teachers and supply and demand tension is sometimes difficult to predict and control.

It is not possible here to do justice to the enduring dilemmas in teacher supply and demand (but see Menter *et al.* 2002). Suffice it to say that there have always been problems in managing this process. However, when New Labour came into government in 1997, they faced a complex set of problems in terms of teaching and teacher education and supply and demand. One dimension of the problem they faced was that they inherited a public discourse where education had been systematically positioned as below par for many years previously (Tomlinson 2005). No new government could afford to disregard the fears and concerns of voters, many of whom were parents. Even though many schools were doing well, the annual 'event' of league tables and the media hunt for 'the worse school in Britain' coupled with media-orchestrated 'events' around GCSE results publication (in August, when news is generally in short supply), meant that the UK had become accustomed to the annual conundrum. This was (and is) that if more students were successful, then the tests were getting easier and standards were falling. If scores went down, then teachers would be 'failing' in their work. In this complex and overheated policy setting, there was no space for slowing the pace of reform. For the New Labour administration, allowing the reforms of the previous government time to bed in was not ever going to be possible. New Labour had to be seen to be 'strong' in the campaign to raise standards, even if they were not actually dropping (see Chapter 4). Simultaneously, there was another pressure for reform. Teachers were leaving the profession in droves.

New Labour's response was to publish a Green Paper (DfEE 1998b) fairly soon into its first administration, *Teachers: meeting the challenge of change*. This report contained some startling statistics that indicated:

> Of every 100 students (who start secondary teacher training in 1999) we estimate that only 58 will start teaching in maintained secondary schools that year and a further six a year later.
>
> (DfEE 1998b para. 18)

New Labour argued that many graduates no longer aspired to teaching as a career. The graduate labour market had expanded rapidly and many careers were and are on offer to graduates. New Labour recognized what they called an 'image problem' – that teachers were working long hours and that their salaries had not held up in comparison with other post-graduate careers. What they didn't directly acknowledge was the impact of relentless change and an almost unremitting stream of mandated reforms and the impact of this on teacher burnout and stress (Smithers and Robinson 2003). In response to the need to recruit more teachers, the Teacher Development Agency (then the Teacher Training Agency) was charged with recruiting more people into teaching. It was argued that there were many people who would want to become teachers if there were more 'flexible' routes into the profession. It was also argued that additional money needed to be offered in shortage subjects to encourage graduates in some disciplines to think of becoming teachers, even if only for a few years. (This policy has had some success, but indirectly signals that perhaps some curriculum areas are of less value than others.) New Labour accepted that teachers were not necessarily going to stay for a lifetime in teaching but would be more likely to want to develop flexible employment portfolios and move in and out of various careers.

Flexibility towards recruitment and diversity in pre-service preparation might be seen as an opportunity (Westcott and Harris 2004). It might also be seen as a sign of pragmatism. The reform outcomes have been that there are now many ways to train to become a teacher. There are the

well-established higher education-based routes (such as the Batchelor of
Education, mainly taken by intending primary school teachers) and the
post-graduate courses (PGCEs) (based in schools for 24 out of the 36 weeks
for secondary teachers). There are other ways in to teaching such as school-
centred training (SCITTs) – a route that is popular with the government but
one that has received less than effusive praise from Ofsted. There are
employment-based routes such as the Graduate Teacher Programme (GTP)
and the Registered Teacher Programme (RTP) that allow individuals to
stay in their work while undertaking their teacher education. For example,
the RTP 'provides a blend of work-based teacher training and academic
study, allowing non-graduates with some experience of higher education
to complete their degree and qualify as a teacher at the same time'
(www.tda.gov.uk). For overseas-qualified teachers there is the Overseas
Trained Teacher programme (OTTP) that helps experienced teachers who
have gained their qualifications overseas to obtain Qualified Teacher Status
(QTS) in England and Wales. There is also the Teach First programme that
only recruits 'outstanding graduates'. It is for 'high flying graduates who
may not otherwise have considered teaching or aren't sure of it as a long-
term career' and it also provides 'the potential to develop a commercially
oriented career' (www.teachfirst.org.uk). This programme is run by an
independent organization. It recruits graduates with a 2.1 degree or better,
offers a short focused training and then places these individuals in inner
city schools facing recruitment problems. There are also new opportunities
in schools for people who do not have QTS, but who will take on some of
the more traditional responsibilities of the teacher (see Chapter 27).

Of course, this flexibility towards issues of supply may well mean that
more people will be drawn to teaching and that flexibility in training routes
will enable more people to enter the profession who have always wanted to
teach, but could not commit to a full-time, one-year course in an institution
of higher education. On the other hand, it may lead to an internally
differentiated occupational setting. Flexibility may well enhance recruitment to teaching in some quarters. At the same time, it may inhibit
recruitment from other cohorts. If becoming a teacher is something that
anyone can do, it might become something that very few will actively seek
to do. From the government's perspective, some routes are significantly
cheaper than others. But recruitment is only one side of the coin. Recruiting
teachers who only stay for two years may not be the best way to meet the
educational needs of children in schools. A rapid staff turnover might not
be the best way to promote systemic reforms such as the 'raising standards'
agenda. Issues of teacher supply have to be considered alongside issues of
retention.

Teacher retention

Two main policies have been set up to promote retention in teaching. One
is related to rewarding teachers financially. The other relates to reforming
the workloads of teachers through what is known as the remodelling

strategy. The 'smart' aspect to these two reforming tactics is that they complement the dominant policy – the raising standards agenda – that lies at the heart of New Labour's educational work. In terms of rewarding teachers financially and encouraging them to stay in the profession, New Labour did appreciate that something needed to be done. However, in line with its core values of 'something for something' and a 'hand-up not a hand-out' (Blair 1996; Whitty 2002), the Green Paper stated that there was now a need 'to provide rewards for success and incentives for excellence'. While the Paper made many proposals, it was the move towards performance management and performance related pay (PRP) that attracted the most attention.

The idea was a straightforward and seductive one; good teachers would be motivated to improve their performance if their individual efforts were rewarded. It is unfair that less successful teachers should be paid the same as their more successful colleagues. Richardson has argued that 'performance related pay makes a lot of sense in many contexts. It succeeds in motivating people as diverse as taxi drivers, garment assemblers, fund managers and sportsmen' (Richardson 1999: 29). However, Richardson went on to state what must seem obvious to many teachers; public sector occupations (like teaching) are complex and not easily reducible to clear and measurable work objectives. Even if student achievement were one measure, there would have to be some way to demonstrate that 'an individual teacher's contribution to pupil performance can be established with confidence' (Richardson 1999: 29). It could be that a student did well in a certain aspect of their work – say mathematics at GCSE – because of successful pastoral support or good teaching at an earlier stage. Teaching is a collaborative venture. Richardson pointed out that there must be a 'suspicion' that performance related pay was not merely concerned with recruiting, retaining and rewarding good teachers. He suggested that it was potentially a strategy to attract and reward a minority while doing 'rather little for the large numbers of average performers' (Richardson 1999: 30). In addition, as Mahony and Hextall (2000) have argued, while PRP may motivate some teachers, it may also have the opposite effect and prove to be counterproductive. However, various forms of performance related pay have been inserted into the teaching profession, notably the performance thresholds (for more details, see Mahony *et al.* 2004).

In terms of reforming teachers' conditions of work (a key factor cited to explain high levels of teacher turnover), a number of changes were implemented in the light of the Workforce Reform Agenda (HM Government 2002). The intentions were to reduce the level of bureaucracy that teachers had to deal with in order to free them up so that they could concentrate on their teaching (www.tda/gov.uk/remodelling). Time limits of 1265 hours per year were set in order to promote a work-life balance. From September 2004, more changes came into effect limiting the amount of classroom cover (for absent colleagues) that individual teachers were supposed to provide. In 2005, every school was required to provide at least 10 per cent of teachers' time as non-contact time for planning, preparation and assessment (PPA time). Even though the Workforce Reform and Remodelling agenda has attempted to reduce the workload and ensure that teaching is an attractive career proposition, 'the evidence would suggest that the workload of teachers is still excessive' (Nixon 2005: 151). However, the remodelling agenda has other potentially far-reaching consequences for teachers' work in schools.

Diversity

If teachers are supposed to be released from their work in the classroom, in order to have sufficient PPA time, the most obvious question is what happens to the students while their teachers are engaged in this necessary work. One outcome is that all state-maintained schools have had to carefully examine the workloads of their teachers and the tasks they are charged with fulfilling. Another outcome is that schools have had to think strategically in terms of who is available and able to provide release, and perhaps supply additional expertise. Westcott and Harris (2004: 33) point out that: 'the current climate is one where the idea of teaching and who teaches is evolving and changing, with a particular emphasis on the role of adults other than teachers within schools'. This diversity is in some ways a double-edged sword. On the one hand, the employment of adults with complementary expertise (linguistic, counselling, career advisers) and adults who offer additional support (teaching assistants, librarians, mentors) will add to the capacity of the school to meet the all round needs of their students. On the other hand, however, if the boundaries between who is/is not a teacher become even more blurred, there could be tension and conflict. Teachers 'have every right to feel that their professional status is hard won' (Westcott and Harris 2004: 35), although they may well be comfortable that others are concentrating on aspects of their work that are secondary to their role as teachers. The issue is where this line is to be drawn. Should classroom teachers have pastoral responsibilities, and if so, to what extent? Should they be responsible for sexual and relationship education, for example, and are they all capable of this (see Chapters 23 and 27 for discussion of these matters).

Obviously there are economic factors that may also come into play. It will almost certainly be cheaper, in terms of staff costs, to employ unqualified staff instead of teachers. Diversity and flexibility in the workforce (and perhaps in entry routes) may add to the capacity of the school to help its students achieve their potential; conversely, they may reduce the status of teaching and inhibit some forms of recruitment. In terms of social justice issues too, it may be the schools facing challenging circumstances that are 'forced' into diverse forms of employment in order to secure acceptable staffing levels. As an aside, it is interesting to conjecture as to what the responses of some parents might be towards unqualified teachers working with their children. However, active and reflexive teams of differently skilled adults, working together, can only enhance the learning and teaching situation. It just takes time, thought, sensitivity and commitment to make these effective and democratic teams. However, diversity and flexibility in terms of the school workforce has another implication. It forces us to ask precise questions about what we understand as a teacher and as teachers' work.

What is a teacher? What is a professional teacher?

In terms of reforming and restructuring the teacher, the central issues turn on the role of the teacher in our society and how that role is currently being shaped by policy interventions (see Chapter 2). In terms of pre-service teacher education (currently called training), Furlong (2005: 130) claims that:

> Individual professional formation is seen as far less critical than it was, especially at the level of initial training. In the lives of young teachers, the state now provides far greater guidance than ever before in the definition of effective teaching, learning and assessment.

Mahony and Hextall (2000: 20) claim that the teacher is now being reconfigured as 'someone who is both being addressed as a "professional" but whose responsibilities, powers and rights are designated as lying well outside realms of policy reflection and deliberation'. To an extent, the teacher is now positioned as a competent, multi-skilled worker, who delivers and assesses a regulated curriculum. Teachers' capacity to influence what they teach, how they assess learning, and even how they organize aspects of their pedagogy, such as student grouping and lesson planning, have been prescribed by government interventions into these areas of the work of teaching.

Teacher education, and what it means to be a teacher, is an important matter for any nation-state. After all, what can be more important than how a nation's young people are educated? Therefore, it is not surprising that teacher education and consequently teaching itself have been subjected to many changes over time. In the past, much of the struggle, within the profession at least, was focused on becoming an all-graduate occupation, thus enhancing the status of teaching. At the same time, issues of supply and demand (pragmatic necessity) have also intervened. There are long-standing tensions between the need for theoretical knowledge (what and how much) and practical experience (how many schools and for how long), as well as the overall length and quality of various routes (Hobson *et al.* 2005). There have always been tensions between professional judgements (of teachers and teacher educators) set against market forces and cost-effectiveness; the needs of individual children and students set against the labour market needs of society.

For the past two decades, however, there have been some discernable patterns in the policy reforms in this area in England, and elsewhere to different degrees (Bates 2004). Perhaps the most persistent theme has been the sidelining of some aspects of theory and the privileging of practical experience. Increasingly, schools have been charged with the professional preparation of teachers – a 'learning on the job' approach, for either part or all of the training period. Clearly, this approach has some potential for effective teacher training. However, this responsibility has not been straightforwardly either devolved to schools, or left to higher education institutions, problematic though either of these extremes would be in our view. For some time now, teacher education has been shaped by the need for compliance with prescribed competencies (standards) that have to be met before qualified teacher status can be attained (Whitty 1997). These 'standards' (DfEE 1998a) refer to levels of competency which have to be met in relation to: knowledge and understanding of subject matter; planning, teaching and classroom management; monitoring, assessment recording, reporting and accountability as well as other professional requirements. Of course these are all good platform attributes for effective teachers, however, in the rush to specify, quantify and assess myriads of 'standards' there are a number of unresolved dilemmas.

First, what are we to make of the paradox that allows the Government to blame poor schools for poor performances yet at the same time may well seek to train teachers in these very institutions? Whitty *et al.* (1998: 77) conclude that:

> School-based initial teacher education, combined with an official list of prescribed competencies, seems likely over time to produce greater consistency of preparation for a narrow set of basic teaching skills alongside increased variation and fragmentation in student experience in other areas.

Bridges (1996: 251) has argued that there are 'limits of experience' in school-based training. He raises important questions about taking a pragmatic approach towards the supply of teachers, although here we are just going to explore one of his arguments. He believes that 'personal observation and experience' cannot provide the 'range, diversity or elaboration of thought available in literature'. And yet, he adds, 'reading seems to be a form of learning which has been rendered almost obsolete in the education of teachers' (Bridges 1996: 254). This is a powerful point that needs more consideration than we are able to offer here. Nevertheless, if the focus is with meeting practical standards, important those these are, what are the potential losses, if teaching is reduced to a non-theoretical occupation? In many ways, your answer to this question will depend on how you have constructed the role of the teacher in our society.

Teaching is a complex, challenging occupation. Indeed Hargreaves and Goodson (2003: ix) call it 'the core profession, the key agent of change in today's knowledge society. Teacher's are the midwives of that knowledge society'. Teachers possess a particular expertise and have an ethical responsibility for their student's well-being. It is these factors, in combination, that will lead them to make claims for some degree of autonomy and control in their professional decision making. In this, we are not arguing for teachers' views to dominate. Rather, with Sachs (2003: 17) we share a belief that 'the concept of teacher professionalism is not static'. Its meaning changes over time, in different contexts. It is struggled over. Currently, it might seem that many governments are trying to 'close down' any debates round what a teacher is or should be. But, the extended professional (Hoyle and John 1995) or McLaughlin's (1997) 'new professional' is someone who engages with professional debates beyond their own classrooms, with parents, students and the wider society.

As Bottery and Wright (2000) would argue, much depends on being and trying to become 'truly professional':

Processes have occurred and are still occurring that have led to a teaching force that may be very competent in teaching academic subjects and in caring at an individual level with pupil's problems, but which generally fails to transcend the problems of the classroom. Being truly professional precisely involves the belief that teaching transcends the classroom, and requires of teachers that they take an active interest and have a duty in participating in issues that affect educational national and global policies ... In other words, ultimately the profession of teaching needs to see itself as a profession for citizen education, a citizen education that reaches beyond the nation state.

(Bottery and Wright 2000: 160)

As this chapter was being written, the *Education Guardian* (Arrowsmith 2006: 1) published an article written by Richard Arrowsmith, a secondary school headteacher who was taking early retirement, aged 57, as he was 'just too fed up with too many things'. He wrote of 'the excessive bureaucracy, ridiculous deadlines and unconvincing consultations ... and, more seriously, the ongoing conflicts between educational ideals and political ideals (that) show no sign of abating. Heads are asked to do far too much where the interest of the child is not the primary motive.' He continued, 'it became a political imperative to meet targets set for specific age groups at specific times, thus dividing children into those who did and those who didn't make the grade.' In these words, it is possible to identify the voice of an extended, professional teacher.

Concluding comments

Finally, we would like you to reconsider some of the key questions that we raised at the start of this chapter. To what degree do you think that teaching is a 'directed profession' (Bottery and Wright 2000) led by the demands of various governments where teachers are trained and prepared in the technicalities and delivery of what has been nationally mandated? To what extent is this a good thing in a democratic society? What purposes does this degree of accountability serve? What else should we be considering in any future reforms of teaching and teacher education (Bates 2005)? Can and should teachers become 'agents of change' (Johnson and Hallgarten 2002), who take control of their professional destinies and influence policy in their area of expertise? What do you think?

References

Arrowsmith, R. (2006) Look back in anger, *Education Guardian*, Tuesday 8 August 2006, pp. 1–2.
Barber, M. (1995) Reconstructing the teaching profession, in H. Bines and J.M. Welton (eds) *Managing Partnership in Teacher Training and Development*. London: Routledge.

Bates, R. (2004) Regulation and autonomy in teacher education, *Journal of Education for Teaching*, 30(2): 117–30.

Bates, R. (2005) On the future of teacher education: challenges, context and content, *Journal of Education for Teaching*, 31(4): 301–5.

Blair, T. (1996) *New Britain. My Vision of a Young Country*. London: Fourth Estate.

Bottery, M. and Wright, N. (2000) *Teachers and the State. Towards a Directed Profession*, London and New York: Routledge.

Bridges, D. (1996) Teacher education: the poverty of pragmatism, in R. McBride, (1996) (ed.) *Teacher Education Policy: Some Issues Arising from Research and Practice*. London: Falmer Press.

Campbell, E. (2003) *The Ethical Teacher*. Maidenhead, Open University Press.

Department for Education and Employment (DfEE) (1998a) *Requirements for courses of Initial Teacher Training*. Circular 4/98. London: HMSO.

Department for Education and Employment (DfEE) (1998b) *Teachers: Meeting the Challenge of Change*. Green Paper. London: HMSO.

Forde, C., McMahon, M., McPhee, A.D. and Patrick, F. (2006) *Professional Development, Reflection and Enquiry*. London: Paul Chapman.

Furlong, J. (2005) New Labour and teacher education: the end of an era, *Oxford Review of Education*, 33(3): 480–95.

Furlong, J., Barton, L., Miles, S., Whiting, C. and Whitty, G. (2000) *Teacher Education in Transition: Reforming Professionalism?* Buckingham: Open University Press.

Gewirtz, S. (1997) Post-welfarism and the reconstruction of teachers' work in the UK, *Journal of Education Policy*, 12(4): 217–31.

Ginsberg, M. and Lindsay, B. (eds) (1995) *The Political Dimension in Teacher Education*. London: Falmer.

Hargreaves, A. and Goodson, I.F. (2003) Series editor preface, in J. Sachs, *The Activist Teaching Profession*. Buckingham: Open University Press.

Hextall, I. and Mahony, P. (2000) Consultation and the management of consent: Standards for Qualified Teacher Status, *British Educational Research Journal*, 26(3): 322–42.

H.M. Government (2002) *A Time for Standards*. London: HMSO.

Hobson, A.J., Malderez, A., Tracey, L. and Kerr, K. (2005) Teachers' experiences of initial teacher preparation, induction and early professional development in England – does route matter? *Journal of Education for Teaching*, 31(2): 133–5.

Hoyle, E. and John, P. (1995) *Professional Knowledge and Professional Practice*. New York: Cassell.

Johnson, M. and Hallgarten, J. (eds) (2002) *From Victims of Change to Agents of Change. The Future of the Teaching Profession*. London: Institute of Public Policy Research.

Mahony, P. and Hextall, I. (2000) *Reconstructing Teaching: Standards, Performance and Accountability*. London: Routledge.

Mahony, P., Menter, I. and Hextall, I. (2004) The emotional impact of performance-related pay on teachers in England, *British Educational Research Journal*, 30(3): 435–56.

McLaughlin, M. (1997) Rebuilding teacher professionalism in the United States, in A. Hargreaves, and R. Evans (eds) *Beyond Educational Reform*. Buckingham: Open University Press.

Menter, I., Hutchings, M. and Ross, A. (eds) (2002) *The Crisis in Teacher Supply: Research and Strategies for Retention*. Stoke-on-Trent: Trentham.

Nixon, J. (2005) Statutory frameworks relating to teachers' responsibilities, in M. Cole (ed.) (2005) *Professional Values and Practice. Meeting the Standards*. London: David Fulton.

Pearce, N. and Hillman, J. (1998) *Wasted Youth: Raising Achievement and Tackling Social Exclusion*. London: Institute for Public Policy Research.

Qualifications and Curriculum Authority (QCA) (2000) *The National Curriculum. Handbook for Secondary Teachers in England Key Stages 3 and 4*. London: HMSO.

Richardson, R. (1999) *Performance Related Pay in Schools. An Evaluation of the Government's Evidence to the School Teachers' Review Body*, Report prepared for the National Union of Teachers. London: London School of Economics and Political Science.

Sachs, J. (2003) *The Activist Teaching Profession*, Buckingham: Open University Press.

Smithers, A. and Robinson, P. (2003) *Factors Affecting Teachers' Decisions to Leave the Profession*. Nottingham: DfES.

Teacher Training Agency (TTA) (2004) *Qualifying to Teach: Professional Standards for Qualified Teacher Status and Requirements for Initial Teacher Training*. London: TTA.

Thrupp, M. (2001) Recent school effectiveness counter critiques: problems and possibilities, *British Educational Research Journal*, 27(4): 443–57.

Tomlinson, S. (2005) *Education in a Post-welfare Society*. Buckingham: Open University Press.

Westcott, E. and Harris, A. (2004) Key issues, opportunities and challenges for new teachers, in V. Brooks, I. Abbott and L. Bills (eds) *Preparing to Teach in Secondary Schools*. Buckingham: Open University Press.

Whitty, G. (1997) Marketisation, the state and the re-formation of the teaching profession, in A. H. Halsey, H. Lauder, P. Brown and A. Stuart Wells (eds) *Education, Culture, Economy, Society*. Oxford: Oxford University Press.

Whitty, G., Power, S. and Halpin, D. (1998) *Devolution and Choice in Education. The School, the State and the Market*. Buckingham: Open University Press.

Whitty, G. (2002) *Making Sense of Education Policy*. London: Paul Chapman.

<table>
<tr><td>8</td></tr>
</table>

Reflection, inspection and accountability

Justin Dillon

Introduction

From now until you decide that it is time to leave teaching, you are going to be watched by a lot of people: pupils, mentors, tutors and inspectors. They will be, in all senses of the word, inspecting you – watching to see what you do, noticing if you can see what they are up to, assessing if you are teaching well and judging what you are wearing. There's something about being watched that can be uncomfortable and, sometimes, unnerving. One of the best pieces of advice that I was given as a PGCE student was 'never wear clothes where the sweat shows'. However, this chapter is not just about being watched, it is also about watching yourself, reflecting during and after teaching, with an aim to be more effective for all your pupils. Reflection is important because, not only are you accountable to others, you are accountable to yourself – to maintain your own standards and to keep faith with your own values. However, if day-to-day reflection is the norm for today's professional teacher, at least in terms of frequency, inspection is at the other end of the spectrum. Inspection, at its best, can offer a rare opportunity for independent insights into your teaching abilities and can catalyse your own reflections. This chapter draws together research into teacher development and related research into school inspection, and, in particular, the impact of the Office for Standards in Education, commonly referred to as Ofsted.

On reflection

Teacher development can be thought of as a mechanism for driving change in education systems, or it can be seen as a strategy for empowering individuals and teams to improve their professional knowledge and pedagogy (Day and Sachs 2004). The literature on teacher development is substantial though it is not, as we will see, unproblematic, and as Munby and Russell also point out, there is a related issue in that:

> the interaction between teachers and those who study and write about teachers and teaching has long been problematic, often sliding too easily into the familiar mode of one person telling another how to improve practice.
>
> (Munby and Russell 1992: 8)

That is not to say that telling someone how to improve their practice does not work – indeed during the early parts of your career, it is something that you will experience frequently. There are other problems with the research into teacher development, such as a lack of evidence of real changes in classroom practices; that is, there's not much evidence that some types of training make you, in any sense, a better teacher (see Chapter 28 for more on this issue).

Although much of the teacher development literature focuses on discrete phases of training, such as pre-service (Reid *et al.* 1994; Boyd 2002; Edwards and Protheroe 2003), or on the induction of Newly Qualified Teachers (for example, Harrison 2002), a growing body of writing has addressed the generic development of teachers (see, for example, Elliott 1993). Claxton *et al.* (1996), for example, examined how teachers' views of themselves as 'learners' impacted on the ways in which they behaved (they found that teachers tended to reproduce their implicit models of learning in the ways in which they treated other learners). Much of the literature on teacher development provides useful insights for beginners even if it focuses on more experienced teachers, so you would be well advised to read widely.

What most researchers and writers in the area of teacher development have in common, is a concern to illuminate the espoused wish of many teacher educators to develop the 'reflective practitioner' (Schön 1983, 1987). Reflection is seen as a strategy that can be used to develop teachers' knowledge, skills and attitudes. The next section examines the idea of the reflective practitioner and looks at key discourses relating to reflection.

The reflective practitioner and the discourse of reflection

The concept of the 'reflective practitioner' has been almost a *sine qua none* of writing about teacher development since the 1960s: it is *the* dominant discourse. Views about the nature of reflection vary, although many writers advocate the process as an essential aspect of teacher development and a key characteristic of effective teaching. The notion of reflection (thinking critically about your own performance, with or without the help of others) holds currency in the UK and elsewhere. It is worth noting here, though, that there are also discourses of the 'reflexive practitioner' (one who reflects on the institutional context as well as on the self) and the 'critical practitioner' (one who reflects on power and authority in relation to one's situation) (see Atkinson 2004 for an interesting discussion of these ideas).

Reflection implies prior experience. It also implies that teachers build knowledge (the exact nature of which is also contested) from their reflection. What is not clear is when the reflection should take place, who should manage it and how is knowledge built from the reflection? Atkinson (2004) points out that many of the assumptions underpinning discourses of reflective practice are often overlooked. Advocates of reflective practice, Atkinson argues, assume that people are able to step outside of their thoughts and feelings and 'reflect' in an almost transcendent way which is both unrealistic and unachievable.

So what does reflecting on your teaching involve? Barnes pointed to the relationship between teaching and reflection when he wrote that: 'teaching depends necessarily upon intuitive judgement, but the intuitions can be reflected upon, sharpened, and related more precisely to long-term goals and values' (Barnes 1992: 10). In effect, Barnes is arguing that teachers' intuition can be developed systematically, through reflection. 'Better teaching', according to Baird, involves the teacher knowing more, being more aware and making better decisions – all in all, being more 'metacognitive', that is, reflecting on their own thinking. Improving teaching involves 'fundamental change in one's attitudes, perceptions, conceptions, beliefs, abilities and behaviors' (Baird 1992: 33). What has to be borne in mind, though, is that we can never reflect in a neutral, abstract manner: systematic, maybe – independently, never. And even people who might hope to give us independent advice can never be wholly objective.

Although there is some measure of agreement in the literature on teacher development that changes come about through reflection, there is less agreement about the nature of that reflection. Some see reflection as something that is done *after* the event (following a lesson), whereas others see it as something that happens *during* the act of teaching. So, what is reflection? In the 1930s, John Dewey wrote that:

> Reflective thinking, in distinction from other operations to which we apply the name of thought, involves (1) a state of doubt, hesitation, perplexity, mental difficulty, in which thinking originates, and (2) an act of searching, hunting, inquiring, to find material that will resolve the doubt, settle and dispose of the perplexity.
>
> (Dewey 1933: 12)

So, the good news is that doubt, hesitation, perplexity and mental difficulty might actually be useful to self-improvement, rather than signs of incompetence. Implicit in Dewey's statement is the notion that reflection happens *during* teaching. Many times I have faced 'doubt, hesitation [and] perplexity' when dealing with challenging questions, difficult behaviour or experiments going wrong. Working in classrooms provides situations that necessitate some element of reflection, whether it be a fleeting thought about the nature of students' ideas about density or someone asking 'Why are we doing this?' Dewey's focus on the act of searching implies the need for an active engagement in reflection in order to develop. Part of the motivation for reflection is a desire to do your best for other people: another reason might be because you are being assessed by others.

Reflection, knowledge and action

Reflective action, as opposed to 'routine' action, 'guided by tradition, *external* authority and circumstance' (Furlong and Maynard 1995: 39), involves 'the active, persistent and careful consideration of any belief or supposed form of knowledge in the light of the grounds that support it' (Dewey 1910: 6). However, reflective thinking on its own does not necessarily lead to teacher development. In this section, the reflexive links between knowing and acting are examined in more detail.

For Schön (1987), knowledge resides in performance. Knowledge-in-action is built up in two ways: reflection-on-action (systematic and deliberate thinking back over one's actions or 'feedback') and reflection-in-action, 'a process with non-logical features, a process that is prompted by experience and over which we have limited control' or 'backtalk' (Munby and Russell 1992: 3). These descriptions begin to go beyond theoretical descriptions and move into strategies that sound achievable or replicable in school and elsewhere. For Loughran (1996), reflection can happen both during and after lessons. Loughran and others advocate using reflection to think of possible alternative approaches and to plan teaching in the light of knowing what happened and why. This approach is posited as an alternative to carrying on with 'business as usual'.

Grimmett (1988: 11–12), putting Schön's ideas 'in perspective', identifies three categories of conceptions of reflection:

- thoughtfulness that leads to conscious, deliberate moves, usually taken to 'apply' research findings or educational theory in order to direct or control practice
- deliberation and choice among competing versions of 'good teaching'
- reconstructing experience, the end of which is the identification of a new possibility for action.

A significant proportion of the literature on teacher development focuses on reflection-on-action (see, for example, Baird *et al.* 1991). Russell and Munby (1991: 164–5) refer to reflection-in-action as 'hearing' or 'seeing' differently, a process that Schön calls 'reframing'. Thus, beginning teachers are encouraged to engage in systematic reflection (sometimes couched in terms of 'evaluate your lesson'), as well as being given opportunities to practice teaching skills, such as identifying problems that children have and then adapting teaching strategies during lessons.

Russell and Munby argue that reflection-on-action 'involves careful consideration of familiar data' whereas 'reflection-in-action presents the data [. . .] in a novel frame' (1991: 164–5). I am not convinced by this dichotomy, nor by the assertion, mentioned previously, that we have 'limited control' over 'reflection-on-action'. One aim of teacher education could be to assist teachers to reflect-on-action *during* their teaching rather than *after* it – that is, to become more systematic about collecting data, patterning it and adapting activities during lessons rather than after them.

For Oberg and Artz, reflection is not 'acquired behaviours or skills; rather [it is] an attitude' (1992: 140). However, Valli, in a study of initial teacher training courses in the USA, reports that 'reflective attitudes' were, in general, tacit rather than explicit goals possibly because of the 'amorphous nature of attitudes' and 'the difficulty of developing or changing' them (1993: 18–19). The job of those tasked with facilitating teacher development, such as mentors and tutors, then, might be to make the tacit more explicit – if this is possible.

The discourse of the reflective practitioner is not without its critics. Indeed, so concerned was Chris Woodhead, the then Chief Inspector of Schools, about the concept, that he attacked it through a talk on 'The Rise and Fall of the Reflective Practitioner' in February 1999. Woodhead concluded that instead of focusing on reflective practice:

> the way forward must be to continue to identify our most effective schools and to find ways to open up the practical knowledge and understanding that they possess to others so the gap between the good and the weak can be narrowed.
>
> (Woodhead 1999)

Woodhead's statement implies a limited, 'common-sense' view of the nature of reflection and of teaching itself. This contrast of knowledge developed through reflection and 'practical knowledge' points to the continued debate over what counts as teacher knowledge. It is appropriate that Woodhead was writing from his position as Chief Inspector, because one of the key drivers of teacher development, it might be argued, has been school inspection, a topic which is considered in the next section.

Inspection

Few people would argue that inspection is a neutral process. Woodhead referred to it as 'disciplined subjectivity' (1999: 5). The chances that you will be observed by an inspector during your teaching practice or in the first few terms of your career are not high. English state-funded schools are inspected, on average, every three years. However, you will almost certainly be unable to escape the influence that inspection, and in particular the Office of Her Majesty's Chief Inspector of Schools in England (Ofsted), has on schooling.

Inspectors have been around for some time. They were first appointed, by the government, in 1839 in response to disquiet about the way in which public funds were being spent by some individuals and by some religious societies (for a history of inspection in England, see Grubb 2000). The remit of Her Majesty's Inspectors included reporting on teaching methods, attainment, organization and discipline, and on the moral training of children, but their powers of intervention were limited. With the introduction of the system of payment by results in 1862, and a national system of free public elementary education under the Education Acts of 1870 onwards, their numbers and their influence increased. The gradual development of secondary schools, under the 1902 Education Act, led to a system of full inspections for secondary schools and subsequently for elementary schools.

During the 1970s, disquiet about educational standards and concerns about a lack of public accountability became a major concern. It found expression in Prime Minister James Callaghan's Ruskin College speech in 1976 (Callaghan 1976) (see, also, Chapter 6, for a discussion of subsequent events). At that time, local education authorities encouraged schools to evaluate themselves (a type of reflective practice in itself), with the help of their advisers, rather than undergo external inspection. By the beginning of the 1990s, political pressure was building for a different sort of inspectorate. HMI was criticized for its lack of published criteria on which judgements were based. The inspectors' independence and objectivity were questioned. They were alleged to be pursuing a pedagogical line through published work, inspection reports and advice to politicians and were 'subject to severe strictures from the "new right" as the major proponents of progressivism' (Fitz and Lee 1996: 18). They were described as representing the interests of the provider rather than the consumer, whose rights were set out in the Citizen's Charter (Cabinet Office 1991). Inspection criteria were now to be made explicit; accountability to the public was expected; more precise statistical information was required; lay members were to be recruited to keep a check on the excesses of the professionals.

The Education (Schools) Act, 1992 established a new organization, the Office for Standards in Education, headed by Her Majesty's Chief Inspector (HMCI). Ofsted was officially set up as a non-ministerial government department, independent from what was then the Department for Education and Employment (DfEE). Its motto is 'Improvement through inspection' and its remit is 'to improve standards of achievement and quality of education through regular independent inspection, public reporting and informed independent advice' (Ofsted 2000).

In the beginning, full-scale (that is, week-long) inspections were to be carried out every four years; now there is a three-year cycle of shorter inspections. The number of HMIs was reduced and inspection teams consisted of independent inspectors not employed directly by Ofsted but trained under its auspices, and operating in a competitive market. A range of private firms and LEAs competed for contracts for the inspections. Ofsted set the framework for these inspections, which are now carried out by the Lead Inspector and a team of up to five inspectors, depending on the size of the school to be inspected.

During the early years of Ofsted inspections, schools could be given as much as four terms' notice or as little as a few weeks. Both of these situations led to considerable stress. In the former, the preparations dominated school life for months, anxiety was often raised to an unreasonable level and an inordinate amount of time was spent by some schools on preparing documentation. In the latter situation, documentation was rushed, and many schools felt that they had not had time to show themselves at their best (Millett and Johnson 1998). A reduction in the notice period to about six weeks was one of the changes made by Ofsted in response to complaints from schools. This period of notice was shortened even further, in 2005, to two days.

Heads' and teachers' views of inspection as being judgemental or developmental affected the way in which inspection was approached. Some schools took a hostile and unco-operative approach, based on critical views of the Ofsted system and the way in which it had been introduced. Some schools saw their inspection as 'free consultancy while others worked extremely hard to conceal any weakness – they aimed for the "perfect week" ' (Ouston and Davies 1998: 14). Some schools employed the services of their local authority in a consultant capacity to help them to prepare for inspection (Dimmer and Metiuk 1998); some went through what amounted to a 'mock inspection'.

Although, in some cases, claims were made by schools that inspection had slowed down ongoing development, in others, the preparation phase was felt to be useful (Ouston and Davies 1998). It was found that individual classroom teachers were more likely than senior staff to admit to anxieties about the forthcoming inspection (Wilcox and Gray 1996). With changes in Ofsted practice (Ofsted 1997) that initiated the reporting to the headteacher of individual teachers' grades using three bands (depending on the quality of their teaching), pressure on individual performance grew. The issue here is that how teachers view inspection affected how they performed and how they interpreted the oral feedback they received and the reports that were written.

The response to inspection

Responses to the process of inspection vary widely and they can be grouped into two main categories – emotional and social, and methodological. Inspection can have a major effect on the professional and personal lives of teachers, leading to feelings of professional uncertainty, loss of self-esteem and change of commitment (Jeffrey and Woods 1998). Although some teachers are very positive about their inspection experiences, there are reports of stress-related illness and even suicide following an Ofsted inspection. Some schools have reported a lowering of morale even after positive inspection results:

> During inspection week fear represses the teachers' ability to act and think – they lose their picture of self-worth. They become irritable at home and can suffer from sleeplessness. Before inspection, people feel screwed down, not able to relax. After inspection a huge sense of relief is followed by deflation.
>
> (A headteacher, quoted in Williams 1999: 12)

It is certainly the case that many schools did report positive experiences, but these did not necessarily receive the same publicity as negative ones (Fidler and Davies 1998). The quality of the inspection team would seem to be a critical factor here. Ofsted's own monitoring (Ofsted et al. 1995) reported a picture of broad satisfaction with the inspection process. Issues that provoked less favourable responses were the match between inspection team members' backgrounds and experience, and the profile of the school;

the contributions of the lay inspector; a lack of professional dialogue with teachers; and the quality of subject judgements.

In early inspections, feedback to individual classroom teachers was non-existent or extremely limited, a fact regretted by inspectors as well as teachers (Jeffrey and Woods 1998). Feedback after lesson observation was incorporated into Ofsted guidance (Ofsted 1997), and although sometimes regarded as inadequate, it was generally welcomed by teachers, who saw it as an improvement. Teachers appreciated guidance on how to handle feedback. They needed to know what form it would take; usually three strengths of the lesson and three weaknesses were given. In terms of feedback at school level, Maychell and Pathak (1997) reported that 94 per cent of secondary headteachers found the oral feedback they had from Ofsted inspectors useful for planning purposes; oral feedback to subject specialists in secondary schools was also popular.

In terms of responses relating to methodology, many writers have questioned the reliability and validity of inspectors' judgements (for example Sandbrook 1996; Wilcox and Gray 1996; Fidler et al. 1998):

> [The] specification of criteria alone does not guarantee validity. Moreover, criteria can never be so tightly defined as to expel the act of judgement completely.
>
> (Wilcox and Gray 1996: 73)

Fitz-Gibbon (1997: 19) considers that:

> the aspect of inspection which is the most expensive in inspectors' time, the most costly to schools in staff stress, and the least validated, is the practice of having inspectors sit in classrooms making amateurish attempts at classroom observation and drawing unchallengeable conclusions about effectiveness.

Ofsted's own research claiming a high level of correlation between the judgements of pairs of inspectors (Matthews et al. 1998) is not viewed as compelling evidence by many critics (Education and Employment Committee, House of Commons 1999).

Opinions clearly differ about the process of inspection. The Market and Opinion Research International (MORI) survey of primary schools, conducted for Ofsted, found overall satisfaction with the process of inspection (MORI 1999). About three-quarters of schools agreed that they were satisfied with the professional knowledge and competence of the inspection team. In cases of disagreement, some schools have felt able to negotiate with inspectors over issues of judgement as well as fact (Fidler and Davies 1998). Schools are now able to pursue complaints about their inspection through an extended complaints procedure, with an external adjudicator, introduced in 1998 (Ofsted 1998).

Inspection is wrapped up in issues of social control and accountability. Attempts to understand inspection from theoretical perspectives have been few and far between. Wilcox and Gray (1996) undertook a three-year study of school inspections and examined four theoretical perspectives: inspection as evaluation; inspection as auditing; inspection as a disciplinary power; inspection as a form of social action. There is not space here to examine these ideas in any detail but the point is that the issues surrounding inspection can be examined from a range of perspectives which may be helpful in finding useful questions to ask of the whole process.

Inspection and development

So, what is the link between inspection and teacher development? Some studies have shown that there would appear to be none:

> Despite the evident intensity of the Ofsted experience, teachers in our study uniformly indicate that, 1 year after inspection, it has had no lasting impact on what they do in the classroom. If Ofsted has questionable direct influence on teaching practice outside nominal compliance with its formal procedures in the run-up to and during the inspection visit, we are left to question what purpose it actually serves. Our conclusion is that, just as teachers 'stage manage' a performance for the visiting inspectorate, the whole Ofsted apparatus itself is little more than a grand political cipher created and maintained to satisfy the imagined scrutinising gaze of a wider public. In short, Ofsted is stage-managed public 'accountability'.
>
> (Case *et al.* 2000: 605)

However, inspection, as with much else in education, cannot easily be evaluated. Some researchers have attempted to gauge schools' and teachers' opinions about the inspection process. Others have looked at the evidence of a direct impact of inspection on student achievement. Some studies have asked whether inspection provides value for money.

Kogan and Maden (1999) evaluated Ofsted inspections using questionnaires to schools; case studies conducted mainly through interviews; interviews with relevant organizations including unions and associations for inspectors, parents and governors; and financial analyses. They reported that stakeholders identified the main benefits of the Ofsted system as including:

- the process of self-examination which leads up to the inspection week (now the inspection team is in school for a maximum of two days)
- the value of external perspectives on the work and running of schools
- the increase in mutual support among staff generated by external inspection and a related recognition of improvements in self-esteem that flow from public affirmation of the work of staff, schools and pupils within schools.

Stakeholders identified some weaknesses, too:

- the system is seen as punitive and fault-finding and generates a climate of fear, which leads to stress and anxiety among staff
- the summative, judgemental outcomes are not effective in promoting reflective professional development within schools
- the system is intolerant of alternative approaches to school improvement and effectiveness.

(Kogan and Maden 1999: 20–1)

Kogan and Maden (1999: 25), in a study that the former Chief Inspector, Chris Woodhead, described as a 'reasonably balanced account' (Woodhead 1999: 5) concluded that 'it is hazardous to assume any connection between Ofsted inspection and improved performance'.

Cullingford and Daniels used a predominantly quantitative study in their research. They looked at the impact of the timing of Ofsted inspections on the GCSE examination performance of a representative sample of pupils throughout England. They reported that 'the time of inspections is significant' and that the 'nearer to the exam period that inspections take place the worse the results' (Cullingford and Daniels 1999: 66). They summarize their findings by arguing that 'Ofsted inspections have the opposite effect to that intended. Year on year they lower standards' (Cullingford and Daniels 1999: 66). Woodhead (1999: 5) quoted an unnamed Ofsted statistician as dismissing the research as 'deeply flawed; ineptly executed and poorly argued'.

Fitz-Gibbon and Stephenson-Forster (1999: 115), reporting on a questionnaire study of 159 headteachers, found that Ofsted had 'failed to win the confidence of headteachers' and had 'caused schools considerable expense'. In response to a question asking 'How much information of use to you in improving schooling did you gain from the inspection?' four heads (of the 85 who had recently been inspected) reported having learned 'nothing'; 14 reported 'not much'; 34 reported 'some' learning; 28 reported 'quite a lot'; and five reported 'a large amount'. These findings point to a wide variation in headteachers' perceptions of the utility of Ofsted.

Surveys conducted by MORI (1999) and by the National Union of Teachers (NUT 1998), focusing on the long-term effect of Ofsted inspection (rather than on the process and judgements made), came to reasonably similar conclusions. In the MORI survey, just 27 per cent of primary schools responding saw inspection as a way to raise standards, and 15 per cent said it helped to improve teaching. In the NUT survey:

> Probably the most significant finding arose from the penultimate question in the survey. Overwhelmingly, head and deputy headteacher members rejected the statement that Ofsted inspections led directly to schools improving. Two-thirds of respondents did not believe that inspections helped school improvement, whereas only 17 per cent agreed with this statement.
>
> (NUT 1998: 3)

Thomas' 1997 survey of the impact of inspection on 80 Welsh secondary schools concluded that 'the weight of evidence indicates that inspection does lead to some improvement in schools; it does not, however, show that inspection brings about large or even medium improvements in many areas' (Thomas 1999: 145). Thomas comments that 'there must be some doubt as to whether [inspection] is a cost-effective method for raising standards' (1999: 146). Gray and Gardner (1999), in a study of 70 Northern Ireland primary and secondary-level schools, commented that there were 'clear reservations about the extent of anxiety induced by the process, the amount of time necessary to prepare for the inspection and the inclusion of lay persons in the inspection team' (p. 455). Lee and Fitz (1998), who interviewed 18 registered inspectors, found that their respondents identified a 'lacuna in the system in that there [was] no easily available source of advice and guidance to help schools meet the Key Issues thrown up by inspection' (p. 239).

So, on balance, it would seem that inspection offers some schools and some teachers a valuable opportunity to reflect on what they are doing. In recent years, Ofsted has appeared to be less of a threat to schools and successive chief inspectors have been keen not to be demonized in the way that Chris Woodhead was. However, two-day inspections every three years by a team of five people does not seem to be the best way to help schools and teachers to improve their own teaching standards given all that we know about teacher development (see Chapter 28 for more details). Systematic reflection, appraisal, peer teaching and mentoring would seem to be more likely than Ofsted inspections to facilitate teacher development, especially if those processes take place in an overall framework of school self-evaluation.

Concluding comments

Although beginning teachers sometimes complain about the amount of time that they are required to spend reflecting, reflection is one of the most powerful tools that we have to improve performance. Reflecting on lessons and other aspects of being a teacher will help you to understand who you are and should lead to you planning more effective lessons. Used well, reflection is a form of formative assessment, helping you to assess your own performance. Used badly, reflection can turn into a process of denial and blame.

Inspection, in theory, should provide few surprises to the reflective teacher and the reflective school. Inspection, in an ideal world, should act as a quality assurance tool, making sure that children and teachers across the country are getting a fair deal. However, it is not an ideal world and inspection is still seen as a somewhat daunting and threatening process by many people. 'Accountability' is seen by some as a dirty word – a surrogate for unnecessary state intervention in public education. By imposing accountability systems on teachers and schools, their professional capacity for self-improvement, it is argued, is diminished. Maybe it is time for teachers to have greater control over their own practices as long as they possess the ability to learn, aided by others, from their own reflections and the resources to effect necessary changes.

Note

Parts of this chapter draw heavily on 'Inspection', Chapter 7 in the second edition of *Becoming a Teacher*. I would like to acknowledge the contributions of Alison Millett and the late Jenny Adey, both of whom co-authored that chapter.

References

Atkinson, D. (2004) Theorising how students teachers form their identities in initial teacher education, *British Educational Research Journal*, 30(3): 379–94.

Baird, J.R. (1992) Collaborative reflection, systematic enquiry, better teaching, in T. Russell and H. Munby (eds), *Teachers and Teaching: From Classroom to Reflection*. London: Falmer.

Baird, J.R., Fensham, P.J., Gunstone, R.F. and White, R.T. (1991) The importance of reflection in improving science teaching and learning, *Journal of Research in Science Teaching*, 28(2): 163–82.

Barnes, D. (1992) The significance of teachers' frames for teaching, in T. Russell and H. Munby (eds) *Teachers and Teaching: From Classroom to Reflection*. London: Falmer.

Boyd, P. (2002) Rose-tinted reflection? The benefits for teachers of initial teacher education in secondary schools, *Journal of In-service Education*, 28(2): 203–17.

Cabinet Office (1991) *The Citizen's Charter. Raising the Standard*, Cmnd 1599. London: HMSO.

Callaghan, J. (1976) The Ruskin speech, *Times Educational Supplement*, 22 October.

Case, P., Case, S. and Catling, S. (2000) Please show you're working: a critical assessment of the impact of OFSTED inspection on primary teachers, *British Journal of Sociology of Education*, 21(4): 605–21.

Claxton, G., Atkinson, T., Osborn, M. and Wallace, M. (eds) (1996) *Liberating the Learner: Lessons for Professional Development in Education*. London: Routledge.

Cullingford, C. and Daniels, S. (1999) Effects of Ofsted inspections on school performance, in C. Cullingford (ed.) *An Inspector Calls*. London: Kogan Page.

Day, C. and Sachs, J. (eds) (2004) *International Handbook on the Continuing Professional Development of Teachers*. Maidenhead: Open University Press.

Dewey, J. (1910) *How We Think*. New York: Heath & Co.

Dewey, J. (1933) *How We Think: A Restatement of the Relation of Reflective Thinking in the Educative Process*. Chicago: Henry Regnery.

Dimmer, T. and Metiuk, J. (1998) The use and impact of OFSTED in a primary school, in P. Earley (ed.) *School Improvement after Inspection? School and LEA Responses*. London: Paul Chapman Publishing.

Edwards, A. and Protheroe, L. (2003) Learning to see in classrooms: what are student teachers learning about teaching and learning while learning to teach in schools? *British Educational Research Journal*, 29(2): 227–42.

Elliott, J. (1993) Three perspectives on coherence and continuity in teacher education, in J. Elliott (ed.) *Reconstructing Teacher Education: Teacher Development*. London: Falmer Press.

Fidler, B. and Davies, J. (1998) The inspector calls again: the reinspection of schools, in P. Earley (ed.) *Improvement after Inspection? School and LEA Responses*. London: Paul Chapman.

Fidler, B., Earley, P., Ouston, J. and Davies, J. (1998) Teacher gradings and OFSTED inspections: help or hindrance as a management tool? *School Leadership and Management*, 18(2): 257–70.

Fitz, J. and Lee, J. (1996) The early experience of OFSTED, in J. Ouston, P. Earley and B. Fidler (eds) *OFSTED Inspections; The Early Experience*. London: David Fulton.

Fitz-Gibbon, C. (1997) OFSTED's methodology, in M. Duffy (ed.) *A Better System of Inspection?* Hexham: Office for Standards in Inspection.

Fitz-Gibbon, C. and Stephenson-Forster, N.J. (1999) Is Ofsted helpful? An evaluation using social science criteria, in C. Cullingford (ed.) *An Inspector Calls*. London: Kogan Page.

Furlong, J. and Maynard, T. (1995) *Mentoring Student Teachers*. London: Routledge.

Gray, C. and Gardner, J. (1999) The impact of school inspections, *Oxford Review of Education*, 25(4): 455–68.

Grimmett, P.P. (1988) The nature of reflection and Schön's conception in perspective, in P. P. Grimmett and G. L. Erickson (eds) *Reflection in Teacher Education*. New York: Teachers College Press.

Grubb W.N. (2000) Opening classrooms and improving teaching: lessons from school inspections in England, *Teachers College Record*, 102(4): 696–723.

Harrison, J.K. (2002) The induction of Newly Qualified Teachers in secondary schools, *Journal of In-service Education*, 28(2): 255–75.

Jeffrey, B. and Woods, P. (1998) *Testing Teachers: The Effect of School Inspections on Primary Teachers*. London: Falmer Press.

Kogan, M. and Maden, M. (1999) An evaluation of evaluators: the Ofsted system of school inspection, in C. Cullingford (ed.) *An Inspector Calls*. London: Kogan Page.

Lee, J. and Fitz, J. (1998) Inspection for improvement: whose responsibility? *Journal of In-service Education*, 24(2): 239–53.

Loughran, J. (1996) *Developing Reflective Practice: Learning about Teaching and Learning through Modelling*. London: Falmer.

Market and Opinion Research International (MORI) (1999) *Schools Inspection Survey. Views of Primary Schools in England Inspected in Summer 1998*. London: Market and Opinion Research International (MORI).

Matthews, P., Holmes, J.R. and Vickers, P. (1998) Aspects of the reliability and validity of school inspection judgements of teaching quality, *Educational Research and Evaluation*, 4(2): 167–88.

Maychell, K. and Pathak, S. (1997) *Planning for Action. Part 1: A Survey of Schools' Post Inspection Action Planning*. Slough: NFER.

Millett, A. and Johnson, D.C. (1998) OFSTED inspection of primary mathematics: are there new insights to be gained? *School Leadership and Management*, 18(2): 239–55.

Munby, H. and Russell, T. (1992) Frames of reflection: an introduction, in T. Russell and H. Munby (eds), *Teachers and Teaching: From Classroom to Reflection*. London: Falmer.

National Union of Teachers (NUT) (1998) *'OFSTED': The Views of Headteachers and Deputy Headteacher Members of the National Union of Teachers*. NUT: London.

Oberg, A.A. and Artz, S. (1992) Teaching for reflection: being reflective, in T. Russell and H. Munby (eds) *Teachers and Teaching: From Classroom to Reflection*. London: Falmer.

Office for Standards in Education (Ofsted) (1997) *Inspection and Re-inspection of Schools from September 1997*. London: Ofsted.

Office for Standards in Education (Ofsted) (1998) Press Notice 98–7, 10 March. London: Ofsted.

Office for Standards in Education (Ofsted) (2000) Press Notices for July 21. http:www.ofsted.gov.uk/.

Ofsted, Keele University and Touche Ross (1995) *Inspection Quality 1994/1995*. London: Office for Standards in Education/Central Office of Information.

Ouston, J. and Davies, J. (1998) OFSTED and afterwards? Schools' responses to inspection, in P. Earley (ed.) *School Improvement after Inspection? School and LEA Responses*. London: Paul Chapman.

Reid, I., Constable, H. and Griffiths, R. (eds) (1994) *Teacher Education Reform*. London: Paul Chapman Publishing.

Russell, T. and Munby, H. (1991) Reframing: the role of experience in developing teachers' professional knowledge, in D.A. Schön (ed.), *The Reflective Turn: Case Studies In and On Educational Practice*. New York: Teachers College Press.

Sandbrook, I. (1996) *Making Sense of Primary Inspection*. Buckingham: Open University Press.

Schön, D. (1983) *The Reflective Practitioner: How Professionals Think in Action*. London: Temple Smith.

Schön, D.A. (1987) *Educating the Reflective Practitioner: Toward a New Design for Teaching and Learning in the Professions*. San Francisco: Jossey-Bass.

Thomas, G. (1999) Standards and school inspection: the rhetoric and the reality, in C. Cullingford (ed.) *An Inspector Calls*. London: Kogan Page.

Valli, L.R. (1993) Reflective teacher education programs: an analysis of case studies, in J. Calderhead and P. Gates (eds) *Conceptualizing Reflection in Teacher Development*. London: Falmer Press, pp. 11–22.

Wilcox, B. and Gray, J. (1996) *Inspecting Schools: Holding Schools to Account and Helping Schools to Improve*. Buckingham: Open University Press.

Williams, E. (1999) Sleeplessness? Irritability? Low self-esteem? You must have Ofsteditis, *Times Educational Supplement* (Mind and Body Supplement), 26 March.

Woodhead, C. (1999) An inspector responds, *Guardian Education*, 5 October.

9

Social justice in schools: engaging with equality

Louise Archer

Introduction

In this chapter I suggest that an understanding of social justice can be a useful tool for teachers who want to work in equitable ways and who wish to foster a classroom environment that is experienced as 'fair' and respectful by pupils from diverse backgrounds. Indeed, teachers are also required to have due regard for equality issues in line with the National Curriculum inclusion statement. In this chapter, I illustrate how the concept of social justice can help us to analyse and address unequal power relations within schools and classrooms and can help professionals to become more attuned to 'hidden' inequalities.

What do we mean by 'social justice'?

The term 'social justice' is increasingly being used by academics as a means for engaging with issues of inequality – although it has perhaps been less commonly employed within policy and practitioner circles. In one sense, the notion of social justice is just another way of talking about and engaging with issues of equality and 'fairness'. Indeed, we could ask why it is even necessary, given the proliferation of terminology within this area in recent years (for example, social exclusion/inclusion; social equity; equal opportunities; equality and diversity; equality of outcomes). However, as I argue below, the strength of 'social justice' is that it provides a robust and comprehensive toolkit for engaging with inequalities – due primarily to the ways in which it has been meticulously theorized.

So how might we conceptualize 'social justice'? In her book, *Action for*

Social Justice in Education, Morwenna Griffiths postulates that 'social justice is a verb' (Griffiths 2003: 55). In other words, it is a dynamic project – never complete, finished or achieved 'once and for all', it is always subject to revision. Drawing on the work of Young (1990) and Fraser (1997), we might usefully identify three key forms of social justice (see also Power and Gewirtz 2001 and Gewirtz 2002 for an example of this framework in practice):

- **Relational justice**: this is about ensuring cultural recognition and respect. It refers to fair and just relationships within society.
- **Distributive justice**: this concerns the allocation and distribution of material and discursive goods and resources within society. It is about making sure that economic, cultural and other resources are shared out equitably.
- **Associational justice**: this refers to people's ability to have a say and participate in decisions that affect their own lives. It is about ensuring that people are enabled to be active and equitable participants in society.

This tripartite conceptualization of social justice offers a complex and holistic approach to identifying and understanding different forms of inequality. Yet as Gewirtz (1998) argues, the three aspects of social justice are not simple, discrete categories. Rather, they overlap, inter-relate and can contradict one another. This alerts us to how the task of promoting social justice within schools will never be simple or straightforward – there is no single, 'one-size-fits-all' approach. However, the three components do provide a useful model for helping to identify the different sorts of equity issues that might be at stake within any given context.

So how might this concept of social justice help us to engage with issues of equality and diversity within schools? The following sections outline and discuss some key features of contemporary debates pertaining to three core axes of social difference within UK society and schools, namely gender, race/ethnicity and social class. Due to constraints of space, I have chosen to concentrate on gender, 'race'/ethnicity and social class – there are other important axes, such as sexuality, dis/ability and so on. Gender, 'race'/ethnicity and social class have been organized here as separate sections purely for ease of presentation and comprehension. This approach should not be interpreted as indicating that I treat them as separate, free-standing social categories. Rather, I would argue that they are all inextricably interlinked (see Archer 2005 regarding my re/theorization of 'difference').

Each section starts by outlining the theoretical and policy context and then moves on to illustrate social justice issues for teachers and schools through a discussion of recent research evidence. It should be noted, however, that the chapter provides merely a brief snapshot and introduction to issues and research in each area – it cannot fully represent the depth and complexity of issues and work within the field.

Gender

Theoretical and policy context

Since the mid–1990s, one of the most high profile educational issues has been the 'boys' underachievement debate'. Newspapers regularly contain headlines expressing concerns about a 'crisis' in relation to boys' under-achievement – and governments around the world have instigated a plethora of initiatives designed to increase boys' attainment at school. Many of these interventions have been substantially funded, for example the $4million 'lighthouse' schools programme in Australia and the $1.2 million study in the USA into whether single-sex teaching can raise boys' achievement (see Francis and Skelton 2005 for a full discussion and overview). In the UK too, there has been a proliferation of research and initiatives, such as the 'Playing for Success' national programme (a football-themed initiative to encourage after-school homework).

Despite the overwhelming media and policy concern with boys' under-achievement, the evidence pertaining to the existence, or the size, of any gender gap in achievement is rather less clear-cut. Indeed, whilst the popular headlines scream out each summer that girls are outperforming boys at GCSE and A level, these overall aggregate figures hide important underlying trends. For instance, girls do not outperform boys at *all* subjects: 'female out performance of boys is strongly connected to their overwhelmingly higher achievement at language and literacy subjects, which somewhat skews the achievement figures overall' (Francis and Skelton 2005: 3).

An international study of achievement across 43 countries (the OECD 2003 PISA study) also found that boys do slightly better than girls in mathematics in almost all countries and that achievement in science is roughly equal (although in some cases boys outperform girls). However, girls were found to perform significantly better in combined reading scales (see Francis and Skelton 2005, for analysis and discussion).

Indeed, it has been argued that the scale of concern with boys' 'under-achievement' in the UK is entirely disproportionate to the issue:

> although there are grave concerns among British policy-makers and journalists about 'boys' underachievement', Britain is actually one of the five countries where the OECD PISA study (2003) identifies the gender gap as narrowest.
>
> (Francis and Skelton 2005: 3)

Serious questions have also been raised about the use of broad-brush statistics within the boys' underachievement debate. For instance, the seminal book by Epstein *et al.* (1998) argues that it is not true to say that all boys are underachieving and all girls are achieving. Rather, they point to complex racialized, classed and gendered patterns of achievement – posing the question as to which boys and which girls are under/achieving? Attention has also been drawn to statistics that demonstrate how boys' achievement is actually rising year on year. Furthermore, data on post-16 employment and earnings indicate that boys tend to be more advantaged than girls in the labour market. Hence feminist academics have argued that the boys' underachievement debate is not only misleading, but is also potentially harmful because it hides the issues and problems experienced by many girls, directs resources towards boys at the expense of girls and deflects attention from more significant achievement gaps in relation to 'race' and social class.

Research evidence: social justice issues for teachers

There is a considerable and wide-ranging body of feminist (and pro-feminist) research pertaining to gender equality in schooling. The journal *Gender and Education* is also an excellent source for current research and thinking. Below, however, are a couple of selected themes together with some illustrations from research, which raise some pertinent issues for teachers wanting to address gender equity within schools.

The popular focus on addressing 'boys' underachievement' within schools has entailed a range of negative implications for girls, whose needs have slipped off the policy agenda. As a study by Osler and Vincent (2003) details, this situation is playing a key role in generating *girls' hidden exclusion*. For instance, the types of social exclusion often experienced by girls (such as verbal/psychological bullying, truancy, self-exclusion and leaving school due to pregnancy) are often overlooked and inadequately resourced because policy makers and practitioners are working with a notion of exclusion that is based on the most common features of boys' exclusion. Hence, Osler and Vincent argue, girls' exclusion has become more difficult for professionals to recognize and address.

Particular attention has also been given to the crucial role played by *teachers' gendered expectations and stereotypes* in reproducing gender inequalities within schools. Teachers' (unwitting) gendered expectations of pupils can impact on their interactions with pupils in class and can play a role in shaping pupils' aspirations and expectations (for instance, steering them towards particular gender-stereotypical aspirations and career expectations – see, for example, Osgood *et al.* 2006). Indeed, there is a wealth of research evidence documenting how teachers are more likely to describe boys as being 'naturally intelligent' and girls as 'plodding achievers', irrespective of the child's actual attainment (see, for example, Walkerdine 1990). Indeed, it has been argued that many professionals work with an implicit (unwitting) model of the 'ideal pupil' that is constructed in masculine terms. Against this, girls may be relegated to a 'helpful', 'sensible' servicing role (see Francis and Skelton 2005); for example, being expected to help facilitate boys' learning and deferring to boys' dominance in the classroom. Numerous studies have also documented how boys continue to take up proportionally more space in schools and playgrounds, dominating these spaces both physically and discursively (see, for example, Connolly 1998; Skelton 2001; Connolly 2003).

Another important area of concern relates to *pupils' constructions of gender identity* – particularly the ways in which the 'coolest' and most popular forms of masculinity and femininity are configured. Research has been particularly instructive in developing our understandings of how gender identities are constructed within matrices of power, and how the dominance of particular hegemonic forms of masculinity and femininity can impact negatively on the lives and experiences of 'other' pupils. Studies, such as those conducted in Australia by Martino and Palotta-Chiarolli (2005), highlight the pain and misery endured by those pupils with marginalized masculinities and femininities, who experience ridicule and relentless pressure to conform to a very narrow dominant form of popular masculinity/femininity. For instance, Martino and Palotta-Chiarolli (2005) detail boys' and girls' accounts of sexualized bullying that is tolerated in schools because the perpetrators are interpreted as 'just being cool' or 'normal'.

The value of schools working to help pupils to deconstruct gender stereo-types and to develop broader, more inclusive gender identity constructions is not 'merely' a social justice issue. Large-scale national research under-taken by Warrington and Younger (2002) demonstrates that boys tend to record higher levels of achievement in schools where gender constructions are less extreme and polarized. It has thus been argued that:

> teachers need to develop ways of getting their pupils to reflect and critique 'taken-for-granted' but gendered assumptions of classroom/ media texts, ways of being organised, managed and assessed, engaging with learning, and so forth.
>
> (Francis and Skelton 2005: 149)

To this end, practical assistance and ideas for professional development activities can be found in the following: Mills (2001) – for tackling dominant forms of masculinity and cultures of violence in schools; Martino and Palotta-Chiarolli (2005) – for challenging gender stereotypes among pupils and staff and reformulating student-welfare policies; Rowan *et al.* (2002) – for addressing gender and literacy; and Francis (2000) – in relation to deconstructing gender stereotyping within secondary schools.

'Race' and ethnicity

Theoretical and policy context

Whilst issues of 'race' and ethnicity tend to occupy the centre-stage of American education policy discourse, they have not achieved such a high-profile status in the UK. This is not to say that questions of 'race'/ethnicity do not feature within UK education debates, but rather that racialized inequalities within schooling have not been positioned as a social justice imperative to quite the same extent. Indeed, it has been argued that there has been a distinct dearth of mainstream discussion and interventions focussing on 'race', ethnicity and achievement in the UK (Gillborn 2001, 2005).

In contemporary education policy, issues around 'race'/ethnicity are predominantly configured in relation to the differential achievement of pupils from minority ethnic backgrounds. Concerns have primarily been expressed about the underachievement (and low rates of progression into post-16 education) of African Caribbean pupils (especially African Caribbean boys) and, to a slightly lesser extent, Pakistani and Bangladeshi pupils (see DfES 2006a/b). Calls have been made, however, to use such statistics with caution – not least because the broad-brush categories employed often lump together groups with very different levels of achievement. For instance, the use of 'White' as a category within official statistics can comprise both White British, Irish and Gypsy/Roma children (all of whom record quite different levels of achievement), and the term 'Asian' can encompass higher-achieving Indian pupils and lower-achieving Bangladeshi pupils (DfES 2005).

Criticisms have also been made of the ways in which much contemporary education policy engages with issues of 'race'/ethnicity. For instance, attention has been drawn to the subtle yet sustained erasure of the language of 'race' and ethnicity from New Labour policies (Lewis 2000). Reviewing statistical evidence and recent policy initiatives, Archer and Francis (2007) argue that issues of 'race'/ethnicity have been subject to a pernicious turn in recent policy discourse. In particular, we have argued that current education policy explanations of (and proposed strategies for engaging with) underachievement among minority ethnic pupils tend to deny or ignore racism as a factor. Instead, emphasis tends to be placed on 'cultural', personal and family factors (for example, the notion of a 'poverty of aspirations' within families). This approach can pathologize minority ethnic pupils and their families and shift the locus of blame/attention away from social structures and institutions and on to minority ethnic families – who are positioned as the primary site of both 'the problem' and any solutions. Furthermore, we have argued that such policy approaches tend to naturalize differences in achievement between ethnic groups and effectively remove the means for engaging with inequalities.

Of course the pathologization of minority ethnic pupils and families within education policy is not a recent or new phenomenon. In the 1960s, minority ethnic pupils were treated as explicit educational problems, who were 'bussed' out to different schools in order to 'spread the burden' of educating them. As Mullard (1985) discusses, a 'compensatory' approach dominated, in which minority ethnic pupils were perceived in terms of 'lack' – hence the primary issue was seen to be how to address and compensate for these pupils' deficits of skills, intelligence, language and so forth. Minority ethnic pupils were framed as 'problems' that need 'solving' – with interventions being designed to speed up pupils' assimilation into the mainstream (for example, encouraging them to 'give up' their 'alien' ways).

There have been various discursive shifts over the years in terms of how education policy has approached the schooling of minority ethnic pupils – although, as critics point out, these have often been built upon problematic conceptualizations of 'race' and ethnicity. For instance, the advent of multiculturalism sought to 'celebrate diversity' yet it attracted criticism for reproducing simplistic, stereotypical views of minority ethnic groups. In particular, the focus upon celebrating aspects of 'culture' has been critiqued for reifying and homogenizing ethnic differences and propagating stereotypical representations of ethnic groups (the 'saris, samosas, steel bands' syndrome). At the same time, this approach also ignored structural inequalities such as racism and could not account for more complex patterns of (under) achievement (see Rattansi 1992 for a discussion).

Anti-racism developed as an alternative to multiculturalism, emphasizing (as the name suggests) the role of racism within minority ethnic pupils' experiences of schooling. Yet this movement also attracted criticism for its homogenization of all minority ethnic groups under a single banner and for its rather simplistic understanding of racism. Indeed, the MacDonald Report (1989) – set up in response to the murder of pupil Ahmed Iqbal Ullah by a white pupil in the playground of his school – delivered a condemning analysis of the ineffectiveness of the anti-racist policies of the school in question at the time.

More recently, the MacPherson Report (1999) – released after the murder of black London teenager Stephen Lawrence – instigated a new policy awareness regarding the role of institutional racism. The report heralded in new legislation, in the form of the Race Relations Amendment Act (2000), which places a duty on public institutions to tackle racism and promote good race relations. And yet, it has been argued that, in general, the New Labour administration has tended to maintain the 'colour-blind' stance adopted by preceding Conservative Governments (Gillborn 2001; Majors 2001). Furthermore, it has been noted that the Government seems not to attach the same importance (and does not devote the same resources) to addressing racial and ethnic differences in achievement as compared, for example, to gender. This, Gillborn (2005) argues, indicates an implicit acceptance of racial inequity within British education policy and reflects 'tacit intentionality' on the part of the Government – that is, an intention to maintain power structures that privilege Whites. Certainly, it might be noted that whilst national policy makers acknowledge issues such as the disproportionate exclusion of black boys (DfES, 2003) and the findings of the MacPherson Report (1999), the Government has still been unwilling to set targets for improvement in relation to any of the statistics outlined.

Research evidence: social justice issues for teachers

Despite the erasure of 'race' and ethnicity from the policy context, a considerable amount of research has been conducted to illuminate the social justice issues within schools. The journal *Race, Ethnicity and Education* also provides a useful reference point for reading further about current research and theory in this area. Detailed below are some core themes that may be of particular interest to teachers wishing to grapple with the issues.

A key issue facing minority ethnic pupils is that of *racist stereotyping*. This not only relates to the tendency for some teachers and schools to hold lower expectations of Black and minority ethnic pupils, but also to more subtle, complex, specifically racialized stereotypical discourses. In other words, popular discursive constructions of particular groups of pupils can result in an array of differential implications for the pupils concerned.

For instance, a number of studies have drawn attention to the disjuncture between teachers' expectations for Black girls, and the views and aspirations of the girls and their parents. As I argue elsewhere, there is dominant popular perception that average achievement is 'good enough' for Black girls and boys – whereas Black pupils and their families often talk about 'wanting more' (Archer 2006). Consequently, aspirational Black pupils may be forced to negotiate circuitous, strategic, 'back-door' routes to achieve educational success (Mirza 1992). For example, Loretta, an 18-year-old Black African student from one study, described her experience of being dissuaded from applying to university:

> I was told not to apply because, you know, I just wouldn't get the grade and whatever . . . and the teacher turned round and said to me 'well I think £14.50 [the application fee] is a lot of money'. And I said, do you know what? When I go to university, whatever I make, I'm sure it will cover that £14.50, so I'll just spend it ahead. I'm really cheeky when I want to be.
>
> (Archer *et al*. 2003: 103)

Loretta did in fact receive three offers of a university place and had achieved the requisite grades at the time of her mock examinations. Loretta's story is, unfortunately, borne out time and again within other research studies. For instance, 16-year-old Analisa described being laughed at by a teacher for her aspirations to go to LSE (Archer *et al*., forthcoming) and Marilyn, a young Black woman from yet another study (Archer *et al*. 2004), recounted:

> I said to Mr W before like, because – you know when we had to go down to the library and do all the Connexions? He goes 'Oh Marilyn, so what do you want to do when you grow up?' And I said I wanted to be a lawyer and he just laughed and he goes 'You!' and I went 'Yes' and he goes 'I don't think so'.

Attention has also been drawn to how dominant stereotypes about Black masculinity operate as pernicious racist discourses. For instance, Sewell (1997) discusses how the identities and behaviours of Black boys in school are often interpreted as being aggressive, problematic and challenging. These images are also underpinned by popular associations of Black masculinity as hyper-heterosexual and 'macho' – a construction that has its root in historical racist representations of blackness (hooks 1992; Mama 1995).

'Asian' and Chinese pupils have also long been subject to particular forms of stereotyping – although these have often taken more 'positive' guises, representing such pupils as 'clever', 'quiet', 'behavers and achievers' (Gillborn 1990; Archer and Francis 2005a). However, even these seemingly 'positive' stereotypes have been shown to be experienced as negative and homogenizing by the young people concerned. More recently, there has been a discursive split within representations of 'Asian' pupils – whereby 'achievers' (Indian, predominantly Sikh and Hindu pupils) have been representationally differentiated from 'believers' – namely Muslim pupils from Pakistani and Bangladeshi backgrounds. The impact of Islamaphobia on representations of Muslims (but particularly boys) as 'problematic' pupils is documented elsewhere (Archer 2003). A sustained critique has also been mounted regarding racist popular constructions of Asian/Muslim girls as

passive and oppressed 'hapless dependants' whose families are more concerned with getting them married off than pursuing an education (for
example, Brah 1996; Basit 1997; Ahmad 2001; Shain 2003).

In addition to the issue of stereotyping, minority ethnic pupils continue
to experience *verbal and physical violence* within schools. For instance,
Muslim young people in a town in the northwest of England recounted
their near-daily experiences of being spat at, insulted and attacked (Archer
2003). They also, however, described more subtle manifestations of racism
from their peers – for instance, explaining their confusion about how their
White peers would be friendly in school but would 'ignore us' in public at
the weekends. A study by Becky Francis and myself also records how British-
Chinese pupils regularly experience name-calling and how British Chinese
boys complain that they are regularly taunted (as 'Bruce Lee') and are forced
to fight by their male peers (Archer and Francis 2005b, 2006). As pupils from
across minority ethnic backgrounds point out, there is still a challenge
for schools in how to resolve incidents of violence. The issue seems particularly acute in the case of those boys who choose to use violence back in
retaliation – with many complaining that an even-handed punishment
of both sides is 'unfair' – not least when the original abuse may remain
unaddressed (and hence is perceived to be sanctioned by the school). This
illustrates the complexity of enacting social justice in schools – although it
does also indicate how addressing racism may also entail a complementary
focus on challenging hegemonic forms of masculinity.

Attention has also been drawn to the importance of ensuring an
equitable *school ethos and organization*, in which parents' and pupils' various
needs and values are valued and respected. Within educational policy, this
is often discussed in terms of the provision of special resources (for example,
halal food, prayer rooms) and the adoption of practices and rules that can
accommodate cultural and religious differences (for example, flexible rules
around uniform, permitting the wearing of hijab, etc). However, critics
have argued that such measures can only go so far, and that additional
efforts may be required with respect to ensuring, for instance, that the
curriculum represents the histories, interests and identities of diverse
ethnic, cultural and religious groups. Debates also continue around the
imbalances that exist in terms of state funding of faith schools – with proportionally far more 'White' faith/denominational schools being supported
as compared, for instance, to Muslim faith schools (see, for example, Parker-
Jenkins *et al.* 2004). Important concerns have also been raised that the
voices of Black and minority ethnic parents remain absent from many
schools at both formal and informal levels (see Crozier and Reay 2005).

Social class

Theoretical and policy context

Within current education policy, issues pertaining to social class tend to be
framed in terms of working-class pupils' (under)achievement and low rates
of progression into post-16 education. Statistics indicate that young people

from poorer socio-economic backgrounds (and those on free school meals) achieve lower academic results than their more affluent peers (DfES 2005). Students from working-class backgrounds also remain severely and persistently under-represented at university level (NCIHE 1997; Archer *et al.* 2003). Consequently, initiatives such as Connexions, Learning Mentors, Aim Higher and the Education Maintenance Allowance (EMA) have been introduced in an effort to support achievement and to encourage more working-class young people to stay on in further and higher education.

It is interesting to note, however, that despite the continued policy interest in 'raising' working-class young people's achievement and post–16 progression, there has been an erasure of the actual language of social class within education policy. Thus, rather than talking about 'working-class' pupils, official publications are more likely to use the euphemistic terminology of 'socially excluded', 'disadvantaged' and/or 'deprived' individuals and communities (see Lewis 2000). As various critics argue, these terms need to be treated with care because they are conceptually loaded and contain a range of normative (and often pathologizing) assumptions.

Whilst it is widely agreed that the achievement and progression of working-class young people is an issue that requires policy attention, there are also quite stark differences of opinion regarding the potential causes of, and solutions to, the issue. For instance, current policies have been criticized for adopting a deficit approach to working-class young people and their families because they assume that lower rates of achievement and post–16 progression are the result of pupils' 'faulty cognitions' and/or lack of information/knowledge (see, for example, Thomas 2001). These assumptions are evidenced within prevalent policy references to pupils' 'low aspirations' and family cultures that do not value education. In contrast, critics have argued that the generation of patterns of working-class achievement and post-16 progression is far more complex, being produced through an interplay of structural and institutional inequalities together with social, cultural, emotional and identity factors (as illustrated further below).

Alongside these policy debates, social class also remains a hotly contested concept within sociological and academic circles. Opinion is divided as to how best to define, understand and theorize social class, and debates rage as to whether the concept of social class is even still relevant and useful. Within these debates it is noticeable that a 'culturalist' approach to theorizing social class is proving attractive (see, for example, Savage 2000; Skeggs 2004), particularly amongst educationalists concerned with promoting social justice (see, for example, Reay 1997, 2002). This approach treats class as a fuzzy concept that is as much to do with people's feelings about their identities and lived experiences as it is to do with their 'objective' position in occupational and economic terms (see also Skeggs 1997; Lawler 1999).

Research evidence: social justice issues for teachers

So what can research tell us about the social justice issues facing schools with respect to working-class pupils? The work of Diane Reay (see, for example, 1997, 2002) provides a particularly useful starting point for reading further about social class inequalities and schooling. The following provides a thumbnail sketch/brief overview of some key themes emerging from recent studies conducted with young people in UK secondary schools.

Attention has been drawn to the social justice implications of the *school as a classed institution*. For instance, various studies record how working-class young people report feeling excluded by the 'middle class', 'posh' language, ethos and curriculum of schools. For instance, interviews conducted with working-class girls in two separate London studies (Archer *et al.* 2004; Archer *et al.* 2005) revealed how the girls felt alienated by their schools' middle-class institutional habitus. They described feeling estranged from the 'high brow' speech of some of their teachers and complained that there was a gulf of understanding between their 'common' selves and 'posh' teachers – who, they felt, were not 'on their level'. This finding has also been noted in relation to working-class students in higher education (see, for example, Read *et al.* 2003). A number of working-class pupils also experienced aspects of the curriculum as irrelevant to their own lives. For instance, a pupil in one study (Archer 2006) was adamant that learning Spanish is irrelevant because 'it's unlikely for me to go out to Spain'. She continued, 'I can't speak enough language anyway, even English, I'm common and that's that' – revealing the psychic damage inflicted on those who are already judged to be 'lacking' and of lesser 'value' within dominant systems.

Various studies have also flagged up how *classed relations between teachers, pupils and parents* are implicated within the reproduction of inequalities. For instance, many working-class young people report experiencing a gulf of understanding and (an albeit sometimes unintentional) lack of respect from teachers/schools due to the disjuncture between the classed backgrounds, identities and assumptions of home and school. For instance, some pupils' report feeling 'misunderstood' by teachers and studies have highlighted how young people's attempts to generate a sense of value and worth in their lives (for example, through particular 'styles' of ways of being) may be interpreted as inappropriate or 'anti-education' by middle-class professionals (see Archer *et al.* 2007). Furthermore, pupils have complained that interactions with their families at parents' evenings can be disrespectful. As one girl put it:

> Some of the things they say . . . it's making them look at my mum stupidly, and I'm like 'don't talk to my mum like that, she's right there, she understands what you're saying, she's not dumb'.
>
> (Cited in Archer *et al.* 2004)

Working-class parents also describe feeling 'looked down on' by schools and are subsequently wary about further contact (Reay 1997). This may, in turn, be interpreted by schools as evidence that these parents do not care sufficiently about their children's education – so feeding into a cycle of bad feeling and/or miscommunication. For similar reasons (and exacerbated by tighter constraints on time and resources), working-class parents also tend to be less fully or less frequently involved in consultations regarding how their children's schools are organized and run (Crozier and Reay 2005). Class differences between home and school can entail a lack of understanding from both sides regarding the identities, motivations and contexts of the other. There is also, of course, evidence of instances of more overt class prejudice – for instance, in one study a teacher's description of working-class families as a 'bolshie and obnoxious', 'underclass' of 'just bloody useless parents' (Archer 2006). All of these examples illustrate the symbolic violence that may be experienced as the result of living in positions of inequality and subordination and how knowing that you are 'looked down on' within society constitutes what Sennett and Cobb (1993) have termed the 'hidden injuries' of class.

A further important consideration concerns the ways in which *material inequalities* can impact on the lives and education of working-class pupils. Less affluent families obviously have fewer economic (financial) resources with which to support their children's learning – whereas middle-class families benefit from having the money to pay for more (or more exotic) school trips, home computers/Internet, reference materials, extra tutoring and a whole host of extra-curricula 'enrichment' activities (see Vincent and Ball 2006). Financial resources are not the only type of resource, however, and working-class families may experience tighter constraints on resources such as time and physical space. For instance, some working-class pupils may find it more difficult to do their homework due to a lack of space at home and/or because they provide important caring responsibilities for parents or siblings. Where families experience different levels of material and cultural wealth, this can also generate symbolic violences; for example, where pupils feel looked down on because they cannot afford to purchase particular uniforms or go on school trips. Disparities in wealth also strongly shape the types of school that pupils attend – an issue exacerbated by current 'school choice' policies (Gewirtz 2002). Indeed, working-class pupils are disproportionately represented in 'sink' and 'demonized' schools with poorer physical environments and resources (Reay and Lucey 2003). They are also less likely to see higher education (particularly the more prestigious institutions) as either open or affordable (Archer *et al.* 2003).

Concluding comments

This chapter has discussed how the concept of social justice can be a useful tool for education professionals. However, this is not to imply that teachers are responsible for either causing or indeed solving all societal problems and injustices! As Gewirtz (2002) discusses, there are no 'purely' egalitarian policies or practices, and the extent to which particular actions are equitable will be mediated by the context and according to the different parties involved. Indeed, it would be unrealistic to expect teachers to be able to change national government policies – and of course we must be mindful that teachers must work within particular sets of requirements, responsibilities and constraints, all of which demand attention, time and resources. However, it is suggested that by developing an understanding of the complexity of enacting social justice in practice and by fostering an awareness of the various types of issues that might be encountered, teachers may be able to create small (but significant) changes in their classrooms and schools. To this end, I have outlined a model for understanding social justice and have tried to draw attention to a few equity issues (in relation to gender, 'race'/ethnicity and social class) which may not otherwise be necessarily apparent – as they often arise as (unintended) implications from wider policies or 'common sense' ways of thinking. This mode of reflection might be particularly valuable for teachers who come from 'dominant' (for example, White or middle-class) backgrounds, because we are rarely obliged to reflect on our privilege and the taken-for-granted assumptions that it can bring. At times this can be a difficult, even painful, process – but it also carries the potential to be incredibly important and fruitful. In sum, the chapter has tried to open up ways of thinking about 'equality' – in all its complexity – as part of a collective project of creating an education system that can be experienced as fair and socially just by all pupils, teachers and parents.

References

Ahmad, F. (2001) Modern traditions? British Muslim women and academic achievement, *Gender and Education*, 13(2): 137–52.

Archer, L. (2003) *'Race', Masculinity and Schooling: Muslim Boys and Education*. Buckingham: Open University Press.

Archer, L. (2005) Re/theorising 'difference' in feminist research, *Women's Studies International Forum*, 27, 459–73.

Archer, L. (2006) The impossibility of girls' educational 'success': entanglements of gender, 'race', class and sexuality in the production and problematisation of educational femininities. Paper for *ESRC Seminar Series 'Girls in Education 3–16'*, Cardiff 24 November 2005.

Archer, L. and Francis, B. (2005a) 'They never go off the rails like other ethnic groups': teachers' constructions of British Chinese pupils' gender identities and approaches to learning, *British Journal of Sociology of Education*, 26(2): 165–82.

Archer, L. and Francis, B. (2005b) British Chinese pupils' and parents' constructions of racism, *Race, Ethnicity and Education*, 8(4): 387–407.

Archer, L. and Francis, B. (2006) *Understanding Minority Ethic Achievement: Race, Gender, Class and 'Success'*. London: Routledge.

Archer, L. and Francis, B. (2007) *Understanding Minority Ethnic Achievement: Race, Class, Gender and 'Success'*. London: Routledge.

Archer, L. Halsall, A. and Hollingworth, S. (2007) Class, gender, (hetero)sexuality and schooling: working class girls' engagement with schooling and post-16 aspirations, *British Journal of Sociology of Education*, 28(2): 165–180.

Archer, L. Halsall, A., Hollingworth, S. and Mendick, H. (2005) *'Dropping out and drifting away: An investigation of factors affecting inner-city pupils' identities, aspirations and post-16 routes*, Final Report to the Esmee Fairbairn Foundation. London, IPSE.

Archer, L., Hollingworth, S. and Halsall, A. (2007) 'University's not for me – I'm a Nike Person. Inner-city young people's negotiations of "new" class identities and educational engagement', *Sociology*, 41(2): 210–237.

Archer, L., Hutchings, M. and Ross, A. (2003) *Higher Education and Social Class: issues of exclusion and inclusion*. London: RoutledgeFalmer.

Archer, L., Maylor, U., Read, B. and Osgood, J. (2004) *An exploration of the attitudinal, social and cultural factors impacting on Year 10 student progression. Final Report to London West Learning and Skills Council*. London: IPSE.

Basit, T. (1997) *Eastern Values, Western Milieu: Identities and Aspirations of Adolescent British Muslim Girls*. Aldershot: Ashgate.

Brah, A. (1996) *Cartographies of Diaspora*. London: Routledge.

Connolly, P. (1998) *Racism, Gender Identities and Young Children*. London: Routledge.

Connolly, P. (2003) Gendered and gendering spaces: playgrounds in the early years, in C. Skelton and B. Francis (eds) *Boys and Girls in the Primary Classroom*. Buckingham: Open University Press.

Crozier, G. and Reay, D. (2005) (eds) *Activating Participation*. Stoke-on-Trent: Trentham Books.

Department for Education and Skills (DfES) (2003) *Using the National Healthy School Stand to Raise Boys' Achievement*. Wetherby: Health Development Agency.

Department for Education and Skills (DfES) (2005) http://www.standards. dfes.gov.uk/ethnicminorities/raising_achievement.

Department for Education and Skills (DfES) (2006a) Ethnic Minority Achievement, accessed on 30 May 2006, at http://www.standards.dfes.gov.uk/ethnicminorities/.

Department for Education and Skills (DfES) (2006b) Black pupils achievement programme, accessed 30 May 2006, at http://www.standards.dfes.gov.uk/ethnicminorities/raising_achievement/bpaprogramme/.

Donald, J. and Rattansi, A. (1992) *Race, Culture and Difference*. London: Sage.

Epstein, D., Elwood, J., Hey, V. and Maw, J. (1998) Schoolboy frictions: feminism and 'failing boys', in D. Epstein, J. Elwood, V. Hey and J. Maw (eds) *Failing Boys?* Buckingham: Open University Press.

Francis, B. (2000) *Boys, Girls and Achievement*. London: RoutledgeFalmer.

Francis, B. (2006) Heroes or Zeroes? The discursive positioning of 'underachieving boys' in English neo-liberal education policy, *Journal of Education Policy*, 21(2): 187–200.

Francis, B. and Skelton, C. (2005) *Reassessing Gender and Achievement*. London: Routledge.

Fraser, N. (1997) *Justice Interruptus*. New York: Routledge.

Gewirtz, S. (1998) Conceptualizing social justice in education: mapping the territory, *Journal of Education Policy*, 13(4): 469–84.

Gewirtz, S. (2002) *The Managerial School*. London: Routledge.

Gillborn, D. (1990) *Race, Ethnicity and Education: Teaching and Learning in Multi-ethnic Schools*. London: Unwin Hyman.

Gillborn, D. (2001) Racism, policy and the (mis)education of Black children, in R. Majors (ed.) *Educating Our Black Children*. London: RoutledgeFalmer.

Gillborn, D. (2005) Education policy as an act of white supremacy: whiteness, critical race theory and education reform, *Journal of Education Policy*, 20(4): 485–505.

Griffiths, M. (2003) *Action for Social Justice in Education: Fairly Different*. Maidenhead: Open University Press.

hooks, b. (1992) *Black Looks*. London: Turnaround Press.

Lawler, S. (1999) Getting out and getting away: women's narratives of class mobility, *Feminist Review*, 63: 3–24.

Lewis, G. (2000) Discursive histories, the pursuit of multiculturalism and social policy, in G. Lewis, S. Gewirtz and J. Clarke (eds) *Rethinking Social Policy*, London: Open University and Sage.

Macdonald, I., Bhavnani, R., Khan, L. and John, G. (1989) *Murder in the Playground*. London: Longsight Press.

MacPherson, W. (1999) *The Stephen Lawrence Enquiry: Report of an Enquiry by Sir William MacPherson*. London: Stationery Office.

Majors, R. (2001) Introduction, in R. Majors (ed.) *Educating Our Black Children*. London: RoutledgeFalmer.

Mama, A. (1995) *Beyond the Masks: Race, Gender and Subjectivity*. London: Routledge.

Martino, W. and Palotta-Chiarolli, M. (2005) *Being Normal is the Only Way to Be: Adolescent Perspectives on Gender and School*. Sydney: University of New South Wales Press.

Mills, M. (2001) *Challenging Violence in Schools*. Buckingham: Open University Press.

Mirza, H. (1992) *Young, Female and Black*. London: Routledge.

Mullard, C. (1985) Multiracial education in Britain, in M. Arnot (ed.) *Race and Gender: Equal Opportunities Policies in Education*. Milton Keynes: Open University Press.

NCIHE (1997) *Higher Education and the Learning Society: The Dearing Report*. London: Stationery Office.

Osgood, J., Francis, B. and Archer, L. (2006) Gendered identities and work placement: why don't boys' care? *Journal of Education Policy*, 21(3): 305–42.

Osler, A. and Vincent, V. (2003) *Girls and Exclusion: Rethinking the Agenda*. London: RoutledgeFalmer.

Parker-Jenkins, M., Hartas, D. and Irving, B.A. (2004) *In Good Faith: Schools, Religion and Public Funding*. Ashgate: Aldershot.

Power, S. and Gewirtz, S. (2001) Reading Education Action Zones, *Journal of Education Policy* 16(1): 39–51.

Rattansi, A. (1992) Changing the Subject? In J. Donald and A. Rattansi (eds) *'Race', Culture and Difference*. London: Sage.

Read, B., Archer, L. and Leathwood, C. (2003) Challenging Cultures? Student Conceptions of 'Belonging' and 'Isolation' at a post-1992 university, *Studies in Higher Education*, 28(3): 261–77.

Reay, D. (1997) *Class Work*. London: UCL Press.

Reay, D. (2002) Shaun's story: troubling discourses of white working class masculinities, *Gender and Education*, 14: 221–33.

Reay, D. and Lucey, H. (2003) The limits of choice: children and inner-city schooling, *Sociology*, 37: 121–43.

Rowan, L., Knobel, M., Bigum, C. and Lankshear, C. (2002) *Boys, Literacies and Schooling*. Buckingham: Open University Press.

Savage, M. (2000) *Class Analysis and Social Transformation*. Buckingham: Open University Press.

Sennett, R. and Cobb, J. (1993) *Hidden Injuries of Class*. Polity Press: Cambridge.

Sewell, T. (1997) *Black Masculinities and Schooling*. Stoke-on-Trent: Trentham.

Shain, F. (2003) *The Schooling and Identity of Asian Girls*. Stoke-on-Trent: Trentham.

Skeggs, B. (1997) *Formations of Class and Gender*. London: Sage.

Skeggs, B. (2004) *Class, Self, Culture*. London: Sage.

Skelton, C. (2001) *Schooling the Boys*. Buckingham: Open University Press.

Thomas, L. (2001) *Widening Participation in Post-Compulsory Education*. London: Continuum.

Vincent, C. and Ball, S. (2006) *Choice and Class Practices*. London: Routledge.

Vincent, C. and Martin, J. (2005) Parents as citizens: making the case, in G. Crozier and D. Reay (eds) *Activating Participation*. Stoke-on-Trent: Trentham Books.

Walkerdine, V. (1990) *Schoolgirl Fictions*. London: Verso.

Warrington, M. and Younger, M. (2002) Speech at the 'Raising boys' achievement' conference, Homerton College, Cambridge, 11 July.

Young, I. M. (1990) *Justice and the Politics of Difference*. Princeton, N.J., Princeton University Press.

10

Education, schools and cities

Meg Maguire and Justin Dillon

Introduction

> Successive governments have failed to resolve the educational problems of the major cities. Standards have been too low for far too long. Raising standards in order to lift opportunities for our children is the key priority for the Government. It is clear that schools in our inner cities demand urgent attention.
>
> (Tony Blair and David Blunkett, foreword, DfEE 1999a: 1)

In this chapter, we focus on the sorts of schools that are currently described as 'facing challenging circumstances' (DfES 2006). These are schools whose intake reflects the higher levels of social deprivation and disadvantage that are usually, but not only, found in large urban areas (DETR 2000). What we want to do is to provide a brief historical background to these schools in order to contextualize them. Then we want to review some earlier policy approaches towards these schools. The chapter then considers some contemporary policies in the area for, as Tomlinson (2005: 108) has put it, 'the long association of inner city schools with disadvantaged, disaffected and disruptive pupils (has) continued to be regarded as a major public policy challenge by New Labour' (Tomlinson 2005: 108).

Schools facing challenging circumstances (SFCCs) often experience higher than average teacher turnover (Menter *et al.* 2002). This means that many beginning teachers will be doing their training and then taking up posts in these predominantly city-based schools as this is where vacancies will tend to occur. Teachers choose to teach in SFCCs for a wide variety of reasons; sometimes because they have done their teacher education in these schools; because they want to enjoy the cultural richness of the city where many of these schools are located; or because they come from the city themselves (Menter *et al.* 2002). Recent research has also shown that some teachers elect to work and stay working in SFCCs because they have a strong desire to make a contribution towards society through 'making a difference' (Riddell 2003; Maguire *et al.* 2006).

In the main, less advantaged and less privileged students attend SFCCs. 'The urban poor, however they are constituted in ethnic, gender or class terms in various societies, and wherever they are located, are a challenge to established institutions' (Grace 1994: 45). This 'challenge' is not always easy for teachers to manage. If trainee teachers and beginning teachers are trying to cope and survive in difficult circumstances, without much more than a cursory understanding of broader structural and material explanations for SFCCs, they may end up 'blaming' their school students for the difficulties they face in their teaching. (This sort of response could indirectly contribute towards reduced expectations and lower achievement.) This chapter is an attempt to help you to theorize and understand the urban context and SFFCs in terms of *social* as well as pedagogical theories.

Brief historical context

Inner city schools have always served a distinct section of society; the working-class urban poor. Their schools 'in and around the inner city stand' as 'beacons and landmarks of working class education' (Hall 1977: 11).

It is important to appreciate that there have always been 'problems' with the 'working-class urban poor' and with their schooling. This is not a new phenomenon. If we go back to the nineteenth century, a period of intense industrialization when state schools were first set up, it is possible to see some continuities with contemporary educational provision (at least in England) (Jones 2003). The nineteenth century was characterized by a move from the land to the town. The new industrializing cities were unable to respond quickly enough to the influx of population and, in consequence, there was a crisis in housing. Poverty, lack of adequate sanitation and poor health provision led to a series of 'panics' on the part of the emerging middle classes. They feared the 'risk' of contamination by the urban working classes (Stedman-Jones 1971). One consequence of this fear and a 'need' for separation was reflected in the growth of the suburbs – an early form of housing-zoning that promoted class segregation. There were other fears: for the middle classes, politicians and the 'gentry', the fear of a revolutionary urban mass was ever present (Fishman 1988).

In 1870, the state reluctantly agreed to provide a form of elementary education to be paid for through taxation. The elementary schools of the nineteenth-century cities were aimed at controlling and disciplining an 'ignorant' and dangerous urban working class. Schools were expected to 'gentle' and school this unruly mob and render them up as good and docile workers for an industrializing nation. Their curriculum was designed partly with this aim in mind and their teachers were trained to this task. Even at their inception, urban schools were seen as 'difficult places' that catered for unruly children. They were not seen as suitable for children from more economically privileged families who needed a different sort of provision and who needed more than an elementary schooling. In terms of class differentiation and segregation, nothing could be starker than the form that state provision of education took in the late nineteenth century. Nevertheless, while the mass provision of elementary schooling might have attempted to control and mould young minds and hearts, this has never been a straightforward task. Schools also produce forms of covert and overt resistance. For example, one of the most famous educational strikes occurred in the early 1900s when elementary school children walked out of their schools all across the UK in protest at being caned by their teachers (Newell 1989).

During the early twentieth century, class segregation continued in schools. Some scholarships were available for 'clever' working-class children who could then go to the local fee-paying secondary schools mainly attended by their middle-class peers. In many cases, this offer could not be taken up. Working-class children often needed to obtain employment to help support their families. In addition, the scholarships did not include money for uniforms and books. So, the meritocratic 'promise' of education as a force for social mobility was not on offer to every working-class child who worked hard. There were no policies of 'widening participation' other than the limited number of scholarships on offer.

Provision of state elementary schooling was extended in the twentieth century and finally became universal by the 1930s. Free compulsory secondary schooling for all was made a legal obligation by the Education Act of 1944. The newly emerging middle-class professionals who were paying increased taxes for state schooling now started to move their children into the local primary schools where they lived. Where there were many other middle-class children (in suburban schools, for example), they moved into the state secondary system. Particularly after the 1944 Education Act when many of the old high-status grammar schools were incorporated into the state sector, middle-class families started to become comfortable with using (some parts of) the state sector for their children. Gradually, state schooling (although largely class-segregated according to location and catchment area) became the 'norm' for the vast majority of children in the UK.

There have always been concerns about 'good' schools and 'bad' schools. From the 1944 Act onwards, secondary schooling was divided into grammar schools (and their high-status, traditional, academic curriculum), mainly attended by middle-class children, and secondary moderns (lower status, more vocationally orientated), attended by the rest. As research in the period put it, 'the dominating class in Britain still underrates the colossal waste of talent in working-class children' (Jackson and Marsden 1966: 16). Gradually, the conviction spread that educating different classes of children together would overcome some of the divisive shortcomings of the past. But, then as now, location played a central part in assuring that while some comprehensive schools had a diverse and comprehensive intake, others did not. Some served communities that had high numbers of unemployed people or were located in 'deprived' housing estates. Not surprisingly, some comprehensive schools became oversubscribed while others were demonized as 'bad schools'.

The history of SFCC is a classed history of segregation, exclusion, poorer resources and greater social need. In 1977 Hall wrote that, 'there has never been, in England, anything remotely approaching a "common" or "comprehensive" school experience for all classes of children. Each kind of school has been absorbed into its socio-geographic segment, and taken on something of that imprint' (Hall 1977: 11). This claim is still supported by contemporary research (Ball 2003). Research studies conducted by Gorard and Taylor (2003) and Taylor (2002) suggest that segregation has declined in some schools, but they conclude that in the most popular and least popular schools (the SFCCs), social class polarization is acute. In the contemporary de-industrializing city of the twenty-first century, the gentrification of some of the more 'desirable neighbourhoods' has involved a displacement of some parts of the older working-class community (Byrne 2001). In these gentrified areas, secondary schools have a more socially mixed intake. In the poorer areas, blighted by higher than average levels of unemployment, higher levels of poor health and higher levels of crime (DETR 2000; Power *et al.* 2002), local schools are, somewhat inevitably, faced with 'challenging circumstances'. What we are suggesting is that SFCC have to do their best in socially (not educationally) constituted circumstances of disadvantage. These schools work hard to support their students in school, but all the research evidence suggests that attainment is highly correlated with socio-economic status (see Mortimore and Whitty 1997 for an excellent review). One question that has to be asked relates to the extent to which contemporary society has the political will to tackle poverty and disadvantage.

Galbraith (1992) has argued that a powerful constituency, what he calls the 'contented electoral majority', actively resists the 'burden' of redistributive taxation. Individuals have the right to hold onto as much of their money as possible, it is argued, while ensuring that they maximize their families' capacity to access state provisions – health, welfare and education (Jordan *et al.* 1994). In the educational context, this can be done through moving house to access a 'good' state school, paying for home tutoring to enhance the likelihood of entrance to a selective state school, or having the capacity (money and transport) to travel further to access a 'good' school (Ball 2003). All these individual measures are less available to inner city working-class families. As Grace (1994: 46) says, the constituency of contentment contains within itself a 'relative unwillingness to look at longer term social, economic, or environmental planning, if these threaten present contentment'. In this way, the 'problem' of poverty and disadvantage becomes individualized and marginalized.

What has been tried in the past?

So far, we have traced some of the historical patterns of segregation, exclusion and also (briefly) the resistance that has characterized the school experiences of many working-class children. In this section, we will examine the forms that policies took in the 1960s and 1970s when there was a serious attempt to reduce the differences in school achievement between middle-class and inner city working-class school children. These approaches have been summarized by an America researcher, Cicirelli (1972), and still have some salience today.

Cicirelli suggested that one major set of public policy approaches drew on notions of 'deficit' based on assumptions that inner city children 'lacked' the ingredients for educational success. For example, living in inadequate housing or experiencing less support within the family could, it was argued, lead to underachievement in education. A 'strong' interpretation of this policy approach would indicate the need to eradicate structural disadvantages through redistribution policies, perhaps through taxation reforms or additional state welfare. A 'weaker' and cheaper approach that located the 'deficit' in the culture/community would be more likely to result in policies based on 'compensating' children for these so-called 'lacks'.

A second key approach concentrated on school disparity. Some successful schools that allegedly shared similar intakes to less successful schools were helping their children to achieve more in education. This approach could be seen as indirectly 'blaming' the less successful inner city school. It could also mean that any national attempts at redistribution might be less likely to be advocated. If some schools were doing well without any additional financial support, then all schools should be able to cope. This is not to say that there is nothing to learn from schools that seem to be succeeding 'against the odds', only that this success might be fragile and hard to sustain over time. In terms of SFCC, while categorizing schools in this way might be useful in some respects, it might also reduce awareness of significant differences *within* these schools.

Cicirelli identified a third major policy approach that was predicated on a need to help inner city children develop their self-esteem in order to fulfil their potential. The emphasis was on helping students to overcome disadvantage through generating positive views about themselves and their capacity to do well in school. However, it could also be suggested that this approach indirectly 'blamed' the individual students and their families for their lack of educational success. It could also be suggested that this policy approach also disregarded the wider social context and the impact of poverty, poor health and poor housing on learning attainment (Power *et al.* 2002).

One of the best-known compensatory-interventionist strategies in the US in the 1960s was the Head Start programme. This involved early interventions for young children such as breakfast clubs and extra pre-school support for learning. Another successful intervention was the Reading Recovery programme developed by Marie Clay in New Zealand (Clay 1982). This was set up in many other countries, including the UK (Rowe 1995). Supporting and developing literacy skills have always been a central issue in raising the achievement of less advantaged children. In the UK, the Educational Priority Area (EPA) schemes, set up in the mid-1960s, aimed to put more money into schools that served 'deprived' areas to compensate for a less advantaged start to life (Halsey 1972). The real difficulty was that the actual sums of money involved were very small indeed so it was very hard to make much difference. As Tomlinson (2005: 18) has argued, the EPA intervention was undertaken without any debate about the 'macro-economic conditions that create poverty or the political failures over redistributive social justice' and thus the fundamental issues were simply not addressed.

Even this short-lived and under-resourced egalitarian moment was not to last for long. During the mid to late 1970s, concerns about poverty and inequality in education were gradually replaced (in policy terms at least) by a market discourse which focused on choice, competition and standards; 'a thin cover for the old stratification of schools and curricula' (Bernstein 1990: 87). In this policy setting, the focus shifted towards individual competition and testing rather than any considerations of social justice. Schools that were seen to be 'failing' in this new high-stakes testing regime were frequently subjected to public derision (Brace 1994). Not surprisingly, the schools that were 'named and shamed' were the sorts of schools now designated as SFCC. In the UK, only 17 per cent of schools were recognized as having 'disadvantaged' students, although 70 per cent of the so-called failing schools taught children categorized in this way (Tomlinson 2005: 80). Ofsted (1993:45, cited in Tomlinson 2005: 78) put it like this:

> Schools in disadvantaged areas do not have the capacity for sustainable renewal . . . beyond the school gates are underlying social issues such as poverty, unemployment, poor housing, inadequate health care and the frequent break up of families.

These contextual factors were discounted and disregarded until the New Labour Government came into power in 1997.

What is being tried today?

In this section, we want to provide an overview of the key policies that have been set up by New Labour in order to tackle long-standing issues of child poverty and disadvantage in society and underachievement in schools. 'Breaking the link between social class and achievement is at the heart of government policy' (Literacy Trust 2006). While New Labour have continued the Conservative agenda of 'market-driven growth' (Jones 2003: 144), they have taken some steps to reduce the inequalities and massive growth in poverty that accompanied the Conservative periods in power (1979–1997).

Immediately after the 1997 election, New Labour established the Social Exclusion Unit in order to start to 'repair the social damage of the previous two decades' (Jones 2003: 145). They set up a complex (and sometimes bewildering) set of measures that attempted to alleviate poverty – that could perhaps be seen as a form of redistribution by stealth. Measures such as the minimum wage, working family tax credits and increased pensioner credits are evidence of this. They also set up the Child Support Agency in an attempt to get more 'absent' parents to financially support their families (and although this agency has had a chequered career, the attempt to achieve this is laudable as many sole-parents live in relative poverty). They have also supported policies of repairing and upgrading social housing that have made a difference to the quality of people's lives (Toynbee 2006). But perhaps their biggest achievement (and biggest gamble) has been the campaign to abolish child poverty in the UK by 2020. Some commentators have said that initial targets have been (almost) met because those closest to the line have just been moved across the poverty divide. In contrast, Toynbee (2006) claims that whereas in 1997 the UK was the worse in the EU for childhood poverty, we are now 'at the EU average and improving fastest'.

New Labour has also enacted policies intended to support educational success more directly. The Sure Start Programme (DfEE 1999b) has been an important lever for change as it initially targeted the key years (0–3) before children start school. Sure Start offers support for families in 'disadvantaged areas' from pregnancy through to when the child is 14. It has increased the availability of childcare and its aims include 'improving health and emotional development for young children' and 'supporting parents as parents and in their aspirations towards employment' (www.surestart.gov.uk). Sure Start includes a focus on early literacy skills. Alongside Sure Start, a number of Children's Centres and Early Excellence Centres have been set up as one-stop shops to offer advice and support in the areas of education, health and welfare. The Children Act (2004) complements this work by facilitating Children Trusts that will help achieve the key strands of Every Child Matters (2003) (see Chapter 18). There are sets of interrelated complementary policies such as the Children's Fund and On Track, a scheme to reduce anti-social behaviour. These sorts of policies are very similar to the US headstart interventions and although it might be argued that they are perhaps based on a concept of 'deficit', the intention is to support and sustain through working alongside families rather than 'correcting' or 'blaming'.

There have also been swathes of policies that have been set up to tackle disadvantage and underachievement within the compulsory school setting. For example, the National Literacy Strategy (DfEE 1997a), which started in primary schools, has been extended into the Key Stage 3 setting. Reading Challenge helps schools provide catch-up provision for students performing at around two years behind the average for their peer group. Extended Schools, offering out of school support (www.everychild-matters.gov.uk) will be provided mainly in areas of disadvantage and the Government has set a target of 1000 primary schools to provide 'wrap-around childcare' from 8am to 6pm. New Labour has put into place some 'foundational policies' designed to combat disadvantage and support schools in challenging circumstances. Many of these policies are about educationally related aspects such as behaviour management or truancy reduction.

Specifically in relation to inner cities, two projects have been designed to tackle disadvantage and spur on social inclusion. These are the Education Action Zone projects and the Excellence in Cities initiative. Education Action Zones (EAZs) were set up in 1997 (DfEE 1997b) in order to raise standards in areas of high disadvantage through drawing on the expertise and funding of local businesses in partnerships with schools. The Government invited interested groups to bid for matched funding in order to support their proposals. Concerns were expressed that education was drifting away from being a welfare provision, towards becoming a profit-making concern for the business partners (Hatcher 1998). Other concerns were expressed: those who made 'successful' bids might not have been in the most needy areas – they might simply have been the best consortia at preparing and writing the bids (Tomlinson 2005). EAZs set up and supported a range of different activities in schools such as breakfast clubs and classes where newly arrived parents could learn English. In many ways, the strategies set up under the EAZ umbrella were similar to the earlier EPAs set up in the UK in the 1960s. Overall, and not surprisingly, there were no significant gains in national test scores in the EAZ schools (Reid and Brain 2003; West *et al.* 2003) and they were incorporated into the Excellence in Cities (EiC) project.

Excellence in Cities (DfEE 1999a) was far more focused and specific in its intentions. The strategy initially specified six large conurbations; London, Birmingham, Manchester, Liverpool, Leeds and Sheffield, where a wide range of tactics were to be deployed. These included some new and smaller EAZs as well as a commitment to provide a learning mentor for 'every young person who needs one, as a single point of contact to tackle barriers to pupils' learning' (DfEE 1999a: 3). There was an emphasis on literacy and numeracy skills, a network of learning centres to be set up and a strengthening of school leadership. Whitty (2002) has argued that one of the potential strengths in Excellence in Cities (EiC) was that it attempted to include *all* children in its remit. Thus, tactics such as streaming and extending opportunities for gifted and talented children could potentially work to keep (the supposedly more supportive and pro-school) middle-class families and their children in city schools. In 2003, the chief inspector of schools reported that although EiC had boosted student confidence, educational gains in terms of test scores were less evident (Bell 2003). EAZs and EiC have made significant contributions in schools through funding additional provisions such as breakfast clubs, parent groups and learning mentors in SFCC. It might be unrealistic to expect short-term, low-cost interventions to achieve much more than this.

New Labour has continued in its attempts to tackle social and educational disadvantage. In its cornerstone policies such as EiC and the Academy schools (see Chapter 3) it has concentrated on raising attainment and tackling underachievement. It has focused on SFCC and set up the London Challenge (DfES 2003). It has also developed strategies such as the Leadership Incentive Grant (LIG) (DfES 2002). This scheme is intended to 'accelerate the improvement in standards' though improving leadership capacity, peer review, reshaping the timetable and a range of other tactics such as 'establishing reliable and high quality school policies and systems which raise expectations of staff and pupils through effective data analysis, target-setting and monitoring for individuals and groups – pupils and staff' (DfES, LIG 2002). So far, the evidence is that provision of increased resources for SFCC, coupled with attempts to engender some local ownership of policy and innovation that have been part of the LIG, have started to produce promising results, where national centre-driven policies have been less effective (Ainscow and West 2006).

In 2004, New Labour set out its 'Five year strategy for Children and Learners' (DfES 2004). This 'radical' policy set out a range of proposals to tackle disadvantage and underachievement at every stage, from under-5 provision through to the 'world of work'. In terms of secondary schools, the strategy included a commitment towards greater personalization of learning and choice. Service provision was to be opened up to 'new and different providers':

> We will build on the achievements of the last seven years, to increase freedoms and independence; to accelerate the pace of reform in teaching and learning; and to extend choice and flexibility in the curriculum [. . .] At the heart of our reforms is the development of independent specialist schools in place of the traditional comprehensive [. . .] We will provide for 200 independently managed academies to be open or in the pipeline by 2010 in areas with inadequate existing secondary schools. Some will replace under-performing schools; others will be entirely new, particularly in London where there is a demand for new school places. We expect there to be around 60 new academies in London by 2010.
>
> (DfES 2004)

One key issue that will need to be carefully documented relates to the sorts of intakes that these (and other new forms of schools) attract. If these schools do indeed become successful, will they become colonized by certain constituencies? Will they need to attract more pro-school students and families to ratchet up their attainment in order to demonstrate their success? What about other policy interventions such as the new specialized diplomas for 14–19-year-olds that 'will suit different learning preferences and motivate all young people to participate and achieve' (DfES 2005)? Will these respect and value differences in learning and lead to outcomes that are equal in status to the more established forms of certification (Hodgson and Spours 2006)?

Concluding comments

In this chapter, we have provided a historical background to schools in challenging circumstances. We have also provided a brief review of the policy approaches that have targeted and continue to target SFCC. In this concluding section, we want to highlight the fact that the 'stark differences in the lives of pupils with different family backgrounds have not gone away, nor has the problem of knowing how to deal with them' (Mortimore and Whitty 1997: 1). Too often government policy making in this area has been expressed in 'deficit' terms that disregard the influences of the wider social setting. There has sometimes been a tendency to 'blame' individual children, their parents, their schools and their teachers for any 'failure' in achievement. Although all teachers face pressures such as the need to meet targets and raise standards, what is distinctive in the inner city context is the catastrophe of poverty that shapes many of the schools in these areas. Rather than an education policy that simply exhorts SFCC to emulate their more privileged neighbours, there is a need to recognize the broader socio-economic contradictions that impact on these schools.

In a competitive environment, the more privileged in society are better placed to gain an edge for their families. When less privileged families are trapped in low wages, poor housing and have limited access to social welfare, it is not surprising that their children fare less well in school. Even where schools have 'succeeded against the odds', a fundamental contradiction needs to be recognized (Harris and Ranson 2005). This is that:

> Inevitably, however, any school improvement that takes place is likely to benefit those from advantaged families – those better able to make use of the new opportunities – more than those from families which are facing difficulties . . . Thus, though overall national standards may rise, the difference between the most and the least advantaged will probably also increase.
>
> (Mortimore 1995: 17)

While this may well be the case, the fact that more children from the 'least advantaged' backgrounds will have gained more from their educational experience is certainly a goal worth pursuing.

Urban policy making, urban pedagogy and teacher education need to directly acknowledge the impact of the urban crisis of poverty and exclusion. As Jones (2003: 172) claims, focusing on raising standards without recognizing contextualized factors 'may well give rise to misdirected pressures, demanding too much of schools, and planning too little for wider sorts of social change'. Equally, there is a need for a politics of education reform that will recognize and respect difference, offer all children the life chances that come with educational success, and promote inclusion and the common good rather than private advantage. School teachers still have some capacity to challenge socially divisive policies through their organizations and at a local level. In their classrooms and schools, they still play a part in mediating education policy and in struggling to enact socially just decisions.

In a period where 'the need to give consideration to the fate of others has been lessened' (Ball 2003: 179), the ethical integrity of those who work and stay working in challenging circumstances needs more recognition. These educators could go to 'easier' schools but they stay where they believe they can make most impact. They stay where they know they are needed. All those who work in schools face tensions between their professional and personal ethics and policies that they do not always recognize as pedagogically appropriate. In SFCC, these tensions make even greater demands on the professional repertoires of all those working to educate young people in settings of higher than average levels of social and economic disadvantage.

Donnelly (2003: 14) believes that 'the greatest challenges in life bring the greatest rewards'. Working with children who sometimes make it 'a triumph of will over adversity that they get to school in the first place' (Brighouse, in Riddell 2003: x) is emotionally costly, but professionally rewarding. Rather than seeing urban schools and children who attend them as 'deficient', the best urban schools are able to realize and celebrate their children's experiences as powerful resources for teaching and learning. The dilemma for the school teacher in SFCC is to be able to recognize the impact of the wider social context and draw on its cultural resources without losing their belief in the power of education to promote and sustain social transformation.

References

Ainscow, M. and West, M. (eds) (2006) *Improving Urban Schools, Leadership and Collaboration*. Maidenhead: Open University Press.

Ball, S.J. (2003) *Class Strategies and the Education Market. The Middle Classes and Social Advantage*. London and New York: RoutledgeFalmer.

Ball, S.J., Maguire, M. and Macrae, S. (2000) *Choice, Pathways and Transitions Post 16. New Youth, New Economies in the Global City*. London and New York: Routledge Falmer.

Bell, D. (2003) Education Action Zones and Excellence in Cities, *Education Review*, 17(1): 10–15.

Bernstein, B. (1990) *The Structuring of Pedagogic Discourse: Class, Codes and Control. Vol. 4*. London: Routledge & Kegan Paul.

Brace, A. (1994) Is this the worst school in Britain? *Mail on Sunday*, 20 March.

Byrne, D. (2001) *Understanding the Urban*. London: Palgrave.

Cicirelli, V.G. (1972) Education models for the disadvantaged, in J. Raynor and E. Harris (eds) *Schooling in the City*. Glasgow: Ward Lock Educational in association with the Open University Press.

Clay, M.M. (1982) *Observing Young Readers*. New Hampshire: Heinemann.

Department for Education and Employment (DfEE) (1997a) *The Implementation of the National Literacy Strategy*. London: DfEE.

Department for Education and Employment (DfEE) (1997b) *Excellence in Schools*. Cmnd 3681. London: HMSO.

Department for Education and Employment (DfEE) (1999a) *Excellence in Cities*. Nottingham: DfEE Publications.

Department for Education and Employment (DfEE) (1999b) *Sure Start: A Guide for Trailblazers*. London: The Stationery Office.

Department for Education and Skills (DfES) (2002) *Leadership Incentive Grant (LIG)*. Nottingham: DfES Publications www.dfes.gov.uk/publications/LIG accessed 6 June 2006.

Department for Education and Skills (DfES) (2003) *The London Challenge Strategy. Transforming London Secondary Schools*. Nottingham: DfES Publications www.dfes.gov.uk/londonchallenge/ accessed 15 August 2006.

Department for Education and Skills (DfES) (2004) 'Five year strategy for Children and learners' www.dfes.gov.uk/publications/5yearstrategy accessed 4 June 2006.

Department for Education and Skills (DfES) (2005) '14–19 Education and Skills White paper' www.direct.gov.uk/EducationAndLearning/Schools/ExamsTests AndTheCurriculum/ExamsTestsAndTheCurriculumArticles/fs/en?CONTENT_ID= 10013915&chk=3Mpk9T accessed 12 August 2006.

Department for Education and Skills (DfES) (2006) 'Schools Facing Challenging Circumstances' www.standards.dfes.gov.uk/sie/si/SfCC/ accessed 18 June 2006.

Department of Employment, Training and Rehabilitation (DETR) (2000) *Indices of Deprivation*. London: DETR.

Donnelly, J. (2003) *Managing Urban Schools. Leading from the Front*. London and Sterling, VA: Kogan Page.

Fishman, W. (1988) *East End 1888: a Year in a London Borough Among the Labouring Poor*. London: Duckworth.

Galbraith, J.K. (1992) *The Culture of Contentment*. London: Sinclair-Stevenson.

Gorard, S. and Taylor, C. (2003) *Secondary School Admissions in London*. London: Institute for Public Policy Research.

Grace, G. (1994) Urban education and the culture of contentment: the politics, culture and economics of inner-city schooling, in N.P. Stronquist (ed.) *Education in Urban Areas: Cross-national Dimensions*. London: Praeger.

Great Britain Treasury (2003) *Every Child Matters*. Norwich: Stationery Office.

Hall, S. (1977) Education and the crisis of the urban school, in J. Raynor and E. Harris (eds) *Schooling the City*. Glasgow: Ward Lock in association with The Open University.

Halsey, A.H. (1972) *Educational Priority, Volume 1*. London: HMSO.

Harris, A. and Ranson, S. (2005) The contradictions of education policy: disadvantage and achievement, *British Educational Research Journal*, 31(5): 571–88.

Hatcher, R. (1998) Profiting from schools: business and Education Action Zones, *Education and Social Justice*, 1: 9–16.

Hodgson, A. and Spours, K. (2006) An analytical framework for policy engagement: The contested case of 14–19 Reform in England, *Journal of Education Policy*, 21(6), 679–696.

Jackson, B. and Marsden, D. (1966) *Education and the Working Class*. London: Routledge.

Jones, K. (2003) *Education in Britain. 1944 to the Present*. Cambridge: Polity Press.

Jordan, B., Redley, M. and James, S. (1994) *Putting the Family First: Identities, Decisions and Citizenship*. London: UCL Press.

Literacy Trust (2006) www.literacytrust.org.uk/socialinclusion/policycontext.html accessed on 15 May 2006.

Maguire, M., Wooldridge, T. and Pratt-Adams, S. (2006) *The Urban Primary School*. Maidenhead: Open University Press.

Menter, I., Hutchings, M. and Ross, A. (eds) (2002) *The Crisis in Teacher Supply: Research and Strategies for Retention*. Stoke-on-Trent: Trentham Books.

Mortimore, P. (1995) Better than excuses, *Times Educational Supplement*, 7 July.

Mortimore, P. and Whitty, G. (1997) *Can School Improvement Overcome the Effects of Disadvantage?* London: Institute of Education, University of London.

Newell, P. (1989) *Children are People Too: the Case Against Physical Punishment*. London: Bedford Square.

Power, S., Warren, S., Gillborn, D., Clark, A., Thomas, S. and Coate, K. (2002) *Education in Deprived Areas: Outcomes, Inputs and Processes*. London: Institute of Education, University of London.

Reid, I. and Brain, K. (2003) Education Action Zones: mission impossible? *International Studies in the Sociology of Education*, 13(2): 195–214.

Riddell, R. (2003) *Schools for our Cities: Urban Learning in the 21st Century*. Stoke-on-Trent: Trentham Books.

Rowe, K.J. (1995) Factors affecting students' progress in reading; key findings from a longitudinal study in literacy, *Teaching and Learning, an International Journal of Early Literacy*, 1(2): 57–110.

Stedman-Jones, G. (1971) *Outcast London: a Study in the Relationship Between Classes in Victorian Society*. Oxford: Clarendon Press.

Taylor, C. (2002) *Geography of the 'New' Education Market: Secondary School Choice in England and Wales*. Aldershot: Ashgate.

Tomlinson, S. (2005) *Education in a Post-welfare Society*. Buckingham: Open University Press.

Toynbee, P. (2006) The fight against poverty is half-won. Now we need a radical plan, *Guardian*, 10 March www.guardian.co.uk/columnists accessed 14 May 2006.

West, A., Xavier, R. and Hind, A. (2003) *Evaluation of Excellence Challenge by Extending and Adding to the Existing Evaluation of Excellence in Cities*. London: Department for Education and Skills.

Whitty, G. (2002) *Making Sense of Education Policy*. London: Paul Chapman.

11 | Teachers and the law

Dylan Wiliam

Introduction

The purpose of the chapter is not to provide a definitive account of the law relating to education – even if such an account could be created, this would take several volumes rather than a single chapter. Rather it is to provide a minimal 'survival guide' to the law for the beginning teacher. For this reason, it does not cover the legal requirements on schools; these affect individual teachers through school policies and, as such, they become part of the teacher's duties as part of their contract of employment. It also does not deal with the specific requirements for out-of-school activities, since it would be most unwise for a beginning teacher to take responsibility for such trips. Instead, the focus is on how the law of England and Wales impacts the regular day-to-day activities of the ordinary class-room teacher.

Sources of law

There are two main sources of law in England and Wales: statute law and common law. Statute law is created by Parliament when it passes Acts like the 1988 Education Reform Act. Common law, on the other hand, has been built up over the centuries from tradition. A teacher's responsibility for children (and by extension that of a student teacher) derives largely from common law, not statute law. The crucial part of this responsibility is the notion of a *duty of care*.

Everyone has a duty of care to everyone else. If a person runs down a busy street and knocks someone over causing injury, that person might well be held liable in a court of law for the injury caused. However, this general duty of care extends only to what one does, rather than what one does not do. If someone has been knocked over in the street, a passer-by has no obligation to help the injured person.

However, the role of teachers (and student teachers) in school is different, because they have taken on what is called a 'special relationship' in respect of the children in the school. If a child is hurt in the school playground, teachers have a duty to help the child because of the special relationship. Being in a special relationship with someone else places a duty of care that includes what one does not do (acts of omission) as well as what one does (acts of commission).

Whether a special relationship exists or not depends on what a person professes to be, rather than what they are. So, for example, if someone says 'Let me through, I'm a doctor' in a crowd of people surrounding a person injured in a road traffic accident, that person assumes a special relationship with the injured person, whether they are, in fact, a doctor or not, and is responsible for what they do not do as well as what they do.

A student teacher taking a class is also responsible for acts of omission as well as commission because the student is implicitly assuming a special relationship with the individuals in that class. Qualified teachers from another school who happened to be visiting, however, would only be responsible for what they did, because they have no such special relationship (that is to say, they are not there as a teacher).

The interpretation of particular laws, whether derived from common law, or brought about by statute, is built up over time by referring to what has been determined in similar cases in the past. This is case law. The 'ground rules' of case law are that if a higher court decides a case in a particular way, then a lower court must follow that ruling and any court at the same level should have regard to it, but a higher court does not have to. So, for example, the High Court would have to follow a ruling decided by the Court of Appeal, but the House of Lords does not. A selection of the most important cases relating to the teacher's role is included at the end of this chapter.

There is a third kind of law called 'delegated legislation'. This is a means by which an Act of Parliament does not specify the details of the legislation, but instead grants powers to some other person or organization to specify the details of the law; for example, through the creation of 'statutory instruments'.

The good news for beginning teachers is that there is no need to keep up with educational legislation, since almost all recent educational legislation has been at a management or a policy level. The task of the ordinary teacher is to carry out any reasonable instruction from the headteacher (this is a part of teachers' standard conditions of service in state schools; in independent schools, conditions are laid down by the governors or equivalent, but invariably include such a requirement) and to discharge a duty of care to the pupils in the school.

Duty of care

The earliest definition of what a duty of care might mean in the context of schools and teaching was established in *Williams v Eady*: 'The duty of a schoolmaster is to take such care of his boys as a careful father would take of his son.' This creates the clear impression that there were neither girls nor female schoolteachers around in these days, but then it is a very old judgment (1893). That was the earliest definition of what exactly that duty of care amounted to in the educational setting – a careful father. Over the intervening years – and certainly over the past 50 years – the duty of care has been interpreted more precisely. That is the strength of common law established through case law: as public perceptions change, interpretations of the law can shift, without changing the 'letter' of the law.

In September 1993, for example, a schoolteacher was suspended for sticking masking tape over a pupil's mouth. Now, that in itself is not surprising because local authorities have the power to suspend people for a range of disciplinary offences, very few of which relate to the law. What was unusual in this case is that the police were involved. The involvement of the police was unusual because in the past they have been rather unwilling to act unless the level of harm to the child was relatively serious. Such action would certainly not have been regarded as a matter for the police (or probably even the education authority) in 1893.

In 1938 the notion of a careful parent was reaffirmed in a judgment that held that 'the courts [would] not put on the headmaster [sic] any higher standard of care than that of a reasonably careful parent'. However, two decades later the requirement had shifted somewhat. Because of the way that case law is built up (as described above), the central notion of a reasonable, prudent or careful parent cannot be overturned, but more recent judgments have provided a gloss on the original judgment. By 1962, the common law duty of a schoolmaster [sic] is held to be that

> of a prudent parent bound to take notice of boys [sic] and their tendency to do mischievous acts, not in the context of home but in the circumstances of school life, and extends not only to how pupils conduct themselves but also to the state and condition of the school premises.

There is an implication here that there are more risks at school than at home and therefore a teacher needs to be aware, and take account, of this. In 1968, it was held that

> it is a headmaster's duty, bearing in mind the propensities of boys and girls [at last!] between the ages of 11 and 18 to take all reasonable and proper steps to prevent any of the pupils under his care from suffering injury from inanimate objects, from actions of their fellow pupils or from a combination of both.

So while the *standard* of care required is the same for teachers and for parents, teachers are expected to take account of the special circumstances pertaining in school in discharging this duty.

The same standard of duty of care applies to student teachers, but the law does recognize that by virtue of their lack of training and experience, they are less able than their colleagues to anticipate events and to take appropriate action. If while a student is teaching a class, something goes wrong and their inexperience leads to a pupil being injured, it could well be the case that the student would not be found negligent whereas an experienced teacher acting in exactly the same way could be. While teachers are in training the law does not expect as much as it does when they are qualified, provided, of course, that they do exercise an appropriate level of responsibility.

Negligence

In practice, most court cases relating to duty of care come under the general heading of negligence. To prove negligence one has to establish that there was a duty of care, that it was breached, that there was damage, that the breach caused the damage, and that the damage was reasonably foreseeable. The latter has been very important in the past. In 1984, a pupil brought an action against a teacher who had tackled the boy around the neck in a 'staff versus students' rugby game, causing the boy severe injuries. The teacher was found to have been negligent because the court held that it was reasonably foreseeable that a 14-stone teacher tackling an eight-stone pupil around the neck would cause injury. As a result, the boy was awarded substantial damages. These were paid by the local education authority (LEA) because although it was the teacher and the school who were actually being taken to court, all local authorities are exposed to what is known as *vicarious liability* as regards the negligence of their employees. Even if a teacher has acted against local authority guidance, the authority can still be liable. And since they tend to have more money than most teachers, most actions are brought against the LEA in addition to the school or an individual teacher.

However, as can be seen from the dates of the important cases relating to negligence (pp 148–9), actions against schools and teachers are rare. Very few actions actually reach the courts. In this sense, teaching is not a 'high-risk' activity (unlike medicine where malpractice suits are much more common). It is important to remember that most teachers never find themselves accused of anything in their whole teaching career. However, it is also important to know what one's professional duties are.

Of the responses that a teacher can make to claims of negligence, the two most important are a) that there was no breach of duty, or b) that what happened would have happened anyway. For example, if one pupil suffers injury as the result of an assault from another pupil during morning break, would the school be held to be negligent? If the attack was unpredictable or completely unexpected, then it is likely that an action for negligence would not succeed – the courts have always held that something that would not have been prevented had there been supervision is not negligence. However, if the attacker was known by the school to be a bully and given to random and unprovoked attacks, then an action for negligence could well succeed, especially if teachers who should have been on duty at break time were not at their allotted posts.

Another response to an action for negligence is illustrated by the following case. A primary school teacher was going to take two young girls out, and had them dressed ready to go when another child came along with a cut hand. The teacher attended to the child with the cut hand during which time one of the two other little children ran out of the school gates and into the road. The driver of a passing car swerved to avoid the child and was killed. The family of the driver sued the teacher and the LEA for negligence. In this case, the teacher was found not to be negligent, because the court held that the teacher had behaved reasonably in dealing with the injury to the other child first. The fact that a teacher is distracted by a more serious or urgent incident is a defence. Although the law places a higher burden on the teacher than on the proverbial person 'on the Clapham omnibus', it still only requires that the teacher behaves reasonably in the circumstances. But even in this judgment, the court was careful to point out that the ruling depended on the fact that it was an *infant* child with a cut hand. A 15-year-old with the same small cut would probably not be grounds for leaving younger children alone, and an action against whoever left the school gates open so that the child could run out into the road might still succeed. The important message here is that the law only requires you to act reasonably – provided you do so, you won't be held liable.

The criterion of reasonableness also governs whether student teachers can teach classes without a qualified teacher present. It would probably not be held to be reasonable to leave a student on her or his own with a class during the first week of teaching practice. A court might also hold that it was unreasonable to leave a teacher on her or his own with a class known to be particularly difficult even towards the end of teaching practice. However, it is widely accepted that there are times when student teachers have to be left alone in the classroom to establish that they can manage a class effectively. The courts have generally followed the principle that the test of what is reasonable in ordinary, everyday affairs may well be answered by experience arising from 'practice adopted generally and followed successfully for many years' (*Wright v Cheshire County Council* [1952] All ER 789).

Sanctions

Another important aspect of educational law is that of sanctions: discipline, confiscation, punishments and so on. Can a teacher confiscate cigarettes from a pupil? The important thing about confiscation is that one must not permanently deprive someone of something – that is theft. So confiscating cigarettes from a pupil may be quite reasonable, but smoking them oneself later is not.

The duty of care also plays a part here, however. If, for example, one discovered that a student had a flick-knife, which was subsequently used to injure another pupil, it is quite possible that one would be found negligent if one had *not* tried to confiscate it, or at least reported the matter to someone else (because of the responsibility for omission as well as commission in a special relationship, and one's duty of care to all the pupils at a school).

Most schools have a procedure laid down for what to do with confiscated items. MP3 players might be kept in the headteacher's office until the end of the day and then returned, cigarettes might be returned only to parents, and flick-knives would probably be handed over to the police. The important thing here is to find out what your school's policy is and follow that.

The same applies to detention. Section 550A of the 1996 Education Act clarified the existing case law that a school may detain pupils after school whether the parents approve of this or not, provided 24 hours' notice has been given. Since this period of 24 hours starts when the parents receive the notice, this means, in effect, that a detention notified on Monday cannot take place until Wednesday. However, the important point is that all teachers at a school must follow the school's policy on detention. Find out what it is, and stick to it.

Use of physical force

The use of physical force is again covered by common law, but because the common law was not well understood, the legal situation was clarified in Section 550A of the 1996 Education Act. The Act allows teachers, and others authorized by the headteacher of a school to have control of pupils, to use reasonable physical force in restraining a pupil when a pupil is:

- committing a criminal offence (including behaving in a way that would be an offence if the pupil were not under the age of criminal responsibility)
- behaving in a way that is likely to injure themselves or others
- causing damage to property (including the pupil's own property)
- engaging in any behaviour prejudicial to maintaining good order and discipline at the school or among any of its pupils, whether that behaviour occurs in a classroom during a teaching session or elsewhere.

The first three of these derive from common law, but the fourth is a specific power available to teachers, and whoever in a school the headteacher authorizes to be 'in control' of students. Whether these additional powers apply to student teachers in a school depends on whether the headteacher has included student teachers in the list of those authorized to be in control of pupils. As with all these issues, it is essential to find out what the school's policy is.

It is also important to remember that the definition of 'reasonable' in this context is that it is the minimum force necessary to achieve what is required. Even for an experienced teacher, a good rule of thumb is never to touch a pupil in anger. Corporal punishment, banned in state schools in 1986, and in all others in 1996, remains illegal. If physical force is used, it should be as a last resort; teachers should always try to resolve the situation in other ways first. The force must be the minimum necessary, and teachers should seek to avoid doing anything that might reasonably be expected to cause injury. Furthermore, teachers should seek to avoid touching or holding a pupil in a way that could be considered indecent. Where the need to restrain students physically can be reasonably foreseen (for example, in the case of some students with emotional and behavioural difficulties) there should be a school policy on the treatment of such students, and teachers should be trained in the use of safe techniques.

Defamation

Most people are familiar with the distinction between slander and libel. Defamatory speech is slander but if it is in any kind of permanent form (writing, audiotape etc) it is libel. Interestingly enough, if someone writes something defamatory on a blackboard, even though it is easily removed, that technically is probably libel rather than slander. The distinction between slander and libel is important, because in order to succeed with an action for slander one generally has to prove some financial loss as a result of the untrue remark, whereas in libel it is necessary to prove only that one's standing in other people's eyes would be lowered. Although actions for defamation are very rare, the safest course is to avoid saying anything 'that would be calculated or likely to reduce somebody's standing in the eyes of their peers', and it is worth remembering that pupils have exactly the same rights under this law as teachers.

Copyright

The area in which teachers are most likely to break the law or run into trouble is copyright. A new agency set up as a result of the 1988 Copyright Designs and Patents Act insists that its poster is displayed by all photocopiers in schools that have signed an agreement permitting limited copying of copyright documents. The poster specifies exactly what one can and cannot copy. One can, for example, make class sets of certain materials for use in teaching provided both the school or the LA and the author of the work are signatories to the agreement. Certain kinds of publications are designed to be photocopied, in which case the copyright agreement might, for example, allow unlimited photocopying within the purchasing institution.

The traditional length of copyright has been 50 years from the death of the author. So, for example, the work of Alfred Lord Tennyson came out of copyright 50 years after the end of the calendar year in which he died. However, published editions have a copyright of 25 years irrespective of the date of the author's death so if one photocopied a page of a book of Tennyson's poems one would not be infringing the author's copyright, but one could be infringing the *publisher's* copyright. This aspect of copyright is particularly important in areas such as music publishing because of the expense of typesetting pieces of music. In January 1996, new legislation was introduced to harmonize copyright legislation across the European Union, which extended the duration of copyright in literary, dramatic, musical and artistic works to 70 years after the death of the author, although the copyright term for broadcasts, sound recordings, films and computer-generated artistic works remained at 50 years. The result of this legislation was that a book written by an author who died in 1940, and which had been out of copyright in the UK since 1990 (50 years after the author's death) would become copyright again until 2010 (70 years after the author's death). However, since the effect of this law is retrospective, it is not clear whether the courts would enforce the revival of copyright in such cases. Nevertheless, the implications for teachers are clear, and similar to the advice on other topics in this chapter: find out what the local circumstances are in your institution.

The area in which schools break copyright laws most frequently would appear to be that of electronic media such as recordings of radio and TV programmes and computer software, not least because of the ease of duplication. As noted above, copyright in TV broadcasts lasts for 50 years from the making of the broadcast, and so, unless it is a programme that is specifically intended for schools to record and use, any playing of a recording of a broadcast would be a breach of copyright. It is also important to note that the conditions under which video-cassettes and DVDs are sold or made available for hire often specifically exclude their use in schools, so permission would be required from the copyright holder before it could be used with a class.

Most computer software is not copy protected and so a single copy of such software can be used on more than one machine quite easily. Schools often reason like this: 'Why should I spend £5,000 buying multiple copies of a desktop publishing package when it's only going to be used by one class for two weeks in the whole year?' Nevertheless, what they are doing is illegal and some LEAs have been 'raided' and, where they have been found to be using software illegally, they have been fined. As far as the new teacher is concerned, the only safe course of action is to ask the member of staff at the school responsible for ICT (information and communications technology) before using any software, and certainly you should not install any software on a school computer without asking the network manager first.

Health and safety at work

Another important piece of legislation is the Health and Safety at Work Act of 1974. This Act makes provision concerning the health, safety and welfare of employees and the health and safety of visitors to any work premises. Strangely, for the purposes of law, pupils count as visitors, rather than workers in educational institutions. This law is important in that it gives the duty of care some 'criminal teeth'. If, for example, there was a nail sticking out of a table, which the teacher knew about, and one day a pupil walked past it cutting his leg, the teacher could well be in breach of the duty of care and there would be a possibility of successful civil action against the teacher and the school or LA. However, the Health and Safety at Work

Act would also allow the Health and Safety Executive to bring a criminal prosecution against the school and the individual teacher for having dangerous premises.

This is exactly what happened in 1986, when a science teacher was fined £500 in a magistrates' court for failing to provide for the safety of the pupils in the laboratory when a flask exploded, showering the pupils with sulphuric acid and glass. Fifteen of the students were taken to hospital, and one was detained overnight. An important factor in the magistrates' decision to convict was that although plastic screens and safety spectacles were available, they were not used. The magistrates were careful to say that they did not wish to curtail the use of practical demonstrations in science lessons, but rather that all reasonable precautions should be taken.

There is sometimes a reluctance to report health and safety issues because they can be disruptive. For example, if a classroom has window catches that do not work properly, the teacher might be unwilling to make too much of a fuss, because the response of the senior management at the school is likely to be to move the teacher to another classroom. Nevertheless, one does have to provide for the health and safety of pupils in one's classes and if one knows about anything that is likely to cause a risk, then one must do something about it. Inconvenience is no excuse, and it is certainly no defence in law.

Inappropriate relationships

One final area of law that teachers need to know about is that of inappropriate relationships. Conducting a sexual relationship with a pupil at the school at which you are working has always been regarded as unprofessional, and could be grounds for dismissal. However, as a result of the Sexual Offences (Amendment) Act 2000, it is now illegal. The Act makes it a criminal offence for anyone over the age of 18 in a position of trust with respect to a person under 18 to engage in any sexual activity with that person. The important point about the Act is that anyone who looks after *any* pupils under 18 at a school or college is in a position of trust in relation to *all* pupils at that institution, whether they teach them or not. The only defences to a charge under this Act are:

- that the person charged did not know, and could not be expected to know that the pupil was under 18
- that the person charged did not know, and could not be expected to know that they were in a position of trust in relation to the pupil
- that the person charged was lawfully married to the pupil.

Concluding comments

Inevitably, this chapter has focused on the 'pathology' of school teaching. As a teacher you will have important responsibilities, but it is important to keep things in perspective. As long as you take care to think through the consequences of your actions and as long as you act reasonably, then you will be OK. No one will sue you or take you to court, and it is extremely unlikely that you will be assaulted in any way. And you will, like most teachers, enjoy the job.

Relevant case law

The extracts from legal judgments given below are taken from *Legal Cases for Teachers* by G. R. Barrell (London: Methuen, 1970).

Negligence

- The duty of a schoolmaster is to take such care of his boys as a careful father would take of his son (*Williams v Eady* [1893] 10 TLR 41).
- The courts will not put on a headmaster any higher standard of care than that of a reasonably careful parent (*Hudson v Rotherham Grammar School and Johnson* [1938] *Yorkshire Post*, 24 March 1938, 25 March 1938).
- The common law duty of a schoolmaster is that of a prudent parent bound to take notice of boys and their tendency to do mischievous acts, not in the context of the home but in the circumstances of school life, and extends not only to how the pupils conduct themselves, but also to the state and condition of the school premises (*Lyes v Middlesex County Council* [1962] 61 LGR 443).
- It is a headmaster's duty, bearing in mind the propensities of boys and girls between the ages of 11 and 18, to take all reasonable and proper steps to prevent any of the pupils under his care from suffering injury from inanimate objects, from actions of their fellow pupils, or from a combination of both (*Beaumont v Surrey County Council* [1968] 66 LGR 580).
- A defendant who through training or experience, may have grounds to visualize more clearly the results of his acts in a particular sphere than would be expected of the proverbial man in the street owes a higher duty of care (*Baxter v Barker and others* [1903] *The Times*, 24 April 1903, 13 November 1903).
- School authorities must strike some balance between the meticulous supervision of children at every moment when they are under their care, and the very desirable objects of encouraging the sturdy independence of children as they grow up; such encouragement must start at quite an early age (*Jeffery v London County Council* [1954] 52 LGR 521).
- The mere fact of the fall of a blackboard is not evidence of negligence (*Crisp v Thomas* [1890] 63 LT756).
- It is negligence for a teacher to order a child to undertake a dangerous operation (*Foster v London County Council* [1928] *The Times* 2 March 1928).
- It is, I think, impossible to avoid the conclusion that it was a most unfortunate, unforeseeable and quite unpredictable thing which

occasioned the accident on this day . . . It appears that this was the first time such a thing had happened. In those circumstances, I find it is impossible to say on the facts than any negligence was shown on the part of the defendant (*Wright v Cheshire County Council* [1952] 2 All ER 789).

- The test of what is reasonable in ordinary everyday affairs may well be answered by experience arising from practices adopted generally and followed successfully for many years (*Wright v Cheshire County Council* [1952] All ER 789).
- Where a course of action follows general and approved practice an action of negligence will not lie (*Conrad v Inner London Education Authority* [1967] *The Times*, 26 May 1967).
- An action for negligence cannot succeed if it is founded on an event which is simply an accident (*Webb v Essex County Council* [1954] *Times Educational Supplement*, 12 November 1954).
- A schoolmaster is not liable for a sudden act which could not have been prevented by supervision (*Gow v Glasgow Education Authority* [1922] SC 260).
- Where there is no evidence of lack of supervision or that, assuming there was supervision, it would not have prevented an accident, there is no liability (*Langham v Wellingborough School Governors and Fryer* [1932] 101 LJKB 513).
- It is not incumbent upon a local education authority to have a teacher continuously present in a playground during a break (*Ricketts v Erith Borough Council and Browne* [1943] 2 All ER 629).
- The duty of a schoolmaster does not extend to the constant supervision of all the boys in his care all the time; only reasonable supervision is required (*Clarke v Monmouth County Council* [1954] 52 LGR 246).
- Even if there is failure of supervision, the question arises whether the best supervision could have prevented the accident (*Price v Caernarvonshire County Council* [1960] *The Times*, 11 February 1960).
- When a class of nine or ten are using pointed scissors, it is not necessary to wait until after a lesson, or to make sure that the rest of the class put their scissors down before giving individual attention to one child (*Butt v Cambridgeshire and Isle of Ely Council* [1969] *The Times*, 27 November 1969).

Further reading

Ford, J., Hughes, M. and Ruebain, D. (2005) *Education Law and Practice* (2nd edn). Bristol: Jordan Publishing Limited.

Fulbrook, J. (2005). *Outdoor Activities, Negligence and the Law*. Aldershot: Ashgate Publishing.

University of Bristol (2005) *Teachers' Legal Liabilities and Responsibilities: The Bristol Guide*. Bristol: University of Bristol Graduate School of Education.

Part 3 | Teaching and learning

John Head

Introduction

The common dictionary definition of adolescence, as the phase of life between childhood and adulthood, gives little hint of the concerns and controversy which surround it. There is little doubt that adolescents often receive a bad press, with lurid tales of blackboard jungles in school, and car theft, drug use and sexual promiscuity, outside school. For reasons such as these, adolescence has been described as a time of 'storm and stress', but is this reputation justified?

There are two limitations in the reports about adolescence in the popular press. They focus on the more sensational news and tend to ignore that which is routine or mundane. Secondly, they tend to offer simplistic explanations. For example, awkward adolescents are dismissed as being 'hormonal'. Of course biological factors are part of the story, but they do not directly and inevitably lead to a particular behaviour. Social factors, the influence of adults and peers, are also involved and sometimes these reinforce the biological factors and at other times they conflict. However, adolescents have minds and can take responsibility for their actions. They do not have to do what others tell them and they are not totally a slave to their biology.

Therefore, we have to unpick each issue in order to understand the underlying causes. A recent concern has been with binge drinking and a 'yob' culture. Presumably adults have to accept some of the responsibility, but precisely how much depends on whether you believe in Original Sin or Original Virtue. The former belief, located in the Bible, in many traditional cultures and vividly described in Golding's *Lord of the Flies*, suggests that children are naturally selfish and aggressive. In this event, adults have to socialize youngsters into more civilized values and the anti-social behaviour reflects a failure by adults to assert appropriate authority. If, however, you subscribe to the concept of Original Virtue, as proposed by Rousseau and taken up by twentieth-century educationalists, such as A.S. Neil, then you will argue that contemporary youth have been corrupted by adults. Maybe the biggest contribution has been a change in policy of sectors of the drink industry. Traditionally bars and pubs catered principally for a more mature clientele but it was then realized that it would be profitable to attract younger people – hence the rise of alcopops and happy hours.

To take another example, we might ask why teenagers are increasingly having sexual intercourse at a younger age than in previous generations (Sharpe and Thomson 2005; Aggleton *et al.* 2006). In this instance, there are both biological and social influences. The former is due to the fact that the age of puberty, for both boys and girls, fell by about three years in the last century. The social factor was increasingly permissive attitudes to sexual behaviour. One way of demonstrating this point is to look at magazines aimed at girls in their mid-teens. A decade or so ago they tended to urge caution, suggesting that girls should not rush into having sex. Nowadays the advice is often about how to have enjoyable sex and the implicit message is that is what they should do. Incidentally, there is no corresponding genre of magazines for boys. Boys either read about things such as sport, cars and computers or go for the 'Lad Mags' which are aimed at an older population (Millard 1997).

There is little new in many of the criticisms made of adolescents. Even in Classical Greece there were complaints about unruly youths failing to show proper respect to their elders. Much later, in *The Winter's Tale*, Shakespeare wrote, 'I wish there were no age between ten and three-and-twenty . . . For there is nothing in the between but getting wenches with child, wronging the ancientry, stealing, fighting . . .' That sentiment certainly sounds familiar!

What is the contemporary evidence? It is mixed: on many criteria, such as physical health, adolescents are a favoured group (Heaven 1996) but there are problems. Among boys the high crime rate for those in their late teens is worrying, with over 8 per cent of the 18-year-old cohort being convicted or cautioned for an indictable offence (that is an offence sufficiently serious to possibly attract a prison sentence). The crime rate for girls is lower and peaks at a younger age, around 15. Among girls, eating disorders are common, but it is difficult to give a precise estimate of the extent of the problem as only the most severe cases are notified to the authorities (Whelan 2002). Recently there has been evidence that a smaller but increasing number of boys suffer from eating disorders (Langley 2005). In their case, they are motivated by the wish to appear athletic and be free of any surplus fat.

Each stage of life presents certain characteristic challenges and problems, and adolescence is not unique, it just presents a particular set of such challenges (Coleman and Hendry 1999). We can attempt to sort out what these issues might be by considering four major ideas related to adolescence: physical development, the 'age between', cognitive and emotional growth, and gaining a personal identity.

Physical development

Adolescence is usually taken to start with puberty. This phase of life not only involves development of the genitalia but several other associated physical changes. Prior to puberty, boys and girls grow at about the same rate – about 5 cm per annum. Girls usually experience puberty first and enter a time when they grow at about 8.5 cm each year. Boys experience puberty about a year to 18 months later, but their growth spurt is more dramatic (height increasing at 9.5 cm per annum) and it lasts longer. Consequently, during Year 8, girls tend to be bigger than their male contemporaries but later on the boys overtake them.

These body changes can produce short-term side effects such as reduced co-ordination and fatigue as skeletal and muscular growth occurs before a corresponding growth of the heart and lungs. The increase in the sex hormones can produce some problems. Boys complain about suffering from acne and about having to shave but the girls suffer most. In a large-scale survey I conducted of teenagers it emerged that the commonest problems reported by girls at 14 involved menstruation. The majority of girls reported considerable distress from menstruation (Prendergast 1992). This sex difference in experiencing puberty tends to temporarily weaken friendships between boys and girls and reinforce same-sex friendships.

Alongside the purely physical effects of puberty are the related psychological effects. Adolescents can now be sexually active, which can be exciting, but also raises a new set of issues, relating to sexual performance, pregnancy, the risk of sexually-transmitted diseases and their sexual orientation. Prior to puberty, children enjoy a latency period, during which they largely overcome the problems of childhood and are able to cope effectively with their everyday living. Then puberty upsets that equilibrium. One of the causes of anorexia among girls is the wish to reverse the effects of puberty in order to escape from menstruation.

The 'age between'

The second idea comes from sociology. It is argued that with both children and adults we have a clear idea about appropriate roles and functions, but with adolescents the position is confused. They receive conflicting messages, firstly telling them to grow up and then reminding them that they are not yet adult. This confusion can make adolescent–adult communication and relationships tricky.

Adolescents tend to envy adults for their perceived freedoms – to drive a car, drink alcohol, or stay out late – and they will tend to pester adults to be allowed as much freedom for themselves. Part of the problem is that they do not recognize the constraints placed on adults. If people did just what they liked, their selfishness would alienate others and lose them friends. Successful living involves negotiation and compromise within the home, workplace and social life. In failing to recognize these constraints, adolescents may carry the battle for independence too far; for example, taking the rule that they can do what they like in their own rooms, they play music at full blast regardless of anyone else in the house. When asked to moderate the volume, they will argue that this request interferes with their freedom.

Probably the wisest course for parents and teachers is to negotiate a progressive position, one in which the adolescent gains increasing freedoms year by year. Certainly a school ought to treat Year 12 or 13 students very differently from those in Year 7.

To compensate for this distancing of themselves from adults, adolescents tend to value their peer group more. To be accepted by a group they have to conform in matters such as dress and leisure interests, including which football team they support (Montemayor et al. 1994; Cotterell 1996). In many respects membership of a group is a positive experience, leading to the formation of life-long friendships, but there can be a negative side. Teenage groups can develop an ethos which demands that members demonstrate that they are cool by taking risks, including some which may involve criminal behaviour. Those who do not conform with the group ethos may be bullied or marginalized. We know that young male car drivers are a high-risk group who have to pay considerable insurance premiums. The risks do not come from physical defects but from showing off their macho driving to their peers.

The youth culture is such that adolescents cannot be seen by their peers to be too submissive to adult authority. In the classroom they may seem hostile but in reality they may be listening and responding to what you are saying. The difficult student in class may be very different in a one-to-one discussion. Traditionally there has been a balance between the influence of adults and the influence of peers, but more recently there has been a strengthening of the latter, leading to what one authority has described as a 'sibling society' (Bly 1996). There are several causal factors. Over 20 per cent of families with children are headed nowadays by a single parent. At the same time, there has been a collapse in provision provided by youth clubs, scouts and guides, hence another site for meeting adults has gone. The reduction in contact with adults occurs at a time when mobile telephones and computers allow youngsters to maintain contact with their peers, creating a virtual community, even when they are at home (Abbott 2000; Abbott et al. 2006).

Cognitive and emotional growth

One of the rewarding aspects of teaching in secondary schools is witnessing students who suddenly 'take off'. Students who recently did the very minimum of work necessary to avoid trouble develop a new interest and enthusiasm for ideas and ideals. They may wish to challenge your beliefs, to ask searching questions, and express commitment to various causes. It might be noted that the commonest age for religious conversion is 16. This discussion can be a stimulating learning experience, one which compares well with the student passively taking notes on what the teacher is saying.

One model of thinking, that of Jean Piaget (Inhelder and Piaget 1958), suggests that there is a qualitative change in thinking during adolescence. Children tend to be concerned with the real immediate world. In adolescence an interest in abstract notions develops. A child may feel unhappy about something tangible – pain, loneliness or hunger. Teenagers may feel unhappy in listening to music or seeing a beautiful sunset. This apparently inexplicable response can worry them. They are likely to be experiencing an emotional flux, falling in love, feeling inexplicable sadness, melancholia, and bursts of enthusiasm and hope.

Children tend to live in their own world and are not too concerned about others. As adolescents decentre (to use the jargon term) they may do so in a lopsided way (Elkind 1967). They may fear that they believe that everyone else is observing and judging them. A more adult stance would be to recognize that other people have their own agenda of interests and concerns and we probably only feature in a very minor way in most of them. Their self-absorption may come across in the classroom as moodiness or even hostility.

Gaining a personal identity

The fourth major idea is that of the need to gain a sense of identity (Erikson 1968; Kroger 2004). It is difficult to define the concept of personal identity, but I have described it as being a life-script (Head 1997 and 1999). Individuals are both the authors of their scripts, which reflect their self-image, and are also like actors, using the script to decide what to say and do.

Identity development occurs at all stages of life, but is important in adolescence. A child's situation, and hence sense of self, is largely determined by others. Their social class is that of their parents. Where they live and go to school and how they spend their leisure time is determined by others. In becoming adults they have to carve out their own lifestyle, to decide on their own careers and develop their own social and sexual relationships (Moore and Rosenthal 1993). The main areas of identity include career plans, personal relationships and having some beliefs which give a sense of purpose and worthwhileness to life.

Successful identity acquisition comes from matching a realistic sense of self, what one is like and is good at, with a sound sense of the world, recognizing what opportunities exist. It is necessary to have some ambitions but they need to be realistic. In essence, there are two processes involved in gaining a sense of identity. The first is to think about issues, trying to match oneself against the possibilities available in life. The second is to make the decisions necessary for planning the way forward.

Within a class you may have adolescents in very different positions in relation to these two processes. Some will, in this respect, still be children, having not thought about the future nor gained a realistic degree of self-knowledge. Others may be more mature and, without much drama, have thought through the issues and decided on where they are heading. A third group may be experiencing what is known as a moratorium, who will be excited by considering all the options open to them but fail to make any lasting decisions. These adolescents will be very changeable, switching from idealism to cynicism, from doubt to a new sense of certainty and then back again. Usually the moratorium phase does not last long as it can be uncomfortable both to self and one's friends. A fourth possibility is fore-closure, the complete opposite to experiencing moratorium. In foreclosure the teenager will attempt to reach maturity by seizing on decisions without giving any thought to the issues. Career choice, leisure interests, beliefs and values will be copied from others, within their friends and family. If they are lucky, these choices prove to be satisfying. Unfortunately many will regret these hasty decisions. People may realize later in life that they have chosen the wrong career, opted for a lifestyle to which they are unsuited or failed to recognize the nature of their sexuality

Occasionally you may encounter teenagers who have acquired a 'negative identity', one in which they have adopted a life-script of the rebel or a loner, to a degree which damages their relationships with both adults and peers. The most common explanation for adopting this stance is that it is employed as a shield, saving themselves from too close contact with others. There may be underlying anger and depression, perhaps from unhappy experiences in childhood. If it proves to be more than a short-term phase then counselling will be needed (Herbert 2005).

What are the implications for the teacher? The first point is to recognize the diversity within a group and seek to be sensitive to their differing con-cerns. Identity acquisition is a personal task but we can help in two ways. First of all, we can provide information, or at least direct attention to sources of information, so they can work with this knowledge. Secondly, we can foster a group ethos in which it is acceptable to talk though the issues, accepting different viewpoints and respecting each other (Matthews 2006; Pellitteri et al. 2006).

Gender differences

Consideration of gender differences is important in itself and also because it reminds us that adolescents are not a uniform homogeneous group. There will be both individual diversity and social diversity, defined by race, social class and gender.

It is in adolescence that gender differences become most marked. In part this situation is due to the earlier maturation of girls. In addition, boys and girls tend to have very different experiences at puberty. For most boys it does not present serious problems, but is seen to add to life's pleasures. As previously noted, for girls, it introduces considerable physical discomfort. The main problem for boys is in *not* experiencing puberty. The late developer tends to have a low status among peers as he cannot compete effectively in sports or defend himself well in a fight. Many such boys go through a depressing time but some develop the social skills to make themselves popular, for example, by being cheeky to teachers and funny within the peer group.

Boys and girls tend to approach sexual relationships with different agendas (Sharpe and Thomson 2005). For boys, sexual activity is often solely a selfish activity, undertaken for physical pleasure and as a right-of-passage to gain the respect of his male peers. Not to enter into sexual activity can lead to a boy being dismissed as 'a wimp' or 'gay' (Holland et al. 1993). Boys report that when they have their first experience of sexual intercourse they are often thinking more about their male friends than their sexual partner. This is not indicative of homosexual desire but a wish to boast to their friends of a success which will enhance their status among their peers. Girls tend to be more ambivalent as the issues are more complex. They are subject to similar peer group pressure to get involved but are aware of the possibility of pregnancy, a prospect that produces mixed feelings, something that is both desired and feared.

These differences in maturity and attitudes towards sexual experience tend to bring short-term separation or even hostility between the sexes. Girls complain of sexual harassment and feel they are in a no-win situation. If they consent to sex they may be labelled a 'slag' and if they do not consent then they are accused of being frigid. Later on in adolescence individuals tend to break away from same-sex groups and the seeing of the other gender in terms of stereotypes in order to form stable one-to-one relationships.

Perhaps the most significant change in respect to gender in recent years has been with academic achievement. The relative success of girls in secondary schools was first evident in the early 1990s and in the intervening years girls have moved further ahead in the language and humanities areas, which have been their long-established strength, and have largely overtaken boys in science and mathematics. In 2004, overall 81 per cent of girls gained A–C grades at GCSE, while only 72 per cent of boys did so (Social Trends 2006). With A levels, 44 per cent of girls gained two or more such grades, compared with 35 per cent of boys. Recruitment into higher education has also been affected. Women made up 42 per cent of undergraduates in 1980, 48 per cent in 1990 and 56 per cent in 2005. In part, the increasing success of girls has come from teachers trying to make the work more 'girl-friendly', but probably the main cause has been a change in expectation and confidence among girls. In the past, many were shunted into poor-paying work, for example, in catering and hair dressing, despite having academic potential. School inspectors have reported evidence that boys tend to be less well organized and less conscientious, particularly in dealing with coursework (EOC/OFSTED 1996).

Additionally, there have been changes in the labour market. Traditionally boys have had access to well-paid work in mining, manufacturing and engineering. Fewer people are employed in these fields in this country nowadays. More jobs have been created in the leisure and service industries where girls can readily compete. Girls have been quicker to move into these new areas of employment while many boys seem to have lost the incentive to succeed.

In the light of this situation attention has been given in more recent years to the recognition of the problems boys commonly face in school (Salisbury and Jackson 1996; Head 1999). Looking at the bigger picture, the academic success for girls holds out the hope that we should be able to devise tactics for enhancing the performance of other low-attaining populations, by demonstrating the relevance of the schoolwork and trying to enhance the expectations and confidence of the students.

What worries adolescents?

I have encountered, through surveys, four main areas of concern with about a third of the respondents reporting a considerable degree of unhappiness with one or more of the four issues (Head 1997 and 1999). The first is with the family, sometimes about a split home, more commonly about arguments relating to money or staying out late at night. The second is with the school. Complaints are mainly about disciplinary procedures, but complaints about the workload are common, too. The third worry is feeling a lack of purpose in their life, and as was already noted, these are indicative of the continuing search for their sense of identity. Finally, there is concern about social and sexual relationships with peers. There may be conflict in recognizing and asserting one's own individuality and being popular with others. There are worries about sexual success and competence and sexual orientation.

Sometimes teenagers find it too difficult to talk about these matters with their parents and may prefer to speak with a teacher. Remembering their self-consciousness it is essential to respect confidence and not do or say anything to embarrass the individual. Ultimately choices have to be made by individuals about their own lives. Our role is to listen to provide factual information, if appropriate, and help the students think through themselves what it is they really believe in and want to do.

Sometimes their problems will be beyond your competence (Herbert 2005). You should be able to call on the school pastoral and PSE (personal and social education) staff to help you – provided the student is willing for you to do so. There are various agencies which deal with specific issues, such as bullying, drug abuse and pregnancy, and it would be sensible to know the names and contact telephone numbers or email addresses of these agencies.

Working with adolescents

What do all the points in this chapter add up to for the inexperienced teacher? Some things are clear. The students respect competence. They accept the need for some discipline. As one boy said to me, 'My job is to muck around. The teacher's job is to stop me.' Asking what makes a good teacher seems to be a boringly self-evident question, so with both trainee teachers and secondary school pupils I have asked them to draw up a recommendation of how one can become a poor teacher. Once they have overcome the initial shock they enter the exercise with gusto. The interesting point is that both groups come up with much the same list: arriving late and being disorganized, mumbling or talking in a monotone while facing the board, avoiding eye contact, failing to return work collected for marking, and so forth.

Some further issues emerge. The students expect a teacher to be fair and consistent. By being fair they mean that all the students are treated equally, there is no favouritism. By consistent they want the teacher to exercise similar procedures and discipline from one lesson to the next. In essence, they need to know the procedures and boundaries used by the teacher. Students can live with both strict and more relaxed classes provided they know what to expect. Also at this age they are open to reason and explanation. A certain amount of running around and jostling each other is only a minor issue in most areas of the school but within a science laboratory it can be a major hazard. The science teacher, therefore, has to insist on appropriate behaviour and once the rationale has been explained to the class they will normally accept the ruling.

A further point is that they both want you to take an in interest in them but also fear being asked intrusive questions in front of the class, about their family, sex life, use of drugs and so on. When these topics are discussed in class you should not permit references to specific people in the school, whether they are teachers or pupils. Similarly, you should not answer direct questions about yourself, such as 'Have you ever taken drugs, Miss?' or 'Have you got a girlfriend, Sir?' Essentially, they are trap questions. Taking the second example, confirming having a girlfriend will lead to further questions containing considerable sexual innuendo. A negative response will lead to comments like 'Oh, so you're gay, Sir', which again will lead on to a mock debate between those telling you they are tolerant and those expressing their disgust. The rule about not referring to specific persons protects everyone.

Working with adolescents can be challenging but it can also be satisfying when you see how they are responding to you. Recalling your own adolescence and that of your friends provides insights for dealing with students. The references given in this chapter have been to specific topics but there a number of general overviews of adolescence (for example, Santrock 2001), while Coleman and Schofield (2005) provide a review of the factual background.

References

Abbott, C. (2000) *ICT: Changing Education*. London: RoutledgeFalmer.

Abbott, C., Detheridge, T. and Detheridge, C. (2006) *Symbols, Literacy and Social Justice*. Leamington: Widgit.

Aggleton, P., Hall, A. and Mane, P. (2006) *Sex, Drugs and Young People: International Perspectives*. London: Routledge.

Bly, R. (1996) *The Sibling Society*. London: Penguin.

Coleman, J. and Hendry, L. (1999) *The Nature of Adolescence*. London: Routledge.

Coleman, J. and Schofield, J. (2005) *Key Data on Adolescence*. Brighton: Trust for the Study of Adolescence.

Cotterell, J. (1996) *Social Networks and Social Influences in Adolescence*. London: Routledge.

Elkind, D. (1967) Egocentrism in adolescence, *Child Development*, 38: 1025–34.

EOC/OFSTED (1996) *The Gender Divide: Performance Differences Between Boys and Girls at School*. London: HMSO.

Erikson, E.H. (1968) *Identity, Youth and Crisis*. New York, NY: Norton.

Head, J. (1997) *Working with Adolescents: Constructing Identity*. London: Falmer Press.

Head, J. (1999) *Understanding the Boys: Issues of Behaviour and Achievement*. London: Falmer Press.

Heaven, P.C.L. (1996) *Adolescent Health*. London: Routledge.

Herbert, M. (2005) *Developmental Problems of Childhood and Adolescence: Prevention, Treatment and Training*. Oxford: BPS Blackwell.

Holland, J., Ramazanoglu, C. and Sharpe, S. (1993) *Wimp or Warrior: Contradictions in Acquiring Masculine Identity*. London: Tufnell Press.

Inhelder, B. and Piaget, J. (1958) *The Growth of Logical Thinking from Childhood to Adolescence: An Essay on the Construction of Formal Operational Structures*. London: RKP

Kroger, J. (2004) *Identity in Adolescence*. London: Routledge.

Langley, J. (2005) *Boys Get Anorexia Too: Coping with Male Eating Disorders in the Family*. London: Paul Chapman.

Matthews, B. (2006) *Engaging Education: Developing Emotional Literacy, Equity and Coeducation*. Maidenhead: Open University Press.

Millard, E. (1997) *Differently Literate: Boys, Girls and the Schooling of Literacy*. London: Falmer Press.

Montemayor, R., Adams, G.R. and Gullotta, T.P. (1994) *Personal Relationships During Adolescence*. Thousand Oaks, CA: Sage.

Moore, S. and Rosenthal, D. (1993) *Sexuality in Adolescence*. London: Routledge.

Pellitteri J., Stern, R., Shelton, C. and Muller-Ackerman, B. (eds) (2006) *Emotionally Intelligent School Counselling*. Mahwah, NJ: Lawrence Erlbaum.

Prendergast, S. (1992) *This is the Time to Grow Up: Experience of Menstruation in School*. Cambridge: Health Promotion Trust.

Salisbury, J. and Jackson, D. (1996) *Challenging Macho Values: Practical Ways of Working with Adolescent Boys*. London: Falmer Press.

Santrock, J.W. (2001) *Adolescence*. New York, NY: McGraw-Hill.

Sharpe, S. and Thomson, R. (2005) *All You Need is Love: The Morality of Sexual Relations*. London: National Children's Bureau.

Social Trends (2006) *Social Trends Number 36*. Basingstoke: Palgrave Macmillan.

Whelan, J. (2002) *Eating Disorders*. London: Hodder Wayland.

13

Learning in and outside of the classroom

Jill Hohenstein and Heather King

Introduction

Learning can be defined as a relatively permanent change in thought or in behaviour that results from experience. In this chapter, we narrow the focus of such a broad topic to present a brief overview of theories of learning and the status of current thinking about learning. We then move on to explore some of the ways in which teachers can support learning both in and outside of the classroom.

Theories of learning

Over the last three centuries, interest in the nature of learning has led to the development of a number of theories which attempt to explain the process by which we learn. In turn, these theories have shaped our approaches to teaching and the mechanisms by which we help learners to learn.

Most theories of learning fall into one of two categories: Behaviourist or Cognitivist (some span both). Behaviourism is based on the view that we should focus on externally observable inputs and outputs to determine what governs learning. This idea is related to the philosophy of Hobbes (1651), who suggested that humans are simply material systems, operating by way of inputs and outputs, and thus constructs such as 'mind' and 'free will' do not affect the way people function.

Extreme Behaviourism claims that infants enter the world as 'blank slates' and learn about the world through various forms of association, including conditioning, both classical (Pavlov 1927) and operant (Skinner 1974). Classical conditioning can be thought of as the training of behaviour on the basis of stimulus and response. For example, a dog has innate responses (salivation) to a stimulus (food), which gradually becomes associated (through repeated pairing) with a new stimulus (a bell). The learned behaviour is then salivating in response to the sound of a bell. Operant conditioning may be defined as shaping behaviour through incentives and punishments. A monkey may learn to press a lever to dispense food by at first giving it food when it approaches the part of the cage where the lever is positioned. Then, as time progresses, food is given only when the monkey touches the lever. Finally, the monkey must actually press the lever to receive food. These principles of conditioning are thought by many to be true of humans in addition to non-human animals.

More modern approaches, such as Connectionism (Rummelhart and McClelland 1986; Elman et al. 1996), would suggest there are structural mechanisms in the brain that assist or constrain learning in various ways but that we should still view learning as a series of inputs and outputs operating in much the same way as a computer programme does. These inputs and outputs are connected via networks which link the concepts that a person has acquired. Building on the analogy between the brain and computers, some researchers have designed computer programmes that are able to learn a language (Seidenberg and Elman 1999); although, admittedly, these programmes have much further to go before they can replicate the powerful learning demonstrated by the human brain. Furthermore, whereas the Connectionist view of learning acknowledges some activity in the brain, these computer models may be more accurately described as Associationist in that they rely primarily on activity in the environment (the inputs) to structure learning.

In contrast to the Behaviourist theories, most contemporary approaches to learning place value on the internal workings of 'the mind'. Some of these Cognitivist theories use forms of introspection to study learning. One such set of theories stipulates that a learner progresses through a series of stages, each affording a greater degree of intellectual ability. Piaget (1952) is perhaps the most well known of the stage theorists. His ideas suggest that when babies are born, and for the first two years of life, a primary objective is to explore the world around them through their developing sensorimotor skills. From age two until age seven, children are said to pass through a period known as the pre-operational stage, in which they tend to be egocentric in their thoughts and not be able to complete 'operations' that older children can do. Once children have entered the concrete operations stage (age 7–12), they are able to operate on the things around them. For example, they can begin to conserve volume, number and mass. A classic Piagetian task involves pouring equal amounts of liquid into two glasses of the same shape and size. After the child has agreed that the glasses contain the same amount of liquid, the liquid from one glass is then poured into a different-sized glass (either taller and thinner or shorter and squatter). Children who can conserve volume will be able to say that there is still the same amount of liquid, supposedly because they can mentally reverse the operation of pouring the liquid from the first glass to the second of differing size. After the age of 12, children pass into the formal operations (or adult) stage of cognitive development. This stage is characterized by the ability to think abstractly about many different concepts and to use logical reasoning. Over the years, many people have challenged the idea that children pass through a set of stages, particularly at the ages Piaget proposed. However, stage theory remains a foundation of developmental psychology today.

Piaget believed that children were able to pass through these stages because their developing brains were more mature at a greater age than at an earlier age. As a mechanism for moving from one stage to another, Piaget and his followers proposed the idea of a cognitive conflict – an encounter with a new construct or experience which would prompt the reorganization, or accommodation, of the new concepts into a mental framework leading to a new stage of mind. In this way, Piaget recognized that children construct their own understandings.

This notion of children constructing their own understanding has been expanded upon by a number of researchers in the field of education and is now known as Constructivism (Phillips 1997). Constructivists believe that a child's learning depends on the way in which they construct new mental schema based on previous knowledge (and/or stage of development) and that their learning is directly correlated with their motivation to learn. Some have interpreted this view of learning as meaning that children need to 'discover' concepts for themselves in order that they can construct their own understanding. However, this idea has been shown to be inaccurate in many situations (Klahr and Nigam 2004). Others have taken the premise of Constructivism to mean that since individuals construct their own understandings about the world, there can be no such thing as one right answer, or absolute fact – for each of us is free create our own explanations. This interpretation has been criticized on the grounds that knowledge, particularly scientific knowledge, is based upon repeated empirical observations of phenomena resulting in objective facts (Osborne 1996). That a learner needs to make sense of these facts is not disputed, instead, the argument is with the notion that learners should be left to construct their own reality rather than be taught the widely accepted scientific explanations.

A variant of Constructivist theory is sometimes called Social-constructivism. This theory holds that children create their own learning through interaction with their environment, often guided by more knowledgeable people around them. Social-constructivism has been linked to the work of Vygotsky (1978), Bruner (1966) and others. This theory suggests that ideas are first encountered by learners in the social environment, mostly in the form of language. After some experience with these ideas, they become incorporated into children's habitual knowledge and become 'second nature'. Knowledgeable others in the environment can guide learning experiences by supporting children's experiences through questions and stimulating commentary. Such support has been termed 'scaffolding' (Wood *et al.* 1976).

Another of Vygotsky's (1978) contributions to ideas of learning is the concept of the Zone of Proximal Development (ZPD). The ZPD defines an individual's potential level of understanding or skill in a more dynamic way than do many forms of assessment. The ZPD may be thought of as the area between what people can accomplish on their own and that which they could achieve with the help of someone more experienced. Take, for example, a child working on problems of multiplication. This child may be able to work through problems that involve single-digit numbers by herself. However, this same child can potentially solve problems involving the multiplication of two-digit numbers with the aid of a teacher or parent. This child's ZPD with respect to multiplication lies between multiplying single-digit numbers and two-digit numbers. The implications for teaching using the ZPD are clear. A teacher will be most effective in helping a child to acquire new understandings when challenging the child to learn concepts at the upper limits of their ZPD, not below or above.

Recently, researchers have begun to expand upon Vygotsky's ideas of development to propose ways that people develop through their socio-cultural experiences (see for example Rogoff 2003). These theories suggest that it is important to take into consideration a person's cultural experiences when determining the elements necessary for learning. For instance, a person in a small village in Guatemala may learn a great deal about weaving, a practice regarded as very important in her society, through watching others work and being physically guided while learning herself. On the other hand, a child in a science classroom in England may learn about the processes of schooling and, we hope, some principles of physics while attending to a teacher and watching an experiment. Sociocultural theory argues that what these two learning experiences share is the intent participation of the learner. In each case, the more engaged the learners are with the material, the more they will advance their skills in the discipline. This notion of engagement or motivation is important, for ultimately learning is dependent upon a learner's response or attitude to new material (Pintrich *et al.* 1993). We now turn to examine a few ideas about motivation as this will become important in our later discussion regarding learning in different contexts.

Learning and motivation

Motivation towards studying a particular domain or topic is related to the affective appeal of that topic. In other words, the more people like a topic, the more they will want to pursue learning in that area. Thus, many teachers would like, and feel the need, to make everything they do with their class inherently interesting (Nisan 1992).

Many theories of motivation can also be labelled Behaviourist or Cognitivist in nature. Behaviourist theories tend to claim that providing positive or negative reinforcement in response to learning behaviours will provide incentive for future learning behaviours. For instance, giving someone praise after getting the answer to a question correct would be seen as motivation to answer other questions correctly. This form of acting in order to receive (or not receive) reinforcement has been called extrinsic motivation. That is, people carry out tasks so that they will receive a reward, not because they choose to do so. Many researchers have criticized this approach for motivating students because it is predicated on the continued presence of rewards. More worryingly, external rewards have even been seen to decrease interest in otherwise motivating tasks. For example, Deci and Ryan (1985) found that when preschoolers were offered a prize for drawing, an activity which they previously enjoyed, they stopped wanting to draw when there was no longer any reward offered.

On the other hand, Cognitivist theories of motivation centre on the stimulation of intrinsic motivation, or the will to learn for learning's sake. One such theory focuses on facilitating people's mastery-orientation as opposed to their performance-orientation (Dweck and Leggett 1988). Mastery-orientation occurs when people pay attention because they want to understand the material at hand. Performance-orientation is related more to extrinsic motivation and is exemplified by the desire to achieve a particular score or grade. Research suggests that students who are mastery-orientated rise to challenges in difficult situations, attribute success to internal causes, and use effective strategies for solving problems, such as in-depth questioning (Alexander *et al.* 1998). Performance-orientation is more complicated, given that most mastery-oriented learners also have some desire to perform well. However, it appears that being performance-oriented without being mastery-oriented may be damaging to learning.

Two pieces of evidence can be used to support the idea that mastery-orientation has advantages over performance-orientation. Firstly, performance goals are often out of a person's direct control. For instance, if two people have the goal of getting the highest score on an exam, unless they both achieve perfect scores, one of them will be disappointed. Secondly, when encountering failure, people who have adopted a mastery-orientation approach tend to continue to attempt to learn and see the experience as valuable, whereas people only concerned with performance-orientation are more likely to be anxious and avoid situations where they will possibly fail in the future (Midgley *et al.* 2001).

Learning environments

We argue in this chapter that no matter which theory one believes best captures the nature of learning, learning is learning, in whatever setting it occurs. That is, people's (children and adults) learning does not depend upon the location or situation in which they find themselves. However, because an individual's goals and motivations may differ in different settings, the learning outcomes will also be different. For example, Hatano and Inagaki (1993) examined the understanding of concepts relating to animal welfare in a two groups of six-year-old students. The first group learned about animal welfare as they took care of classroom animals as part of their school routine. The second group had pets at home and thus were intimately involved in their care. The second group was found to have a more sophisticated understanding of animals due, the researchers claimed, to their personal motivation to care for their pets.

In addition to the home context, museums and other out-of-school settings offer a set of environments which may stimulate an individual's interest and personal motivation to learn. In the formal school system, gaining good grades constitutes an omnipresent extrinsic motivation. But, in the absence of externally imposed pressures of examinations and assessments, learners are free to engage with content as and when they wish. Such learning has been defined as informal, or free choice (Falk and Dierking (1992) and described as voluntary and self-directed. Wellington (1990) offers the following characterizations of in-school and out-of-school learning:

In-school or formal learning	Out-of-school or informal learning
Compulsory	Voluntary
Structured	Unstructured
Sequenced	Unsequenced
Assessed	Non-assessed
Evaluated	Unevaluated
Close-ended	Open-ended
Teacher-led	Learner led
Teacher-centred	Learner centred
Curriculum-based	Non-curriculum based
Fewer unintended outcomes	Many unintended learning outcomes
Empirically measured outcomes	Less directly measurable outcomes
Solitary work	Social intercourse
Teacher-directed	Non-directed or learner directed

However, it should be noted that these lists are merely generalizations. Whilst many in-school experiences are sequenced, teacher-centred and involve solitary work, this is not the case for all in-school learning. In contrast, not all out-of-school learning is as open-ended, non-assessed and voluntary as is implied by Wellington's characterization. In fact, developing such lists may lead to the establishment of a false dichotomy between what constitutes learning in and out of school.

To illustrate, the lack of a formal assessed curriculum does not automatically mean that a learner will choose to engage with the content on offer in the museum or out-of-school context. Learners still need to be motivated to learn, and their learning will be enhanced if it is supported or mediated in some way. Perry (1992), for example, argued that an exhibit or museum experience will only be intrinsically motivating to visitors if it inspires curiosity, confidence and feelings of competence, a challenge or something to work toward, control and a sense of self-determination, play and enjoyment, and communication by engaging in meaningful social interaction.

Such a list of factors can also apply to experiences in the school context and indeed many teachers seek to intrigue and challenge their students, whilst aiming to develop their confidence and competence in a particular area. Thus, rather than contrast the nature of learning in-school with out-of-school settings, we argue that it makes more sense to build on the opportunities provided by each to enhance and extend learning in the other.

One of the advantages of out-of-school learning experiences, such as visits to museums or field centres, is that the environment offers a different set of learning objectives. Indeed, most non-school environments will not have been designed with explicit content objectives in mind. Instead, the primary goal of most museums is to provide an affective experience in which a learner is inspired, enthused, sensorially intrigued and ultimately entertained. Museums also acknowledge their role in enabling visitors' access to the cultural capital of the wider society and providing opportunities for individuals to acquire skills associated with inter-generational, cross-community social interaction (Schauble *et al.* 1997). Yet the educational value of an entertaining experience should not be underestimated. Studies have shown that attitudes towards a topic can be enhanced if that topic is approached in a manner which affords practical investigation in real-life settings. For example, attitudes toward ecology and agricultural science have been shown to be enhanced following field trips to farms and outdoor centres (Dillon *et al.* 2006). Unfortunately, enhanced attitudes have not been found to consistently correlate with higher test scores. Nonetheless, positive attitudes play an important role in prompting intrinsically motivated, mastery-orientated learning.

Out-of-school learning environments may have the potential to enhance attitudes by virtue of the novel experience, but to maximize the learning opportunities, learners still need support and the experience needs to be mediated. In the museum context, exhibitions are designed to help visitors compare objects and appreciate patterns and trends. Museum educators, meanwhile, encourage students to examine objects and question their selection for display. In this way, a visitor's experience is scaffolded as they learn how to make sense of the museum's content.

The novel experience provided by unfamiliar contexts may ignite a learner's curiosity and motivation to learn, but too much novelty can be a distraction or impairment to learning. For example, Falk, Martin and Balling (1978) found that exposure to a novel learning environment, in this instance a field centre, without preparation of what to expect, reduced children's conceptual recall of the various activities. The children were so preoccupied in learning about their new environment – the physical space, its amenities – that they were not able to concentrate on the specific content objectives. The authors concluded that learners would benefit from preparation or advanced organisers (Ausubel 1968) about what to expect in order to decrease the novelty affect.

Whilst the value of out-of-school environments for enhancing attitudes is important, the potential for conceptual learning should not be ignored. Even when ostensibly just having fun, individuals can be observed to exhibit learning-type behaviours. Such behaviour largely refers to a person's actions and talk that support the making of connections between concepts or objects. In museums, this 'meaning-making' has been observed in incidences of systematic and purposeful looking back and forth between exhibits (vom Lehn *et al.* 2001), and by explicit or implied content of visitor talk. For example, in her analysis of visitor talk, Allen (2002) was able to characterize conversations that were conceptual and connective in nature ('they remind me of the frogs we saw on holiday'), in addition to contributions that were simply perceptual and affective ('wow, look at that'). However, due to the ephemeral nature of most visits to museums, field centres or other out-of-school learning environments, it is clear that there is limited opportunity for learners to gain substantial amounts of new knowledge *in situ*. But the value of the out-of-school context may still be realized if connections continue to be made back in the classroom. In this way, the attitudes cultivated in the out-of-school context may be harnessed in schools, and the experiences of the different setting may be consolidated and connected to the curriculum by a teacher in the classroom. In the next section, we discuss the ways in which teachers can support the connection of learning experiences.

Connecting learning experiences

Forming connections between different concepts and learning experiences is arguably one of the most important factors in learning (Vosniadou and Ortony 1989). Regardless of which learning theory one aspires to, the idea that one should build new learning into existing knowledge structures makes sense. Therefore, it becomes imperative for teachers and other people involved with education to make explicit the relevance of different principles and concepts that are encountered in different learning experiences.

Incorporating new knowledge into a person's existing knowledge (or making a person's misconceptions salient) can be seen as integral to developing a person's understanding of any given topic (Ausubel 1968). As Alison King (1994: 339) notes:

> During the process of reformulating information or constructing knowledge, new associations are formed and old ones altered within the individual's knowledge networks or structure. These links connect the new ideas together and integrate them into that individual's existing cognitive representations of the world. Adding more and better links results in a more elaborated and richly integrated cognitive structure that facilitates memory and recall.

That is, by relating what is being learned with previously learned knowledge, learners have greater opportunities for both understanding and remembering the material.

A number of strategies for integrating new and old knowledge have been proposed. For instance, a common process in learning that directly relates old understandings with new ones is analogy. Learning through analogy involves comparing a familiar (or source) concept with a new (or target) concept, where the two are related in some form. Analogy can be especially powerful as a learning tool when the two concepts are similar in structural, rather than superficial, ways. To illustrate, noticing the superficial similarities in the colour of a deer and an antelope may be less helpful to learning about the functional attributes of these animals than noticing that a snake and a shrimp both shed their outer layers. Analogy has been studied as a natural occurrence in the work atmospheres of scientists (Dunbar 1995). But it has also been shown to be effective in teaching students at varying levels (Bulgren *et al.* 2000; Gentner *et al.* 2003).

Another set of strategies for connecting knowledge from one situation to another includes the use of guiding questions and explanations. In a study by A. King (1994), one group of students engaged in a process of peer questioning whereby classmates encouraged each other to apply concepts to a new situation, relate new materials to known materials, provide justifications for concepts and draw personal conclusions. In contrast, a second group were not encouraged or supported to interrogate the subject matter learned. In analyses of test results, the first group scored more highly in understanding, applying and retaining the information that they were learning than did the second.

Many learners find establishing connections between content across topics or subject matter to be difficult, and it is the particular skill of a teacher to remind students about past content, or the application of content to different disciplines. Connecting content encountered in informal environments also requires support. Unfortunately, researchers have found that out-of-school learning experiences are rarely supported by pre-visit preparation or post-visit follow-up work. For example, Griffin and Symington (1997), in their study of 12 Australian schools planning museum visits, found that few students knew of the purpose of the visit, had any expectations of learning or experienced any follow-up teaching after the visit. To support and consolidate the experiences of out-of-school learning opportunities, and to minimize the effect of novel environments, Griffin and Symington offer the following advice: orient students to the setting before the visit, plan pre-visit activities aligned with curriculum goals, provide students with the opportunity to plan aspects of the visit themselves, allow time for self-exploration and discovery during the visit, and conduct post-visit classroom activities to reinforce the experience.

Finally, in supporting the construction of connections, across environments, topics or lessons throughout the year, teachers can employ a variety of verbal strategies. They can repeat a student's statement to emphasize its contribution to the discussion and its role in connecting ideas. Teachers can also rephrase or reformulate a student's contribution so that the idea is more explicitly aligned to a particular position. To ensure that students are making sense of content, teachers can also employ a framework known as reciprocal teaching (Palinscar and Brown 1994). This involves the teacher provoking a discussion about a piece of material as a way of identifying and then clarifying problems in understanding. In the context of reading, students are then encouraged to predict what will follow based on their understanding of what has gone before. In this way, the student's response or answer shapes the subsequent communication and exchange of ideas and ensures that the teacher can keep track of the way in which the learner is making connections in content. Alexander (2005) defines this type of teaching as dialogic teaching and, in addition to the sharing of ideas and the collective rather than isolationist completion of tasks, notes that this structure allows for ideas to be cumulative and to be linked into coherent lines of thinking.

Concluding comments

As we have discussed here, there are many different theories to describe the manner and process by which people learn. These theories suggest a range of ways in which learning can be enhanced and/or mediated by a teacher or more expert individual. What most of these theories share, however, is the premise that learning involves making connections between content and experience. Recall is then supported by virtue of the many links connecting a variety of stimuli to particular piece of content. It follows that learning can be facilitated by providing learners with as many opportunities as possible to build new connections between existing concepts, and to establish connections between new content and prior experience. In addition to connecting content and topics in school, learners can also benefit from new, content-rich experiences in out-of-school settings. Such experiences are also valuable in that their novelty can ignite learner curiosity, whilst the different format – such as the sensory stimulation offered by the outdoor environment, or the object-rich environment of a museum – can enhance attitudes towards particular content areas. In turn, the learner may become personally motivated to learn more about a particular subject.

In this chapter we have argued that learning is learning wherever it occurs. More importantly, we have argued that the learning which takes place in one environment has the potential to complement the learning which takes place in another. In this way, out-of-school learning plays an active part in supporting learning that goes on in the classroom and vice versa. The integration of different learning environments should therefore be supported as much as possible in order to maximize a student's education.

References

Alexander, P., Graham, S. and Harris, K. (1998) A perspective on strategy research: progress and prospects, *Educational Psychology Review*, 10: 129–53.

Alexander, R. (2005) *Towards a Dialogic Teaching: Rethinking Classroom Talk*. York: Dialogos.

Allen, S. (2002) Looking for learning in visitor talk: a methodological exploration, in G. Leinhardt, K. Crowley and K. Knutson (eds) *Learning Conversations in Museums*. Mahwah, NJ: Lawrence Erlbaum Associates.

Ausubel, D. (1968) *Educational Psychology: A Cognitive View*. London: Holt, Reinhart & Winston.

Bruner, J. (1966) *Towards a Theory of Instruction*. New York: Norton.

Bulgren, J. Deshler, D., Schumaker, J. and Lenz, K. (2000) The use and effectiveness of analogical instruction in diverse secondary content classrooms, *Journal of Educational Psychology*, 92: 426–41.

Deci, E. and Ryan, R. (1985) *Intrinsic Motivation and Self-determination in Human Behavior*. New York: Plenum Press.

Dillon, J., Rickinson, M., Teamey, K., Morris, M., Choi, M., Sanders, D. and Benefield, P. (2006) The value of outdoor learning: evidence from research in the UK and elsewhere, *School Science Review*, 87(320): 107–11

Dunbar, K. (1995) How scientists really reason: scientific reasoning in real-world laboratories, in R. Sternberg and J. Davidson (eds) *The Nature of Insight*. Cambridge, MA: MIT Press.

Dweck, C. and Leggett, E. (1988) A social-cognitive approach to motivation and personality, *Psychological Review*, 95: 256–73.

Elman, J., Bates, E., Johnson, M. *et al.* (1996) *Rethinking Innateness: A Connectionist Perspective on Development*. Cambridge, MA: MIT Press.

Falk, J.H. and Dierking, L. (1992) *The Museum Experience*. Washington: Whalesback Books.

Falk, J.H., Martin, W.W. and Balling, J.D. (1978) The novel field-trip phenomenon: adjustment to novel settings interferes with task learning, *Journal of Research in Science Teaching*, 15(2): 127–34.

Gentner, D., Lowenstein, J. and Thompson, L. (2003) Learning and transfer: A general role for analogical encoding, *Journal of Educational Psychology*, 95: 393–408.

Griffin, J. and Symington, D. (1997) Moving from task-oriented to learning-oriented strategies on school excursions to museums, *Science Education*, 81: 763–79.

Hatano, G. and Inagaki, K. (1993) Desituating cognition through the construction of conceptual knowledge, in G. Salomon (ed.) *Distributed Cognitions*. New York: Cambridge University Press.

Hobbes, T. (1651/1968) *Leviathan*. Harmondsworth: Penguin.

King, A. (1994) Guiding knowledge construction in the classroom: Effects of teaching children how to question and how to explain, *American Education Research Journal*, 31: 338–68.

Klahr, D. and Nigam, M. (2004) The equivalence of learning paths in early science instruction: Effects of direct instruction and discovery learning, *Psychological Science*, 15: 661–7.

Midgley, C., Kaplan, A. and Middleton, M. (2001) Performance-approach goals: good for what, for whom, under what circumstances, and at what cost?, *Journal of Educational Psychology*, 93: 77–86.

Nisan, M. (1992) Beyond intrinsic motivation: Cultivating a 'sense of the desirable', in F. Oser, A. Dick, and J. Patry (eds) *Effective and Responsible Teaching: The New Synthesis*. San Francisco, CA: Jossey-Bass.

Osborne, J. (1996) Beyond constructivism, *Science Education* 80(1): 53–82.

Palinscar, A.S. and Brown, A.L. (1994) Reciprocal teaching of comprehension – fostering and comprehension-monitoring activities, *Cognition and Instruction*, 1(2): 117–75.

Pavlov, I. (1927) *Conditioned Reflexes*. New York: Dover.

Perry, D. (1992) Designing exhibits that motivate, *ASTC Newsletter*, 20(2): 9–10.

Phillips, D. (1997) How, why, what, when, and where: perspectives on constructivism in psychology and education, *Issues in Education*, 3, 151–94.

Piaget, J. (1952) *Origins of Intelligence in Children*. New York: International Universities Press.

Pintrich, P., Marx, R. and Boyle, R. (1993) Beyond cold conceptual change: the role of motivational beliefs and classroom contextual factors in the process of conceptual change, *Review of Educational Research*, 63: 167–99.

Rogoff, B. (2003) *The Cultural Nature of Human Development*. Oxford: Oxford University Press.

Rummelhart, D. and McClelland, J. (eds) (1986) *Parallel Distributed Processing: Explorations in the Microstructure of Cognition. Volume 2. Psychological and Biological models*. Cambridge, MA: MIT Press.

Schauble, L., Leinhardt, G. and Martin. L (1997) A framework for organising a cumulative research agenda in informal learning contexts, *Journal of Museum Education*, 22(2 & 3): 3–8.

Seidenberg, M. and Elman, J. (1999) Networks are not 'hidden rules', *Trends in Cognitive Sciences*, 3: 288–9.

Skinner, B.F. (1974) *About Behaviorism*. New York: Alfred A. Knopf.

vom Lehn, D., Heath, C. and Hindmarsh, J. (2001) Exhibiting interaction: conduct and collaboration in museums and galleries, *Symbolic Interaction*, 24(2): 189–216.

Vosniadou, S. and Ortony, A. (1989) *Similarity and Analogical Reasoning*. Cambridge: Cambridge University Press.

Vygotsky, L. (1978) *Mind in Society: The Development of Higher Psychological Processes*. London: Harvard University Press.

Wellington, J. (1990) Formal and informal learning in science: the role of the interactive science centres, *Physics Education*, 25(5): 247–52.

Wood, D.J., Bruner, J.S. and Ross, G. (1976) The role of tutoring in problem solving, *Journal of Child Psychology and Psychiatry*, 17: 89–100.

14

Classroom management

Jeremy Burke

Introduction

> As she enters the classroom for the first time, music blaring, students
> are sitting on desks, talking and rapping, oblivious to her entry.
>
> Ellsmore (2005: 75)

In her book on teachers in film Susan Ellsmore describes the entry of
Lou-Anne Johnson into her English class in *Dangerous Minds* (1995). Here
the US Marine turned English teacher faces perhaps the toughest challenge
of her life: to teach these kids. Now the emphasis on the tough element of
this challenge is actually to *teach* the students. Gaining their attention
might not be all that hard, although clearly a necessary precursor to any
teaching. Keeping students' attention, sometimes proves more difficult.
The title of this chapter is 'classroom management' and that is because the
problem of gaining and retaining attention from an audience can be
planned and managed. This is just as well, since the tricky part of teaching
is actually teaching.

When people start teaching they bring a number of preconceptions
with them from various sources. Films and media are interesting in their
portrayal of teacher/student relations. Classrooms are often presented as
riotous and dangerous places, with streetwise kids and the threat of aggressive and potentially violent incidents. The myth of school chaos is compounded with press articles such as the *Mail on Sunday's* 'Is this the worst
school in Britain?' (Brace 1994) and reports of schools being 'out of control'
(*Education Guardian* 2005). A recent Teachers' TV presentation. 'The Great
Behaviour Debate' (Coleman 2005) looks again at whether school students
can be 'controlled' in schools. This focus on 'behaviour' constructs an ideal
of a school student as quiet, acquiescent and studious, a restatement of
being 'seen' but not 'heard'. On the other hand, the recent Training and
Development Agency for Schools advertisements to attract people into

teaching show pupils as lively, excited and, albeit under specific conditions, noisy. There is a potential balance to be struck between the targets of discipline which aims to control 'behaviour', and discipline which aims to promote study.

In this chapter I am presenting an analysis which gives a description of the way institutions, and in particular secondary schools, subject people within them to what are deemed to be 'normal' modes of doing and saying. This chapter does not seek to give a list of witty remarks and put-downs when engaging with students, but rather to look at the way that a strategic engagement might work.

I want to consider classroom management as a strategy to encourage pupils to study and consequently, I want to differentiate between the two targets of discipline.

Two discourses

I think it is productive to consider classroom management from the point of view of issues of comportment and issues of the subject of study. Bernstein (1990: 183; 2000: 32) distinguishes these two approaches as the regulative discourse (RD), which is concerned with the establishing of 'order, relations, identity' that is, the rules which mark out students' behaviours, comportment, style of dress, manner of address and so on; and the instructional discourse (ID), which addresses the 'specialized skills' and competences, that is, the school subjects being taught and learnt.

The term 'discourse' has become subject to much discussion over recent years and I want to define it in terms of Paul Dowling's 'Activity' which 'is to be understood as the contextualizing basis of social practice' (Dowling 1998: 131); in other words, to outline what is do-able and what is say-able in particular social contexts.

Bernstein, himself, says that the ID is embedded in the RD, producing only one discourse. However, for our purposes maintaining the separation is a productive distinction to make in terms of classroom management. A teacher will always be able to call on aspects of the RD if 'school rule' flouting is adopted as an oppositional strategy in a lesson.

Foucault and discipline

Michel Foucault (1977) in his book *Discipline and Punish* looks at an analysis of 'power', which he argues occurs only in social interaction and has no materiality. It is descriptive of hierarchies in social relations and, for our purposes, the strategies used in social institutions. Foucault introduces a number of analyses of social strategy adopted in a variety of institutions including the army, prisons, hospitals and schools which, in their own ways, are concerned with 'discipline'. The aim of disciplinary action is to bring about an acceptance of the regulations laid down by the institution on the part of its subjects. Subjectivity is realigned and recast through the process of disciplinary strategy. This might sound grim, but education is concerned with transformation. A student should be different, in some respects, at the end of a course.

The strategies which Foucault outlines are prevalent in schools. This does not mean that there has to be utter oppression, but schools are concerned with redirecting students' understanding of the do-able and the say-able. Foucault describes how 'technologies of the social' are used to achieve this through:

1 the systematic use of the layout and arrangement of space;
2 systems of punishment and privilege to state and restate the expected normal behaviours and actions of conscripts, inmates, patients and students;
3 the hierarchical 'gaze' which leads people to feel under constant surveillance;
4 the production of evidence to produce 'case notes' which describe and position individuals and all go towards constructing a network of regulation.

We can look at how these aspects of the systematic organization of a disciplinary institution apply in schools, although this is a very brief outline of Foucault's work.

The organization of space

School are organized into spaces for learning: classrooms, laboratories, art rooms, drama theatres, sports grounds and so on, and each of these spaces will have its own organization. In a classroom there are many possible seating arrangements from rows, to groups, to a horseshoe and each of these arrangements will facilitate different types of engagement between the student and teacher and student and student. Moreover, individual students might be assigned particular seats and, consequently, who they sit next to and might interact with during a lesson. Student teachers are often recommended to make a seating plan in order to place each student – and possibly to help learn their names. Foucault observes that the organizing of educational spaces moved from the traditional model of the master working with an apprentice whilst others simply looked on, to a 'learning machine, but also as a machine for supervising, hierarchizing and rewarding' (Foucault 1977: 147). The organization of the classroom becomes a resource for the teacher to establish authority, and also to manage students' engagement with the activities set.

Normalizing judgement

'Disciplinary power' is used to induce people into following certain actions, within the institution, through a system of small punishments and privileges. The punishments that are used should reinforce the desired action – if a student fails to produce a piece of written work, then the punishment is to write. The punishment reinforces the desired action. Similarly, privileges may be given which recognize conformance with the desired actions, and withdrawn if a student fails to continue to carry them out.

One example of this might be the use of 'quiet work' and 'silent work'. A class is asked to get on with their activity in a focused and quiet way. If the noise level rises the teacher will comment, 'The noise level is too high. Will you get on with work more quietly please?' This lets students know the limit of classroom noise. If students continue to be too noisy, a period of silent work is implemented. Here students work in silence for an announced period of time – say two minutes – but any transgression of the silent work is met with serious punishment – for example, a telling off, a detention, a letter home or the withdrawal of some privilege. Thereafter a period of 'quiet work' is permitted where students may once again talk to each other, but without raising their voices. The repeated implementation of this kind of strategy inducts students into the required level of noise permitted in that classroom.

Schools will frequently be concerned to institutionalize certain comportments, which teachers will be expected to check on (surveillance) and promote. Some typical examples will include:

- **dress** – specified school uniform, hair styles, permitted jewellery, exclusion of trainers, etc.
- **comportment** – sitting up straight in lessons, silence, lining up, walking on the left in corridors, etc.
- **styles of address** – calling teachers 'Sir', or 'Ma'am' or 'Miss', not using derogatory names for classmates, etc.
- **time and location** – the school timetable requires students to be in particular places at particular times of the day, detentions demand a time and place attendance, etc.

Here we can note that these things are more like the RD than the ID. For the purposes of students' learning a subject, then the classroom discourse has to focus on learning action. This might be directed through forms of engagement with the topic, the use of particular equipment, the kind of response to questions, problems or situations presented. Students are also inducted into a way of working in particular subjects.

The gaze

Here Foucault draws on the metaphor of the *Panopticon*, a prison designed by Jeremy Bentham which, built in the round, has cells on the perimeter of the building and a watch tower in the centre. Light enters the building from windows in the cells, but the central watch tower remains in relative darkness. The prisoners are exposed, backlit, to the *gaze* of the guards in the watch tower. Now, because the prisoners cannot see the watch tower, they do not know whether they are being observed, or not, and consequently learn to act as though they were under constant surveillance. The Gatso Speed Camera has much the same effect on motorists. The analogy to this in a classroom is the notion that teachers have 'eyes in the back of their heads'. Even if the teacher is not obviously looking at a student, the student must still feel subject to their gaze. School teachers learn very early on to 'scan' their classes. Their eyes will move to look at every student in the room even if they are actually talking to only one. This gives the opportunity to check on anyone acting in any way which is significantly off task and, according to this theory, leads students to *feel* as though off-task action will not go unnoticed. The 'gaze' is an important concept, as it is part of an almost unseen mechanism through which people adjust, modify and internalize their actions.

The examination

In schools various forms of assessments are used all the time. Pupils are measured, commented on, given targets and a whole panoply of data are produced and recorded. This is potentially strong stuff. The 'examination' might be a formal subject test, or it might be marking homework, or commenting on a student's progress during a lesson. The recording of observations; exam, exercise and homework marks; targets; and 'attitude' make each individual student 'a case'.

Foucault describes the theatre of the examination and the widespread acceptance that it generates a 'truth' about the student. It becomes an effective tool in classifying students according to criteria which typically include 'ability' and 'effort'. Foucault argues that disciplinary power is invisible and the techniques of normalization and surveillance lead to the internalization of the required comportments, behaviour and utterances by the subjects. The examination in school creates 'a case', much as a medical examination creates a case. The examinee is invited to accept the individualizing judgement of the examination as a representation of themselves, and the process objectifies and subjugates them (Foucault 1977: 191).

Frequently, the most effective action a teacher can take when dealing with a recalcitrant student is simply to write a report. This, alongside the other data held about the student, makes it possible to call the student to account at a chosen time. It constructs a case-to-answer. Foucault points out the economy of the examination is in uniting the 'gaze' and 'normalizing judgement'. Students, in school, are presented with an image of themselves measured alongside a scale of 'normal' action, and effectively invited to conform to the norm. We can now turn to look at how 'all this theory' might inform classroom management in practice.

Establishing a classroom discourse

If the teacher wants to establish what might count as the classroom discourse, the do-able and say-able, authority has to be established by the teacher. Although schools as institutions are designed to promote the authority of teachers, this is not necessarily totally uncontested by students, and authority has to be claimed and maintained. In fact, each time teachers take on a new class, whether they are new or experienced teachers, their authority has to be reasserted. However, care needs to be taken when drawing on the established norms of the school, in terms of comportment, dress and so on, that authority is not merely focused on teacher as enforcer.

We might take the ID as also marking out the classroom space, from other subject classrooms, or the corridor or dining hall, and this also has to be established. Discussion about coats and trainers is a distraction from the topic in hand. Prolonged struggles over outdoor coats, trainers and so on will effectively prevent the shift from RD to ID. An effective strategy might be to deal with these issues quickly at the outset of a lesson. In terms of the classroom discourse, the do-able and say-able might be restricted to the subject of the lesson. So in science, talk about science, in maths, talk about maths and in Spanish talk about (or in) Spanish. This way non-subject talk becomes un-sayable.

Having determined that the only talk and discussion can be about the subject of study it would seem reasonable to ensure that students were not barred from engaging in study. By this, I mean that differentiation practices should lead to pupils being able to gain entry to the subject of study, and not have it simplified to the point of becoming infantile. If students are effectively barred from engaging in the full range of subject study, then it might not be surprising if they become disenchanted and oppositional.

Managing a lesson

I shall take a lesson as having four parts, or stages, in terms of managing students' learning. These are: starting the lesson; introducing the topic/activity; maintaining student engagement; and managing the end of the lesson.

I want to exemplify the progress of a lesson from the approaches of two teachers drawn loosely from the documentary *The Lion's Den* (Morse 1992), which looks at how a new teacher, a teacher of eight years' experience and a teacher of 22 years' experience work with the same group of Year 10 pupils in a typical mixed, multicultural, multi-ethnic inner city London comprehensive school. I am interested in marking out the differences in approach between the new teacher, trying to establish himself with the class, and the very experienced teacher who seems to gain positive engagement from the same class that the new teacher has difficulty with. For the new teacher this is his form and he takes them for PSHE. The experienced teacher is their head of year and their English teacher.

Starting the lesson

Typically lessons begin with the teacher announcing his or her authority. This is simply to say, following Dowling (2001), that any pedagogic relation requires an author and audience, where the authority resides with the author. In our terms, the teacher has both the authorial voice and authority over the practice.

The way that teachers may address their classes and gain attention will vary considerably. Rogers (1997) suggests using an analogy, or Cowley (2003) suggests writing something on the board, and there are other self-help books which give lists of strategies that have worked for their authors. However, it is important to consider that any strategy is contingent on the place, time and participants, so teachers have to be prepared to adjust what they do and say in the light of responses from their classes. Strategies can be planned, tried and amended over a number of lessons.

It is at the opening of the lesson that it is most profitable to recruit wider school rules so some restatement about expected comportments might be made, including such standards as taking off outside coats, having books, pens and so on out and being ready to begin work. The experienced teacher might include these rules as part of her general commentary, and in our example school, the experienced teacher enters the classroom and simply says that she expects pupils to be getting on with their (preset) work rather than making a lot of noise. In saying this at the outset she announces her presence, her authority and the desired practice in her classroom. The statement expresses what is held to be the norm in that classroom. Punishment or privilege might follow a failure or concordance with the norm. Over a period of time, students are inducted into the classroom discourse. They know what is expected and respond to the slightest prod in its direction. What is important then, is for the teacher to be as clear as possible about what the classroom discourse should be. This can be difficult when one first sets out as a teacher, but can be thought through and planned for, nevertheless.

In our example school the new teacher calls for the class to be quiet. However, he says 'I'm getting sick of this now. Can you stop chattering on?' This has the effect of both focusing on himself, he is the one that is troubled because he needs to be the centre of attention, and diminishing his students by using 'chattering on' in a derogatory way. This is a negative approach which positions the students as engaging in an oppositional practice, making him 'sick'. Instead the teacher could have been more inclusive with a phrase along the lines, 'Will everyone please stop what they are doing and pay attention.' This means that the teacher can focus on 'the stopping' as a precursor to giving the message. This will often entail calling individuals to account, such as, 'Karl, will you pay attention, please?', and *always* waiting for complete quiet before starting to give your message.

The kind of language that a teacher uses requires thought and reflection. As the ID is established students will need to see a place for themselves and understand the rules of engagement. The experienced teacher has set up such a regulation. The new teacher needs to do so.

Surprisingly, calling for people to be quiet and listen, in all sorts of circumstances, might be quite easily achieved. However, if the message is dull or if the audience does not recognize its value, then keeping people's attention can become quite difficult. It is to this that we now turn.

Introducing the activity

In our example school the new teacher takes his form for PSHE and has to teach a lesson on drugs and alcohol. PSHE is not his main subject and it is likely that he has not encountered drugs and alcohol as a topic in which to engage Year 10 pupils. This highlights what is referred to as a 'subject knowledge' issue.

I want to refer again to Dowling's (2001) Social Activity theory, which describes a pedagogic relation as one where the author has access to a privileged domain of knowledge and the audience is yet to be inducted into that knowledge domain. In other words, the teacher will have access to the knowledge which, through pedagogic action, will be made available to students. If teachers do not have the knowledge, then they really do not have much to say and nothing to teach. The only thing they can do is to resort to RD action.

Moreover, in pedagogic relations, it is teachers who are able to judge whether something which is produced within the subject is good enough – that is, to judge whether their own explanation or a students' production meet the requirements of the subject. The logical converse of this is when the principles of evaluation of the performance reside with the audience. This is quite important, because at the outset of teaching a class, the group might not be quite prepared to accept or run with what is being offered to them. If a new teacher approaches things in a different way to the class's last teacher the students might well say, 'This is not the way things are done.' Alternatively, students will often ask, 'What are we learning this for?' As a teacher presents a topic which is new to the class, so there is an element of marketing involved, as the new knowledge is shown to be of interest, benefit or worthwhile in some way. Our new teacher facing a new class and teaching them about drugs did not really attempt to 'sell' the topic, but simply asked the students to discuss it. The students respond by saying that they do not know anything about drugs, which is probably a sensible thing to say under the circumstances. They very well might not want to discuss whatever they do know about drugs. The point here is that the teacher has to look for a way in with the students. This is a difficult issue, which according to a recent Ofsted report is still not handled sufficiently well in schools (Ofsted 2006). The teaching challenge is to clarify the main message and to consider what will get students to a point where they can receive it. An opener might well be to find out what students actually do know already.

So, the teacher needs to consider lesson starters, small activities, open questions or other activities to enable the class to engage in some meaningful way with the topic. It would be unsurprising if students were not willing to take on something which makes little sense to them. In turn this might lead to them adopting oppositional strategies. It is important for a teacher to find an understanding with the groups that they teach. Indeed, as Bernstein has argued: 'If the culture of the teacher is to become part of the consciousness of the child, then the culture of the child must first be in the consciousness of the teacher' Bernstein (1974: 199). Teaching might be considered as a dialogue, in which case both author and audience need to understand each other. Classroom management, if it is to achieve the move to an ID, needs to be focused on developing a dialogue.

As students start to get on with their tasks there will need to be some consideration about working methods – with whom students can work, what they can talk about, where they can move to and how much noise they can make. These methods will differ from lesson to lesson and between subjects depending on what is being taught and the type of activity selected. These rules need to be set out clearly in the explanation of the activity.

Maintaining engagement

Once students have been set off to work on an activity, then it becomes important to make sure that they are able to sustain this. Some may not have fully understood what it is they are being asked to do. Some might not understand the principle which ostensibly has just been explained. Some might be thinking about some other aspect of their lives, hanging on for their next text message about the play of events amongst their friends and so on. It is at this point that focus needs to be on the ID, where the classroom discourse is about study and not about other aspects of behaviour. We might analyse this part of the lesson in terms of Foucault's gaze and normalizing judgement. Let's look at some typical actions by pupils and consider possible counter strategies.

Firstly, the rules for the activity need to be adhered to for effectiveness or for health and safety issues. This means that the teacher has to be aware of what is going on, and this is achieved simply by looking. Teachers have to scan the class frequently, perhaps nearly all the time, to see that students are engaged and not off task. This does not mean that every pause, sigh, glance out of the window needs to be addressed, but that there has to be some sensitivity about whether students are able to engage with the activity.

If scanning reveals a student is doing something other than their work, then this might invite a comment. However, some consideration should be given to the effect the utterance is likely to have. Teachers' comments such as, 'Don't be silly' or 'I'm fed up with your lack of effort' or 'Why can't you do as you are told?', all offer the possibility of replies which lead away from the subject of study. Students can stand on their dignity about being called silly. If a teacher says that they are 'fed up' this can elicit the student response, 'Am I bothered, though?' A strategy then might be to focus comments on the desired norm for the lesson. So a teacher could say to a student, 'Do you need some help with your work?', or more encouragingly, 'Ask me a question which will help you to get on.' This focuses attention on what is aimed for, and not on what is deemed as deviant.

Perhaps a more significant concern is when students disengage from their task and become what is called 'disruptive'. This is perhaps the media-fuelled populist image of schools. Here, rather than drift off, as it were, students might engage in oppositional action to that which is being offered. Calling out, being disagreeable, throwing paper planes, pens or equipment all serve to disrupt the planned flow of the lesson. Initially this can be a real difficulty with some classes, and a planned and managed approach is what is required. Where there is a significant number of students who are being 'difficult' then seeking support and advice from more experienced colleagues is a sensible strategy. However, the outcome has to be that the class teacher deals with all the members of the class, and authority ultimately has to be claimed by the class teacher. Sending students out of the room, or sending them to someone else, such as a head of department or head of year, means that authority has not been able to be established yet. Strategies for (re)establishing authority will have to be planned.

Dealing with students who are being disruptive can also be achieved through action which focuses on their work. Instead of complaining about a paper aeroplane, for example, the student might be asked to explain how throwing it helped them get on with their work. Perhaps less confrontational would be to ask the student to come and show their work to the teacher. This then positions the teacher as the holder of the principles of evaluation – is this student's work good enough? The action restates the teacher's authority in terms of the ID.

Ultimately, students and teachers have to form an alliance, that is to be speaking the same language, travelling the same path. Telling students off, unthoughtful put downs, sarcasm and so on, all have the effect of casting the student as Other to the ideal presented by the teacher. It places them in an oppositional position. The effective teacher has to form an alliance. This means that it is a sensible strategy to assume that the students are able to learn what it is that is going to be taught. If they are not learning, then the teacher has to make an adjustment to what they do – it is a planning and re-planning issue.

At this point we can make a link with formative assessment and dialogic teaching. Black and Wiliam (2001) show that learning is enhanced through the use of formative assessment and we might consider this as opening and maintaining a dialogue with students. The discussion will be about students' work and progress and the teacher will gradually form some understandings about the students and vice versa. As the teacher gets to know the students' work better, so it becomes an easier task to refer to some item of their learning. This keeps the conversation focus firmly on the classroom discourse, the subject and students' progress. Although teachers will inevitably develop a set of 'put downs' as students try to amend lesson trajectories, keeping these focused on the trajectory is doubly effective.

Managing the end of a lesson

Teachers' classrooms are, in some ways, an indicator of their authority in terms of their organization and being in control of their presentation. Goffman (1990: 32) uses the term 'front' and this can apply to a classroom. In order to maintain the 'front' the room needs to give the desired impression. Usually this will be a place which is neat and orderly, which means as well as having books and equipment ready for the beginning of a lesson, everything needs to be cleared away at the end. This includes leaving table tops and the floor as spotless as possible, because this provides the final impression for students leaving the room and, in turn, provides the initial impression for the next class entering

Part of planning for a lesson should include planning how the lesson will end. Enough time needs to be allowed for packing away and tidying up. Too much time will eat into the lesson, so plan and organize for this to be fairly quick. A teacher will need to know what was handed out and what should be collected in – a list could help. Making use of students to help collect in books, paper and equipment and asking someone to take the bin round so that all bits of paper and other debris can be picked up and thrown away can help speed things up. As the teacher now directs clearing-up operations so the discourse shifts from ID to RD, and it is RD authority which is now claimed. As we have seen this is an easier claim than for ID authority, but the leaving message is one of the teacher being in charge. This is good as the private sphere of the classroom becomes public when the door opens. If the view is of an orderly classroom with students standing behind their chairs waiting to be dismissed, a small group at a time, then it looks like the teacher is 'in control'. This might be a positive thing to enjoy, at least at the end of every lesson.

Concluding comments

We have observed that we can consider the strategies used in a classroom for managing the audience and the engagement with the subject of study. Schools are disciplinary institutions which are concerned about students' comportments, actions and utterances. However, students can take oppositional action to the rules and oppositional action to a subject being offered in a subject lesson. Here it is suggested that the focus of disciplinary strategy should be on the subject being taught. This has the effect of fore-grounding the instructional discourse which, in turn, might be considered as passing a normalizing judgement which promotes engagement in the lesson activity. However, the lesson activity is then crucial to the process which, in turn, suggests that lesson planning is the key to classroom management.

References

Bernstein, B. (1974) *Class, Codes and Control, Volume I: Theoretical Studies Towards a Sociology of Language* (2nd edn). London: Routledge & Kegan Paul.

Bernstein, B. (1990) *The structuring of Pedagogic Discourse, Vol IV: Class, Codes and Control*. London: Routledge.

Bernstein, B. (2000) *Pedagogy, Symbolic Control and Identity: Theory, Research and Critique*. Oxford: Rowman & Littlefield.

Black, P. and Wiliam, D. (2001) *Inside the Black Box: Raising Standards through Class-room Assessment*. King's College London http://www.kcl.ac.uk/depsta/education/publications/Blackper cent20Box.pdf last accessed July 2006.

Brace, A. (1994) Is this the worst school in Britain? *Mail on Sunday*, 20 March.

Coleman, D. (2005) *The Big Behaviour Debate*. http://www.teachers.tv/oneOff Programme.do?transmissionProgrammeId=187789 last accessed July 2006.

Cowley, S. (2003) *Getting the Buggers to Behave 2*. London: Continuum.

Dowling, P.C. (1998) *The Sociology of Mathematics Education: Mathematical Myths/Pedagogic Texts*. London: Falmer.

Dowling, P.C. (2001) *Social Activity Theory*. http://www.ioe.ac.uk/ccs/dowling/sat2001.htm last accessed July 2006.

Education Guardian (2005) *Out of Control*. educationguardian.co.uk http://education.guardian.co.uk/classroomviolence/story/0,,1446969,00.html accessed 22 July 2006.

Ellsmore, S. (2005) *Carry on Teachers! Representations of the Teaching Profession in Screen Culture*. Stoke-on-Trent: Trentham Books.

Foucault, M. (1977) *Discipline and Punish: The Birth of the Prison*. London: Penguin Books.

Goffman, E. (1990) *The Presentation of Self*. London: Penguin.

Morse, O. (1992) *The Lion's Den*, Windfall Films.

Ofsted (2006) *Healthy Schools, Healthy Children? The Contribution of Education to Pupils' Health and Well-being*, London: Office for Standards in Education.

Rogers, B. (1997) *Cracking the Hard Class: Strategies for Managing the Harder than Average Class*. London: Paul Chapman Publishing.

Further reading

Rogers, B. (1997) *Cracking the Hard Class: Strategies for Managing the Harder than Average Class*, London: Paul Chapman Publishing.

Steer, A. (2005) *Learning behaviour: The Report of The Practitioners' Group on School Behaviour and Discipline*. http://publications.teachernet.gov.uk/eOrdering Download/STEER-FINAL.pdf last accessed July 2006.

15

Differentiation in theory and practice

Simon Coffey

Introduction

Differentiation is a philosophy of education which recognizes that pupils learn differently. This chapter addresses the what, why and how questions which face teachers across the curriculum as they seek to embed differentiated teaching into their practice. The need to ensure that each pupil experiences meaningful and successful learning often seems a daunting challenge given material and time constraints, but differentiation *is* manageable when viewed as flexibility in planning, teaching and assessing. The range of strategies which constitute differentiation also underpin recent conceptual innovations in education such as 'personalised learning' (DfES 2004) and 'assessment for learning' (Black *et al.* 2003), sharing the aims of empowering pupils through developing the learning skills which work best for them. There is no great mystery to differentiation, yet it often appears to be an elusive concept. I asked 50 training teachers nearing the end of their PGCE year to report on their experiences of differentiation and most had not heard of the term before starting the course, unless they had encountered it in pre-course reading. Almost all agreed with the principles of differentiation but still felt that they were unsure how to implement these in their lessons. Similarly, subject mentors often report that training teachers do not adequately consider individual learners' needs. Yet, differentiation is not an 'extra' dimension to teaching, rather, it represents a set of principles and practices which *are* teaching in the modern classroom.

What is differentiation?

To differentiate means, according to my dictionary, 'to perceive, show or make a difference (in or between); to discriminate'. This definition serves us well in the classroom context where teachers *perceive* difference in styles of learning, in aptitude, in interests and in a range of other motivational criteria. Teachers *show* sensitivity to this difference through the range of activities that they plan, in how these are structured, both incrementally and by type, and through the variety of ways pupil participation is facilitated in order to offer challenge and optimal learning. The learning process therefore *makes* differentiated learning feasible, allowing all pupils to engage to the best of their ability. Most schools now include 'differentiation' explicitly or implicitly in their stated learning goals, acknowledging that teaching needs to reflect the highly individual needs of learners. Consider, for example, these two aims extracted from school mission statements:

- We believe that every pupil can succeed and we challenge pupils to achieve their full potential by building differentiated targets into our teaching.
- We will develop pupils' individual talents and encourage them to work positively on improving identified areas for development.

These statements reflect the remit of education in the twenty-first century: to prepare pupils for a lifetime of flexible 'learnability'. Skills and knowledge are no longer, if indeed they ever were, viewed as finite entities or attributes, things that some people can do or know and which will continue to serve them in their professional life. We cannot know which skills will be in demand in the future or which personal qualities will be privileged in the workplace and so the emphasis is now on developing flexible skills and approaches to learning. Differentiation – offering the appropriate level of challenge – allows pupils to understand their own learning styles and to negotiate their own targets. In other words, it encourages positive involvement and increased autonomy.

Why differentiate?

Differences in aptitude and learning styles have long been recognized. In the past such differences were understood as being immutable characteristics inherent within pupils and it was believed that pupils of different aptitudes would benefit from structural segregation by 11-plus filtering or by streaming, banding and setting by ability groups within a school. Of course, even where groups are set by ability there is a range of varying aptitude within the group, as well as different learning styles and motivations, so even the most rigorous selection process will never produce a truly homogenous group of learners. It is for this reason that the term 'mixed ability' can be somewhat misleading. However, the remit of this chapter is not to discuss the arguments for or against ability group setting (for this, see Wiliam and Bartholomew (2004) or Chapter 16 in this book), but I am making a distinction between differentiation through systemic separation and flexible, differentiated teaching. It is the latter which is referred to throughout this chapter, that is, teaching which allows pupils to discover for themselves their own capacities for getting involved in learning. The move away from setting toward completely 'mixed ability', that is, *unset* groups seemed a natural extension of the egalitarian ethos of comprehensivism and required teachers to rethink issues of organizing and planning for pupils' different learning needs. The ethos which underpins *explicit* differentiation as it is now interpreted in the UK[1] is therefore closely tied to a belief in mixed ability teaching, not least of all the importance of the social dimension.[2]

As the term 'differentiation' became established in educational discourse in the 1990s, it denoted an attitude to pupils and a repertoire of practices which many experienced teachers already recognized as 'good', child-centred teaching. As the focus on differentiated teaching and learning became more explicit, through in-service training and initial teacher education, many experienced teachers welcomed the acknowledgement of what had long been their experience in the classroom:

> Defining the word and operationalising it was something new, although the actual practices were old, something which was part of experienced teachers' professional expertise and craft knowledge.
>
> (Kersher and Miles 1996: 19)

At last, the open discussion about difference and how to support different pupils meant that ideas could be cross-fertilized and new strategies developed to cater for different needs. Differentiation no longer needed to be dependent on anecdote and conventional wisdom but could take its place as a major cornerstone in the way lessons were planned and taught. Similarly, teachers new to the profession welcomed the range of differentiating strategies to support their management of the sometimes overwhelming diversity of any pupil cohort.

In summary, then, many teachers have always implicitly had different expectations from different students, especially as their personal knowledge of pupils grew, and these expectations often affected choices made about which pupils to ask what, which pupils to pair off together for an activity and so forth. Now, however, differentiation enjoys full recognition as it has become increasingly understood and codified, although of course any

---

[1] It is worth remembering that the differentiation ethos and strategies described here are the product of specific cultural beliefs about the aims of education and these are not universal. For example, a review of research looking at differentiation reported: 'the literature revealed that differentiation is interpreted quite differently (both in the UK and the US)' (NFER 2003). In the UK the focus is on differentiating the curriculum to cater for mixed ability classrooms whereas in the USA the emphasis is on streamed classes for gifted children. Furthermore, in France, where equality is seen as a cornerstone of republican democracy and is enshrined institutionally in national education, the idea of giving pupils different work to do seems inequitable to many teachers (Raveaud 2005).

[2] Although some schools have recently reintroduced setting for pupils in specific subjects, notably maths and modern foreign languages (NFER 2003).

codified practices which assist learning are only valid inasmuch as they constitute and support 'good practice'.

Differentiated learning

The different ways in which pupils learn result from complex cognitive, genetic and social differences, which we are still only beginning to understand (see Chapter 13). It is important to emphasize that differentiation in teaching is only as important as differentiation in learning. A traditional view of school learning was that, metaphorically speaking, pupils were receptacles and the job of the teacher was to fill them with knowledge. The process was conceived as linear, that is, incremental, so 'good' pupils retained more knowledge. In such a case, it was often seen that this type of pupil had a good memory, was motivated and paid attention, while 'bad' pupils did not retain knowledge, lacked motivation to learn and were easily distracted. Unsurprisingly, 'co-operation' and docility therefore became conflated with notions of intelligence.

We now recognize that learning is a much more complex process than the retention of information and that the traditional classroom privileged certain, culturally-shaped ways of learning, interacting and seeing the world. There is still some dispute over terminology to describe difference; for example, less able, SEN, different needs, gifted and talented – see Cigman (2006) for a defence of the concept of the 'gifted child'. However, modern educationalists, faced with increasing diversity, unite in acknowledging that the 'one-size-fits-all' model of learning is no longer credible and so we are left with no alternative which can claim to be just and equitable other than to integrate into our teaching a flexibility that allows *all* pupils the opportunity to succeed.

How to differentiate

Providing optimal challenge

As teachers differentiate between classes according to a broad set of variables (for example, age, set, previous learning, maybe gender ratio, even the time of day), so, within a class, teachers know that there are a range of pupil learning styles, levels, competences and so forth. Whether the class has been 'set' or not, *all* classes require sensitivity to differentiated needs, although, of course, where there is broad mix of ability this breadth needs to be reflected in the scope of the teacher's differentiation strategies. Differentiation does *not* mean teaching individually tailored lessons to 30 individuals; no teacher is expected to provide private tuition on this scale! Even if this were feasible logistically, such exclusively individualized learning would undermine the richness of the group dynamic which characterizes in-school learning. The social aspect of learning in a group with pupils offering different types of help to each other through modelling, explaining, collaborating (peer coaching, scaffolded learning) is a dimension which is to be capitalized on by teachers.

Indeed, as exemplified at the end of this chapter, peer collaboration and modelling offer important mechanisms for providing differentiated support, and research has shown that such scaffolding does lead to improved competence (Tudge 1992). Clearly, social cohesion and a belief in pupil–teacher shared goals are important elements in ensuring a feeling of belonging and a positive attitude to the subject and, indeed, to school (Ireson and Hallam 2005). Differentiation strategies therefore always need to be underpinned by an environment of warmth and security in which pupils work together.

Differentiation means offering pupils *optimal* challenge, so that each child can experience success. The role of the teacher is to sustain appropriate levels of interest and engagement. During the thousands of lessons I have both taught and observed I have concluded that the single most striking yardstick for measuring sustained pupil engagement (for which read 'successful learning') is sensitivity to the appropriate *level*, *pace* and *type* of learning to ensure optimal challenge. To unpack this statement let us consider each of the three components.

Level of learning

Clearly, pupils need to be set activities which are within their reach but which are not too easy. Both work that is too difficult and that which is too easy are likely to lead to distraction and, in the long term, to disaffection. If work is perceived to be too difficult, pupils will feel that they are not up to the task. This may be because the task does not build on the frame of knowledge and skills that has previously been developed, or it may be that the task has not been 'scaffolded' adequately with support material, further explanation or other sources of support, such as group work. Pupils often feel that the task is intrinsically too difficult for them rather than thinking that they need to enlist support. Indeed, they may not know what type of support is available or how to gain access to it. Provision of adequate support, or clear signposting toward it, is incumbent upon the teacher. Pupils in this case, faced with a task which they perceive as too hard, are likely to switch off. They may then display some form of bravado to parade an indifference to learning ('this is stupid – I don't care about this') or will simply remain quiet and internalize their confusion. In either case, the effects on personal self-esteem as well as on class morale are decidedly negative.

At the other extreme, if pupils are repeatedly set work which is too easy they will soon realize that they are not being stretched and will also become bored. Here the danger is that teachers set work toward the middle of the ability band without allowing pupils with more aptitude in the subject the scope for challenge at the upper level. It is a common mistake for beginning teachers to set work that is too easy in the hope that it will 'please' pupils and keep them occupied. In fact, the opposite happens. I firmly believe that pupils enjoy the level of challenge that allows them, with effort, to succeed. This has a confidence-boosting effect on the individual and is good for class morale; differentiation is therefore tightly linked to the goal of pupil motivation (Miller 1998).

So, how do we know where to pitch the level? Borrowing a metaphor from linguist Stephen Krashen (1984), input should be 'i + 1', which means slightly above the existing level. Of course, this is never going to be an exact science, so Krashen allows that content input will be 'roughly-tuned'. In order to be able to provide the appropriate level of input teachers need to know what pupils have done before, that is, new input needs to build on previous learning. Some National Curriculum attainment target levels suggest that pupils' knowledge/skill-base is developed in a linear, hierarchical fashion; however, the building process is not purely incremental. Rather, previous learning is constantly revisited, checked and integrated into new learning to provide a qualitatively expanded and highly individualized experience of the subject. Short-term and long-term plans (lesson plans, schemes of work, whole school curricula) need to take a broad perspective of learning aims to ensure that key overarching themes dovetail over time. Ollerton and Watson describe this type of planning as a 'three dimensional activity that (takes) account of the student's passage through school' and advocate a 'spiral curriculum' which sees pupils revisiting 'ideas from different perspectives, different directions at different times' (Ollerton and Watson 2001: 55).

The ways in which new knowledge is integrated into existing cognitive schemata are personal yet shaped by cultural frames as well as neurobiological patterns. The Vygotskian ZPD (zone of proximal development) metaphor emphasizes individualized appropriation of new concepts through joint participation in an activity. Differentiation strategies support this view of learning as a process of social engagement, that pupils learn not through being *told* but through 'problem solving under adult guidance or in collaboration with capable peers' (Vygotsky 1978: 86, cited in Daniels 2001: 57).

Pace of learning

Pace refers to the speed at which new items are presented sequentially and the time allowed for their assimilation. Different pupils need different time frames and different levels of support to digest new information but, again, this is not only about speed but also about the level of conceptual sophistication. If more able pupils are expected to work too slowly, they will soon become bored and if less able pupils are not given adequate time to understand and assimilate a concept, they will become frustrated as they are less likely to grasp the follow up. Teachers will use different levels of explanation and different levels of support to modify the input that pupils receive. *All* pupils, of course, require clear exposition of concepts and clear modelling and guidelines for tasks that they are asked to complete. No matter how able pupils may be it is important not to obscure 'content' by presenting the mechanics of the task in a confusing or ambiguous way.

Type of learning

The type of learning that is taking place needs to be clear in the teacher's mind if varied learning styles are to be addressed. Classifying different learning styles and teaching inclusively to bring in pupils who may not excel in traditionally valued school learning patterns now constitute a far-reaching, though not uncontested, discourse affecting educational theory and practice. Stemming largely from Howard Gardner's (1993) highly contested theory of multiple intelligences, recognition of different learning styles has now become widely entrenched in educational planning,[3] for example Lazear (1997), Larsen-Freeman (2000). While I do not believe it is necessary to cater explicitly for all 'intelligence types' and learning styles in every lesson, it soon becomes clear to any new teacher that different pupils can develop their own effective strategies for learning when given adequate scope to do so, and this is why engendering autonomy and self-awareness through teaching learning skills is so important. Differentiation is all about equity of opportunity and so planning a range of different types of activity values personal styles of learning and preferred modes of participation. For example, combining speaking and writing activities (public and personal acts) into a lesson, or allowing pupils preparing for a presentation to work in allocated roles which play to the personal strengths of each group member.

A convenient way to build these differentiated elements into our teaching is by the now classic dyad: *differentiation by task/differentiation by outcome* and it is to these that we now turn. However, it is vital to remember that differentiation is not simply a top and tail reflection which concerns only the planning phase and the outcome of a task or lesson. Rather, it affects everything about the task *while* it is underway, that is, in terms of the support provided through ongoing help and variation in pace and level of explicitness. Essentially, 'differentiation by task' means that pupils in the same class are given different tasks to do, whereas 'differentiation by outcome' means that all pupils are given the same task but that this task has been designed to allow for a range of variable outcomes to offer different levels of challenge. Many other types of differentiation are often described, for instance differentiation by support or by resource; however, teacher choices facilitating differentiated learning can be adequately discussed under the two types: by task and by outcome.

Differentiation by task

Differentiating by the setting of different tasks can mean planning completely different activities for pupils so that they are almost following parallel curricula and, clearly, this is necessary where pupils have specific needs such as bilingual or near-bilingual children in a modern languages

---

[3] Gardner's categories of 'intelligence' have been repeatedly adapted, including by Gardner himself, and remain contested conceptually (for example see Richards and Rodgers 2001).

class (McLachlan 2002), or if isolated pupils within a class are being fast-tracked to take an exam early. However, this extreme version of individualized task setting is unusual because of practical limitations. Task differentiation usually means modifying resources in some way to provide more or less support (scaffolding) to groups within a class. In written work this could take the form of graded exercises, moving from maximum guided support to freer pupil production. Some pupils may not need to do preliminary exercises, which are worked through by average or less able pupils, and so can move directly to a higher level of challenge to match their aptitude in the subject. In other cases, the teacher might set *core* then *optional* activities, which serve as an extension for early finishers or more able pupils. It is important to give due thought to the nature of extension tasks: these should not simply be 'more of the same' but should be *qualitatively* stretching. Being given an increased quantity of unchallenging tasks just to stay occupied can demotivate even the most enthusiastic pupil.

However, differentiation by task is not limited to graded worksheets and individual activities. One preparation-intensive but extremely enriching alternative to traditional teaching is the carousel approach (Cajkler and Addelman 2000) which enables individuals, pairs or groups to work around the room at different work stations structured to both challenge different skills sets and to facilitate different levels of challenge. In this case, the teacher and other staff present have very much a facilitating, supportive role. Pupils of all levels generally respond well to this type of learning, enjoying the high degree of autonomy that is afforded.

The 'learning how to learn' agenda – see, for example, Black *et al.* (2006) and Pedder (2006) – plays a key role in developing pupil autonomy and can be furthered by open discussion of learning styles ('what works for me is . . .'). It is a good idea to allow pupils the time and space to share their own approaches to work and study as well as to benefit from the teacher's guidance. When giving revision work, for instance, it is useful to discuss a range of strategies that pupils might employ, for example, mind maps, redrafting, testing each other aloud, pictorial prompts and so forth. Unsurprisingly, research has shown that pupils feel best supported in doing 'self-regulated' or semi-autonomous tasks where there is an explicit focus on the learning *how* to learn (van Grinsven and Tillema 2006).

Differentiation by outcome

Tailoring learning outcomes

The most time-efficient and practical way of differentiating is to set pupils a common task which is open-ended and flexible so that the expected outcomes are staggered. This strategy also has the enormous benefit of keeping learning across the class on track. Differentiated outcomes are now built into teachers' planning, as reflected in the QCA's recommended format for lesson plans and schemes of work, that is:

All pupils will be able to . . .
Most pupils will be able to . . .
Some pupils will be able to . . .

The key here is to make expected outcomes explicit, often negotiated by pupils themselves with guidance from the teacher. It is very clear when, in an English lesson for example, two peers produce markedly different creative compositions from the same assigned title that pupils' inter-pretation of the task is extremely divergent. When faced with such an open-ended task, therefore, pupils need help in understanding what is expected, so minimal outcomes must be clearly stated and understood; in the English lesson this might be a writing frame or a prescribed set of elements which must be included in the text. This use of frames and models provides all pupils with a sense of security but does not restrain more able pupils from going beyond the minimum requirements.

Interacting with pupils

Given that much class time is spent speaking, the nature of this spoken interaction also represents a valuable opportunity for differentiation. The way new concepts are introduced, building on previous learning, and the way in which pupils are encouraged to revise previously covered items usually rely on teachers asking questions to the class. In a traditional setting questions are asked, an answer is then given by a pupil and the teacher then provides feedback (usually saying if the answer is right or wrong). The restrictive nature of this traditional interaction routine (input-response-evaluation) has been recognized for some time – see Black *et al.* (2003) on formative assessment and Wragg and Brown (2001) on explanation strategies. Some creative forethought into the way questions might be asked in class to stimulate thinking at different levels ensures that all pupils can make a contribution corresponding to their current level and their preferred mode of participation. For example, questions can be directed to particular pupils or can be addressed to the whole class; questions can be open or closed to varying degrees – see Revell (1995) for a full discussion of effective questioning strategies for differentiated learning. Open questions clearly offer pupils more opportunities for creative expression, enabling them to structure their own responses. Open questions might also be particularly appropriate where there is a range of possible solutions. This type of questioning also provides the teacher with useful formative feedback. How-ever, more closed answers can bring specific elements (key words and key themes) into focus and can reaffirm existing knowledge, allowing a larger number of pupils to experience success, especially where pupils chose from a range of given answers. Consider these question types:

- Who were the Luddites? (to class)
- Who can tell me something about the Luddites? (to class)
- Lucy, can you tell us something about the Luddites? (to one pupil)
- Maia, if you described somebody as a Luddite, would you mean that that person is conservative or that they embrace change? (to one pupil) . . . Yes, I agree. Well done. Can you say where the word comes from?

- I would like each of you to think of at least one fact about the Luddites – more if you can – and note it down. You have one minute from now. (to class)
- In pairs, write one sentence using the words Luddites and mechanization.

Alternative questioning strategies include re-framing questions by giving an answer for pupils to think of an appropriate question or, for longer answers, asking pupils to present questions or use role play to present different points of view. This might work well, for example, in understanding the motivations of different historical characters such as the Luddites versus the factory owners or the mill hands.

There is also some research evidence (Myhill 2006) that reference-framing strategies in teacher–pupil interactions have a determining effect on pupil participation. For instance, pupils respond more positively when invited to draw on their own experience rather than with reference to an abstracted reality. This is true of all pupils but has been shown to be especially effective in increasing participation of disaffected, low-achieving boys (Myhills' research showed that this group was three times more likely to refer to personal, out-of-school experiences).

Let us now turn to an example of differentiation in practice. The lesson described here posits models of good practice for differentiation with reference to a particular subject – French – although the principles which underlie the differentiation strategies described are general and can clearly be applied across the curriculum.

Differentiation with a Year 9 mixed ability group: a French lesson

This lesson was taught by 'Lis' to a Year 9 mixed ability group. The topic is within the scheme of work unit on illnesses, parts of the body, remedies and the primary language objective is *j'ai mal au/à la . . .*, with the imperative tense being a secondary objective. Pupils had previously learnt parts of the body, although many make mistakes with the gendered article and some struggle with pronunciation. The whole lesson lasted one hour. Lis identified the following objectives for the lesson:

- all pupils will revise parts of the body with gendered article and combine parts of the body with *j'ai mal au/à la . . .* to express some basic ailments: I've got a headache, I've got a sore throat, my leg hurts etc.
- some pupils will understand and say some basic remedies: stay in bed, take these tablets, drink plenty of water, get plenty of rest.
- some pupils will be able to extend the minimal dialogues with conjunctions, present perfect phrases and extra turns using *si ça continue*.
- some pupils will be able to say affected body parts but may not be able to use *au/à la* correctly and may only remember key vocabulary items from the chunk-learnt phrases.

After greeting the class, Lis discussed the objectives, written on the board, with pupils. She then presented the new language to the whole class by holding up pictures showing people suffering from affected body parts and repeating clearly key phrases: *j'ai mal à la jambe, j'ai mal au dos* and so forth. Once the expressions had all been modelled by Lis, she used pupils with more confidence in French to model for others, *j'ai mal au* __, each pupil finishing the phrase according to the picture being held up. This led pupils to incorporate previously learnt vocabulary into new phrases. Lis chose different pupils to answer in quick-fire succession, moving from more to less confident pupils. This differentiated routine was then repeated but with a different prompt from Lis (*Qu'est-ce que tu as?*) which required pupils to respond using a whole phrase beginning *j'ai mal au/à la*. It is a common strategy to instigate peer modelling by starting off routines with more confident pupils in this way, however, it is important not to overuse particular pupils when deploying this strategy as this can be perceived as favouritism. Such a risk can be avoided by using alternating strategies such as starting some activities with simpler, more closed questions and targeting less confident pupils to answer.

Next, pupils listened to a series of short, recorded dialogues of different people being asked and answering questions about what is wrong with them. Pupils were given one of three different worksheets to complete during the listening activity, each offering different levels of challenge. For example, one sheet required pupils to write a sequence number next to a picture while others required pupils to fill in a gap as well. This activity exemplifies how the same resource, in this case recorded dialogues, can be exploited differently.

Lis then led a whole-class review. She went through the answers from the listening activity and as pupils answered some kept textbooks closed ('Look if you need to'), while others looked up the vocabulary item or its gender. There was a focus on pronunciation as pupils gave answers. Then all new expressions were reviewed through miming ailments, starting teacher to pupil (*Qu'est-ce qu'il y a?*), then pupils to each other in pairs. Pupils were able to look at a simple, gapped dialogue on a PowerPoint slide if necessary, although most did not need this support. As she circulated in the room, Lis encouraged many pupils to go beyond the modelled dialogue. This teacher-focused part of the lesson allowed Lis both to assess pupils' progress and to reinforce the key objectives of the lesson.

The next activity aimed at developing reading skills. Each pupil was given a handout consisting of a series of patient–doctor dialogues, each more complex than the last.

Referring to the first three dialogues, pupils were invited to respond, at speed, to some true/false (*vrai/faux*) questions using mini-whiteboards; for example, Sandrine's leg hurts – *vrai ou faux?* The doctor advises M Viret to stay in bed – *vrai ou faux?* Mini-whiteboards allow all pupils to offer an answer without the risk to self-esteem of getting it wrong. This maximizes pupil participation and allows the teacher to check comprehension instantly. Next, some reading comprehension questions were given on PowerPoint for pupils to work through on their own, graded to become gradually harder ranging from *vrai/faux* to eliciting full responses. Lis asked the class to 'do as many as you can'. A time limit was set for the whole class. Early finishers were given the following extension: write your own dialogue using the picture prompts at the bottom of the handout. The questions and the written texts were prepared to be progressively more challenging, some pupils would only do a few and others would finish. When Lis went over the answers with the class, she expected pupils who are more able in French to give fuller answers. She again did a quick assessment of how far pupils were progressing ('Hands up if you've answered 5/6/7 questions correctly'). All pupils were praised for their effort.

The match-up 'game' which followed was to give pupils the opportunity for speaking practice. Pupils worked in groups, some with light and dark blue cards and some with light and dark yellow sets. Blue cards showed a picture of an ailment to be matched to its written phrase. Yellow cards also showed a picture of an ailment to be matched up to a phrase but the picture card also had a 'suitable remedy' picture which pupils were asked to express in words to win the pair, for example *Reposez-vous! Prenez deux aspirines!* The children had played this type of match-up activity with Lis before and so were familiar with the routine and always enjoyed the game. Lis, a learning support assistant and a foreign language assistant all circulated among pupils during the card game activity to monitor and support. Some pupils were encouraged to go beyond the minimum turns from the cards, that is, to add an extra, unscripted turn such as *Qu'est-ce que s'est passé? – J'ai eu un accident* or to add *et si ça continue?* The activity was timed and lasted for ten minutes.

The final activity was a writing task which was started off in class to be finished for homework. Pupils were asked to write a postcard to a French pen pal describing a holiday where a lot of things have gone wrong. Pupils were asked *to choose* between two writing frames, one with gapped out phrases and picture prompts or one that only had picture prompts. Pupils using only picture prompts were also asked to add their own unprompted sentences.

At the end of the lesson, after pupils had packed their bags and were waiting to be dismissed, Lis asked differentiated questions using a combination of flashcard pictures, mime and requests for remedies. She revisited the key objective of the lesson, asking different pupils to give examples using *j'ai mal au/à la* . . . This was the fundamental goal of the lesson (the *base* or *minimal* outcome) and so it was important for Lis to reinforce this expression with body parts vocabulary, so that *all* pupils would leave the room with this key phrase in mind, having a clear idea of the lesson's aims and feeling that they had achieved these. However, Lis also built into the plenary review opportunities to reinforce elements of the extended dialogues that some pupils had covered in the lesson.

Concluding comments

In this chapter we have seen how differentiation (in the UK) emerged as a result of decreasing structural setting by ability – both of schools and within schools – which led to increasing mixed ability teaching. Faced with a broad range of different pupil needs and ability levels teachers needed to develop new strategies as well as to formalize existing 'craft knowledge' (Kersher and

Miles 1996) in order to create optimal learning opportunities for different pupils within a single lesson. We have explored the conceptual principles underlying the notion of optimal learning within the learning level-pace-type trichotomy, which enables us to modify lesson content and to plan activities to suit a range of learning styles. While differentiation may often require more detailed and lengthy planning, I have tried to emphasize in this chapter that differentiation is about building in flexibility and this does not always entail *extra* planning and materials but rather a broader and more creative vision of learning outcomes and how these can be achieved. In schools which prepare pupils effectively for greater personalized learning, differentiation strategies are shared within and across departments not only informally but as an integral part of professional development. Similarly, differentiation in lesson planning will dovetail with differentiated goals built into schemes of work and these, in turn, reflect a whole school ethos which acknowledges diversity and opportunity for all.

References

Black, P., Harrison, C., Lee, C., Marshall, B. and Wiliam, D. (2003) *Assessment for Learning: Putting it into Practice*. Buckingham: Open University Press.

Black, P., McCormick, R., James, M. and Pedder, D. (2006) Learning how to learn and assessment for learning: a theoretical enquiry, *Research Papers in Education*, 21(2): 119–32.

Cajkler, W. and Addelman, R. (2000) *The Practice of Foreign Language Teaching*. London: David Fulton.

Cigman, R. (2006) The gifted child: a conceptual enquiry, *Oxford Review of Education*, 32(2) 197–212.

Daniels, H. (2001) *Vygotsky and Pedagogy*. London: RoutledgeFalmer.

Department for Education and Skills (DfES) (2004) *A National Conversation about Personalised Learning*. Annesley: DfES Publications.

Gardner, H. (1993) *Frames of Mind: The Theory of Multiple Intelligences* (2nd edn). London: Fontana Press.

Ireson, J. and Hallam, S. (2005) Pupils' liking for school: mobility grouping, self-concept and perceptions of teaching, *British Journal of Educational Psychology*, 75: 297–311.

Keogh, B. and Naylor, S. (2002) Dealing with differentiation, in S. Amers and R. Boohan (eds) *Aspects of Teaching Secondary Science*. London: RoutledgeFalmer.

Kersher, R. and Miles, S. (1996) Thinking and talking about differentiation, in E. Bearner (ed.) *Differentiation and Diversity in the Primary School*. London: Routledge.

Krashen, S. (1984) *Principles and Practice in Second Language Acquisition*. Oxford: Pergamon Press.

Larsen-Freeman, D. (2000) *Techniques and Principles in Language Teaching* (2nd edn). Oxford: OUP.

Lazear, D. (1997) *Seven Ways of Teaching: The Artistry of Teaching with Multiple Intelligences*. Arlington Heights, IL: Skylight Publishing.

McLachlan, A. (2002) *New Pathfinder 1. Raising the Standard: Addressing the Needs of Gifted and Talented Pupils*. London: CILT.

Miller, D. (1998) *Enhancing Adolescent Competence*. London: Thomas Nelson.

Myhill, D. (2006) Talk, talk, talk: teaching and learning in whole class discourse, *Research Papers in Education*, 21(1): 19–41.

National Foundation for Educational Research (NFER) (1998) *Learning from Differentiation*. Slough: NFER.

National Foundation for Educational Research (NFER) (2003) *What Works for Gifted and Talented Pupils: A Review of Recent Research*. Slough: NFER.

Ollerton, M. and Watson, A. (2001) *Inclusive Mathematics 11–18*. London: Continuum.

Pedder, D. (2006) Organizational conditions that foster successful classroom promotion of Learning How To Learn, *Research Papers in Education*, 21(2): 171–200.

Revell, M. (1995) *The Differentiation Handbook: A Guide to Differentiation in Secondary Science Teaching*. Northants: Northamptonshire Inspection and Advisory Service.

Richards, J. C. and Rodgers, T. S. (2001) *Approaches and Methods in Language Teaching*. Cambridge: CUP.

Tudge, J. R. H. (1992) Processes and consequences of peer collaboration: a Vygotskyan analysis, *Child Development*, 63: 1364–79.

van Grinsven, L. and Tillema, H. (2006) Learning opportunities to support student self-regulation: Comparing different instructional formats, *Educational Research*, 48(1): 77–91.

Wiliam, D. and Bartholomew, H. (2004) It's not which school but which set you're in that matters: the influence of ability grouping practices on student progress in mathematics, *British Educational Research Journal*, 30(2): 279–94.

Wragg, E.C. and Brown, G. (2001) *Explaining in the Secondary School*. London: RoutledgeFalmer.

16

Setting, streaming and mixed-ability teaching

Jeremy Hodgen

Introduction

How should pupils be grouped for teaching? Should they be grouped according to some notion of general ability or should children be taught in mixed ability groups? Should pupils of different 'ability' be offered different curricular opportunities? What are the effects of different forms of ability grouping on teaching and learning? Are some sorts of pupil grouping more appropriate to particular school subjects?

In this chapter, I review the research that has been conducted on ability grouping in the UK and elsewhere. I look at the impact of different forms of ability grouping on pupils' learning, achievement and attitudes. Finally, I examine alternative approaches to grouping and teaching pupils at different levels of attainment.

Ability and ability grouping in the UK

The ideology of 'ability' is particularly powerful in UK educational policy and practice. There is a widespread belief both within and outside the education profession that individuals have a fixed 'ability' with a strong genetic component (Sukhnandan and Lee 1998). According to this belief, ability can be measured accurately and is a significant determining factor in educational achievement. (See White 2005 for an interesting philosophical discussion as to why the ideology of ability is so powerful in the UK.) This focus on ability is in marked contrast to many of the countries that out-perform the UK nations in international comparative studies of educational performance (Stigler and Hiebert 1999). In China, for example, a much greater emphasis is placed on the notion of effort.

A discourse of ability underpins the common forms of classroom organization in the UK:

- **streaming**, where pupils are differentiated according to general ability and taught in the same 'ability' classes for all subjects
- **setting**, where pupils are allocated to 'ability' groups within particular subjects
- **mixed ability**, where classes include the range of ability and attainment in a particular year group. Pupils may be placed in 'ability' groups within classes.

Until the late 1960s, the UK secondary education system was predominantly selective. Pupils were allocated to grammar and secondary modern schools according to their performance on the 11-plus examination. In addition, almost all secondary schools and many large primary schools operated an internal system of streaming. In a study conducted in the early 1960s, for example, Jackson (1964) found that 74 per cent of schools had placed pupils in different classes on the basis of inferred ability by the age of seven.

In the 1970s and 1980s, the move towards comprehensive schooling was accompanied by an increasing use of mixed-ability grouping in secondary schools, although setting was commonplace in GCSE classes and subjects such as mathematics and modern foreign languages. Latterly, there has been an increasing use of setting in both secondary and primary schools. A number of factors have contributed to this change, including teachers' perceptions of the requirements of the National Curriculum and pressure from middle-class parents (Gewirtz *et al.* 1993; Reay 1998). At the same time, there has been an increased emphasis on targets and comparing schools on the basis of league tables, whilst the school inspection regime has encouraged the use of more ability grouping (Ofsted 1998).

Currently, there is a consensus amongst the main political parties on the need for more ability grouping in schools (*Guardian* 2006). The Education White Paper, *Higher Standards, Better Schools for all, More Choice for Parents and Pupils*, states that:

> Grouping students can help to build motivation, social skills and independence; and most importantly can raise standards because pupils are better engaged in their own learning. We have encouraged schools to use setting since 1997.
>
> (DfES 2005: 58)

Ability grouping is a very hot topic in education.[1] Indeed, there have been no fewer than four substantial research reviews published in the UK during the past decade (Sukhnandan and Lee 1998; Harlen and Malcolm 1999; Hallam 2002; Kutnick *et al.* 2005). So what are the arguments for grouping by ability and what are the arguments against it?

---

[1] As I write this chapter, the 'Thought for Today' on the BBC Radio 4 *Today* programme (6 July 2006) by Dr Jeevan Singh Deol, an academic at the School of Oriental and African Studies, is a polemic in praise of ability grouping in schools in order to stretch the most able students.

The arguments for and against ability grouping

The main arguments for ability grouping are that groups of homogenous ability enable teachers to tailor their teaching more closely to all the pupils' needs. This enables more whole-class teaching making more efficient and effective use of teachers' time. There is a widespread belief that mixed ability grouping has caused underachievement (Sukhnandan and Lee 1998). Many believe that high attainers, in particular, are 'held back' in mixed-ability classes and that setting (or streaming) stretches these pupils. (See Loveless 1999 for a forthright statement of this position from a US perspective.) The opponents of ability grouping point to setting and streaming as one of the principal causes of underachievement (Gillborn and Youdell 2000). They believe that grouping by ability creates and maintains inequality, arguing that low achievers, in particular, receive a poorer educational experience. They contend that heterogeneous grouping provides a richer learning environment for the majority of pupils. Slavin (1990: 473) summarized the debate as follows:

> In essence, the argument in favour of ability grouping is that it will allow teachers to adapt instruction to the needs of a diverse student body and give them an opportunity to provide more difficult material to high achievers and more support to low achievers. The challenge and stimulation of other high achievers are believed to be beneficial to high achievers. Arguments opposed to ability grouping focus primarily on the perceived damage to low achievers, who receive a slower pace and lower quality of instruction, have teachers who are less experienced or able and who do not want to teach low-track classes, face low expectations for performance and have fewer positive behavioural models.

It seems that the more a subject is viewed as a fixed and structured body of knowledge, the more likely teachers of the subject and others in the field are to perceive ability grouping as necessary (Harlen and Malcolm 1999). For example, a survey by the National Foundation for Educational Research (NFER) in the UK found that 47 per cent of mathematics teachers believed mixed ability teaching to be inappropriate compared to 16 per cent of science teachers and only 3 per cent of English teachers (Reid *et al.* 1981, cited in Ruthven 1987).

The debate over ability grouping has important consequences for individuals and groups of pupils in terms of learning, achievement and attitudes. If the proponents of setting and streaming are correct, then mixed ability grouping will reduce educational attainment, particularly for the highest attaining pupils. But is this at the expense of the low attainers? What is ability and can it be measured? What does research have to say about these issues? Is there evidence to support the notions that setting creates inequality or that setting diminishes or enhances attainment for certain students?

Measuring 'ability'

The notion of a general 'fixed' ability, as measured by IQ tests, has come in for a great deal of criticism in recent years for cultural, class and racial bias. Sternberg (1998) argues that IQ tests measure current attainment and expertise rather than a general ability. Moreover, such tests can predict future attainment to a degree, but this predictive validity is limited.[2] Typically, measures of a child's general ability at the age of, say, 11 account for less than half of the variability in students' achievements at age 16. Social and economic status appears to be at least as important a factor as measured 'ability' in predicting future performance (Nash 2006).

The evidence suggests that teachers place a high degree of trust in the mechanisms for measuring pupils' abilities within subjects (Hallam 2002). In a substantial review of the literature, however, Sukhnandan and Lee (1998) found that the allocation of pupils to ability groups is frequently made on a subjective and inconsistent basis and there is considerable evidence of a high degree of group misplacement, where pupils are allocated to the wrong sets (Neave 1975; Winn and Wilson 1983). Indeed, some studies have found the practice of ability grouping did not reduce the range of ability in groups to any significant extent (see, for example, Oakes 1995). In a study of within class grouping in primary schools in the UK, Macintyre and Ireson (2002) found that the overlap in attainment between the lowest and highest ability groups was very considerable, with some in the lowest groups outperforming some in the highest.

But even the most carefully constructed tests have limitations. Any system of measurement *by its very nature* involves inaccuracy and error. On a theoretical exercise, assuming a selection test with a predictive validity of 0.7 and a reliability of 0.9, Black and Wiliam (2006) calculate that 50 per cent of students would be placed in the wrong set.[3] In a similar exercise based on the GCE A-level examination, Please (1971) estimated that 46 per cent of candidates were likely to have been wrongly graded. It is worth emphasizing that these errors are not due to the quality of the tests but reflect fundamental limitations in examinations per se. Thus, even the best constructed tests are likely to result in a relatively large proportion of pupils being allocated to the 'wrong' ability group. Yet, the evidence suggests that the movement between groups is very limited. (See, for example, Devine 1993.) In Macintyre and Ireson's (2002) study, although the majority of teachers said that they believed individual pupil's ability to be changeable, the researchers found that the actual movement between groups was very small. This is particularly surprising given that MacIntyre and Ireson's study focused on within-class grouping where movement

---

[2] Predictive validity indicates the degree to which a test predicts future performance.

[3] Reliability broadly indicates the extent to which individual scores on one occasion would be exactly the same on another occasion. Individuals' performance may vary from day-to-day or according to the particular questions asked or because markers allocate marks differently. Black and Wiliam's (2006) calculation is rather conservative, since the figures of 0.7 for predictive validity and 0.9 for reliability are at the limits of what can currently be achieved on most tests.

between groups would be relatively free from organizational and institutional constraints.

The effects of setting and streaming

Effects on attainment

One of the most important and widely reported reviews of research was conducted by Slavin (1990). Slavin reviewed a total of 29 studies and found the effects of ability grouping on achievement to be zero for pupils of all levels and all subjects.[4] In a more recent research project, Linchevski and Kutscher (1998) compared the attainment of pupils in 12 setted schools with their expected attainment, based upon entry scores. This research showed that ability grouping had no effect on attainment in ten of the schools and a small negative effect in the other two.

The weight of evidence indicates, as Terwel (2005) argues, that ability grouping has no meaningful effect on the overall mean performance of pupils. Although Slavin's review found negligible differences between the attainment of high and low ability pupils, other studies do suggest some differential impact. In an earlier review, Kulik and Kulik (1982) found a slight advantage for initial high achievers who studied in mixed ability groups. Linchevski and Kutscher (1998) compared the achievements of two groups of pupils at the same school assigned either to setted or mixed-ability groups. This study showed that the average scores of the most able pupils placed in setted groups were slightly, but not significantly, higher than the most able pupils placed in mixed ability groups. However, the scores of pupils in the two lower setted groups were significantly lower than similar ability pupils in the mixed ability classes.

Linchevski and Kuscher also examined the thinking and performance of pupils of similar attainment who were assigned to different groups. While the initial differences in attainment between the highest-scoring pupils in the lower band and the lowest-scoring pupils in the upper band were very small, the subsequent attainment differed greatly, with the pupils assigned to the higher groups attaining significantly more than pupils of a similar ability assigned to lower groups. Linchevski concluded from this that the achievements of these pupils were largely dependent on their arbitrary assignment to either the lower or higher group.

In a UK study involving 955 pupils in six schools, Wiliam and Bartholomew (2004) examined the effect of pupils of the same initial attainment being placed in different ability sets. They found that pupils placed in top sets averaged nearly half a GCSE grade higher than those in the other upper

[4] Slavin (1990) examined the effect sizes of the 29 studies and found that the median effect size was +0.01 for high achievers, −0.08 for average achievers and −0.02 for low achievers, none of which are significantly different from zero. The effect size is the difference between group means, divided by the standard deviation, resulting in a measure of effect in standard deviations. Effect sizes are commonly used to evaluate the impact of educational initiatives and interventions. Effect sizes of less than 0.2 are generally regarded as small or negligible.

sets, who in turn averaged a third of a grade higher than those in lower sets, who in turn averaged around a third of a grade higher than those pupils placed in bottom sets. In a study of seven US high schools, White *et al.* (1996) found that average achievers' chances of successfully completing high school (secondary education) varied enormously according to the group in which they were placed: from 2 per cent if placed in the course designed for low achievers and 23 per cent if placed in the course for average achievers, up to 91 per cent if placed in the course designed for high achievers.

Other studies that have found differences in achievement between homogeneous and heterogeneous groupings have tended to replicate the finding of a widening differential between low and high attainers (Hallam and Ireson 2005). Studies show some small, statistically insignificant increases for pupils in high ability groups together with large, statistically significant losses for pupils in low ability groups (Dar and Resh 1994). In short, grouping by ability widens the attainment gap and low attaining pupils lose more than high attaining pupils gain. Moreover, simply being placed in a lower set appears to reduce pupils' achievement, whatever their initial ability.

Nevertheless, the belief that high attainers are significantly disadvantaged in mixed-ability groups is very persistent. Burris *et al.* (2006) set out to investigate this issue. In a longitudinal study involving 985 pupils, they examined the effects of providing an accelerated mathematics curriculum in heterogeneously mixed classes in a diverse US school district.[5] They compared pupil progress both before and after the introduction of the accelerated curriculum and found that the proportion of pupils successfully completing mathematics courses increased significantly and markedly for pupils at all attainment levels. In particular, there was no statistical difference in the performance of initially high-achieving pupils in heterogeneous and homogenous ability groups. They concluded that the higher performance associated with high-ability groups resulted from better teaching and higher expectations rather than from the sorting of pupils.

Effects on teaching

There is considerable evidence that higher ability sets get the best qualified and most experienced teachers (Sukhnandan and Lee 1998). There is also evidence to suggest that the practice of ability grouping alters the ways in which teachers interact with their pupils. In a survey of 1500 teachers in the UK, Hallam and Ireson (2005) found considerable differences in the teaching of high and low ability groups. In contrast to both mixed ability classes and high ability sets, lower ability sets were offered a curriculum with more rehearsal and repetition, more practical work, less discussion, less detailed feedback, less homework, less access to the curriculum and easier work at a slower pace. There is considerable research evidence to support the claim that different ability groups receive a different curriculum

[5] The notion of accelerated curriculum has a long history in the US. Broadly, the term refers to a curriculum designed to stretch the most able pupils.

delivered in a different mode (Harlen and Malcolm 1999). A more surprising result in Hallam and Ireson's study was that these differences were
found to be apparent even amongst groups taught by the same teacher.
They conclude that grouping practices are a very powerful influence on
teaching practices. It would seem that low ability sets tend to be offered a
'remedial' curriculum, whatever the individual skills and beliefs of their
teacher. This may be partly because teachers assume that the pupils are
homogeneous and all learn at the same pace. As a result, they teach to
what Dallöf (1971) calls a 'reference group'. It may also be partly due
to differences in teachers' expectations. Repeated studies in a variety of
educational contexts have shown strong correlations between teachers'
expectations and pupils' academic progression (Rosenthal and Jacobson
1992).

Effects on attitudes

One of the arguments against grouping pupils by ability is that being placed
in lower ability groups has a negative effect on pupils' attitudes to learning.
Three seminal studies of schooling in the 1960s and 1970s provide support
for this view. Hargreaves (1967), Lacey (1970) and Ball (1981) all found that
placing pupils into high and low streams also created a polarization of
pupils into pro- and anti-school factions. Abraham (1995) investigated
whether the polarization of pupils according to their social class occurred as
a result of setting as well as streaming. He studied a comprehensive school
that made extensive use of setting, and found that, just as in the studies of
streaming, pupils were polarized into pro- and anti-school factions in
response to the groups in which they were placed.

On the other hand, in a meta-analysis of 13 studies, Kulik and Kulik
(1992) found that ability grouping tended to raise the self-esteem of low
attainers, whilst lowering the self-esteem of high attainers.[6] Boaler's (1998,
2002) work suggests that high attaining pupils may react in very different
ways to ability grouping. She conducted an in-depth study in the UK of
pupils over three years that focused upon the pupils' attainment and
attitudes. She studied two cohorts of pupils, matched in terms of ability and
socio-economic status. One of the cohorts was taught mathematics in
mixed ability groups using an investigative teaching approach, the other
in ability sets with traditional teaching. The study showed that top set
pupils responded in different ways to ability grouping. Some students
benefited from the setting arrangements. But, a significant number of
pupils, particularly some of the able girls, appeared to be disadvantaged,
developing negative attitudes and underachieving in GCSE examinations.
The pupils related their negative responses to the pressure and fast pace of
lessons in the top set.

In a UK study involving 3000 pupils, Ireson et al. (2002) found that pupils
in schools with moderate levels of setting had more positive self-concepts
than those in either schools with high levels of setting or mixed-ability

---

[6] Meta-analysis is a statistical technique that combines the effects of a number of related
studies.

schools. In addition, they found that setting in English tended to raise the self-concept of low attainers and lower the self-concept of high attainers, although they found no similar effects in mathematics and science. In a qualitative study of ability grouping in mathematics involving 96 pupils in Australia, Zevenbergen (2005: 317) found a considerable difference between pupils in high and low sets typified by the following quotations:

> I am so glad to be in these classes. We get the best teachers and you know that they tell us we are clever. They bring out the best in us, and I know that I will be able to do the hard maths in Year 11 and 12 because they bring out the best in us.
>
> (Pupil in high ability group)

> I don't like being in this class [because] it is the only one I feel dumb in. I mean English or workshop, I am doing OK, but in maths, I feel like a 'retard'. The teacher treats us as if we know nothing.
>
> (Pupil in low ability group)

The contrast between these two pupils' responses to ability grouping is stark. However, they do suggest that these pupils' attitudes may be affected by a range of secondary factors interacting with the practices of ability grouping: the quality of teaching, the breadth of the curriculum and the level of teacher expectations.

Effects on equity

In an extensive review of the research relating to educational inequality, Gillborn and Mirza (2000) conclude that there is considerable evidence that setting and streaming tend to disadvantage black and working-class pupils. A range of factors other than 'ability' affect the placement of pupils in sets or streams:

> Although ability is supposedly the major criterion for placement in subject and examination levels, ability is an ambiguous concept and school conceptions of ability can be affected by perceptions that pupils are members of particular social or ethnic groups and by the behaviour of individual pupils. Factors related to class, gender, ethnicity, and behaviour can be shown to affect the placement of pupils at option time, even those of similar ability.
>
> (Tomlinson 1987: 106)

Pupils of similar ability are frequently placed in different sets or streams according to their social class, their gender or their ethnic origin, thus creating and perpetuating a cycle of social and educational disadvantage. Nash (2006) found that this educational disadvantage is reinforced at every stage of the educational system. In a study focused on two secondary schools, Gillborn and Youdell (2000) found that the schools focused most of their available teaching resources on those pupils judged likely with help to achieve five A–C grades at GCSE, leaving those judged unlikely to achieve this level with only limited help, thus further widening the attainment gap. This latter group contained a disproportionate number of black and working-class pupils.

Concluding comments

To sum up, although the current political consensus is in favour of more setting and ability grouping in schools in order to raise standards of educational achievement, there is little research evidence to support this view. In fact, the evidence strongly suggests that grouping by ability is unlikely to raise attainment overall. Setting and streaming create and exaggerate differences in attainment between pupils. Small academic benefits for high attainers are achieved at the expense of large disadvantage for low attainers. There is conclusive evidence that setting and streaming create and perpetuate social inequalities amongst pupils. The research concerning the effects of ability grouping on pupils' attitudes is more equivocal although there is some evidence to suggest that some of the teaching associated with lower sets – lower expectations coupled with a more limited and poorly delivered curriculum – have a negative impact on pupils' attitudes.

The research evidence reviewed here suggests that a high quality curriculum coupled with high expectations delivered within heterogeneous mixed ability groups has the potential to produce educational benefits for pupils at all levels of attainment. Nevertheless, as Hallam and Ireson (2005) argue, mixed ability teaching is far from straightforward. Responding to the needs of pupils at different attainment levels requires a considerable degree of skill on the part of a teacher in terms of differentiating the curriculum whilst providing a high quality curriculum for all. Several studies suggest that key to doing this is the adoption of a more fluid attitude to pupils' abilities. (See, for example, Hart et al. 2004.) For example, in a study of primary numeracy, Askew et al. (1997) found that one characteristic of effective teachers (as measured by gains in pupils' attainment) was a belief that all pupils have the potential to learn mathematics.

The evidence supporting the benefits of collaborative group work and discussion between different pupils is considerable (Slavin 1988; Mercer et al. 2004). In a study of Key Stages 1 to 3, Blatchford et al. (2005) found that working in groups produced significant gains in pupil attainment. However, they argue that, in order for these gains to occur, pupils need to be taught the necessary social and emotional skills to collaborate with others. Pupils often learn more from other pupils' explanations than from teacher instruction (Adey and Shayer 1994). But, in groups with a narrow range of attainment, pupils appear to be discouraged from asking for or giving explanations. Hence, groups function best when they are mixed ability: low ability pupils ask questions, high attaining students help the group to function whilst benefiting from giving explanations to others (Hallam 2002). In a review of the literature relating to mathematics education, Askew and Wiliam (1995) argue that in groups with a wide attainment range, pupils of middle attainment lose out, because they neither ask for nor give help. They suggest that the most appropriate form of grouping is 'near' mixed ability grouping, where high attainers are grouped with middle attainers and middle attainers with low attainers. This form of grouping maximizes the opportunities for all pupils to be involved in giving and receiving explanations.

The research on pupils' learning suggests that pupils do not learn in a neat, orderly and sequential manner (see, for example, Denvir and Brown 1986). By listening to, and engaging in, dialogue with pupils, teachers can tailor the teaching to all pupils' learning needs. Evidence from the research on formative assessment suggests that by listening to pupils, teachers can help to produce significant gains in attainment (Black *et al.* 2003; see also Chapter 17 on assessment for learning). Indeed, there is evidence to suggest that this kind of dialogic teaching not only increases pupils' learning but also increases their capacity for future learning (Mercer *et al.* 2004). This would indicate that we need to be exploring dialogic teaching approaches rather than continuing with a policy of ability grouping that seems to have little to offer in terms of raising standards or promoting effective learning for all.

References

Abraham, J. (1995) *Divide and School: Gender and Class Dynamics in Comprehensive Education*. London: Falmer Press.

Adey, P.S. and Shayer, M. (1994) *Really Raising Standards*. London: Routledge.

Askew, M., Brown, M., Rhodes, V., Johnson, D.C. and Wiliam, D. (1997) *Effective Teachers of Numeracy*. London: King's College.

Askew, M. and Wiliam, D. (1995) *Recent Research in Mathematics Education*. London: Ofsted.

Ball, S.J. (1981) *Beachside Comprehensive*. Cambridge: Cambridge University Press.

Black, P., Harrison, C., Lee, C., Marshall, B. and Wiliam, D. (2003) *Assessment for Learning: Putting it into Practice*. Buckingham: Open University Press.

Black, P. and Wiliam, D. (2006) The reliability of assessments, in J. Gardner (ed.) *Assessment and Learning*. London: Sage.

Blatchford, P., Galton, M. and Kutnick, P. (2005) *Improving Pupil Group Work in Classrooms: A New Approach to Increasing Engagement and Learning in Everyday Classroom Settings at Key Stages 1, 2 and 3*. Teaching and Learning Research Programme (TLRP) Research Briefing, 11. London: TLRP. (Available at: http://www.tlrp.org/pub/documents/no11_blatchford.pdf#search=%22Improving%20Pupil%20Group%20Work%20in%20Classrooms%22.)

Boaler, J. (1998) Open and closed mathematics: student experiences and understandings, *Journal for Research in Mathematics Education*, 29: 41–62.

Boaler, J. (2002) *Experiencing School Mathematics: Traditional and Reform Approaches to Teaching and their Impact on Student Learning*. Mahwah, NJ: Lawrence Erlbaum Associates.

Burris, C.C., Heubert, J.P. and Levin, H.M. (2006) Accelerating mathematics achievement using heterogeneous grouping, *American Educational Research Journal*, 43: 105–36.

Dallöf, U. (1971) *Ability Grouping, Content Validity and Curriculum Process Analysis*. New York: Teachers College Press.

Dar, Y. and Resh, N. (1994) Separating and mixing students for learning: concepts and research, *Pedagogisch Tijdschrift*, 19: 109–26.

Denvir, B. and Brown, M. (1986) Understanding number concepts in low attaining 7–9-year-olds. Part II: The teaching studies, *Educational Studies in Mathematics*, 17: 143–64.

Department for Education and Skills DfES (2005) *The Education White Paper: Higher Standards, Better Schools for All, More Choice for Parents and Pupils*. Norwich: The Stationery Office.

Devine, D. (1993) A study of reading ability groups: primary school children's experiences and views, *Irish Educational Studies*, 12: 134–42.

Gewirtz, S., Ball, S.J. and Bowe, R. (1993) Values and ethics in the education market place: the case of Northwark Park, *International Studies in Sociology of Education*, 3: 233–54.

Gillborn, D. and Mirza, H.S. (2000) *Educational Inequality. Mapping Race, Class and Gender: A Synthesis of the Research Evidence*. London: Ofsted.

Gillborn, D. and Youdell, D. (2000) *Rationing Education: Policy, Practice, Reform and Equity*. Buckingham: Open University Press.

Guardian (2006) Extend ability setting to every school, says Cameron, *Guardian*, 9 January.

Hallam, S. (2002) *Ability Grouping in Schools: a Literature Review*. London: Institute of Education.

Hallam, S. and Ireson, J. (2005) Secondary school teachers' pedagogic practices when teaching mixed and structured ability classes, *Research Papers in Education*, 20: 3–24.

Hargreaves, D. (1967) *Social Relations in a Secondary School*. London: Routledge & Kegan Paul.

Harlen, W. and Malcolm, H. (1999) *Setting and Streaming: a Research Review*. Edinburgh: The Scottish Council for Research in Education.

Hart, S., Dixon, A., Drummond, M.J. and Mcintyre, D. (2004) *Learning Without Limits*. Maidenhead: Open University Press.

Ireson, J., Hallam, S., Hack, S., Clark, H. and Plewis, I. (2002) Ability grouping in English secondary schools: effects on attainment in English, mathematics and science, *Educational Research and Evaluation*, 8: 299–318.

Jackson, B. (1964) *Streaming: An Education System in Miniature*. London: Routledge & Kegan Paul.

Kulik, C. and Kulik, J.A. (1982) Effects of ability grouping on secondary school students: a meta-analysis of evaluation findings, *American Educational Research Journal*, 19: 415–28.

Kulik, J.A. and Kulik, C. (1992) Meta-analysic findings on grouping programs, *Gifted Child Quarterly*, 36: 73–7.

Kutnick, P., Sebba, J., Blatchford, P. *et al.* (2005) *The Effects of Ability Grouping: a Literature Review*. DfES Research Report RR688. Nottingham: Department for Education and Skills (DfES).

Lacey, C. (1970) *Hightown Grammar*. Manchester: Manchester University Press.

Linchevski, L. and Kutscher, B. (1998) Tell me with whom you're learning, and I'll tell you how much you've learned: mixed-ability versus same-ability grouping in mathematics, *Journal for Research in Mathematics Education*, 29: 533–54.

Loveless, T. (1999) *The Tracking Wars: State Reform Meets School Policy*. Washington DC: Brookings Institute.

Macintyre, H. and Ireson, J. (2002) Within-class ability grouping: placement of pupils in groups and self-concept, *British Educational Research Journal*, 28: 249–63.

Mercer, N., Dawes, L., Wegerif, R. and Sams, C. (2004) Reasoning as a scientist: ways of helping children to use language to learn science, *British Educational Research Journal*, 30: 359–77.

Nash, R. (2006) Controlling for 'ability': a conceptual and empirical study of primary and secondary effects, *British Journal of Sociology of Education*, 27: 157–72.

Neave, G. (1975) *How They Fared: the Impact of the Comprehensive School on the University*. Henley: Routledge & Kegan Paul.

Oakes, J. (1995) Two cities' tracking and within-school segregation, *Teachers College Record*, 96: 681–90.

Ofsted (1998) *Setting in Primary Schools*. London: Office for Standards in Education.

Please, N.W. (1971) Estimation of the proportion of examination candidates who are wrongly graded, *British Journal of Mathematical and Statistical Psychology*, 24: 230–8.

Reay, D. (1998) Setting the agenda: the growing impact of market forces on pupil grouping in British secondary schooling, *Journal of Curriculum Studies*, 30: 545–58.

Rosenthal, R. and Jacobson, L. (1992) *Pygmalion in The Classroom: Teacher Expectation and Pupils' Intellectual Development*. New York: Irvington Publishers.

Ruthven, K. (1987). Ability stereotyping in mathematics, *Educational Studies in Mathematics*, 18: 243–53.

Slavin, R.E. (1988) Research on co-operative learning: consensus and controversy, *Educational Leadership*, 47: 52–4.

Slavin, R.E. (1990) Achievement effects of ability grouping in secondary schools: a best evidence synthesis, *Review of Educational Research*, 60: 471–99.

Sternberg, R. (1998) Abilities are forms of developing expertise, *Educational Researcher*, 27: 11–20.

Stigler, J.W. and Hiebert, J. (1999) *The Teaching Gap*. New York: Free Press.

Sukhnandan, L. and Lee, B. (1998) *Streaming, Setting and Grouping by Ability: A Review of the Literature*. Slough: NFER.

Terwel, J. (2005) Curriculum differentiation: multiple perspectives and developments in education, *Journal of Curriculum Studies*, 37: 653–70.

Tomlinson, S. (1987) Curriculum option choices in multi-ethnic schools, in B. Troyna (ed.) *Racial Inequality in Education*. London: Tavistock.

White, J. (2005) Puritan intelligence: the ideological background to IQ, *Oxford Review of Education*, 31: 423–42.

White, P., Glamoran, A., Porter, A.C. and Smithson, J. (1996) Upgrading the high school mathematics curriculum: mathematics course-taking patterns in seven high schools in California and New York, *Educational Evaluation and Policy Analysis*, 18: 285–307.

Wiliam, D. and Bartholomew, H. (2004) It's not which school but which set you're in that matters: the influence of ability grouping practices on student progress in mathematics, *British Educational Research Journal*, 30: 279–93.

Winn, W. and Wilson, A.P. (1983) The affect and effect of ability grouping, *Contemporary Education*, 54: 119–25.

Zevenbergen, R. (2005) The construction of a mathematical habitus: implications of ability grouping in the middle years, *Journal of Curriculum Studies*, 37: 607–19.

17 | Making assessment work in the classroom

Christine Harrison

Introduction

Assessment is intricately bound up in the teaching–learning cycle. When people begin to train as teachers, their personal focus is usually on their performance as a teacher, while their tutors and mentors try to refocus their attention onto the students' learning that is taking place in the classroom. As a result, assessment tends to be neglected in the early stages of teacher development and, when it suddenly looms, rather than being embedded in the developing practice, assessment is tacked on. It is not surprising, therefore, that in a recent Ofsted report on initial teacher training at secondary level, one of the main findings was that, 'Trainees' standards in professional values and practice and subject knowledge are generally good, but their assessment of pupils is usually weaker' (Ofsted 2004: 77). The report went on to outline, in more detail, trainees' strengths and weaknesses:

> Most trainees structure their lessons carefully and manage classes confidently. Trainees plan particularly well in history, ICT and RE. In a number of subjects, including geography, design and technology, science and English, the effectiveness of their teaching is sometimes reduced by a rigid adherence to the three-part lesson structure at the expense of the flexibility that could result in lessons being more varied and stimulating. The assessment of pupils' work continues to be a relative weakness across subjects. Pupils' work is marked regularly but some trainees have limited skills in assessing work at examination levels, including that associated with post-16 examinations.
>
> (Ofsted 2004: 77)

So, it's not just a matter of knowing about assessment, you need to unravel the complexities of how assessment works in order to inform teaching and learning. First, we need to consider the various uses to which assessment is put in classrooms and in schools and to understand how these purposes interact and, at times, clash with one another. Then we need to look at the range of tools that teachers can use to carry out assessments. Finally, we need to outline some of the consequences of assessment, and begin to suggest ways of using assessment practices to foster effective learning environments.

Purposes of assessment

There are three main purposes of assessment:

- assessment for learning
- assessment for reporting attainment
- assessment for accountability.

Teachers, at various times, need to assess for each of these reasons, but it is essential that, before they start, they ask themselves, 'assessment for what purpose?' While the assessment tools a teacher might use for these three purposes could be the same, the ways in which a teacher would use them would differ depending on the purpose. The issue is not the type of assessment tool, nor the procedure that is selected, but rather the way in which the assessment data are collected and used.

In assessment for learning, teachers need to use a variety of tools to find where students are in their learning. From these data, they can make judgements that can help the student to decide on the next step in learning, and so guide them towards improvement. This process is known as formative assessment and at its heart is effective feedback. It involves the teacher and the learners in pinpointing the leading edge of learning and deciding what the next learning steps should be. This process requires a rich source of data for judgements to be made. It also requires students being open to advice about what they should do next, and being motivated to develop their understanding.

In assessment for reporting on attainment, the need is different. This type of assessment is used to check on whether individuals have reached a certain point in their learning or to compare the performance of one student against another. It is generally carried out at the end of a learning period or at a key point within the learning. The process is called summative assessment or assessment *of* learning, since its purpose is to measure what learning has taken place. This type of assessment might be needed for mapping a student's progress in order to report to parents or for the purposes of aiding transfer to another class or school. It is also needed to award certificates and qualifications such as the General Certificate of Education (GCSE) at age 16.

The final category, assessment for accountability, has taken greater prominence since the introduction of the National Curriculum. This form of assessment is used to check that schools are providing adequate educational provision for their students. In recent years, the government has chosen to do this by comparing school examination results in the form of 'league tables'. The current system provides comparative measures of success and progress. While it is not unreasonable for schools to demonstrate to the public, who fund them, that they are providing good educational standards, the practice in England of publishing school examination results has had a detrimental effect on the other two types of assessment. Accountability pushes teachers into 'teaching to the test' rather than 'teaching for understanding', which, in turn, creates a performance environment rather than a learning environment. At its extreme, the system might lead teachers to advise children to rote learn. In a recent project that investigated the assessment of science learning for the 16–19 phase, one teacher reported that he frequently found himself advising students: 'Don't worry if you don't understand. If this comes up in the exam then just write . . .' (Black *et al.* 2004: 13). More worryingly, a review by Harlen and Deakin-Crick (2002), on testing in schools, indicated the negative effect that current 'high stakes' testing regimes had on student motivation, which, in turn, had significant consequences for future learning. In particular, the review showed that one impact of tests was to reduce the self-esteem of those students who did not achieve well. The review also revealed that the effect of 'high stakes' tests on teachers was to lead them to adopt teaching styles that emphasized knowledge transmission rather than more active and creative pedagogies. In Wales, league tables have never been used to compare school examination results, despite their external measures for assessment of learning (that is, their examinations) being similar to those used in England. While the government still use assessment for accountability purposes, it is unlikely to affect the other purposes of assessment to the same degree that it does in England, where league tables dominate the assessment scene.

The assessment repertoire

Formative assessment

Once teachers have established what the main purpose of their assessment will be, they can then select from the tools available. For the majority of the time in classrooms, the main purpose will centre on assessment for learning. Here the main challenge will be selecting a tool and a way of using it to obtain rich data on which to make judgements for future guidance. The goal is to find what students know, what they partly know and what they do not know (Black and Harrison 2004). The idea is to try to locate student understanding, teachers need to explore what's happening in students' heads. This process requires activities that encourage students to talk about their learning, and to apply whatever knowledge they have, from which teachers can gauge their level of understanding.

Many studies have mapped the type of talk that happens in classrooms (Barnes and Todd 1995; Mercer 2000; Alexander 2004). If we look first at who does the most talking, it seems that in most British classrooms, the teacher is responsible for most of what is said. In the King's Medway

Oxfordshire Formative Assessment Project (KMOFAP), which ran from 1999–2001 with science, mathematics and English secondary school teachers, teachers often began lessons with question and answer sessions intended to link the lesson with previous learning experiences. At the start of the project, teachers dominated talk in most of the lesson starters by a factor of 10:1. When teachers did try to engage learners, by asking questions, the answers tended to be limited to one-word or one-sentence responses and the focus was on recall; such questions are not useful in tapping understanding. This approach restricted learners' opportunities to express their ideas and created difficulties for teachers in collecting evidence of strengths and weaknesses in student understanding.

With support from the research team, teachers began to address this imbalance in classroom talk. By the end of the project, most of the teachers had introduced techniques that reduced this dominance of teacher talk. This result was achieved by helping students to find a voice (Black *et al.* 2002, 2003) through working on strategies to help students raise ideas. This process began by improving 'wait time' (Rowe 1974) – the time a teacher takes between asking a question and accepting an answer. It was also enhanced by many teachers allowing students to rehearse and construct answers in groups, prior to the whole-class discussion, and working on techniques that encouraged the continuation of themes and ideas within the talk. This strategy involved teachers planning scenarios and situations that the class could talk about, instead of using classroom talk as a series of questions to check whether some students knew the answers or not.

A helpful way of understanding the dynamic of the classroom, and the constraints and affordances it offers for dialogue and feedback, is through Perrenoud's (1998) concept of the regulation of learning. He describes two different types of classrooms – the 'traditional' and the 'discursive or negotiated' classroom. In traditional classrooms, lessons are highly regulated with activities tightly defined and, consequently, learning is prescribed. The outcomes tend to be content driven and predetermined, with little opportunity for the students to play an active role in their own learning. From these types of lessons, teachers can only glean what students cannot do, according to the narrowly defined terms of reference (Marshall and Wiliam 2006).

In a discursive, or negotiated, classroom, the tasks are more open-ended. The scope for students to be active in their learning, and to govern their own thinking, is greater. Teachers can gauge understanding and provide meaningful feedback for learners. Learners co-construct knowledge through such learning experiences, and the teacher's role is both instigatory and facilitatory. A starting point in this process is formulating questions that make students think and which motivate them to want to discuss ideas. For example, questions such as, 'Is it always true that green organisms photosynthesize?' are better at generating talk than, 'Which types of organisms photosynthesize?' Questions that require students to predict or consider alternatives are better than those leading to a set answer. For example, 'What might the wolf have done if the grandmother had been out?' is a far better question for active discussion and thought than, 'What happened to the wolf in the Red Riding Hood story?' Sometimes playing on the ambiguities that puzzle learners can be a good starting point. For example:

Which one of these statements is true?

a) 0.33 is bigger than 1/3
b) 0.33 is smaller than 1/3
c) 0.33 is equal to 1/3
d) You need more information to be sure

(Hodgen and Wiliam 2006: 6)

This question would be unacceptable in a summative test, because there are several possible answers that depend on the way the question is approached. The question is not designed to check on a specific understanding, but rather to generate talk to explore a number of different understandings. Learning can benefit greatly from the talk that is generated from good questions, and teachers need to put planning time aside to generate questions and to share effective questions with colleagues (Harrison 2006).

It is also possible to use test questions and papers that were initially designed for summative purposes, in a formative way. One science teacher on the KMOFAP project gave his class an end-of-topic test in the first lesson of the unit. The students' task was to browse quickly through the test and to indicate their confidence with the questions using a traffic light system. Students indicated their confidence levels by putting a green, amber or red dot by each of the questions. Green meant that they felt confident about answering the question, amber meant that they knew something about the answer, but were not too sure they were fully correct, and red meant that they had never come across that bit of learning previously. For a good proportion of the questions, there was some consensus on whether the children were green, amber or red. The teacher used this information to plan the lessons for the topic. He knew that he could omit, or quickly cover, parts of the topic that had been judged green and that he could then spend more of the time on the amber areas and on introducing the red areas. His planning was informed by assessment data from the students. Other teachers on the KMOFAP project used similar techniques to help students effectively plan revision for summative tests.

Sadler (1989) conceptualizes formative assessment as the way in which judgements about student performance can be used to hone and improve their competence by short-circuiting the randomness and inefficiency of trial-and-error learning. This approach enables teachers to make 'programmatic decisions with respect to readiness, diagnosis and remediation' (p. 120). Teachers, therefore, are able to feed back information from assessments into the teaching process and take decisions about the next step in the learning for individual students (Gipps 1995). This is a two-fold process in that teachers have to make a judgement about the next learning step for the student and about the appropriateness of the next task, so that an effective match can be achieved. Implicit in the choice of task is an understanding of the progression within the subject domain, which enables decisions to be made about the learning goal that the teacher considers is attainable by each student.

Summative assessment

As the name suggests, summative assessment comes at the end of the learning period, or at key points in the learning. Its purpose is to provide a snapshot of where the learning is, at that specific time. The form that the data for summative assessment need to take will depend on their exact purpose. If the assessment is needed for providing information about learners when they transfer from one teacher to another, then relatively detailed data are needed across a range of content and skills. However, when learners transfer to very different environments, such as from school to higher education, detailed information of their learning will not be that useful as the style of learning and focus of the work is very different to that in school. Therefore, less detailed data are needed for summative assessment. However, whether grades are sufficient data for this process is not clear and there is some debate about selection procedures for university places based on predicted grades.

The emphasis on psychometrics (the theory and techniques of psychological measurement) throughout the history of summative assessment, has affected the way that teachers, schools and the government look at data. The emphasis on relative ranking, rather than actual accomplishment (Gipps 1995), on individual performance rather than on the success of collaborative group tasks, and the misplaced belief that objectivity conveys with it accuracy of measurement of a student's capabilities, distract teachers from investigating what summative assessments have to offer. Assessment is not an exact science (Gipps 1995), and the best that we can do is make ourselves aware of the confidence levels of the assessment tools that we use and knowledgeable about how we can make assessments as accurate as possible within the confines of the time, tools and school contexts.

Confidence in a specific assessment can be divided into two aspects – reliability and validity. Reliability focuses on the subjunctive approach:

- What if the paper was taken on a different day?
- What if different questions were selected?
- What if different markers assessed it?
- What if different grade boundaries were set?

Each of these factors, in different ways, may affect the final score that a student achieves. The students will have the same capabilities whatever the test paper, but the score that they achieve will be determined to a large intent by the particular test that they take; this includes all the conditions of when and where the test took place, and by whom, or how, the test paper is marked.

Validity is a measure of how close the assessment is to measuring the capabilities it hopes to assess. If a modern foreign language qualification was only given for writing and reading, and there was no assessment of speaking French, despite it being part of the curriculum, then the validity would be lowered because only part of the taught curriculum was being assessed. Similarly, if all of the questions on the test paper used sport and food as the main context for questions, then only part of the curriculum is tested and this again would reduce the validity.

Sometimes, in attempting to improve reliability, the validity is lowered.

For example, a test consisting of 30 multiple-choice questions is likely to have greater reliability than three essay questions but if these are set in religious education, where some of the aims are to develop argument, elaborate nuanced explanations and compare and contrast ideas, then essays provide a more valid way of assessing these skills. It is important to consider carefully what and a test is assessing and how this is done. Whereas formative assessment drives the learning, the final, summative assessment should serve the learning and not predetermine it. If teachers allow themselves to be seduced into teaching to the test, then they change the classroom ethos from a learning orientation to a performance orientation. The consequence of this change is that students will not make any effort in their learning unless they can see clearly that it will help them achieve a higher test score. More damaging than this consequence is that they may refuse to attempt challenging activities because they see any struggle as failure rather than an opportunity for learning (MacBeath and Mortimore 2001).

Teachers rarely evaluate their test papers or the test papers that other agencies provide. Sometimes it is possible to spot 'rogue' questions that are ambiguous or are strange ways of asking a student to do something straightforward, and these questions can be omitted, adapted or replaced. It is also simple to pre-test questions on students in other classes to check that the questions are doing what the test constructor hoped they would do. So you might want to select questions from a Year 8 test as a class activity for your Year 9 class, to check on the questions and, at the same time, provide you with formative data to decide where to take the Year 9 students next. These methods will improve the confidence levels of your test papers.

To improve the reliability of the paper, you will need to get a class to do the paper and then look at the results of all candidates question by question. If you work on the premise that stronger candidates will do well on most questions and weaker candidates will tend to perform badly on most questions, then you need to consider whether this pattern occurs for specific questions. If it does, then the question can be described as discriminatory. Let us exemplify this by looking at the results of a class of 12 students taking a seven question test, with each question having ten possible marks. First, you need to rank the class results and then look at the spread of marks on the individual questions.

Student	Q1	Q2	Q3	Q4	Q5	Q6	Q7	TOTAL
AH	9	9	4	7	9	10	10	58
VB	9	8	4	6	8	9	10	54
JJ	8	9	5	5	9	7	10	53
CH	9	7	4	6	7	8	10	51
DR	8	8	5	5	5	5	10	46
OL	8	8	5	6	5	4	10	46
WS	7	7	4	6	6	3	10	43
PY	7	9	3	5	5	4	9	42
MJ	8	5	7	5	4	4	9	42
WW	8	3	8	3	2	4	9	37
MT	7	1	7	4	2	3	9	33
TB	9	6	6	4	3	2	0	30

To help focus, look at the range of marks per question, but focus on the first four students, AH, VB, JJ and CH, who we'll call 'high attainers' and MJ, WW, MT and TB, who we'll call 'low attainers'.

All students do reasonably well on question 1; high attainers get 8 or 9 marks while low attainers get 7 or 8. While this question is not very discriminatory, it is common practice to have a question that most students can do as the first question. Question 7 is similar, but it may be that you would ask yourself whether it is useful having the last question on the paper as one where most students score full marks. Student TB scored zero for question 7 which could be because TB has no understanding of the learning that question 7 demands. Equally, it could be the case that TB worked slowly through the first six questions and failed to reach question 7 or even, that TB did not turn the final page and realize that there was a seventh question to answer. It might, therefore, be safer not to have a high scoring question as the last question on the paper next time and so question 7 could be omitted or moved earlier in the paper.

Question 2 has the high attainers scoring between 7 and 9 marks, while the lower attainers manage 1 to 6 marks. This question is discriminatory. Question 3 proves to be a strange question in that high attainers do worse than low attainers. This can happen sometimes when more capable learners feel that the answer is so obvious that they may start to look for an alternative explanation and end up failing to answer part of the question. This is therefore a 'rogue' question and should be considered for omission, adaptation or replacement the next time this test is given.

Questions 4 to 6 are also discriminatory. Question 6 covers a wide range of marks, while question 4 uses the range 2 to 7. You would want some questions to be widely discriminatory, while with others you may want most students to score at least 4 of the marks and only part of the question to discriminate. Only careful scrutiny of the results and the details of the question will allow you to decide on this. However, unless teachers actually set time aside to evaluate examination papers in this way, to check how well they have fulfilled the purpose of assessing the capabilities of students, then the assessment data that are produced will lack reliability.

Another form of reliability that needs attention, particularly if the data and judgements from the summative test are to be used for important decisions, is inter-marker reliability. The reliability here can be improved if teachers construct mark schemes together, enter into professional dialogue at some during the marking process, and instigate some sampling techniques to pair-mark some papers and come to an agreement about the intricacies of the marking and the judgements made.

Summative assessments need not be tests. Sometimes a product is generated at the end of the learning in subjects such as in technology, art, music, drama, media, English and humanities. The general issues with regards to validity and reliability apply to these just as they do to tests, but with these alternative forms of assessment, other confidence issues arise. How can the assessors judge how much of the work is the student's and how much of the product results from someone who helped the student? This point is of particular concern with coursework for GCSE and A-level qualifications. Does feedback from a teacher or a relative on the first draft of an essay constitute cheating? Is allowing a music student three attempts, rather than one, at recording their prepared piece, and then selecting the best performance fair? Should a drama assessor judge each player individually, or award the same mark to everyone in the performance, no matter how large or complicated their part? Is using the Internet something we should reward a student for because it is a skill we hope they will acquire, or should we ban all Internet use because we are frightened that it will encourage youngsters to plagiarize work?

Such questions need to be openly debated and this process has begun in the current Assessment Reform Group project, 'Assessment Systems for the Future'. This group believes that the systemic weaknesses in our assessment system could be tackled by changing the balance between external and school-based summative assessments and through dependable quality in teachers' summative assessments. Northern Ireland, Scotland and Wales already give more weight to teachers' summative assessments than is the case in England. However, research shows that whilst some innovations have improved teachers' summative assessments, others have clearly failed. Several attempts both to improve the ways in which teachers collect and interpret evidence from their students and to secure alignment between standards and practices between schools, show a patchwork of success and failure. However, they do indicate ways that have potential for success. An example of the possibilities is the established teacher assessment practices in Queensland, Australia (Cumming and Maxwell 2004), where there are no external examinations. Teachers carry out their own summative assessments; quality issues are assured through a state-wide moderation system, where teachers meet in groups and agree the quality of samples from each other's schools.

Assessment consequences

Assessment practices are a product of our historical context (Black 1995) and they are driven by social and professional change. Assessment pervades all aspects of the work that teachers do, and we need to be clear that the assessment practices in the classroom today are not established because of educational needs from a former era. While the media might wish to focus on the 'gold standards' (Baird *et al.* 2000) of yesteryear, teachers need to focus on current assessment practices and how these relate to successful teaching and effective learning.

Formative assessment is part of teachers' day-to-day work; it supports them in dealing with the individual successes and needs of their students. Summative assessment provides a means for reporting on progress, for providing information for transfer purposes and for awarding certification at the end of a learning period. These two purposes could work side-by-side quite well, if it were not for the overriding effect of accountability. As Gipps (1995: 4) writes:

> the task assessment specialists must address is how best to design accountability assessment which will provide good quality

information about pupils' performance without distorting good teaching (and learning) practice.

In our current, high-stakes testing regime, it is difficult for schools and teachers to escape the tyranny of assessment for accountability. Whereas the focus of schools should be on assessment for learning, many schools feel forced to focus on assessment for accountability and invest considerable time and money in continuously collecting masses of performance data, in the hope that taking account of this evidence will result in success. Such an approach needs to be cautioned against, since a strong drive for accountability can undermine effective formative and summative assessment practices. While successful resolution might be difficult for schools to find, they need, at least, to enter into debate with teachers, students, parents and governors about the assessment model they hope to set up, maintain and sustain within their school. A model that allows for the flexibility and individuality of formative assessment, while preparing for summative assessment and providing for accountability. Teachers are key to making such a system function and assessment practices will only improve if the central role of teachers in assessment is recognized and their expertise is trusted.

References

Alexander, R. (2004) *Towards Dialogic Teaching: Rethinking Classroom Talk*. Cambridge: Dialogos.

Assessment Systems for the Future (ASF) (2004) *ASF Working Papers and Interim reports*. Available from the ARG website http://arg.educ.cam.ac.uk/ASF.html.

Baird, J., Cresswell, M.J. and Newton, P. (2000) Would the real gold standard please step forward? *Research Papers in Education*, 15(2): 213–29.

Barnes, D. and Todd, F. (1995) *Communication and Learning Revisited*. London: Heinemann.

Black, P. (1998) *Testing: Friend or Foe? The Theory and Practice of Assessment and Testing*. London: Falmer.

Black, P., Harrison, C., Lee, C., Marshall, B. and Wiliam, D. (2002) *Working Inside the Black Box: Assessment for Learning in the Classroom*. London: NFERNelson.

Black, P., Harrison, C., Lee, C., Marshall, B. and Wiliam, D. (2003) *Assessment for Learning: Putting it into Practice*. Maidenhead: Open University Press.

Black, P. and Harrison, C. (2004) *Science Inside the Black Box: Assessment for Learning in the Science Classroom*. London: NFERNelson.

Black, P., Harrison, C., Osborne, J. and Duschl, R. (2004) *Assessment of Science 14–16: a Report Prepared for the Royal Society*. London: Royal Society.

Cumming, J. and Maxwell, G. (2004) Review of assessment practices in Queensland, *Assessment in Education*, 11(1): 89–108.

Gipps, C. (1995) *Beyond Testing: Towards a Theory of Educational Assessment*. London: Falmer.

Harlen, W. (2004a) A systematic review of the evidence of reliability and validity of assessment by teachers used for summative purposes (EPPI-Centre Review), in *Research Evidence in Education Library. Issue 3*. London: EPPI-Centre, Social Science Research Unit, Institute of Education.

Harlen, W. (2004b) A systematic review of the evidence of the impact on students, teachers and the curriculum of the process of using assessment by teachers for summative purposes (EPPI-Centre Review), in *Research Evidence in Education Library. Issue 4*. London: EPPI-Centre, Social Science Research Unit, Institute of Education.

Harlen, W. and Deakin-Crick, R. (2002) A systematic review of the impact of summative assessment and tests on students' motivation for learning (EPPI-Centre Review), *Research Evidence in Education Library. Issue I*. London: EPPI-Centre, Social Science Research Unit, Institute of Education.

Harrison, C. (2006) Banishing the quiet classroom, *Education Review* 19(2): 67–77.

Hodgen, J. and Wiliam, D. (2006) *Mathematics Inside the Black Box: Assessment for Learning in the Mathematics Classroom*. London: nferNelson.

MacBeath, J. and Mortimore, P. (2001) *Improving School Effectiveness*. Buckingham, Open University Press.

Marshall, B. and Wiliam, D. (2006) *English Inside the Black Box: Assessment for Learning in the English Classroom*. London: nferNelson.

Mercer, N. (2000) *Words and Minds*. London: Routledge.

Office for Standards in Education (2004) *Standards and Quality 2002/03. The Annual Report of Her Majesty's Chief Inspector of Schools*. London: The Stationery Office.

Perrenoud, P. (1988) From formative evaluation to a controlled regulation of learning processes: towards a wider conceptual field, *Assessment in Education: Principles, Policy and Practice*, 5(1): 85–102.

Rowe, M.B. (1974) Wait-time and rewards as instructional variables, their influence on language, logic, and fate control: part one – wait-time, *Journal of Research in Science Teaching*, 11(2): 81–94.

Sadler, R. (1989) Formative assessment and the design of instructional systems. *Instructional Science*, 18(2): 119–44.

18

Aiming for inclusion: removing barriers and building bridges

Chris Abbott

All children, wherever they are educated, need to be able to learn, play and develop alongside each other within their local community of schools.

(DfES 2004: 3)

Introduction

The most recent government policy document on special educational needs (DfES 2004) is titled 'Removing Barriers to Achievement'. It is the latest in a line of developments in this area which have themselves traced an arc of understanding across a wide vista of educational change. Like all recent educational policy statements, current SEN policy is linked to the strategies for intervention and for integration of services in 'Every Child Matters' (DfES 2003). This document outlines the key rights of all children, and these also underpin all support for those who are faced with barriers to learning.

The rights outlined in 'Every Child Matters' are that children should:

- be healthy
- stay safe
- enjoy and achieve
- make a positive contribution
- achieve economic well-being

(DfES 2003: 6–7)

This chapter examines the recent history of the response of the educational system to learners who have often been characterized as having special educational needs (SEN). The use of the term SEN is itself contested since it raises issues related to labelling and low expectations (Billington 2000). Within the UK, for example, Scotland no longer uses the term and prefers to talk about ASN: Additional Support Needs. It should be noted, of course, that the term ASN in Scotland is intended to cover a much wider range of issues than has traditionally been covered by SEN. In the absence of a fully acceptable terminology, this chapter will reflect common usage among teachers by using the term SEN, albeit with an enhanced awareness of the contestability it carries with it. The chapter considers a range of responses from teachers, policy makers and other relevant groups. All teachers need to be aware of SEN issues, and they have particular duties laid out in the SEN Code of Practice. The code is discussed in order that you can consider its implications for your teaching.

This chapter is not, however, a practical guide to supporting learning needs in your classroom. Many such guides are available, and these go into much more detail than is possible in one short chapter. Such guides are often aimed at the SENCO – the Special Educational Needs Co-ordinator in the school (Cowne 2003) – but much of use to the subject teacher will also be found in such publications. The needs of trainee teachers and NQTs are considered by a more recent publication (Spooner 2006), which contains detailed practical guidance for beginning teachers on this complex and evolving area.

The current SEN Code of Practice (DfES 2001) and its predecessor followed the influential Warnock Report (DES 1978), and the 1981 Education Act (DES 1981), both of which came down firmly in favour of inclusive education. At the time of publication of the Fish Report (Committee to Review Special Educational Provision 1985) on the future of SEN provision in London, the arguments for inclusive education seemed compelling and any opposition to them risked being labelled as divisive and inequitable. The authors of the report were unequivocal:

> [I]ntegration in society is a process not a state. It is not simply a question of placement in the same groups and institutions as others. It is a process which requires continued and planned interaction with contemporaries and freedom to associate in different groups. The potentially adverse effects of isolation and segregation, in whatever context, including comprehensive institutions, are now well known, including the risks to social competence and to the development of a positive self-identity.
>
> (Committee to Review Special Educational Provision 1985: 5)

Many special needs teachers, particularly those in inner London (the focus of the Fish Report) expected that within a few years most special schools would be closed, almost all children would be educated together and segregated schooling would become an historical anomaly. That almost none of this has yet happened is explained by several factors, but is particularly related to the arrival of the National Curriculum and, subsequently, league tables of schools. As league table results and positioning become ever more crucial to the perceived success of a school, so has inclusion become a much less urgent target.

The integration debate of the 1980s became the inclusion debate of the latter years of the twentieth century, as it became clear that only inclusion offered an equitable and socially just aim. Integration too often implies that the person concerned should change in some way in order to become integrated. Others (Clough 1998; Allan 1999; Daniels and Garner 1999; Lunt and Norwich 1999; Slee 1999; Thomas and Vaughan 2004) have considered inclusion in far greater depth than is possible in this chapter.

Prior to the publication of the Fish Report, the 1981 Education Act had led to increasing numbers of young people being considered as having special educational needs at some point during their school career. A figure of 20 per cent of all children, quoted in the Warnock Report (DES 1978), was highly influential in changing attitudes, freeing resources and ensuring that serious attention was paid to the issue. At the time, special schools were educating approximately 2 per cent of the school population; the current figure is 1.1% (DfES 2004: 34). The 20 per cent figure has disappeared from current government policy documents, to be replaced by the more general (although decreased) 'nearly one in six' (DfES 2004: 5).

The mid-1980s was a time of great expectations for those involved in special needs education. The old barriers were to be swept away, young people were to be educated together and mainstream schools would have to become more inclusive. Inclusion, however, was overtaken by events, more particularly by one event: the publication of the 1988 Education Reform Act and all that followed from it. Suddenly, schools and local education authorities were faced with fundamental changes, changes that carried the force of law and the insistent voice of a timetable of implementation, neither of which were true of the 1981 Act.

The early years of this century have seen a further level of attention given to legal frameworks, with the Special Educational Needs and Disability Act (UK 2001) building upon and adding duties to the earlier Disability Discrimination Act (UK 1995). This has led to a resurgence of interest in this area of education, with the issue of the future of special schools, in particular, much discussed during the 2005 General Election.

Withdrawal or in-class support?

Prior to the events of the mid-1980s, the fundamental controversy regarding special needs provision in mainstream schools had been the one that has since reappeared: is it more desirable to educate young people seen as having special needs by withdrawing them from the lessons where they are experiencing difficulty and educating them elsewhere, or should support teachers be provided to enable such young people to learn alongside their more able peers in ordinary schools? The support system approach has much more in common with the aims and beliefs of the 1981 Act than does the practice, formerly widespread, of withdrawing children and educating them in small groups with specialized resources in the care of a teacher whose only role is to work with those children. Implicit in the latter approach is an assumption that children can be categorized. Although the rapid rise in the number of learning support assistants in schools can be welcomed as an indication of a further strengthening of in-class support, the pressure to withdraw is always present, especially in schools where test results are giving cause for concern. The misleadingly-named 'opportunity classes' and 'special classes' of the 1980s may be being recreated in some of the Pupil Referral Units and Exclusion Units of the present day. Although the number of special schools continues to decline, the numbers of pupils placed in them is dropping only slowly. At the same time, influential voices within political circles and elsewhere are beginning to question the validity of inclusion for all, including most surprisingly one of the main advocates for inclusion in the 1980s (Warnock 2005).

Categories of need

Teachers entering the profession in the 1970s would have met terms such as 'mentally handicapped', 'maladjusted' and 'physically handicapped'. These terms, stark though they may seem, replaced others that were even more uncompromising. The British education and health systems have a long history of placing people in categories and, until the turn of the last century, the categories in general use were terms that would today be entirely inappropriate:

- **Idiots** – [P]ersons so deeply defective in mind from birth . . . [as to be] unable to guard themselves against common human dangers . . .
- **Imbeciles** – [M]ental defectiveness not amounting to idiocy . . . incapable of managing themselves or their affairs . . .
- **Feeble-minded** – . . . require care, supervision and control for their own protection . . . permanently incapable of receiving proper benefit from the instruction in ordinary schools . . .
- **Moral imbeciles** – . . . some permanent defect coupled with strong vicious or criminal propensities on which punishment has had little or no effect . . .
- **Acute lunacy** – . . . has been excluded from the definitions.
(adapted from Great Britain 1886)

The categories now in use are based on a belief that special educational need is a product of context rather than an innate state situated within the child. Teachers still talk about categories of need, however, and it may be useful to consider these before discussing the influence of context. The categories of need referred to in the first version of the SEN Code of Practice (DfE 1994), and still widely used by teachers, are:

- learning difficulties
- specific learning difficulties
- emotional and behavioural difficulties
- physical disabilities
- sensory impairment: hearing difficulties
- sensory impairment: visual difficulties
- speech and language difficulties.

The tendency to adopt the labelling of children as a strategy for meeting need has been described by Feiler and Gibson (1999) as one of the four main threats to the inclusive movement (the others being lack of precision in definitions of inclusion, the lack of research evidence and the tendency for some children to be excluded even if they are within the school environment). The 2001 Code takes the process of generalizing and grouping rather further and 'does not assume that there are hard and fast categories of special educational need' (DfES 2001: 85). This echoes the point made above, that an understanding of special educational needs should be focused on the context in which a child is educated rather than on a supposed innate deficit within that child.

Children will have needs and requirements which may fall into at least one of four areas, although many children will have inter-related needs which encompass more than one of these. The impact of these combinations of need on the child's ability to function, learn and succeed should be taken into account. The areas of need identified in the current Code of Practice are:

- communication and interaction
- cognition and learning
- behaviour, emotional and social development
- sensory and/or physical.

(DfES 2001: 85)

The next sections examine each of these four areas in more detail.

Communication and interaction needs

It has become increasingly clear that difficulties with speech and language, if noted early enough in a child's school career, need not be lifelong in duration. Language units have been set up, often in schools, to provide early intervention during a child's first years at school and these have often been remarkably successful. It is unlikely that many secondary teachers will have to deal with this range of needs.

In recent years there has been a large increase in the number of children described as suffering from attention deficit disorder (ADD), sometimes linked to hyperactivity (ADHD). This is an area of controversy in the USA, where many young students have been prescribed drugs to control the behaviour linked to the disorder. Drug therapy has been seen as a last resort in Britain but is now on the increase. The terms ADD and ADHD seem to be gaining acceptance among professionals and many teachers will have children so identified in their classrooms. Criticism of the use of terms such as ADHD tends to be similar to that of dyslexia as a catch-all description, in that the term signifies a model of special educational need as a medical condition for which a cure, or at any rate relief, can be prescribed. Others (Place *et al.* 1999) have argued that ADHD may be a root cause of some of the behaviour difficulties observed in schools.

Cognition and learning needs

By far the largest group of children described as having special educational needs are those with learning difficulties. These difficulties may be minimal, moderate or severe, depending upon the context in which the young person is being taught and the task involved. All teachers will have students with learning difficulties in their classrooms, although it is unlikely that these difficulties will be of a severity that causes the young person involved to be unable to speak or communicate. Children with such needs are still most likely to be found in special schools.

Some children display a range of difficulties with learning that seem at odds with what also appears to be a high level of understanding in other contexts. They are able to learn in other ways very quickly, but reading, writing and spelling in particular appear to give them great difficulty.

Many people have regarded this collection of difficulties as a specific trait and have termed it 'dyslexia'; others resist the notion of one kind of difficulty and prefer to use the general term 'specific learning difficulties'. Whatever the personal perspective on this argument, it is true that some young people do appear to have particular difficulties with language, especially in its non-verbal forms, and teachers need to be adept at dealing with this. It is unfortunate that the many different agencies seeking to support people with dyslexia are not able to agree on the most appropriate action for teachers to take, or even an accepted definition of the term.

Behaviour, emotional and social development needs

Perhaps above all other categories of need, this is the one that is most affected by context. It is also probably the area of need which classroom teachers feel is more difficult to meet within the mainstream classroom than any other. Children can appear to be extremely disruptive, unmotivated or withdrawn, and a whole range of behaviours can be seen as falling within this area. At the present time, many young people whose needs relate to this area are educated separately, often within a school that operates a behavioural management ethos. Government initiatives, particularly Excellence in Cities (DfEE 1999; see also Chapter 10), are seeking to address this issue and to find ways of enabling mainstream schools to meet this range of needs.

Sensory and/or physical needs

The assumption too easily made about physical disability is that children can be included in mainstream provision provided that structural alterations are made to the building. This is too simplistic and fails to take account of the psychological and sociological hurdles that are involved in the successful inclusion of such young people into mainstream schools.

It is often those young people who have hearing difficulties or who are deaf who have the greatest struggle to be included in mainstream education. Where children have developed a confident grasp of signing they are likely to feel much more comfortable talking to others who are similarly bilingual. Talking to a hearing person may involve learning to lip-read and this can be very difficult for some young people. Technology is beginning to offer support in this area and it is likely that speech-to-text hand-held devices, for example, will become available in time.

Some children with visual difficulties have been successfully included in mainstream schools for many years. This may have been achieved through the sensible use of computers and other specially adapted aids, but in many cases a willing teaching force and a well-prepared group of students are the most important factors. Children with colour vision difficulties may not be able to cope with certain colour combinations when reading; with many computer programs this can be amended, but printed materials present insuperable problems. Teachers need to be sensitive to the particular needs of the children in their class and should be given clear advice on this by medical authorities involved with the child.

Children and their needs in context

The issue of context-related need was mentioned earlier and it is this issue that has dominated thinking about SEN in recent years. To reiterate: it is generally accepted that special educational needs arise often from the contexts in which we place children, rather than from the child itself. A child who exhibits signs of emotional and behavioural disturbance in a mainstream school may be entirely calm and at ease in another setting such as a small special school or an off-site unit. A student who is disruptive in science may be a model of good behaviour in English, solely because the teacher involved offers a different context for learning. Factors such as the size of a school, the pressure of being one of such a large student body or a bewildering variety of tasks and directives when joining a new school, can cause special educational needs to become noticed, or cause them to become so important that they cannot be ignored. It follows from this argument that an essential requirement for schools is to produce contexts that do not aggravate or create special educational needs among the student body. This is a task not only for the senior management of the school but also for all staff (teaching and support) and students.

Differentiation – strategies for support

Tasks given to learners should always be capable of differentiation to meet the different needs and capabilities of those students. Chapter 15 of this book covers differentiation in depth but it is appropriate here to pick out the key points as they apply to the topic of special educational needs. In too many cases teachers use the strategy of differentiation by outcome; at its simplest level this means that one task is given to all students so that some of them produce a range of responses while others struggle to produce anything at all.

A more appropriate strategy involves differentiation by task; a careful teacher will allow for a range of tasks to be offered. There are many ways in which this can be done, and the use of a variety of strategies is likely to be more effective than an over-reliance on the same methodology. Some teachers prepare alternative versions of a task, particularly where an activity is based around the use of worksheets. Others may prepare different tasks for different groups in the classroom, although this has the built-in danger of leading to permanent setting within the classroom, which is unlikely to be appropriate (see Chapter 16). Students who find difficulties with one task will not necessarily react in the same way to another; as with special needs in general, the difficulty will be related to the context – in this case, the learning activity – rather than to the learner. It is unrealistic to expect that teachers will always be able to provide a differentiated range of activities, but it should be the aim of a good teacher to do so whenever possible and as often as possible.

The SEN Code of Practice

Following a wide-ranging consultation exercise, a Special Educational Needs Code of Practice (DfE 1994) was introduced and followed by all schools and teachers. It was then updated and superseded in late 2001 by a revised version, in which the importance of context-created need was underlined through a change in the sections of the Code. It is useful to consider here the fundamental principles quoted in the Code of Practice as these underpin the proposals it contains:

• a child with special educational needs should have their needs met
• the special educational needs of children will normally be met in mainstream schools or settings
• the views of the child should be sought and taken into account
• parents have a vital role to play in supporting their children's education
• children with special educational needs should be offered full access to a broad, balanced and relevant education, including an appropriate Curriculum for the Foundation stage and the National Curriculum.

(DfES 2001: 7)

The Code of Practice recommends a two-stage process of identification of special educational needs by schools and teachers, a reduction from the previous five stages in the 1994 Code. The proposed reduction was suggested in the hope that it would streamline the process of needs identification and avoid some of the delays inherent in the previous system.

Subject teachers have a particular role in the first of these stages, as the code indicates that one of the triggers for *School Action*, the first phase, could be concern expressed by a teacher that a student is not making progress (DfES 2001: 68–9). This suggests that not only should subject teachers be sensitive to such situations as they arise, but that they should share their concerns with others and be ready to make the necessary evidence available that will demonstrate the nature of the difficulty.

If a particular student seems to be experiencing difficulties and is not known to have special educational needs, it is the responsibility of that child's subject teachers to spot the difficulty, contact the special educational needs co-ordinator (SENCO) and attempt to describe the nature of the needs that have been noted. Following their consultations with the SENCO, subject teachers then need to take the action agreed, and this may form part of the written IEP (individual education plan) for that student. It may be that a change as simple as a move to a different part of the classroom has been suggested, or that the teacher should speak more clearly and face the child concerned. This can lead to a dramatic improvement in communication where a child with a hearing difficulty is concerned. The SENCO may wish to attend a lesson in order to make an informal assessment of the situation prior to any formal process that the school may have developed.

A particular focus during the school action phase of identifying special needs is the collection of information and evidence. This process will be extremely valuable if it is necessary to progress to the second phase, *School Action Plus*. Here, the main responsibility for action lies with the SENCO, although it is essential that the subject teacher gives enthusiastic support and co-operation, without which there is little hope of improving the situation. The school may decide to provide support in the form of technology, a support teacher or an assistant, if these are available. The job of the learning support assistant is made much easier when subject teachers keep them fully informed about the work in hand and offer to assist them in devising suitable activities. It may be that, following this process of gathering information, the school decides to seek outside assistance and to consider the need for a statement of special educational needs, but this will not always be the case.

SEN statements were an outcome of the 1994 Code of Practice and have become widely used, although there has been criticism of the number of statements written, the length of time taken to prepare them and the differing patterns of statementing in various local education authorities (LEAs). The revised code contains clear expectations that statements in future will be much fewer in number and will be in place for shorter periods of time, although only limited progress has been made in this area to date.

Information and communication technology and SEN

The 1994 Code of Practice highlighted the ways in which information technology could assist schools and students in the meeting of special educational needs. IT in this case usually meant computers and the various pieces of hardware that could be attached to them. The 2001 Code of Practice is much less specific in this area but includes a number of general statements implying the use of information and communications technology (ICT), as it is now generally described, and there is a growing literature in this area (Blamires 1999; McKeown 2000; Abbott 2002; Florian and Hegarty 2004).

Children with learning difficulties, for example, can use overlay keyboards or onscreen keyboards to access an activity that for other students involves the use of a standard keyboard. An overlay keyboard is a device on which paper sheets containing words or pictures are placed. Pressing on the words or pictures sends commands to the computer, since the overlay has an associated file containing the instructions devised by the teacher. Many teachers also use overlay keyboards to speed up the writing process for learners whose writing is slowly and laboriously produced. In a science lesson, for example, some teachers might use overlays that create the phrases and concepts frequently included when writing up an experiment. Pressing on the area concerned will cause these to be written to the screen, and the student can then concentrate on the novel parts of the activity.

There has been a rapid increase in recent years in the use of graphical symbols by people with learning disabilities (Abbott 2000; Detheridge and Detheridge 2002). Initially, the aim of this use was predominantly communication, but as the software has become more sophisticated, real progress has been made in giving non-text readers access to literacy through symbols (Abbott, Detheridge and Detheridge 2006) and much more detailed research has now been completed into the nature of current symbol use (Abbott and Lucey 2005).

Children with visual difficulties may be helped by magnification software, or by the use of other magnification technology to deal with printed material. Such devices are very portable and make it possible for a student with a visual difficulty to be placed on an equal footing with others. Screen readers can offer access to a wide range of information sources including the Internet, and web browsers can easily be set to display text in large formats.

Children with hearing difficulties sometimes communicate using email, and the rapid increase in the number of schools with Internet access continues to open up the range of possibilities. Children who become very ill and have to spend long periods in hospital or at home can keep in touch with their schools through email, and be set homework in this way too. Many children are therefore able to keep up with their exam coursework, and the ready availability of computers may result in a vastly improved amount of work being done during a period as an inpatient than was previously the case.

There are some difficulties, though, that arise from the use of a computer itself, and these can be a source of stress or frustration. This is often the case when a child has a slight loss of fine motor control and finds that the mouse is very difficult to control. In such cases, it is possible to substitute a trackerball, sometimes described as an upside-down mouse, which enables the two mouse actions of clicking and moving to be separated rather than having to be done simultaneously. More importantly, the trackerball itself remains stationary – the movement being controlled by the large ball on top.

Many other devices can be substituted for a mouse, and children with physical disabilities are then able to use head switches, puff switches (controlled by blowing) or even control the computer with eye movements. Where the degree of difficulty is not so great, the perceptive teacher will use the inbuilt control facilities of the software to alter the mouse tracking speed and rate at which double clicks must be made. Such small changes, which take only a few seconds and are reversible for the next user, can transform a frustrated learner into one who is able to become increasingly confident.

Although all these uses of ICT, and many others, have always been explored by inventive teachers in enlightened classrooms and schools, the impetus has sometimes come from outside agencies. This support can no longer be relied upon, as the major change in this area since the Code of Practice came into being has been the requirement that schools investigate the use of ICT for a particular need before outside experts are called in. This means that all teachers, but special educational needs co-ordinators in particular, must become familiar with the different ways in which ICT, which may not only mean computers, can offer support. It is to the SENCO that a teacher should turn if advice is needed about meeting a particular need, or if a teacher has concerns of any kind about the progress or lack of it made by particular students.

Concluding comments

The two concepts that teachers should bear in mind with regard to SEN are context and differentiation. Teachers must be able to plan activities that can be offered in a range of different forms so as to provide a learning context that will meet the needs of all the students in their classes. They need to be perceptive observers of students, noticing where they have difficulties, and attempting to record and describe those situations so that, in consultation with colleagues, they can attempt to improve the situation. Where difficulties are obvious, they must not focus on why the student cannot do something, but on whether the learning environment provided is appropriate for that student's needs. Some aspects of the environment may be outside their control, but important factors such as their attitude, the provision of differentiated work and their awareness of student reaction, may not.

Inclusive education should not just be a worthy aim or a statement of policy, but a goal towards which teachers, parents and other agencies are striving. The LA, in particular, has an important role to play, and it has been shown that inclusive practices must become a 'corporate priority which is reflected in global targets within the LEA' (Ainscow *et al.* 1999: 137). It will never be easy to make an education system inclusive but it will always be indefensible to accept that it should be otherwise. Inclusion 'trips easily off the tongue but can be without meaning or substance' (Wade 1999: 81) but this must be avoided if education is to be a benefit which is truly available to all: a bridge and not a barrier.

References

Abbott, C. (ed.) (2000) *Symbols Now*. Leamington Spa: Widgit.

Abbott, C. (ed.) (2002) *Special Educational Needs and the Internet: Issues in Inclusive Education*. London: RoutledgeFalmer.

Abbott, C., Detheridge, T. and Detheridge, C. (2006) *Symbols, Literacy and Social Justice*. Leamington: Widgit.

Abbott, C. and Lucey, H. (2005) Symbol communication in special schools in England: the current position and some key issues, *British Journal of Special Education*, 32(4): 196–201.

Ainscow, M., Farrell, P., Tweddle, D. and Malki, G. (1999) The role of LEAs in developing inclusive policies and practices, *British Journal of Special Education*, 26(3): 136–40.

Allan, J. (1999) *Actively Seeking Inclusion*. London: Falmer Press.

Billington, T. (2000). *Separating, Losing and Excluding Children: Narratives of Difference*. London: RoutledgeFalmer.

Blamires, M. (ed.) (1999) *Enabling Technology for Inclusion*. London: Paul Chapman.

Clough, P. (ed.) (1998) *Managing Inclusive Education: from Policy to Experience*. London: Paul Chapman.

Committee to Review Special Educational Provision (1985) *Educational Opportunities For All: Report of the Committee Reviewing Provision to Meet Special Educational Needs* (The Fish Report). London: Inner London Education Authority.

Cowne, E. (2003) *The SENCO Handbook: Working within a Whole-School Approach* (4th edn). London: David Fulton Publishers.

Daniels, H. and Garner, P. (eds) (1999) *Inclusive Education (World Yearbook of Education 1999)*. London: Kogan Page.

Department for Education (DfE) (1994) *Code of Practice on the Identification and Assessment of Special Educational Needs*. London: DfE.

Department for Education and Employment (DfEE) (1999) *Excellence in Cities*. Nottingham: DfEE.

Department for Education and Employment (DfEE) (2001) *SEN Code of Practice on the Identification and Assessment of Pupils with Special Educational Needs*. London: DfES.

Department of Education and Science (DES) (1978) *Special Educational Needs: Report of the Committee of Enquiry into the Education of Handicapped Children and Young People* (The Warnock Report). London: HMSO.

Department of Education and Science (DES) (1981) *Education for All*. London: HMSO.

Detheridge, M. and Detheridge, T. (2002) *Literacy Through Symbols: Improving Access for Children and Adults* (2nd edn). London: David Fulton Publishers.

DfES (2003) *Every Child Matters*. London: Stationery Office.

DfES (2004) *Removing Barriers to Achievement: The Government's Strategy for SEN*. London: Stationery Office.

Great Britain (1886) *Classification of Defectives Under the Mental Deficiency, Lunacy, Idiots and Education Acts*. London: HMSO.

Feiler, A. and Gibson, H. (1999) Threats to the inclusive movement, *British Journal of Special Education*, 26(3): 147–52.

Florian, L. and Hegarty, J. (eds) (2004) *ICT and Special Educational Needs: A Tool for Inclusion*. Maidenhead: Open University Press.

Lunt, I. and Norwich, B. (1999) *Can Effective Schools be Inclusive Schools?* London: Institute of Education.

McKeown, S. (2000) *Unlocking Potential: How ICT Can Support Children with Special Educational Needs*. Birmingham: The Questions Publishing Company Ltd.

Place, M., Wilson, J., Martin, E. and Hulsmeier, J. (1999) Attention Deficit Disorder as a factor in the origin of behavioural disturbance in schools, *British Journal of Special Education*, 26(3): 158–63.

Slee, R. (1999) *The inclusive school*. London: Falmer Press.

Spooner, W. (2006) *The SEN Handbook for Trainee Teachers, NQTs and Teaching Assistants*. London: David Fulton Publishers.

Thomas, G. and Vaughan, M. (eds) (2004) *Inclusive Education: readings and reflections*. Maidenhead: Open University Press.

United Kingdom (UK) (1995) *Disability Discrimination Act*. London: Stationery Office.

United Kingdom (UK) (2001) *Special Educational Needs and Disability Act*. London: Stationery Office.

Wade, J. (1999) Including all learners: QCA's approach, *British Journal of Special Education*, 26(2): 80–3.

Warnock, M. (2005) *Special Educational Needs: a New Look*. London: Philosophy of Education Society of Great Britain.

19

English as an Additional Language: challenges of language and identity in the multilingual and multi-ethnic classroom

Roxy Harris and Constant Leung

The demographic context

Becoming a teacher in contemporary Britain means developing effective practice with regard to pupils who come from ethnic and linguistic minority families. According to statistics produced by the Office for National Statistics for the DfES, in 2004, approximately 17 per cent of pupils in Primary and Secondary Schools in England were described as belonging to minority ethnic groups with roughly 11 per cent of those in primary schools and 9 per cent in secondary schools said to use English as an Additional Language (EAL) (TSO 2004). These figures, though, need to be treated with some caution since they contain certain inadequacies which will be examined later. However, we will first look at the way the broad figures disguise striking regional variations. To quote directly from other statistical analyses utilized by the DfES:

> According to the Pupil Level Annual School Census (PLASC) the proportion of minority ethnic pupils varies across England in maintained schools from 4 per cent of the school aged population of the North East to nearly three quarters of the school aged population of Inner London (of whom 17 per cent are Black African; 12 per cent Black Caribbean; 11 per cent Bangladeshi; 9 per cent Any other White background; 8 per cent Mixed Heritage background). The range by Local Education Authority (LEA) [shows] that the school aged minority ethnic population ranges (maintained schools) from 1.5 per cent of East Riding of Yorkshire LEA to 84 per cent of Hackney LEA. London has a high

proportion of England's minority ethnic pupils compared to other areas. Nineteen per cent of England's minority ethnic pupils go to school in an Inner London LEA compared to four per cent of White British pupils; 44 per cent of minority ethnic pupils attend schools in either an Inner or Outer London LEA compared to eight per cent of White British pupils.

(DfES 2005(a): 3–4)

This regional variation in relation to ethnicity is matched by comparable differences with respect to the figures for English as an Additional Language. For instance in primary schools pupils with EAL vary in proportion in the following way – North East (3.3%), North West (7.4%), Yorkshire and Humber (9.5%), East Midlands (6.9%), West Midlands (13.4%), East of England (5.2%), Inner London (50.2%), Outer London (27.9%), South East (5.2%), South West (2%). When it comes to secondary schools the variation is as follows – North East (2.2%), North West (5.2%), Yorkshire and Humber (7.3%), East Midlands (6.3%), West Midlands (10.4%), East of England (4.4%), Inner London (45.3%), Outer London (25.7%), South East (4.8%), South West (1.6%) (TSO 2004).

Once teachers have developed an awareness of the demographic picture they should begin to seek out information that will build a more specific local awareness. For instance, a study of the languages of London's school-children (Baker and Eversley 2000: 5) states that in Greater London the range of home languages spans more than 350 language names, with English dominant at 67.86 per cent of the 850,000 schoolchildren surveyed. Of the remaining third, the 'top ten' are Bengali and Sylheti, Punjabi, Gujarati, Hindi/Urdu, Turkish, Arabic, English-based Creoles, Yoruba, Somali and Cantonese. Again, these global figures do not reveal the particularly heavy weightings of languages, other than English, in specific London local education authority areas such as Brent (Gujarati 23.85 per cent), the City of London (Bengali and Sylheti 56.37 per cent), Ealing (Punjabi 20.12 per cent), and Tower Hamlets (Bengali and Sylheti 53.81 per cent) (ibid.:12). Of course teachers, after analysing these figures, should then go on to develop a progressively finer awareness of what the proportions might be both for their particular school and their particular class-room. This task will be assisted by the acquisition of some background knowledge and understanding of the historical context within which the issue of pupils for whom English is an Additional Language has become nationally important.

The historical context

The EAL issue became an important one in the education system in England as a result of the inward migrations and settlement of peoples and languages since 1945, particularly in the 1950s, 1960s and 1970s. Martin-Jones (1989) usefully characterizes these migrations as principally of people entering Britain as either migrant workers or as refugees. At the same time, she sees a significant divide between those entering from other parts of

Europe and those from former colonies and Third World nations. It has been the languages of people from these latter nations which have had the greatest impact on EAL policy and practice in Britain. We are speaking here of people who migrated to Britain in relatively large numbers from India, Pakistan, Bangladesh, the Caribbean, Hong Kong, East Africa (principally Kenya, Tanzania and Uganda), West Africa (mainly Nigeria and Ghana), Vietnam, Ethiopia and Eritrea, Somalia and Cyprus (see Peach 1996) and brought with them languages such as Punjabi, Urdu, Gujarati, Hindi, Bengali and Sylheti, Cantonese and Hakka Chinese, Caribbean Creoles, Yoruba, Twi, Cypriot Greek and Turkish, Kurdish, Tigrinya, Amharic and Somali (see ILEA 1989; Alladina and Edwards 1991).

Unfortunately, the entrance into the UK of migrants from former colonies and so-called developing countries was accompanied by a considerable amount of racial hostility and contempt for their languages. This led, in earlier years, to an official assimilationist approach (Department of Education and Science 1971), based on the idea that schools should set about erasing the languages and cultural practices of the children of new migrants as a precondition for their educational success. This position was later modified following the Bullock Report (1975: 286), which stated that:

> No child should be expected to cast off the language and culture of the home as he (sic) crosses the school threshold (and) ... the school should adopt positive attitudes to its pupils' bilingualism and wherever possible should help maintain and deepen their knowledge of their mother tongues.

Despite this declaration, the Bullock Report did not indicate how schools were to give practical expression to this aspiration. A decade later another official report, the Swann Report (1985), while reaffirming a positive attitude, in general terms, to the home and community languages of ethnic minority pupils, firmly ruled out any role for what it described as the 'mainstream' school in relating these languages to the learning process and the official curriculum:

> We find we cannot support the arguments put forward for the introduction of programmes of bilingual education in maintained schools in this country. Similarly we would regard mother tongue maintenance, although an important educational function, as best achieved within the ethnic minority communities themselves rather than within mainstream schools.
>
> (Swann Report 1985: 406)

However, one principle upon which the Swann Report insisted, was that ethnic minority pupils for whom English was an Additional Language should at all times be educated in the mainstream classroom alongside their peers to avoid segregated provision and to guarantee equal access to the curriculum. In recent years the profile of pupils with EAL has changed rapidly, for instance as a result of the arrival of new migrant populations from Eastern Europe and elsewhere stimulated by major global economic and military upheavals. (For a fuller treatment of historical developments relevant to EAL, see Rampton *et al.* 2001.) In the contemporary educational system in this country, access to the curriculum means access to the National Curriculum. It is to the relationship between English as an Additional Language and the National Curriculum that we now turn.

English as an Additional/Second Language (EAL/ESL) and the National Curriculum

Many of the ethnic minority pupils whom we have described so far are in the process of learning to use English for both social and academic purposes. At present, with the possible exception of some short-term English language induction courses, all pupils with EAL are expected to follow the National Curriculum (CRE 1986; NCC 1991; SCAA 1996; DfES, 2002 (a), 2005 (b)).[1] This means that additional language learning opportunities, particularly for academic purposes, are to be provided in mainstream classes or subject lessons. Hence, 'the teaching of English is the responsibility of all teachers' (SCAA 1996: 2).

Within the National Curriculum, EAL, unlike English or science, is not regarded as a discipline in its own right; therefore, there is no dedicated curriculum specification for it. EAL is seen as a pupil phenomenon with implications for teaching and learning. At the same time, for all intents and purposes, the curriculum specifications and assessment criteria for (the National Curriculum subject) English are used for both mother tongue English speaking pupils and those who are still in the process of learning EAL.[2] It is emphasized that the programme of studies for Key Stages 1–4 should be used to develop all aspects of EAL pupils' English. Official English curriculum documents also advise teachers that they should 'plan learning opportunities to help pupils develop their English and should aim to provide the support pupils need to take part in all subject areas' (DfES and QCA, 1999: 49).

[1] For a detailed discussion of the development of this approach to EAL, see Mohan *et al.* (2001); suffice it to say at this point that a number of official documents have argued for the mainstreaming of EAL provision. For instance, in a landmark investigation into the EAL provision and practice of the Calderdale education authority, the CRE (1986) found the practice of providing separate non-mainstream schooling for pupils with EAL to be racially discriminating and contrary to 'the prevailing educational view' (p. 6) and recommended that 'provision for second language speakers is made in conjunction with mainstream education . . .' (p. 16). The term EAL itself is of relatively new coinage; previously it was referred to as ESL (English as a Second Language). Indeed in other parts of the English-speaking world, the term ESL is still preferred. For some the notion of an 'additional' language is generally held to be ideologically more positive than 'second' language, which might encourage a deficit view of pupils' linguistic repertoire. For this reason, sometimes pupils with EAL are also referred to as bilingual pupils. Also see relevant parts of the Swann Report (1985) and Bullock Report (1975).
[2] For details of pre-Level 1 and adapted Level 1 EAL assessment descriptors see QCA (2000).

A glimpse of professional reality

In order to understand how EAL provision is organized in schools it is important to know something about funding and staffing in schools. EAL provision is non-mandatory (unlike subjects such as English and mathematics). Since 1966, EAL funding came from a special grant. Up until the late 1990s this grant was commonly known as Section 11, earmarked 'to support the cost of employing additional staff to help minority ethnic groups overcome linguistic and other barriers which inhibit their access to, and take up of, mainstream services' (Ofsted 1994: 1). Since 1998 the monies have been administered under a DfEE/DfES grant scheme, currently known as Ethnic Minority Achievement Grant (EMAG). This grant is time limited, often two or three years at a time. The actual amount of funds available to a school, via the local education authority, can vary from one grant period to another depending on the total size of grant and competing demands from other schools. A vast majority of EAL teachers, often referred to as language support teachers, are employed through this funding.

Although since the 1960s this grant has been regularly renewed, the time-limited nature has meant instability for schools in terms of even medium-term curriculum response, and for individual EAL staff in terms of their career and professional development. The shortage of funds has also meant that, generally, EAL staff are very thin on the ground.[3]

Given that EAL is not a curriculum discipline with its own programme of study and timetable slots, EAL teachers are expected to work alongside their mainstream colleagues in the classroom and in the school, in a variety of ways. Broadly speaking, the roles EAL teachers are expected to play include the following:

- as a classroom teacher, working in partnership with class or subject teachers, with a special regard for EAL development within the context of the school curriculum
- as a curriculum adviser and developer to promote a more inclusive and whole-curriculum planning approach to responding to the needs of pupils with EAL
- as a day-to-day adviser and in-service professional development provider to other colleagues on EAL matters
- as a liaison person, particularly applying to those EAL teachers who are speakers of a community language such as Turkish and Urdu, with minority parents and community organizations (for a fuller account, see Bourne and McPake 1991).

The extent to which any individual EAL teacher can contribute to the above roles depends on a number of individual and school circumstances. Professional experience has shown that, given the shortage, EAL teachers can only meet some of the teaching and curriculum development demands in school. Many class or subject teachers working in classrooms with a

---

[3] In one official press release it was reported that 'the proportion of specialist staff with appropriate qualifications is now as low as 3 per cent in some LEAs' (Ofsted 2002).

high number of EAL pupils receive no assistance from EAL specialists. It is therefore important for all teachers to have some knowledge about some of the key concepts and principles which have been influential in shaping EAL teachers' classroom strategies. A knowledge of these principles may enable non-EAL teachers to begin to understand the teaching and learning issues involved.

Pedagogic principles and classroom strategies

Earlier we pointed out that EAL is a cross-curricular teaching concern. Within this cross-curricular perspective two linked pedagogical principles have been applied in the professional literature:

First, making learning activities and tasks personally meaningful and understandable by encouraging children to use their own knowledge to solving group problems, and providing timely 'support that might be needed by individual children to acquire curriculum concepts and the language needed to express them' (Bourne 1989: 64).

Translated into lesson planning, two questions should be asked:

- Do I plan clearly defined and staged tasks which are purposeful, practical and geared towards the pupil's experience?
- Do I plan for collaborative work with visual and contextual support?

(Travers 1999: 7)

(See Chapter 3 in Edwards and Redfern 1992 for a more detailed discussion.)

Second, using learning activities which encourage active engagement; it is generally held that pupils':

second language skills develop well when . . . they have opportunities to model the second language used by peers in small group collabora-tive activities, where talk and interaction are central to the learning going on . . .

(Hampshire County Council 1996: 2)

These principles are broadly consistent with a constructivist view of education which puts a great deal of premium on hands-on experiential learning. They also require the teacher to have a very clear understanding of at least two language development issues in the classroom context:

- the link between curriculum knowledge and the language used to express that knowledge
- the link between spoken and written English (and other languages) used for interaction in the classroom, including teacher talk and teacher writing, and the development of spoken and written English for assignments, assessments and tests in different subject or curriculum areas.

In the actual classroom EAL (and class/subject) teachers have to interpret these broad principles with reference to their EAL learners who may be at different stages of English language development. In general terms, they are concerned with providing, at least, the following three elements.

Contextual support using physical movements/actions, visual/audio material and realia

Unfamiliar concepts and complex ideas can often be made more comprehensible by using pictures, diagrams and visual and other sensory representations. For instance, the central ideas in the topic of paper making may be visually supported by a series of pictures or drawings showing the process involving tree logging, making pulp and so on. Even ephemeral and often domain-specific concepts such as cynicism and sarcasm in a particular narrative context may be exemplified by drama activities. In many ways the value of this kind of contextual support is quite well understood. An important issue here is not to assume that contextual support of this kind can be understood by all pupils. It is possible that sometimes even the most obvious picture, to the teacher, may not make any sense to some pupils. For some very young pupils, the picture of an inkwell or the image of a vinyl record, may mean very little. The usefulness of any contextualization material and activity has to be constantly evaluated in relation to the pupils involved. A further issue is that while contextual support may lead to a degree of understanding, this understanding of the content meaning does not automatically mean understanding or even being aware of the associated language.

Opportunities for language development by teaching and modelling language in context

Cummins' (1992) distinction between basic interpersonal communication skills (BICS) and cognitive academic language proficiency (CALP) has been useful in helping teachers see how to analyse language demands for their pupils. A teacher asking pupils to choose a colour by holding up a colour chart is a classroom example of BICS. From EAL pupils' point of view, even if they do not understand the question or the names of the colours, the immediate meaning of the activity can be worked out by observing others. The physical context of the activity and the active engagement in the activity (by having to choose a colour) can provide an opportunity for highly focused language modelling by the teacher, and conscious noticing and active use by the pupil. The value of this observation can be made more obvious if we picture a different scenario – this time the teacher asks the same question but without holding up the colour chart. This kind of use of highly contextualized language supported by visual and other materials can be helpful for pupils at all stages of developing listening, speaking, reading and writing in EAL, but its benefits are immediately obvious to those teachers who are working with pupils at an early stage of learning English.

Opportunities to move from the here-and-now language to
academic genres

Meaning in speech in social situations can be interactionally built up.
Imagine the following:

Pupil 1: What are we doing?
Pupil 2: Miss said we have to write down what we said.
Pupil 3: Like what we did on Monday.
Pupil 1: What, like we write down the things we made up?

Classroom conversations, even when they are curriculum-related, are full
of examples of this kind of joint focus forming and meaning making. This is
indeed one of the main characteristics of everyday spoken language.
Furthermore, spoken language is often informal in that it is not necessarily
made up of well-formed sentences; the phrase or the clause is more likely to
be the unit of utterances (Kress 1994). Spoken language in social situations
also tends to use lots of referring and pointing words such as '*it*', '*this*', '*here*'
and '*there*', for example, '*I think it's 20 degrees here and that's 40 degrees*' when
a pupil tries to estimate the temperatures of different substances as part of a
science activity. Some of these characteristics of everyday spoken language
are not found in formal academic English. The ability to read and write
effectively in an academic style cannot be assumed, even when a pupil
appears to be able to handle here-and-now spoken English, and can
read and produce some everyday texts such as simple stories and factual
accounts.

The ability to read and understand academic texts, especially in the
senior years of schooling, requires more than a knowledge of curriculum-
related vocabulary and grammar (which is already quite a challenge for
some pupils with EAL anyway). Pupils have to develop a knowledge of text
types or genres. That is, they need to know something about the conventionally established ways of selecting and structuring information in
specific formats for different purposes (for example, a narrative, instructions for games, a letter of complaint, a technical report), and the specific
features of language expression involved (for example, the use of slang in a
play dialogue or technical terms in a report). Furthermore, pupils need to be
able to go beyond the literal meaning. Some texts, and not just literary
texts, cannot be fully appreciated without an ability to understand and
decipher humour, cynicism, sarcasm, irony and other culturally supported
meanings. In face-to-face situations some of these implied meanings may
also be signalled by physical actions, contextual clues and facial expressions
which can assist interpretation.

Some of the knowledge and skills involved in the process of writing are
sometimes 'hidden', so to speak; only the outcomes are visible. In the
school, curriculum writing tasks tend to be about representing ideas or
describing events (for example, telling a story or reporting on the results of
an experiment.) The purpose of a great deal of writing in school is to show
that one can communicate one's ideas and thoughts without the benefit of
either contextual support or immediate contributions and feedback from
others (as in a conversation). This involves pupils drawing on their existing
knowledge and expertise to package ideas and produce a piece of text by

themselves. This is a complex process. Beyond the level of knowing vocabulary, learning to write involves:

- using different types of phrases and sentences to represent ideas
- organizing sentences into sequences and sections (paragraphs)
- selecting, organizing and presenting information and ideas in conventionally recognizable ways.

Gibbons (1998: 101) provides a highly illuminating example of how language features change as pupils move from group talk to individual writing:

> Text 1: (spoken by three 10-year-old students and accompanying action)
> this . . . no it doesn't go . . . it doesn't move . . .
> try that . . .
> yes it does . . . a bit . . . that won't . . .
> won't work it's not metal . . .
> these are the best . . . going really fast.

> Text 2: (spoken by one student about the action, after the event)
> We tried a pin . . . a pencil sharpener . . . some iron filings . . . the magnet didn't attract the pin . . .

> Text 3: (written by the same student)
> Our experiment was to find out what a magnet attracted. We discovered that a magnet attracts some kinds of metal. It attracted the iron filings, but not the pin . . .

The above discussion shows that a great deal of the academic use of written English in school is different from classroom spoken English in a number of ways; some of the differences are related to vocabulary and grammatical choice; some are concerned with information structuring; and others are related to the properties and constraints of the different modes of language. These differences often reflect the different purposes served by spoken and written language in different contexts. Thus harnessing the knowledge and understanding achieved through classroom activities mediated by the spoken language provides a mere starting point (for a fuller discussion on developing reading and writing in EAL, see Leung 2001; for a further discussion on EAL provision see Leung, 2005).

Concluding comments

In educational practice, questions concerning EAL are inextricably connected to questions of ethnicity, which themselves are far from simple. Earlier a reference was made to the need to treat collected figures for the number of ethnic minority pupils in the school system in England with caution. Some years ago the then DfEE identified a particular problem in this area. In the first place, according to the DfEE (1995: 1), 'There are serious weaknesses with the quality and usefulness of data provided by the current Ethnic Monitoring Survey.' One immediate problem was that as far as ethnic origin was concerned 'there is a significant proportion of pupils shown in the unclassified category' (ibid.:2). The ethnic origin of 35.9 per cent of pupils was left as unclassified because either the parent or the school failed to complete the survey. It is possible to argue that this failure reflected an ideological objection to supplying the requested information. However, a more likely explanation is that it has become increasingly difficult to fit real pupils in real schools into neat, tidy and discrete ethnic categories. The complexities involved were fully reflected in a number of commentaries following the 1991 UK Census. For instance, there was the fact that among ethnic minority males aged 16 to 34, 40 per cent of those designated as Black-Caribbean, 7 per cent of Indians, 6.2 per cent of Pakistanis, 16 per cent of Chinese, 18 per cent of Other-Asian, 19.2 per cent of Black-African and 60 per cent of Black-Other are 'currently living with a white partner' (Berrington 1996: 199–200). Furthermore, as Peach (1996: 24) states:

> A significant proportion of the ethnic minority population is derived from mixed unions and new ethnic identities are being forged which will be increasingly difficult to capture within the existing census categories . . . Indeed, one of the lessons to be derived from the 1991 Census, is that new ethnicities are emerging in Britain.

Later, we will examine this question of new ethnicities a little more, but first it is necessary to look at the second reason for exercising caution concerning figures on the ethnic origins of pupils. In the DfEE's 1999 collected figures, the ethnic group categories used are as follows: White, Black Caribbean Heritage, Black African Heritage, Black Other, Indian, Pakistani, Bangladeshi, Chinese, Any Other Minority Ethnic Group. The inadequate nature of these categories lies in the way that the different labels appear to be trying to measure different things. There is a colour category – White, Black Caribbean Heritage, Black African Heritage, Black Other. There is a nationality category – Pakistani, Bangladeshi. There is also an ethnic category – Indian, Chinese.[4] In addition, there are the problems associated with what the catch-all category 'White' hides and oversimplifies. Finally, there is no guidance as to what the practising teacher is to do with the category of apparently unclassified pupils represented by labels such as Black Other, or Any Other Minority Ethnic Group. In recognition of these problems, the DfES issued further guidance on more nuanced ways of collecting ethnicity data in schools following refinements introduced in the UK National Census in 2001 (DfES 2002(b)); and although the census did not contain a language question, schools have now also been given advice on the collection of language data (DfES 2006).

For anyone becoming a teacher there is a need to find ways of thinking about these issues which have some practical utility for day-to-day interactions with pupils. There are a number of central problems that require attention. First of all, schools and teachers have experienced some difficulty

---

[4] Although Indian and Chinese could also indicate nationality referring to India and mainland China, in British educational discourse they are just as likely to be ethnic markers referring to a wide variety of people of Indian or Chinese extraction including, say, those from East Africa or Hong Kong and Vietnam respectively.

in accommodating the idea that pupils belonging to 'visible' minority groups are members of ethnic formations which far from being fixed, stable, homogeneous and comfortably knowable, are instead complex, fluid and heterogeneous. Secondly, there has been a difficulty in envisioning these ethnic minority pupils as cultural and linguistic insiders rather than permanent outsiders in the UK. Thirdly, many schools and teachers have struggled to see how these pupils might be at one and the same time aligned to *both* UK/English/British ethnic identities *and* those associated with other global locations. Some help is available in the work of theorists operating generally in the field of what has come to be known as British Cultural Studies. Space does not permit a full exploration here of the ideas involved, but it is worth mentioning briefly a number of concepts which may be useful. Gilroy (1987) depicts the refusal to allow for change and variation in representations of broader British and minority ethnic identities as ethnic absolutism. Hall (1988) suggests that minority individuals, rather than seeking to preserve their ethnic identities unchanged, are actively and continuously engaged in a process of creating new ethnicities. Mercer (1994), amongst others, sees significant numbers of young members of UK-based 'visible' minority groups as being intimately connected *both* with the everyday mores of their UK locations *and* wider, African, Caribbean and Asian derived diasporas. Hall provides a useful summary of the general position being described here when he identifies the concept of translation which:

> describes those identity formations which cut across and intersect natural frontiers, and which are composed of people who have been *dispersed* forever from their homelands. Such people retain strong links with their places of origin and their traditions, but they are without the illusion of a return to the past. They are obliged to come to terms with the new cultures they inhabit, without simply assimilating to them and losing their identities completely. They bear upon them the traces of the particular cultures, traditions, languages and histories by which they were shaped. The difference is that they are not and will never be *unified* in the old sense, because they are irrevocably the product of several interlocking histories and cultures, belong at one and the same time to several 'homes' (and to no one particular 'home'). People belonging to such *cultures of hybridity* have had to renounce the dream or ambition of rediscovering any kind of 'lost' cultural purity, or ethnic absolutism. They are irrevocably *translated* . . . They are the products of the new *diasporas* created by the post-colonial migrations. They must learn to inhabit at least two identities, to speak two cultural languages, to translate and negotiate between them. Cultures of hybridity are one of the distinctly novel types of identity produced in the era of late-modernity, and there are more and more examples of them to be discovered.

(Hall 1992: 310)

To put it briefly, the essential point for new teachers to grasp is that the majority of young ethnic minority pupils in England are daily engaged in the active construction of what Back (1996) terms 'new forms of working class Englishness'. Harris (2006) offers a detailed treatment of one example of this phenomenon. There are specific linguistic consequences of relevance to classroom teachers. More precisely, one of the factors with which any teacher needs to come to terms, is that there are two aspects of the actual patterns of language use of many pupils for whom English is an Additional Language, which are little commented upon:

- Many such pupils with EAL are more linguistically comfortable with a local urban spoken English vernacular rather than with an ethnic minority 'community' language which they might encounter in family contexts (see Leung *et al.* 1997; Harris 1997, 1999, for examples of this phenomenon).
- Even where these pupils begin their school careers in England with very limited English language proficiency, their entry to English tends to be connected with a local urban spoken vernacular English, learned informally, rather than with the spoken or written Standard English associated with the formal aspects of the school curriculum.

Hewitt made a number of perceptive observations on the significant ways in which urban youth, in their routine language use, participate in the 'destabilisation of ethnicity' (1991: 27). He suggested that an important but often overlooked part of their language use is what he describes as a 'local multi-ethnic vernacular' or a 'community English'. This language use is 'the primary medium of communication in the adolescent peer group in multi-ethnic areas' (ibid.: 32). For Hewitt (1995: 97) the sources of this language use are diasporic and global as well as local, and contribute to:

the obliteration of pure language forms deriving from a single cultural source, evident in some inner city areas (in the UK) and ... the diasporic distribution of communicative forms which, whilst generated from and based in local communities, nevertheless reach out and extend lines of connection in a global way. The local penetration and mixing of language forms evident in some urban settings in the UK should, in fact, be seen perhaps as a reflex of the broader linguistic diasporic processes.

The view of reality sketched by Hewitt tends not to have been shared by very many schools and teachers in England, who have preferred to project onto pupils with EAL what Harris (1997) has called a Romantic Bilingualism, referring to:

... the widespread practice, in British schools and other educational contexts, based on little or no analysis or enquiry, of attributing to pupils drawn from visible ethnic minority groups an expertise in and allegiance to any community languages with which they have some acquaintance.

(Harris 1997: 14)

In preference to this approach it might be useful for new teachers encountering pupils with EAL to begin to work with a framework offered by Harris (1999) as a prelude to developing effective classroom pedagogies suited to differing linguistic needs of individual pupils. In this framework there may well be three broad groups of pupils with EAL.

The 'new' arrivals

These pupils may be relatively recent arrivals in the country possessing a limited acquaintance with, and low levels of expertise in, the English language together with little familiarity with contemporary British cultural and educational practices.

The low-key British bilinguals

- Pupils born and brought up in a multilingual home in a British urban area. They have regular routine interaction with family and community languages other than English without claiming a high degree of expertise in these languages. They are entirely comfortable with the discourse of everyday English, particular local vernacular Englishes and with contemporary British cultural and educational practices. They have, however, along with fellow pupils of all ethnic backgrounds, including white British ones, difficulty in reproducing accurate and fluent written Standard English in the preferred written genres favoured in specific school subject disciplines.
- Pupils born and brought up in British urban areas who enter early years schooling with a dominant spoken language proficiency in a 'home'/ 'community' language originating from outside the UK, but not in English.
- Pupils born in another country who enter the British schooling system some time between the ages of 5 and 16 and appear to gradually move from the 'new' arrival to the low-key British bilingual category
- Pupils of Caribbean descent who perhaps constitute a special case of point one in terms of their patterns of language use. That is, they may have substantial experience and expertise in a Caribbean Creole language such as Jamaican Creole, which while having a lexical relationship with English is often not intelligible to English-speaking outsiders.

The high-achieving multilinguals

These pupils have a good level of expertise or an untapped potential to rapidly acquire expertise in 'home'/'community' language(s) other than English. At the same time they also have a high degree of proficiency in the kinds of written Standard English required for school success.

It should be evident that each of these distinct groups of pupils will require distinct approaches to language and learning developed by sensitive teachers. The pedagogic principles discussed earlier should be translated into classroom strategies and teaching activities with reference to the actual pupils in the classroom. To sum up, for many teachers, as Garcia (1996) has commented from a North American standpoint:

> it has become necessary to cope with a process of change whereby the ethnolinguistic identity of children is itself undergoing rapid change . . . The greatest failure of contemporary education has been precisely

its inability to help teachers understand the ethnolinguistic complexity of children, classrooms, speech communities, and society, in such a way as to enable them to make informed decisions about language and culture in the classroom.

(Garcia 1996: vii)

References

Alladina, S. and Edwards, V. (1991) *Multilingualism in the British Isles*, vol. 2. London: Longman.

Back, L. (1996) *New Ethnicities and Urban Culture*. London: UCL Press.

Baker, P. and Eversley, J. (2000) *Multilingual Capital: The Languages of London's Schoolchildren and their Relevance to Economic, Social and Educational Policies*. London: Battlebridge Publications.

Berrington, A. (1996) Marriage patterns and inter-ethnic unions, in D. Coleman and J. Salt (eds) *Ethnicity in the 1991 Census*, Vol. 1. London: HMSO.

Bourne, J. (1989) *Moving into the Mainstream: LEA Provision for Bilingual Pupils*. Windsor: NFERNelson.

Bourne, J. and McPake, J. (1991) *Partnership Teaching. Co-operative Teaching Strategies for English Language Support in Multilingual Classrooms*. London: HMSO.

Bullock Report (1975) *A Language for Life*. London: HMSO.

Commission for Racial Equality (CRE) (1986) *Teaching English as a Second Language*. London: Commission for Racial Equality.

Cummins, J. (1992) Language proficiency, bilingualism and academic achievement, in P.A. Richard-Amato and M.A. Snow (eds) *The Multicultural Classroom*. New York: Longman.

Department for Education (DfE) (1995) *Ethnic Monitoring of School Pupils: A Consultation Paper*. London: DfE.

Department for Education and Employment (DfEE) (1995) *Ethnic Monitoring of School Pupils: A Consultation Paper*. London: DfEE.

Department for Education and Employment (DfEE) (1999) *Minority Ethnic Pupils in Maintained Schools by Local Education Authority Area in England* – January 1999 (Provisional). DfEE Statistical First Release (SFR 15/1999). www.DfEE.gov.uk. Government Statistical Service.

Department for Education and Skills (DfES) (2002a) *2002/2002 Guidance for Local Education Authorities on School's Collection and Recording Data on Pupils' Ethnic Background*. London: DfES.

Department for Education and Skills (DfES) (2002b) *Key Stage 3 National Strategy – Unlocking Potential: Raising Ethnic Minority Attainment at Key Stage 3*. London: DfES.

Department for Education and Skills (DfES) (2005a) *Aiming High: Guidance on Assessment of Pupils Learning English as an Additional Language*. Nottingham: DfES.

Department for Education and Skills (DfES) (2005b) *Ethnicity and Education: the Evidence on Minority Ethnic Pupils. Research Topic Paper: RTP01–05*. London: DfES.

Department for Education and Skills (DfES) (2006) *2006-DOC-EN Pupil Language Data: Guidance for Local Authorities on Schools' Collection and Recording of Data on Pupils' Languages*. London: DfES.

Department for Education and Skills (DfES) and the Qualifications and Curriculum Authority (QCA) (1999) *English – the National Curriculum for England*. London: DfES and QCA.

Department of Education and Science (DES) (1971) *The Education of Immigrants: Education Survey 13*. London: HMSO.

Edwards, V. and Redfern, A. (1992) *The World in a Classroom: Language in Education in Britain and Canada*. Clevedon: Multilingual Matters.

Garcia, O. (1996) Foreword, in C. Baker, *Foundations of Bilingual Education and Bilingualism* (2nd edn). Clevedon: Multilingual Matters.

Gibbons, P. (1998) Classroom talk and the learning of new registers in a second language, *Language and Education*, 12(2): 99–118.

Gilroy, P. (1987/1991) *There Ain't No Black in the Union Jack*. London: Routledge.

Hall, S. (1988) New ethnicities, in A. Rattansi and J. Donald (eds) (1992) *'Race', Culture and Difference*. London: Sage/The Open University.

Hall, S. (1992) The question of cultural identity, in S. Hall, D. Held and T. McGrew (eds) *Modernity and its Futures*. Cambridge: Polity Press/Open University.

Hampshire County Council (1996) *Bilingual Learners Support Service: Service Guidelines* (2nd edn). Hampshire: Hampshire County Council.

Harris, R. (1997) Romantic bilingualism: time for a change? in C. Leung, and C. Cable (eds) *English as an Additional Language: Changing Perspectives*. Watford: NALDIC.

Harris, R. (1999) Rethinking the bilingual learner, in A. Tosi and C. Leung (eds) *Rethinking Language Education: From a Monolingual to a Multilingual Perspective*. London: CILT.

Harris, R. (2006) *New Ethnicities and Language Use*. Houndmills, Basingstoke: Palgrave Macmillan.

Hewitt, R. (1991) Language, youth and the destabilisation of ethnicity, in C. Palmgren, K. Lovgren and G. Bolin (eds) *Ethnicity and Youth Culture*. Stockholm: Stockholm University.

Hewitt, R. (1995) The umbrella and the sewing machine: Trans-culturalism and the definition of surrealism, in A. Alund and R. Granqvist (eds) *Negotiating Identities*. Amsterdam: Rodopi.

Inner London Education Authority (ILEA) (1989) *Catalogue of Languages: Spoken by Inner London School Pupils: RS 1262/89*. London: ILEA Research and Statistics.

Kress, G. (1994) *Learning to Write*. London: Routledge.

Leung, C. (2001) *Developing Reading and Writing in English as an Additional Language*. Cheshire: United Kingdom Reading Association.

Leung, C. (2005) English as an additional language policy: issues of inclusive access and language learning in the mainstream, *Prospect*, 20: 95–113.

Leung, C., Harris, R. and Rampton, B. (1997) The idealised native-speaker, reified ethnicities and classroom realities, *TESOL Quarterly*, 31(3): 543–60.

Martin-Jones, M. (1989) Language education in the context of linguistic diversity: differing orientations in educational policy making in England, in J. Esling (ed.) *Multicultural Education Policy: ESL in the 1990s*. Toronto: OISE Press.

Mercer, K. (1994) *Welcome to the Jungle*. London: Routledge.

Mohan, B., Leung, C. and Davison, C. (eds) (2001) *English as a Second Language in the Mainstream: Teaching, Learning and Identity*. Harlow: Longman.

National Curriculum Council (NCC) (1991) *Circular Number 11: Linguistic Diversity and the National Curriculum*. York: NCC.

Office for Standards in Education (Ofsted) (1994) *Educational Support for Minority Ethnic Communities*. London: Ofsted.

Office for Standards in Education (Ofsted) (2002) Training on minority ethnic achievement has improved, but more mainstream staff need to be involved, says OFSTED. Press release NR 2002–178, 08 October 2002. www.ofsted.gov.uk/press releases/index.cfm?fuseaction=news.details&id= 1365.

Peach, C. (1996) Introduction, in C. Peach (ed.) *Ethnicity in the 1991 Census*, vol. 2. London: HMSO.

Qualifications and Curriculum Authority (QCA) (2000) *A Language in Common: Assessing English as an Additional Language*. London: QCA.

Rampton, B., Harris, R. and Leung, C. (2001) *Education and Languages Other than*

English in the British Isles. Working Papers in Urban Language and Literacies. London: King's College.

School Curriculum and Assessment Authority (SCAA) (1996) *Teaching English as an Additional Language: a Framework for Policy*. London: SCAA.

Swann Report (1985) *Education for All*. London: HMSO.

The Stationery Office (TSO) (2004) *Statistics of Education: Schools in England*. London: TSO.

Travers, P. (ed.) (1999) *Enabling Progress in a Multilingual Classroom: Towards Inclusive Education*. London Borough of Enfield: Language and Curriculum Access Service.

Part 4 | Across the curriculum

20

Literacy

Bethan Marshall

Introduction

Literacy dominates most educational debates. Whether it is the need to be literate, the means by which we become literate or the fear that we are becoming less literate, some aspect of literacy is never far away from the news headlines. In a way this is hardly surprising. Access to the world of print is the foundation of most schooling and a prerequisite for most employment. To be illiterate is to be virtually disenfranchised as a twenty-first century citizen. Its importance and newsworthiness make it a subject that politicians cannot ignore and since New Labour came to power in 1997, there has been an unprecedented number of initiatives aimed at raising attainment in this key area of the curriculum.

1998 saw the first national literacy strategy (NLS) for primary schools (DfEE 1998). Three years later, a similar framework was introduced for secondary school English departments (DfEE 2001). The following year, guidelines were made available for literacy across the curriculum (DfEE 2002). In 2003, the primary national strategy was launched, under which umbrella the NLS was now to work. And 2006 saw the publication of the Rose Report, commissioned to inform future policy. This set out the precise method to be used in teaching young children to read – a strategy known as synthetic phonics which will be discussed below (DfES 2006).

With the possible exception of the cross-curricular document, all these publications share a common tone. They are immensely detailed and pre-scriptive, particularly the Rose Report (2006). Each characterizes literacy as a series of competencies that need to be acquired before an individual can become literate; most come with a clear set of targets. The primary national strategy, for example, requires schools to set specific and agreed targets (with the local authority) as to the number of pupils who are to achieve a level 4 in national tests at age 11; the national target is 80 per cent. All these documents are, as yet, non-statutory, unlike the National Curriculum. They gain their force in schools from the rubric of Ofsted, which inspects the ways in which schools have negotiated and implemented the strategies.

Yet, while the flurry of initiatives of the past ten years is unusual in its scope and intensity, the focus on literacy, in this fashion, is not new. There are possible reasons why policy makers are so exacting in the requirements for teachers when tackling literacy: a fear that standards are falling and a desire to be seen to be doing something vigorous about it.

The standards debate

Concern about falling standards, for example, is a common feature of almost every official report throughout the twentieth century (see Marshall 2000) and one of the most frequently cited sources of those concerns are employers. The seemingly annual complaints from the Institute of Directors about falling standards echo much earlier reports such as the Newbolt Report of 1921. Citing Boots Pure Drug Co. it commented that, 'The teaching of English in present day schools produces a very limited command of the English language' (Newbolt Report 1921: 72). In the same report, all but a few employers complained that they had found difficulty in 'obtaining employees who can speak and write English clearly and correctly' (ibid.: 72). Successive reports make similar observations. Yet research comparing standards over the last 30 years carried out by the National Foundation for Educational Research (Brookes 1997) has shown that no such decline in standards has occurred.

Debates about how to put right the so-called decline are similarly well rehearsed. In terms that are eerily familiar, Katherine Bathurst, an Inspector for the Board of Education in 1905, describes the process of learning to read from a new boy's point of view:

> A blackboard has been produced, and hieroglyphics are drawn upon it by the teacher. At a given signal, every child in the class begins calling out mysterious sounds: 'Letter A, letter A' in a sing-song voice, or 'Letter A says Ah, letter A says Ah', as the case may be. To the uninitiated I may explain that No. 1 is the beginning of spelling, and No. 2 is the beginning of word building. Hoary headed men will spend hours discussing whether 'c-a-t' or 'ker-ar-te' are the best means of conveying the knowledge of how to read cat. I must own an indifference to the point myself, and sympathise with teachers not allowed to settle it for themselves.

> (cited in Van der Eyken 1973: 121)

The return, in 2006, to a very particular form of phonics teaching, to the exclusion of all others, comes, as with the perception of declining standards, supported by little research evidence. The Rose Report based its recommendation on a small, but highly publicized study in Clackmannanshire, which appeared to find that synthetic phonics worked better than all other methods in the teaching of reading. But the study was not actually designed to assess this question and the pupils involved were exposed to a raft of other initiatives, which may well have also contributed to their success (Ellis 2005). A much larger and more systematic survey carried out by the American Reading Panel, which reviewed hundreds of studies, found that there was no difference between children taught either by analytic or synthetic phonics (National Institute of Child Health and Human Development, NIH, DHHS 2000).

Language and learning

Dominating the construction of literacy underpinning current policy, however, is the idea that it is about decoding print. Another way to understand what it means to be literate is to focus attention on the way print conveys meaning through language. Concentrating on the part played by language in literacy broadens the debate into a consideration of the role of language in learning. In this way, literacy becomes about much more than decoding print. Through talk pupils can, for example, gain access to difficult and demanding texts that otherwise they might struggle to read.

The NLS does state, near the very beginning of the document that: 'Literacy unites the important skills of reading and writing. It also involves speaking and listening which, although they are not separately identified in the Framework, are an essential part of it' (DfEE 1998: 3). Yet it moves away from understanding language as a vehicle for learning in the following comment by narrowly focusing on knowledge about language itself: 'Good oral work enhances pupils' understanding of language in both oral and written forms and of the way in which language can be used to communicate' (ibid.: 3).

The idea that language is essential to the learning process gained currency in this country through the writing, amongst others, of James Britton, Douglas Barnes and Harold Rosen in books such as *Language, the Learner and the School* (Barnes, Britton and Rosen 1972) and *Language and Learning* (Britton 1974). Their work built on the writing of the Russian psychologist Vygotsky. Although Vygotsky's research was carried out in the 1930s, it was not translated in the West for nearly 30 years. Vygotsky argued that language was an essential cognitive tool.

> [By] focusing attention on the interaction between speech and the child's social and cultural experiences, Vygotsky provides us with a model of learning which emphasises the role of talk and places social discourse at the centre. Most significant is the notion that children can learn effectively through interaction with a more knowledgeable other (which may be a peer or adult).
>
> (Corden 2000: 8)

This notion underpinned Vygotsky's pivotal learning theory of the zone of proximal development (ZPD) (Vygotsky 1978a). In essence, he argued that as each new learning situation arises, we move from a state where we do not understand to a position where we can understand, if supported through interaction with the more knowledgeable other (the ZPD), to a situation where we are independent. The aim of the teacher is to support the pupil through this process either through class or group discussion. The theory of ZPD has often been connected in practice with the work of Bruner. He coined the term 'scaffolding' (Bruner 1985) to describe the process by which children need initial support on engaging in a new activity and then have that support gradually withdrawn as they become more independent and are able to work unaided.

Implementing Vygotsky and Bruner's theories effectively in the class-room demands what Dewey would call, 'high organisation based upon ideas' (1966: 28–9), whereby teachers have 'the difficult task to work out the kinds of materials, of methods, and of social relationships that are appropriate' (ibid.: 29) to help pupils learn. In other words, they orchestrate classroom activities where dialogue and discussion become essential exploratory tools to extend and develop thinking. More recently Robin Alexander has stressed the significance of talk in learning in his pamphlet *Towards Dialogic Teaching: Rethinking Classroom Talk* (2006a).

But to view literacy in this way is to take a very particular educational stance. Literacy, which everyone is agreed is important, provokes considerable controversy. While this chapter has thus far presented the idea of language and learning as an essential component of literacy, extending it beyond simply decoding print, for others this is taking a very radical, possibly subversive stance. One way of understanding the passion that the literacy debates provoke is to see how closely our view of what it means to be literate relates to our view of the purpose of education and, through education, our beliefs about the nature of society and our place within in it.

Literacy and the purpose of education

This elision between what might be called a progressive philosophy of education and vision of how society should be organized is evident in the title of Vygotsky's work *Mind in Society* (1978b) and in Dewey's most famous work *Democracy and Education* (1916). It is present also in another of Alexander's pamphlets called *Education as Dialogue: Moral and Pedagogical Choices for the Runaway World* (2006b). In it he notes that:

> In some countries education has been required to mould individuals into compliant subjects; in others it has attempted to develop active and questioning citizens [. . .] Thus, education may empower and liberate, or it may disempower and confuse.
>
> (Alexander 2006: 5)

It is evident on which side of the debate he sits for he wishes actively to promote dialogue in the classroom because it:

> Requires willingness and skill to engage with minds, ideas and ways of thinking other than our own; it involves the ability to question, listen, reflect, reason, explain, speculate and explore ideas . . . [it] lays the

foundations not just of successful learning but also social cohesion, active citizenship and the good society.

(Alexander 2006: 5)

His views chime with those who advocate what is known as critical literacy.

> Literacy becomes a meaningful construct to the degree that it is viewed as a set of practices and functions to either empower or disempower people. In the larger sense, literacy must be analysed according to whether it promotes democratic and emancipatory changes.
>
> (Freire and Macedo 1987: 41)

For such writers the type of literacy required by government documentation is simply 'schooled literacy' (Street and Street 1991), an ability to decode the print on the page but little else. By contrast:

> Critical literacy responds to the cultural capital of a specific group or class and looks to ways in which it can be confirmed, and also at the ways in which the dominant society disconfirms students by either ignoring or denigrating the knowledge and experiences that characterise their everyday lives. The unit of analysis is social and the key concern is not individual interests but with the individual and collective empowerment.
>
> (Aronowitz and Giroux, cited in Ball, Kenny and Gardiner 1990: 61)

Others, such as Shirley Bryce Heath, have problematized the issue still further by examining the literacy of different social groups and noting how children from certain communities are disadvantaged by narrow definitions of 'schooled literacy' (Heath 1983). As Gee notes, such a perception of what it means to be literate means that 'the ability to talk about school based sorts of tasks is one way in which Western-style schools empower elites: they sound like they know more than they do' (Gee, cited in Corden 2000: 27).

Even those with a less overtly radical agenda use the term 'critical literacy' to describe a form of literacy that goes well beyond the basics. Richard Hoggart in his essay 'Critical Literacy and Creative Reading' writes:

> The level of literacy we now accept for the bulk of the population, of literacy unrelated to the way language is misused in this kind of society, ensures that literacy becomes simply a way of further subordinating great numbers of people. We make them literate enough to be conned by the mass persuaders [. . .] The second slogan has to be 'Critical Literacy for All'. Critical Literacy means [. . .] teaching about the difficulties, challenges and benefits of living in an open society which aims to be a true democracy.
>
> (Hoggart 1998: 60)

For all these writers, to varying degrees, literacy becomes a means of 'reading' the society in which we live. Integral to this task is a demand that we do not take 'authority' at face value, but question and challenge it as part of the democratic process. They do not want passive subjects but active citizens.

But the relationship between literacy and society is not simply the property of the left. T.S. Eliot, whose views were well to the right, made a similar connection. In his essay, *On Modern Education and the Classics*, Eliot describes education as:

> A subject which cannot be discussed in a void: our questions raise other questions, social, economic, financial, political. And the bearings are on more ultimate problems even than these: to know what we want in education we must know what we want in general, we must derive our theory of education from our theory of life.

> (Eliot, cited in Tate 1998: 3–4)

The progressive, Dewey, defines 'the main purpose and objective' of traditional education, such as that espoused by Eliot, as the preparation of:

> The young for future responsibilities and for success in life, by means of acquisition of the organised bodies of information and prepared forms of skill which comprehend the material instruction. Since the subject matter as well as standards of proper conduct are handed down from the past, the attitude of the pupils must, upon the whole, be one of docility, receptivity, and obedience.

> (Dewey 1966: 18)

The societal and moral implications associated with this position become clearer when we apply Eliot and Dewey's observations to the literacy debate. John Rae, the former headteacher of Westminster School, wrote, for example, in the *Observer* in February 1982:

> The overthrow of grammar coincided with the acceptance of the equivalent of creative writing in social behaviour. As nice points of grammar were mockingly dismissed as pedantic and irrelevant, so was punctiliousness in such matters as honesty, responsibility, property, gratitude, apology and so on.

> (Rae, cited in Graddol, Maybin, Mercer and Swann 1991: 52)

In identifying progressive teaching so closely with the permissive society, Rae appears to locate a problem with literacy developing somewhere around the mid-1960s. As we have seen, his observation is misplaced and there is little evidence that standards have altered over time. Yet such an opinion has found credence with more recent social commentators, including the journalist Melanie Phillips. In her book *All Must Have Prizes*, written as an invective against what she sees as the failings of the liberal educational establishment, she comments, 'The revolt against the teaching of grammar becomes a part of a wider repudiation of external forms of authority' (Phillips 1996: 69). In a chapter ironically sub-titled 'Proper literacy', she lays the blame at the door of radical English teachers:

> English, after all, is the subject at the heart of our definition of our national cultural identity. Since English teachers are the chief custodians of that identity we should not be surprised to find that revolutionaries intent on using the subject to transform society have gained a powerful foothold, attempting to redefine the very meaning of reading itself.

> (Phillips 1996: 69)

Both Rae and Phillips' analysis of the problem is almost certainly more to do with their view of society than literacy standards in schools. There is a subtle but significant elision between rules of language and standards of behaviour where anxiety about the latter requires greater emphasis on the former. Grammatical rules become societal laws. Any suggestion that these might be redefined or abandoned becomes a threat to civil order. For Phillips and Rae, literacy is to be taught as a set of rules in order to reinforce an orderly society.

Literacy, economic growth and phonics

If the battle lines over literacy and the good society are clearly drawn, there seems apparent harmony over the notion that high levels of literacy are needed for economic growth. Yet scratch the surface of the consensus and the same divisions appear. The relationship between the individual's need for literacy and the needs of the economy are made clear at the beginning of the NLS framework. David Blunkett, then Secretary of State for education, writes: 'All our children deserve to leave school equipped to enter a fulfilling adult life. If children do not master the basic skills of literacy and numeracy they will be seriously disadvantaged later' (DfEE 1998).

Yet, the way the literacy framework is conceived owes much more to Dewey's definition of traditional education than it does to a more progressive vision. As we have seen, it currently omits any notion of talk as part of literacy. Underpinning the strategy is the notion that there are three elements required in children becoming literate – word level, which to a greater or lesser extent involves the teaching of phonics; sentence level, which looks at grammar, and text level. While the developers of the strategy insist that these are integrated, the term 'levels' implies a hierarchy or rather a teaching order and it is this, along with the sheer weight of the content that must be delivered, that has given the NLS its traditionalist feel.

This criticism is even more true of the new proposals for the teaching of early reading – synthetic phonics, and it is worth digressing for a moment to look at the debate to appreciate the extent to which the understanding of the beginning of literacy has narrowed. The NLS recommended a blend of approaches to early reading. This included 'real books'; children learning to read using picture books rather than reading schemes. Margaret Meek, one of the best-known advocates of real books, takes what she calls a social constructivist, or Vygotskian perspective on early reading (see, for example, Meek 1988 and 1991). In other words, she has sought to build on what young children already know, which includes their knowledge of how books work and how print conveys meaning. In this way, reading and writing are always taught within a clearly defined context. The work of the Centre for Language in Primary Education (CLPE) has built on this work. Research publications such as *The Reader in the Writer* (Barrs and Cork 2001) show how children use their readerly knowledge of how stories and texts work in their writing.

More dominant, however, has been the teaching of phonics as a gateway to literacy. The type of phonics to be used, has, until the publication of the Rose Report, never been specified. Analytic phonics, currently the more commonly used method, encourages pupils to make sense of print alongside the teaching of sounds. It asks children to focus on the initial word sounds – onset, and then make analogies about the second half of the word based on their knowledge of the pattern of sounds. The books of Dr Seuss are a good example of teaching phonics using onset and analogy through the way they play with sound and rhyme.

Those advocating synthetic phonics break the English language down into 44 phonemes, or units of sounds. These are then taught through drills and then put together to form words. Purists of the synthetic phonics approach recommend that children do not attempt to read a book for themselves until they have mastered all 44 phonemes. They are then introduced to carefully graded reading schemes, which stage the introduction to words of increasing complexity.

Of course the fundamental problem in this country with any reading programme that relies totally on phonics is that English is a notoriously unphonetic language. How, for instance, is the word 'was' taught phonetically? Think of the permutations of pronunciation of the letters 'ough'. How do we make sense of the difference between read and read or tear and tear unless we understand from the context of the sentence whether we are looking at a noun or a verb? Children taught by using phonics alone are confronted by a myriad of exceptions and variations to the rule every time they look at a page. As a method, however, it is closer to Dewey's definition of traditional education in that it requires the 'acquisition of the organised bodies of information and prepared forms of skill which comprehend the material instruction' (Dewey 1966: 18).

But it is not just the impracticality of phonics that poses a problem for its critics. If we return to the economic imperative of literacy we find writers such as Gunther Kress (1995, 1997) arguing that the model of literacy apparently endorsed by the NLS will not fit pupils for the economy of the future. Part of his contention is that traditional 'schooled literacy' does not pay sufficient attention to the demands of the new technologies. But his argument is more significantly dependent on the notion that the new economies, built on 'fast capitalism', demand adaptable and flexible workers. He writes:

> The question I am posing is simply this: in relation to the economic and social futures such as these, what is the English curriculum doing? [. . .] If jobs are moveable with the speed of global fiscal markets, then certain requirements of a fundamental kind follow the kind of person whom we are preparing for that world. Somehow they will have to be prepared not just to cope, but to control their circumstances.
>
> (Kress 1995: 18)

However, his agenda is most clearly seen when he attempts to define the literacy necessary to achieve this end. In terms that clearly echo Dewey's definition of traditional education, he writes:

If we represent literacy, in the curriculum, as a matter of fixed, immutable rules, we encourage a different attitude to the one suggested by a representation of literacy as a set of resources shaped by society and constantly reshaped by each individual reader and writer. The former encourages an acceptance of what is; a certain attitude to authority; a limitation accepted and internalised by the individual. The latter encourages curiosity about how things have come to be as they are; a certain attitude to individual responsibility and agency; and an internalisation of the individual as active, creative and expansive.

(Kress 1995: 75)

In other words, to produce the flexible worker of the future, to create the learning society we need to cope with an ever-changing economic landscape, we need a theory of literacy that incorporates a vision of an active participant rather than a passive receiver of predetermined rules. And it is this notion of the individual as active that governs his view both of the way in which we need to learn and the beginnings of literacy in pre-school children. He does not assume, however, that all children will engage in the process in the same way, but wants to understand what they are doing in order to develop them further: 'My preference is for intervention, for aiding and abetting, for making sure that children have to hand what will make that possible' (Kress 1995: 37).

In his advocacy of the importance of dialogue in the classroom Robin Alexander shows how education can be used to shape the moral questions that lurk behind this economic future. Globalization, he argues, means that we have to think beyond our country's own economic needs and 'address international challenges' (Alexander 2006b: 6). For him, this means, 'acknowledging that global interdependence carries moral obligations from which no country is immune; and that education can serve to unite rather than divide' (Alexander 2006: 6).

Considerations of literacy, then, extend far beyond the best method of teaching young children to read or how pupils might gain access to a science textbook. Our views on what it means to be literate are shaped by what we think education is for and what role we believe the children in the classroom today should play in the society of tomorrow. And this is the last element of literacy that needs to be discussed. For some it involves an element of futurology.

Concluding comments

Writers such as Kress argue that not only do we need to address the economic needs of the future but also that to confine literacy to the printed word is to misrepresent the complexity of what it now means to be literate. He has coined the term 'multi-modality' to represent what he means by this new type of literacy (see, for example, Kress and van Leeuwen 2001; Kress 2003). Children, he observes, are growing up in a world of web pages, blogs, MSN and texting. Traditional conventions of print do not apply to the type of reading and writing that uses images and symbols as an integral part of the way meaning is conveyed. More importantly, Kress argues, this new literacy provides valuable opportunities to extend the type of learning offered by simple print literacy.

> If the limits of the imagination imposed by one mode of representation are reached it seems a decidedly positive situation to be able to move to another mode, which extends these limits in certain ways, or offers a different potential. This offers an enormous potential enrichment, cognitively, conceptually, aesthetically and affectively.
>
> (Kress 1997: 29)

Pahl and Rowsell (2005 and 2006) have researched how young children explore and represent their ideas in a range of modes:

> Each mode contains its own meaning making potential, its affordance. Children, when they make texts, explore the affordances of modes, that is they draw on the potential in the 'stuff' [i.e. different modes and materials] from which they make meaning.
>
> (Pahl 2006: 21)

Classrooms, they argue, are places where this type of experimentation and expression needs to be encouraged.

Literacy lies at the heart of education, however we understand it; as a finite skill to be acquired or as a process that lies at the heart of teaching and learning. This chapter has attempted to explore how complex a subject it is and the extent to which our view of education, and through education our beliefs about the type of society we wish to create, govern our understanding of what it means to be literate. There are sides in this debate and while they may more often be represented as shades of grey it is important, when listening to the latest initiative or literacy fad and fashion to ask from which perspective it comes. And perhaps most importantly of all, we need to ask ourselves where we stand and what this says about how we view what education is about.

References

Alexander, R. (2006a) *Towards Dialogic Teaching: Rethinking Classroom Talk*. Cambridge: Dialogos.

Alexander, R. (2006b) *Education as Dialogue: Moral and Pedagogical Choices for a Runaway World*. Cambridge: Dialogos.

Ball, S.J., Kenny, A. and Gardiner, D. (1990) Literacy policy and the teaching of English, in I. Goodson and P. Medway (eds) *Bringing English to Order*. London: Falmer.

Barnes, D., Britten, J. and Rosen, H. (1972) *Language, the Learner and the School*. Harmondsworth: Penguin Books.

Barrs, M. and Cork, U. (2001) *The Reader in the Writer*. London: Centre for Language in Primary Education.

Britton, J. (1974) *Language and Learning*. Harmondsworth: Penguin Books.

Brooks, G. (1997) *Trends in Standards of Literacy in the United Kingdom 1948–1997*. Conference paper. British Educational Research Association, University of York, 11–14 September.

Bruner, J. (1985) Vygotsky: a historical and conceptual perspective, in J. Wertsch (ed.) *Culture, Communication and Cognition: Vygotskian Perspectives*. Cambridge: Cambridge University Press.

Corden. R. (2000) *Literacy and Learning Through Talk*. Buckingham: Open University Press.

Departmental Committee of the Board of Education (1921) *The Teaching of English in England: Being the Report of the Departmental Committee Appointed by the President of the Board of Education to Inquire into the Position of English in the Educational System of England* (The Newbolt Report). London: HMSO.

Department for Education and Employment (DfEE) (1998) *The National Literacy Strategy*. London: HMSO.

Department for Education and Employment (DfEE) (2001) *Framework for Teaching English: Years 7, 8 and 9*. London: HMSO.

Department for Education and Employment (DfEE) (2002) *Literacy Across the Curriculum*. London: HMSO

Department for Education and Skills (DfES) (2003) *Excellence and Enjoyment – A Strategy for Primary Schools*. London: HMSO.

Department for Education and Skills (DfES) (2006) *Independent Review of the Teaching of Early Reading: The Final Report (The Rose Report)*. London: HMSO.

Dewey, J. (1916) *Democracy and Education*. New York: Macmillan.

Dewey, J. (1966) *Experience and Education*. London: Collier Books.

Ellis, S. (2005) *The Wider Context for Synthetic Phonics in Clackmannanshire: Evidence to the Rose Committee of Inquiry into Methods of Teaching Reading*. Glasgow: University of Strathclyde.

Freire, P. and Macedo, D. (1987) *Literacy: Reading the Word and the World*. London: Routledge.

Graddol, D., Maybin J., Mercer, N. and Swann, J. (eds) (1991) *Talk and Learning 5–16: An Inservice Pack on the Oracy for Teachers*. Milton Keynes: Open University Press.

Heath, S. (1983) *Ways With Words*. Cambridge: Cambridge University Press.

Hoggart, R. (1998) Critical literacy and creative reading, in B. Cox (ed.) *Literacy is Not Enough: Essays on the Importance of Reading*. Manchester: Manchester University Press.

Kress, G. (1995) *Writing the Future: English and the Making of a Culture of Innovation*. Sheffield: NATE Papers in Education.

Kress, G. (1997) *Before Writing*. London: Routledge.

Kress. G. (2003) *Literacy in the New Media Age*. London: Routledge.

Kress, G. and van Leeuwen, T. (2001) *Multimodal Discourses: the Modes and the Media of Contemporary Communication*. London: Arnold.

Marshall (2000) *English Teachers – The Unofficial Guide: Researching the Philosophies of English Teachers*. London: Falmer Routledge.

Meek, M. (1988) *How Texts Teach What Readers Learn*. Stroud: Thimble Press.

Meek, M. (1991) *On Being Literate*. London: Bodley Head.

National Institute of Child Health and Human Development (NIH, DHHS) (2000) *Report of the National Reading Panel: Teaching Children to Read* (00–4769). Washington DC: US Government Printing Office.

Pahl, K. (2006) Blue frogs, blue skies and sheep: an investigation, *English in Education*, 40(1): 20–36.

Pahl, K. and Rowsell, J. (2005) *Literacy and Education: Understanding the New Literacy Studies in the Classroom*. London: Sage Publications.

Pahl, K. and Rowsell, J. (2006) Introduction, in K. Pahl and J. Rowsell (eds) *Travel Notes from the New Literacy Studies: Instances of Practice*. Clevedon: Multilingual Matters Ltd.

Phillips, M. (1996) *All Must Have Prizes*. London: Little, Brown & Co.

Street, B. and Street, J. (1991) The schooling of literacy, in D. Barton and R. Ivanich (eds) *Writing in the Community*. London: Sage.

Tate, N. (1998) *What is Education for? The Fifth Annual Education Lecture*. Department for Education and Professional Studies, King's Collage London, November 1998.

Van der Eyken, W. (1973) Education, the Child and Society: A Documentary History. London: Penguin Education.

Vygotsky, L. (1978a) *Thought and Language*. Cambridge, MA: MIT Press.

Vygotsky, L. (1978b) *Mind in Society*. Cambridge, MA: MIT Press.

Ann-Marie Brandom

Introduction

In 1999, the publication of the *National Curriculum Orders for Citizenship* established a new foundation subject in the revised National Curriculum. The inclusion of citizenship as a discrete subject was a direct result of the publication of the *Final Report of the Advisory Group on Citizenship*, now known as the Crick Report (Advisory Group on Citizenship 1998). When the Qualifications and Curriculum Authority (QCA) drew up the Orders, which included the programmes of study and end of key stage descriptors, the then Department for Education and Employment (DfEE) set up a Ministerial Working Party in 2000 to oversee the introduction of the new subject.

At Key Stage 1, citizenship was introduced as part of the non-statutory framework for personal, social and health education (PSHE) in August 2001 (see Chapter 23). In August 2002, citizenship was introduced as part of the non-statutory PSHE framework at Key Stage 2 and as part of the National Curriculum at Key Stage 3. It was introduced as part of the statutory National Curriculum at Key Stage 4 in August 2004. The establishment of the Ministerial Working Party gave secondary schools two years to audit their practice and devise their individual responses to citizenship provision at Key Stage 3, in preparation for its introduction at Key Stage 4.

In fairness to many schools, provision for the subject already existed, either for historical reasons or because schools had implemented the non-statutory cross-curricular themes of the National Curriculum. These themes had been introduced in 1990 to augment the subject-based content of the National Curriculum. The five themes were: health education, citizenship, economic and industrial understanding, careers education and guidance, and environmental education. Schools were encouraged to include these 'themes' across the curriculum. In reality, with no official time allocation, no reporting instructions and no assessment requirements, the themes had not been generally prioritized in schools (Kerr 1999; Beck 2000: 128).

The new statutory orders provided a framework, an assessment obligation and the inclusion of the subject at inspection level. Schools were galvanized into action at the same time as having to make provision for the Key Stage 3 Strategy with its emphasis on numeracy and literacy, and the revised National Curriculum in the form of Curriculum 2000. Secondary schools now had to fit another subject into an already crowded curriculum, which according to Curriculum 2000, had been slimmed down. What motivated the addition of citizenship as a new subject at Foundation Level in the National Curriculum?

A rationale for the introduction of citizenship education in England

According to the QCA Handbook on Citizenship:

> Citizenship gives pupils the knowledge, skills and understanding to play an effective role in society at local, national and international levels. It helps them to become informed, thoughtful and responsible citizens who are aware of their duties and rights. It promotes their spiritual, moral, social and cultural development, making them more self-confident and responsible both in and beyond the classroom. It encourages pupils to play a helpful part in the life of their schools, neighbourhoods, communities and the wider world. It also teaches them about our economy and democratic institutions and values; encourages respect for different national, religious and ethnic identities; and develops pupils' ability to reflect on the issues and take part in discussions.
>
> (QCA/DfEE 1999: 12)

The government argued for the centrality of citizenship at a time when there were 'worrying signs of alienation and cynicism among young people about public life and participation, leading to their possible disconnection and disengagement from it' (Kerr 1999: 3). Social issues in the late 1990s:

> appeared to confirm what many had already assumed or suspected: that there were deteriorating social and cultural conditions in England and that political and voluntary participation in the affairs of society was in decline.
>
> (Arthur and Wright 2001: 6)

Osler (2000) also argues that the introduction of the legislated study of citizenship was a means of addressing the deep-seated inequalities resident in society, as evidenced in the Macpherson Report, published as result of the Stephen Lawrence Inquiry (Macpherson 1999). Bottery (2003) claims that citizenship education was a direct response to the contentious notion of identity, as the concept of the nation-state continues to unravel in current global contexts. This context may, in part, explain the government's approach and determination to establish citizenship as a discrete subject. It certainly explains the emphasis on a form of active citizenship rather than a merely theoretical examination of modes of government. The model of citizenship education put forward in the Orders emphasizes the need for pupils to have knowledge, skills and understanding of their role in society in order that they might better understand what participation in a variety of arenas might actually look like.

For pupils to know what citizenship is, the government argued, they must be given access to a curriculum that will give them confidence to begin the examination of what it is to be a respectful member of society. They must be encouraged to critique the status quo using a range of skills in order to understand better the diverse value systems of the local, national and international society to which they belong. Finally, pupils, it suggests, need to be given the physical opportunity to participate in some form of community-based work to enable them to reflect on the role they will play in their adult life.

The evolution of citizenship education in England

Until 1999, education for citizenship had not held a statutory place in the school curriculum. As such, England was unique among its European, North American and Australian counterparts where civics or citizenship education had played an explicit role in education. This is not to say that individual schools in England had not been active on this front, nor that constituent lobbying for the inclusion of citizenship had not taken place, it is simply acknowledging the insignificant role that citizenship played in national legislation until this time.

There had been periods of time when citizenship had been advocated in English schools (Batho 1990). Two significant instances are related to the crises of war. After the First World War, Frederick Swann published the *Primer of English Citizenship* in 1918 to endorse the moral character of the British citizen. In 1935, the Association for Education in World Citizenship (AEWC) was established to preserve the democratic fabric of society in response to the rise of totalitarianism. The association was built upon the desire to emphasize the social responsibility of the individual citizen, to foster an allegiance to the principle of freedom and to raise awareness of the political and economic factors that shape the modern world. These principles will begin to sound familiar when we compare them to the current National Curriculum guidelines for citizenship.

Attention was paid to the AEWC's definition of citizenship in the post-war years but no official programme was ever advocated at a national level. The subject was not taken forward and it was not until the introduction of the comprehensive school system in the mid-1960s, and the appearance of social studies courses such as sociology, social studies and politics, that citizenship was recognized, albeit at a low level, in the school curriculum. Although voluntary work in the community and participation in the broader life of a school were hallmarks of many educational institutions, it tended to be as a result of the enthusiasm of individual teachers (Fogelman 1997).

The National Curriculum

With the introduction of the 1988 Education Reform Act, citizenship was given some form of legislative recognition. The National Curriculum contained not just an explanation of what was to be taught in each subject area, excluding the content for religious education (which was to be part of the 'basic curriculum'), but also a framework of guidance for 'cross-curricular themes'. The themes were provided as a means of augmenting the National Curriculum and were designed to give coherence to the educational experience of the pupil. As previously stated, the five themes were: health education; careers education and guidance; environmental education; education for economic and industrial understanding; and education for citizenship (NCC 1990a).

Non-statutory guidance was published for each theme (NCC 1990b). Schools were encouraged to develop their own policy document in response to the statement, 'Education for Citizenship develops the knowledge, skills and attitudes necessary for exploring, making informed decisions about and exercising responsibilities and rights in a democratic society' (NCC 1990b). Some schools did produce policy documents but it quickly became apparent that the pressure on curriculum time was so great that citizenship education had fallen by the wayside.

Even after the publication, in 1990, of the report of the Speaker's Commission on Citizenship, *Encouraging Citizenship*, and the National Commission on Education report (NCE 1993), there was little practical application of the blueprints on offer. Both reports endorsed the significance of citizenship and the former even attempted a definition of citizenship by referring to the work of the sociologist T.H. Marshall. Marshall had recommended that citizenship should be compulsory from the age of seven, but it was still up to schools to ensure provision and this was too problematic.

The review of the National Curriculum by Sir Ron Dearing in 1994 (Dearing 1994) could not find a formal place for citizenship. Representations were made to him but the slimming down of the subject content took priority (Fogelman 1997). The lack of any evidence of much good practice in citizenship education in schools did not, however, hinder research into the arena. In 1991, for example, the Centre for Citizenship Studies in Education was established at Leicester University. Surveys were carried out to ascertain schools' provision of citizenship and one such review, carried out in 1995, found that:

> 43 per cent of primary schools and 62 per cent of secondary said that it is an essential or very important part of the curriculum . . . on the other hand it was still the case for almost all schools that there was no mention, or only a very brief one, of citizenship education in the school development plan. About two thirds of schools (both phases)

stated that pressures on the timetable had been a major constraint on their ability to provide citizenship education; lack of funding for resources and lack of staff expertise were also mentioned by significant numbers.

(Fogelman 1997: 93)

The election of a Labour government in May 1997 provided an opportunity for change. The White Paper, *Excellence in Schools* (DfEE 1997) proposed that the teaching of democracy and education for citizenship be strengthened. To this end, the Secretary of State for Education initiated the formation of an advisory group to establish the aims and function of citizenship in schools; to define in broad terms what effective citizenship should be; and make practical recommendations to the QCA in the light of the authority's review of the National Curriculum. The group was to be chaired by Professor Bernard Crick and the group's recommendations were to provide the framework for what citizenship education has become.

The *Final Report of the Advisory Group on Citizenship*, was submitted in 1998 (Advisory Group on Citizenship 1998). The 'Crick Report' recommended that 5 per cent of curriculum time should be given over to the subject across the key stages. Subsequently reviewed by the QCA working party, known as Preparation for Adult Life, the recommendations in the report formed the framework for citizenship in the revised National Curriculum 2000.

As well as the recommendation of 5 per cent of curriculum time, the report suggested that there should be a degree of interpretation permitted in the programmes of study, in order to provide schools with a means of adapting the guidelines to the particular situation they were in. The report also suggested that provision for citizenship education, whilst not statutory, should be made available in the post-16 sector.

The Crick Report

The Crick Report outlined the rubric of citizenship along three lines:

• understanding social and moral responsibility
• becoming involved in the community
• developing political literacy.

The report leans heavily on Marshall's definition of social citizenship (Marshall 1950, 1964); a citizenship that involved three inter-related elements, the civil, the political and the social. The civil element stemmed from an understanding of 'individual freedom – liberty of person, freedom of speech and the right to justice'. The political element referred to 'the right to participate in the exercise of political power as a member of a body vested with political authority or as an elector of the members of such a body'. The social element referred to 'the whole range from the right to a modicum of economic welfare and security to the right to share to the full in the social heritage . . . prevailing in society' (all quotations from Marshall 1964: 78). These three strands form the basis of the current definition of what constitutes the effective education of citizenship: first, the social and moral responsibility given to, and expected of, pupils in school; second, their community involvement, learning about and becoming responsibly involved in the life and concerns of the community; third, the notion of themselves as politically literate, in other words aware of the scope of what it means to be an active citizen in society.

Underpinning Marshall's three-stemmed approach is the progressive notion of the child as a future citizen. In other words, his model anticipates the active engagement of the pupil in the decision-making process. This position contrasts with a view that assumes a more passive model of learning in which pupils need to receive information to enable them to participate in adult life.

Thus the Group prefaced their report with the statement:

> We aim at no less than a change in the political culture of this country both nationally and locally: for people to think of themselves as active citizens, willing, able and equipped to have an influence in public life and with the critical capacities to weigh evidence before speaking and acting; to build on and to extend radically to young people the best existing traditions of community involvement and public service, and to make them individually confident in finding new forms of involvement and action among themselves.
>
> (QCA 1998: 7)

National Curriculum 2000 requirements for citizenship

The three strands of understanding social and moral responsibility; becoming involved in the community; and developing political literacy have been incorporated into broad programmes of study at Key Stage 3 and Key Stage 4. As a result of citizenship education, pupils are to:

- become informed citizens
- develop skills of enquiry and communication
- develop skills of participation and responsible action.

(QCA/DfEE 1999: 6)

To become an informed citizen, a pupil is required to have the opportunity to learn about a myriad of key political, social and cultural aspects. The requirements, which are content laden, include learning about the law and the human rights and responsibilities that underpin society. Pupils are to be taught about the diversity of national, regional, ethnic and religious identities in society and they should understand the function of local and central government, with the aim of appreciating the importance of their own participation now and when they are able to vote. They should understand how the voluntary sector operates and how significant the media is in affecting opinion. Finally, they should learn about the global community and about resolving conflict (QCA/DfEE 1999: 14). Thus, the model of citizenship is defined less through a conceptual process or framework but rather, as with the numeracy and literacy strategies, as a body of knowledge to be acquired. There is, however, obvious progression from Key Stage 3 to Key Stage 4. The same topics are covered again at Key Stage 4, but in more depth and with more scope for analysis. This approach is designed to encourage further enquiry and provide the opportunity to form reasoned opinion.

In addition, although the programmes seem to focus on the content, rather than the process, it is the emphasis on skills that offers much scope for training pupils in intercultural dialogue. Pupils are to be taught to think, to justify, to contribute, to use their imagination, to negotiate and decide, and to participate responsibly in school and in community-based activities. It is this last element that distinguishes the rubric on citizenship. Schools must provide opportunities for pupils to participate in voluntary work. The framework is not just theoretical, it is active and practical (QCA/DfEE 1999).

In providing such a framework for the subject, schools have had to wrestle with the issue of citizenship in their respective unique and individual situations. Responsibility now lies with the school to demonstrate how they provide for citizenship education within curriculum time. Crick endorsed the freedom of the orders, which carried no advice about the methods of delivery or teaching methods appropriate to citizenship. Pedagogically, schools and teachers were free to interpret the nature of the programmes of study.

The importance of individual and corporate responsibility and participation, within the framework, is consistently emphasized. The learning outcomes are designed so that pupils have the opportunity to identify the many factors that influence society and begin to understand their own position within the political framework. As a result, they should be able to justify their personal opinion on these matters in the light of the issues they have studied – hence the focus on becoming politically literate. An outline is provided to indicate how citizenship can promote pupils' spiritual, moral, social, and cultural development as well as the key skills. Subsequent schemes of work were published to demonstrate how schools could integrate the subject, as they saw fit, in their context.

Much of the content provides detailed cross-curricular links. Science, modern foreign languages, information and communication technology, music as well as English, history, art and design and geography are all mentioned. For example, requirement 1i 'pupils should be taught about: the world as a global community, and the political, economic, environmental and social implications of this' is linked with Sc2/5a, Hi/13, Gg/3b and MFL/4c (QCA/DfEE 1999: 14).

Assessment of citizenship takes the form of end-of-key-stage descriptors rather than the eight-level scale. The movement from knowledge of the mechanisms of a democratic society at Key Stage 3 to the broader understanding of what constitutes the support and development of such a society, through active participation by Key Stage 4, is a measure of the progression expected of school-based schemes of work as they sustain an education into citizenship. The means of assessment are again left open to innovation and individual school interpretation. There are now GCSE syllabuses for citizenship; however, these cannot address the active citizenship rubric of the Orders, nor are they legislatively proscribed. They do provide a route to report on pupil progress in the subject. The process of assessment of citizenship is an area that has generated much debate with the introduction of the subject. However, as there is no set format for reporting and recording progress, schools are struggling to develop ways of enabling pupils to self-assess as well as be more objectively assessed (Gearon 2003).

Implications of the programmes of study

Citizenship must be taught, but there is no proscribed approach to the implementation of the subject at any key stage. This approach encourages schools to adapt to their own needs, plans and communities. Kitson (2004) helpfully outlines a number of approaches that schools have taken when integrating citizenship into the curriculum. Kerr (1999) has undertaken longitudinal research to map the response of schools in England to the citizenship initiative. He, too, documents a number of different models of provision (Kerr and Cleaver 2006). His findings have thrown up a myriad number of questions, not least surrounding the actual definition of citizenship, of which there are apparently over 300. Kerr's (1999) literature review is probably one of the most comprehensive surveys of the current status of citizenship. He identifies three areas of research: the organization of citizenship education in schools; the issues affecting students undertaking citizenship education; and the issues surrounding teachers and the teaching of citizenship education.

Apart from the autonomy of interpretation written into the orders on citizenship, one of the most significant elements of the statutory framework is the emphasis on pupil participation. Schools must be able to offer some form of voluntary programme to students, in order to allow them the opportunity to develop their commitment to their community. This could be in the form of a school council or voluntary community work. If citizenship is to be integrated into the present curriculum, schools must be prepared to examine the value system they uphold through the ethos of the school – because the school itself is a community and therefore acts as a model of citizenship. Pupils will automatically be acquiring knowledge, understanding and skills to cope in their school. They will very quickly glean the role they are to play in school, the extent of their rights and responsibilities and the nature of what is and is not valued. As Burkmisher says:

> If the school is a model ... what is the school's vision? What is its purpose? Are the aims clear and understood and subscribed to by all? Is there clarity about values which underpin the aims? Do members of the school share in the discussion of these values? Do they measure their own practice against values? Are the values understood and shared by the wider community which the school serves? Given that we see our state as democratic, how democratic are our schools and in what ways can we make them more democratic?
>
> (Burkmisher 1993: 8)

Hart (1997) has also developed a helpful 'ladder of participation' in order to judge (metaphorically) active citizenship. Hart does not advocate that the final rung is the final goal to aim for; he offers the ladder as a means of assessing democratic opportunity in a school community. By discussing the notions of tokenism, consultation and child-initiated versus adult-initiated decisions, Hart emphasizes that power must be actively shared in a democratic community, not just assumed. Deakin-Crick *et al.* (2004) state, in their literature review on research into citizenship education, that 'the teachers' own beliefs and value systems were found to contribute to their choice of strategy [in the classroom], leading to the conclusion that the development of the teachers' own reasoned, comprehensive and flexible socio-moral credo is important' (Deakin-Crick *et al.* 2004: 64). The authors suggest that all schools should examine the ethos and values attached to their system of government, as only through interrogation of this could the school honourably meet the requirements of the orders. This self-reflection is necessary if open and trusted dialogue is to take place, and power is to be understood and shared effectively.

Underlying the programmes of study is a commitment to respect both the individual and the diversity of communities in society. Yet, through their experience in and outside school, pupils will already be aware that there are structures in society that dictate authority. Citizenship can provide a means for pupils to reflect on their moral and personal development while learning how to acknowledge the value system that is in operation underpinning the society in which they live.

Since pupils will then be aware of their place in society, the Crick Report suggests it will become apparent that pupils have responsibilities to others in the community, hence the emphasis on the second aspect of effective citizenship, that of community involvement. This approach is not designed to be limited to the pupil's time in school, either, this is education for life. The intention is to demonstrate to pupils the role the community plays and their life-long part in it. They need, therefore, to be made aware that personal decision making and conflict resolution also have implications for all levels of society, from within families, to local community level through to the national, European and international level.

The nature of citizenship

The nature of citizenship continues to be a contentious issue. What does citizenship mean, what does the teaching of citizenship entail? Is it a conglomeration of facts about the democratic system of government in the UK which are be learned, or an opportunity to participate in the democratic process, or a mixture of both, which is certainly how the Home Office present their documentation on becoming a citizen of the UK (HMSO 2000). How is citizenship to be defined; on a local, national, European, international or global level? What constitutes a good education in citizenship, what is to be the outcome of such an education? These are not new questions. Aristotle was driven to declare in *The Politics* that 'there is no unanimity, no agreement' over the nature of citizenship (Aristotle 1981: 168).

In the pluralistic, secular society in which we live, citizenship needs to promote a liberal democratic form of education. Such a model, in and of itself, is of course not neutral but underpins the values expressed in the National Curriculum. Accordingly, the Foreword to the Orders on Citizenship states that 'education in citizenship and democracy will provide coherence in the way in which all pupils are helped to develop a full understanding of their roles and responsibilities as citizens in a modern democracy' (QCA 1999: 4). What then is the aim of citizenship education: social cohesion, preparation for participation in democracy – to ensure that young people will vote, inclusion in and understanding of what is meant by society, an understanding of rights and responsibilities?

The government finally gave a formal place to citizenship in the National Curriculum in 2000. Evidence of two models of learning, one progressive and one content-laden, lies within it, but the government's solution to the potential tension between these two approaches may not be to everyone's liking because of the amount of prescribed content. Nor is there, necessarily, wholehearted acceptance for the underlying rationale of this programme of citizenship. However, the emphasis given in the documentation on the skills of enquiry, communication, participation and intercultural discourse enables us to respond to the question of what it means to be educated for citizenship.

Concluding comments

The implications of Marshall's three strands, as translated into the programmes of study for citizenship, are not without their problems. The nature of the term 'active' citizenship demands response by the individual, yet any inherent inequality within society means that the response of some is curbed. Yes, lobbying Parliament in a democracy is your right, but it does not necessarily imply that things will change. In the same way, if pupils are to be offered a context for decision making in a school, a context which, more often than not, takes the form of a student council, what powers, if any, does the council actually wield?

What kind of model of democratic rights are we promoting when we dictate, in the first instance, a certain moral code of acceptable behaviour? What right do we have as teachers to dictate to students what the QCA have defined as good citizenship education? We are back to questions again. To find answers, we need to examine the underlying values operating in our educational system. Our educational system is caught up in the same dilemma; according to which value system has our national curriculum been developed? This question echoes the current debate over a 'liberal political theory . . . confronted by a diversity of beliefs and values' (Beck 2000: 136) (see also Chapter 4).

At no point in time is citizenship education advocating an anarchic model for pupils, yet our democratic society promotes, in fact demands, open debate concerning claims to possessing the 'right' understanding. Consequently, sources of truth are actively interrogated and scepticism reigns supreme. This, in turn, invites people to doubt authoritative institutions, preventing them forming allegiances, encouraging them to ask the question 'Why?' and subsequently providing their own alternatives to the dominant assumptions of the day. If this approach is coupled with a diverse, multicultural society that has clusters of people who define their own authority structures separately, then there is confusion as to what makes a good citizen, let alone what makes for good citizenship education.

The key question here is how teachers are to deal with controversial issues in the classroom. There is no rubric for the presentation of the topics on citizenship, but an endorsement to engage pupils with complex concepts and create an environment for healthy debate, discussion, respectful disagreement and critical thinking. The danger of this is that to engage pupils' thinking capacities is to allow them to question, and if you allow them to question, they will begin to interrogate the autonomy they are permitted in school, they will challenge the status quo and they will perhaps lobby for change. The advocacy of education for citizenship is an exciting move forward in educational terms, if, by education, we mean the freeing of the child to question. (Some suggestions about teaching controversial issues can be found in Oulton *et al.* 2004a and b.)

On a final note, it is the ethos of the school which will ultimately determine the provision of effective citizenship education. The ethos of the school is upheld by members of its community. As a member of the school community you, as a teacher, must ask yourself what your understanding of citizenship is in order to make explicit your own value system. In doing this, you will be more confident in addressing the issues of citizenship because you will have answered the questions for yourself.

Since pupil self-confidence is a vital ingredient to establish, it should also be the case that teachers are confident in the material they are handling and the critical thinking processes they are advocating. If you provide pupils with the skills with which to assess and analyse their role in society, you may well be giving them the opportunity of a lifetime. If you simply ensure that they have learned how the United Nations Declaration of Human Rights came about, you may never hear them mention its significance again. Pupils need to own the process of democracy, not just be taught about it.

References

Advisory Group on Citizenship (1998) *Education for Citizenship and the Teaching of Democracy in Schools: Final Report of the Advisory Group on Citizenship.* London: Qualifications and Curriculum Authority.

Aristotle (1981) *The Politics* (rev. edn) T.J. Saunders (ed.). Harmondsworth: Penguin.

Arthur, J. and Wright, D. (2001) *Teaching Citizenship in the Secondary School.* London: David Fulton.

Batho, G. (1990) The history of the teaching of civics and citizenship in English Schools, *The Curriculum Journal,* 1(1): 91–107.

Beck, J. (2000) Citizenship and education for citizenship, in J. Beck and M. Earl (eds) *Key Issues in Secondary Education*. London: Cassell.

Bottery, M. (2003) The end of citizenship: the Nation State threat to its legitimacy and citizenship education in the twenty-first century, *Cambridge Journal of Education*, 33(1): 100–22.

Burkmisher, M. (1993) Creating a climate for citizenship education in schools, in J. Edwards and K. Fogelman (eds) *Developing Citizenship in the Curriculum*. London: David Fulton.

Commission on Citizenship (1990) *Encouraging Citizenship. Report of the House of Commons Commission on Citizenship*. London: HMSO.

Deakin-Crick, R., Coates, M., Taylor, M. and Ritchie, S. (2004) *A Systematic Review of the Impact of Citizenship Education on the Provision of Schooling*. London: EPPI Centre: Social Science Research Unit, Institute of Education.

Dearing, R. (1994) *The National Curriculum Council and its Assessment: Interim Report*. London: NCC/SEAC.

Department for Education and Employment (DfEE) (1997) *Excellence in Schools*. London: DfEE.

Department for Education and Science (DES) (1988) *Education Reform Act*. London: HMSO.

Edwards, J. and Fogelman, K. (1993) *Developing Citizenship in the Curriculum*. London: David Fulton.

Fogelman, K. (1997) Citizenship education in England, in K. Kennedy (ed.) *Citizenship Education and the Modern State*. London: Falmer Press.

Gearon, L. (2003) Developing schemes of work in citizenship, in L. Gearon (ed.) *Learning to Teach Citizenship in the Secondary School*. London: RoutledgeFalmer.

Hart, R. (1997) *Children's Participation; The Theory and Practice of Involving Young Citizens in Community Development and Environmental Care*. London: Earthscan Publications Ltd.

HMSO (2000) *The Immigration and Asylum Appeals (Procedure) Rules 2000. Statutory Instruments 2000 No. 2333 (L.21)*. London: HMSO.

Hogan, D. (1997) The logic of protection: citizenship, justice and political community, in K. Kennedy (ed.) *Citizenship Education and the Modern State*. London: Falmer Press.

Kitson, A. (2004) Citizenship, in V. Brooks, I. Abbott and L. Bills (eds) *Preparing to Teach in Secondary Schools*. Maidenhead: Open University Press.

Kerr, D. (1999) Re-examining citizenship in England, in J. Torney-Purta, J. Schwille and J-A. Amadeo (eds) *Civic Education Across Countries: 22 Case Studies from the Civic Education Project*. Amsterdam: Eberon Publishers for the International Association for the Evaluation of Educational Achievement.

Kerr, D. and Cleaver, E. (2004). *Citizenship Education Longitudinal Study: Literature Review. Citizenship Education One Year On: What Does It Mean? Emerging Definitions and Approaches in the First Year of National Curriculum Citizenship in England* (DfES Research Report 532). London: DfES.

Macpherson, W. (1999) *The Stephen Lawrence Inquiry*. London: Stationery Office.

Marshall, T.H. (1950) *Citizenship and Social Class*. Cambridge: Cambridge University Press.

Marshall, T.H. (1964) *Class Citizenship and Social Development*. Chicago, IL: Chicago University Press.

National Commission on Education (NCE) (1993) *Learning to Succeed. Report of the National Commission on Education*. London: Heinemann.

National Curriculum Council (NCC) (1990a) *Curriculum Guidance 3: The Whole Curriculum*. York: NCC.

National Curriculum Council (NCC) (1990b) *Curriculum Guidance 8: Education for Citizenship*. York: NCC.

Osler, A. (ed.) (2000) *Citizenship and Democracy in Schools: Diversity, Identity, Equality.* Stoke-on-Trent: Trentham Books.

Oulton, C., Day, V., Dillon, J. and Grace, M. (2004a) Controversial issues – teachers' attitudes and practices in the context of citizenship education, *Oxford Review of Education*, 30(4): 489–507.

Oulton, C., Dillon, J. and Grace, M. (2004b) Reconceptualizing the teaching of controversial issues, *International Journal of Science Education*, 26(4): 411–23.

Qualifications and Curriculum Authority (QCA) (1998) *Education for Citizenship and Teaching of Democracy in Schools.* London: QCA.

Qualifications and Curriculum Authority (QCA) and the Department for Education and Employment (DfEE) (1999) *Citizenship.* London: QCA/DfEE.

22

Spiritual education

Ann-Marie Brandom, Mike Poole and Andrew Wright

Introduction

To achieve qualified teacher status (QTS) new teachers must demonstrate that they can 'plan opportunities to contribute to pupils' personal, Spiritual, Moral, Social and Cultural development' (DfEE 1998: 12). This chapter deals solely with the topic of spirituality. Why? Because in the first instance, although there are issues around definitions of what constitutes moral, social and cultural development, there are very specific difficulties in defining spirituality, not least being the fact that it is not necessarily a subject of comfortable public discourse. Second, although there are resources to support the delivery of spirituality across the curriculum, they do not address the issue of teacher confidence in handling spirituality in the classroom.

The requirement to be able to 'plan opportunities to contribute to pupils' personal, spiritual, moral, social and cultural development' (DfEE 1998: 12) reflects government concern that 'insufficient attention has been paid explicitly to the spiritual . . . aspects of pupils' development' (DfE 1994: 9). The 1988 Education Reform Act requires the promotion of 'the spiritual, moral, cultural, mental and physical development of pupils at school and of society' (DES 1988: 1). This requirement is reinforced by the Office for Standards in Education's (Ofsted) *Framework for the Inspection of Schools* (Ofsted 1993a) which expects inspectors to report on the provision made by schools for the spiritual development of children.

What exactly is 'spiritual development'? Is it merely a rhetorical reference to the conglomeration of experiences that constitute postmodern 'identity'? Or does it have a more substantial and critical role to play in the education of our pupils? We suggest that spiritual development is at the heart of the educational process since authentic education is inextricably bound up with ultimate questions of the meaning and purpose of life.

This chapter develops a working definition of spirituality, explores the developing place of spirituality in education, considers spirituality as a whole-school issue, and finally, presents a case study designed to stimulate reflection on classroom practice.

What is spirituality?

Effective spiritual education in schools requires a clear understanding of what teachers are being asked to deal with. 'Spirituality' is a notoriously ephemeral concept; although it has something to do with the ultimate meaning and purpose of life, attempts at a tighter definition tend to prove elusive. The traditional equation of spirituality with Christian piety, in which the task of spiritual education was to nurture children into a confession of the Christian faith, seems disturbingly narrow in the context of our multi-faith and multicultural classrooms. However, there is a real danger that, in resisting such Christian exclusivism, schools will inadvertently embrace a bland inclusive spirituality that, in trying to be all things to all people, ends up having nothing of value to say to anybody. Consequently, spiritual educators have embarked on a search for a flexible definition of spirituality, one acceptable to the broad sweep of public opinion yet at the same time open to the insights of specific spiritual traditions.

A frequent starting point in the search is the ambiguous relationship between spirituality and religion. For many, genuine spirituality is rooted in the sphere of the sacred, bound up with a desire to locate the ultimate meaning and purpose of life in some form of transcendent reality above and beyond the universe. The religious disciplines of prayer, worship and meditation enable the believer to enter into a spiritual relationship with God, Nirvana or some other conception of ultimate reality. Though the religious quest resonates with contemporary New Age sensibilities – in sharp contrast to the earlier rationalistic rejection of religious discourse as meaningless superstition – it is not without its problems. If we accept a necessary relationship between spirituality and religion, which specific religious tradition(s) ought we to teach in schools? In doing so, do we not effectively disenfranchise the spiritual lives of atheists and agnostics?

A second starting point is the dualism between the physical or material and spiritual or immaterial. Plato viewed the material world as transient and contingent, contrasting it unfavourably with the eternal and stable realm of spiritual forms (Hamilton and Cairns 1961). The ultimate meaning and purpose of our lives lies not in our physical bodies, which are destined to return to dust and ashes, but in the flourishing of our immortal souls. This Platonic dualism gave birth to an anthropology in which our spiritual selves are represented as 'ghosts in the machine' and 'spirits in the material world'. This dualism leads to forms of spirituality rooted in the ascetic renunciation of the physical world, such as a decision to resist the materialistic values of consumer capitalism or to follow the eight-fold path of Buddhism. A mirror image of this ascetic spirituality is to be found in the

Epicurean celebration of the brute fact of human sensuality, sexuality and physicality.

A third starting point can be found in the idea of human freedom which places the introspective and self-conscious individual at the spiritual centre of the universe. This positioning can lead to the equation of spiritual health with psychological well-being and an ultimate concern for self-awareness, self-understanding and self-acceptance. Such introspective spirituality is cultivated by a variety of modern techniques such as therapy, meditation and counselling. Two important observations need to be made about this perspective: in the first place, there is an increasing consensus that we are relational creatures, and that our self-understanding is as much dependent on our external relationships with society, culture and nature as it is on our internal self-understanding. Second, postmodern philosophers, such as Foucault, argue that our identities are in constant flux and, consequently, spiritual health depends not on our ability to 'find ourselves' but rather on our ability constantly to construct and celebrate multiple identities (Gutting 1994).

These three approaches to the complex question of spirituality are best seen as complementary and interconnected rather than as mutually exclusive: our ultimate spiritual concern needs to take account of our religious or secular world views, of the relationship of our inner selves to our bodies and to the material world, and of our developing identities as we seek to relate both to ourselves and those around us. This leads us to propose the following working definition of spirituality:

> Spirituality is the relationship of the individual, within community and tradition, to that which is – or is perceived to be – of ultimate concern, ultimate value and ultimate truth, as appropriated through an informed, sensitive and reflective striving for spiritual wisdom.
>
> (Wright 2000: 104)

Some comments will help clarify this definition:

- Spirituality here is intimately linked with personal identity as formed both by inner self-understanding and by our developing relationships with the world about us.
- The distinction between the way we see the world and the way the world actually is opens up the possibility of our spiritual values being either in harmony or dissonance with the actual order of things.
- It follows that our ultimate concerns may be pathologically misdirected; for example, in a desire to dress in the latest fashion or in a more sinister need to victimize others on the basis of their race or sexual orientation.
- Spiritual truth is not neutral but value laden and demanding of our full engagement.
- Wisdom rooted in an ability to reflect in-depth on our experience of life, rather than abstract rationality or unrestrained emotivism, is the appropriate means of examining our spiritual commitments.
- The definition deliberately leaves the question of the substantial content of spirituality hanging in the air, not because the issue is unimportant but because the issue is too important prematurely to close down any options.

- The definition is offered not as a final statement but as a working model intended as a heuristic tool to enhance the possibility of cultivating spiritual literacy in schools.

Spirituality and education

There is no easy route from establishing a working understanding of spirituality to successful classroom practice. As a teacher you need to begin this journey by taking account of the legislation concerning spirituality, and of a range of approaches to spiritual education – traditionalist, progressive and critical (Wright 1998; Copley 2000).

When the 1944 Education Act referred to the spiritual dimension of education, it had in mind a specifically Christian spirituality. The context was that of a partnership between the state and the established Church of England that sought to utilize education as a means of bringing about the moral and spiritual rejuvenation of the nation in the aftermath of the horrors of the Second World War. The Act adopted a traditionalist model of education as cultural transmission that has its roots in the educational philosophy of John Locke ([1693] 2000). If the immediate task was to transmit knowledge through the traditional disciplines, the overriding aim was to cultivate those moral and spiritual virtues and habits of mind necessary for pupils to find their proper place in a civilized society. This fundamental task was to be achieved through compulsory religious education and daily acts of collective Christian worship. Pupils were to be nurtured into a Christian value system drawn from the Sermon on the Mount and the Ten Commandments. Spirituality was narrowly and exclusively Christian spirituality.

The 1960s saw a reaction against this traditionalist Christian pedagogy, driven by the recognition that – given the reality of an increasingly secular and pluralistic society – Christian values were being transmitted in an authoritarian manner which effectively silenced the voices of alternative spiritual traditions. The reaction against Christian traditionalism reconceptualized rather than rejected the task of spiritual education. In effect, the source of spiritual values was relocated; no longer rooted in Christian revelation, they were instead to be found in the innate spiritual insight of children uncorrupted by society. Spiritual values were to be discovered introspectively rather than imposed externally. The task of the emergent progressive child-centred education that came to dominate the 1960s was to free children's spirituality from external constraint and enable them to discover their own inner spiritual selves. It was to Rousseau's romantic pedagogy rather than Locke's traditionalism that teachers turned for philosophical inspiration (Rousseau [1762] 1986).

The 1970s and 1980s saw a reaction against child-centred progressivism linked to sustained attempts to recover a traditional subject-centred education, a process exemplified in the introduction of the National Curriculum. The 1988 Education Reform Act (ERA) adopted a minimalist approach to spiritual education: schools must offer a balanced and broadly based curriculum in such a way that it 'promotes the spiritual, moral, cultural, mental and physical development of pupils at the school and of society' (DES 1988: 1). When the legislation was enacted, many observers assumed that this fleeting reference to spirituality would be treated as a mere rhetorical flourish that would have little direct impact on schools. The fact that, on the contrary, there has been a renaissance in spiritual education in schools since 1988 requires some explanation. Two key factors appear to have influenced this process. The first is the traditionalist concern of successive governments to utilize education as a tool for the moral rejuvenation of society (aided by the decision of Ofsted to report on the provision made by schools for the spiritual development of their pupils rather than the outcomes of this provision). The second factor was the response of teachers concerned with the rigid subject-centred nature of the National Curriculum who found in the reference to spirituality a Trojan horse that opened up the possibility of recovering a more flexible form of progressive child-centred pedagogy. As Tate observes, nobody 'wants their child to leave school clutching a handful of certificates, but no idea of how to be a human being' (Talbot and Tate 1997: 2).

The result has been a flourishing of spiritual education, coupled with a fundamental confusion concerning its nature, material content and pedagogical processes. There is an impasse between those traditionalists who wish to transmit clear spiritual values to children (either in the form of an inclusive liberal humanism or an exclusive Christian pietism) and those progressives who see spiritual education as a means of undermining the incipient authoritarianism of the 1988 legislation (by freeing children to create their own spiritual identities against the backdrop of a child-centred education reconstituted within a postmodern framework). In recent years there has been an attempt to break the traditionalist–progressive deadlock through the development of a critical spiritual pedagogy based around five key principles.

- **Spirituality is a controversial issue**. Since there is no public consensus regarding the ultimate meaning and purpose of life, teachers should acknowledge a range of competing and conflicting spiritual traditions. This strategy rejects a relativistic education that treats all spiritual perspectives as equally valid and invites pupils to create their own spiritual values on the basis of their untutored desires and inclinations. Such a move ignores the possibility that our ultimate concerns can be both morally unacceptable and intellectually inadequate.
- **Spirituality enhances human freedom**. Critical spiritual pedagogy seeks to maximize the spiritual freedom of pupils by rejecting the paternalistic pedagogic strategies of both traditionalists and progressives. Traditionalists are paternalistic in imposing a single dominant spiritual tradition on pupils, while progressives are paternalistic in imposing on pupils the postmodern ideology that their immediate spiritual preferences are always valid. Authentic spiritual freedom, it is claimed, requires that pupils learn to engage critically with the ambiguous nature of spirituality.
- **Spirituality is rooted in nurture**. Critical spiritual pedagogy accepts that spiritual nurture – understood as the induction of pupils into a

specific value system – is an inevitable outcome of formal schooling. It rejects the myth that schools can be spiritually neutral institutions: they will always work – if only implicitly – with a set of ultimate values that will help shape the spiritual lives of pupils. It follows that schools should openly embrace their role as transmitters of spiritual value and strive to bring spiritual integrity in all aspects of the life of the community.

- **Spirituality must be appropriated critically**. The process of spiritual nurture must always be supplemented with a process of critical spiritual education. Nurture alone will produce only spiritually contented pigs while critical education will strive to form spiritually discontented philosophers. Pupils will need to be led towards a critical awareness of their own spiritual horizons, of the spiritual horizons of the school as an institution and of the spiritual horizons of a range of alternative spiritual traditions.
- **Authentic spirituality demands spiritual literacy**. Critical spiritual pedagogy requires schools to equip pupils with appropriate levels of spiritual wisdom, thus enabling them to engage with spiritual questions in an informed, sensitive and intelligent manner. Pupils must be taught spiritual discernment, insight and understanding if they are to have the freedom to flourish as spiritual beings.

Spirituality in the whole school

It is time to ground the abstract discussion of the previous two sections in the concrete reality of schools and classrooms. Any discussion of the place of spirituality in the whole school needs to take account of the politics of education. The final two decades of the last century saw a polarization of authority and responsibility away from local educational authorities into both central government and individual schools. The current system gives central government the role of setting the broad educational agenda, and – via a complex system of surveillance and inspection – ensuring that individual schools successfully conform to this agenda. At the same time individual schools have significant levels of responsibility for their own development as they seek to organize and structure themselves to meet the demands of central government. This increase in local autonomy has led to a structural pluralism in which an increasingly diverse range of schools plough their own individual furrows. The minimalist nature of the legislation covering spirituality offers schools a fair degree of autonomy in developing their provision for spiritual education.

Government advice on the implementation of spiritual education, presented in *Spiritual and Moral Development* (SCAA 1995), reinforces this picture of the autonomy of individual schools in their provision for spiritual development. The document offers no more than a generalized understanding of spirituality: spirituality is presented as being fundamental to the human condition, transcending ordinary everyday experience and concerned with the search for identity and meaning in response to death, suffering, beauty and evil; spirituality may be encountered in our beliefs, sense of awe, wonder and mystery, feelings of transcendence, search for meaning and purpose, self-knowledge, relationships, creativity and feelings and emotions; the promotion of spiritual development requires the nurturing of curiosity, imagination, insight and intuition (Wright 1998: 17). It is clear that this understanding leaves room for engagement with a broad range of specific spiritual traditions, both religious and humanistic, and does not preclude traditionalist, progressive or critical approaches. There is, though, a clear expectation that spiritual provision will be encountered in the school's ethos, its collective worship and in its explicit curriculum.

The spiritual ethos of the school will need to be a reality rather than an aspiration. The Department for Education and Employment (DfEE) expects schools to include a mission statement in their documentation that provides an opportunity for schools to make explicit their specific spiritual visions of the ultimate meaning and purpose of life, in general, and of education, in particular. Mission statements vary from school to school, depending on each school's foundation. A state-sponsored Muslim school, for example, is likely to have a very different spiritual vision than that of a multicultural school that grounds its values in the tradition of liberal humanism. The mission statement needs to be public property, articulated, owned and implemented by the whole school community. Gold and Evans claim that research demonstrates 'that a school where the purpose of education is clearly articulated and communicated is a far more effective school than one in which there is no obviously agreed purpose' (1998: 14).

The quality and integrity of a school's provision for spiritual education is likely to be reflected in its response to the vexed question of collective worship. A healthy mark of any community is its ability to celebrate its spiritual achievements and aspirations. All too often, collective worship reflects spiritual sickness rather than health. An apologetic attempt to appease Ofsted inspectors through a hesitant act of worship with which few can identify introduces a spiritual vacuum into the very heart of the school community. A school's core spiritual values need to be celebrated with dignity and integrity. This may take the form of either a religious act of worship or a secular assembly, since the legislation regarding collective worship is extremely flexible and makes available a range of religious and secular options.

The contribution of individual teachers to the spiritual life of the school will be reflected in their engagement with the institution's ultimate values. This need not – indeed frequently ought not – be a process of blind acquiescence. A healthy spiritual community will be open to self-criticism if its spiritual values are either inappropriately formulated or implemented. More specifically, individual teachers will need to reflect on the place of spirituality in the classroom in their roles as form tutors and subject teachers.

Effective promotion of spiritual development in individual subject areas needs to respond to the ultimate questions about the meaning and purpose of life that are integral to each academic discipline. This applies to a geography teacher teaching about the weather system, to an English teacher addressing Keats' suggestion that 'Beauty is truth and truth beauty', and to a PE teacher inviting students to reflect on the importance of physical fitness. In each subject area there is opportunity to allow students to step back and see the larger picture of life, rather than simply knuckle down and improve their grades. Classroom teachers will need to ensure that the broader spiritual picture informs their lesson planning so that their classroom teaching effectively stimulates the critical, imaginative and creative dimension of their pupils' spiritual lives.

Science education – a case study

Ofsted (1993b: 17) emphasized that 'The promotion of pupils' spiritual, moral, social and cultural development is a "whole school" issue . . . other subjects [than religious education] can play no less significant a part in inviting pupils to reflect on the purpose and meaning of life'. There is not the space here to consider the spiritual dimension of every subject, so our discussion is limited to a single case study, science. Some science teachers have found difficulty in 'promoting' the spiritual dimension of their subject and some have resented the requirement as an intrusion into 'teaching the facts'. However, far from adulterating science with metaphysics, the requirement is better seen as having a corrective role in showing science with a human face. It serves to redress some of the scientific imperialism of the early part of the twentieth century, which still lingers on as one strand of popular culture. As the foregoing discussion has indicated, the category 'spiritual' has many facets, several of which can help teachers show pupils the scientific enterprise in ways that neither exaggerate nor undermine its capabilities. They can be placed in four groups:

Awe, wonder and mystery

Young pupils find aspects of the natural world quite breathtaking, but increasing age is often accompanied by a blasé attitude. There is some justification for this change of attitude since something remarkable may seem like magic to a young child who has not yet understood the physical structures and processes involved. There is no good reason, however, why the sensations of awe, wonder and mystery generated by gazing into the night sky or studying how our bodies work should be diminished through increased learning, as though 'explaining' scientifically somehow 'explains away' non-scientific perspectives. Such sensations are most likely to be fostered and preserved if science teachers themselves experience and refer to them and are constantly aware of how little anyone knows of what there is to be known.

Curiosity, creativity and imagination

The role of curiosity in initiating scientific investigation needs no comment, but an understanding of the roles of creativity and imagination in scientific discovery has, over recent decades, grown considerably.

The place of metaphor and conceptual models in promoting understanding of theoretical structures is now widely acknowledged in science as elsewhere. Teachers might help pupils to see how this has worked by introducing them to such examples as the water circuit model of electricity flowing in a wire or the solar-system model of the hydrogen atom.

Meaning, purpose and identity

The question 'Why do I exist?' can have several meanings. It can be answered by reference to parental desires; it can be answered by a mechanistic description of the biology of human reproduction; it can be answered with reference to the purpose of a transcendent agent, God. The first two answers come from the behavioural and life sciences. The third answer lies outside the remit of science. Pupils sometimes ask for scientific proof that God exists. They have not spotted that it is no use going to science, the study of nature, for answers to religious questions about whether anything other than the natural world exists and to which the world owes its existence. It is beyond the competence of science to answer such questions and *Science in the National Curriculum* indicates that 'Pupils should be taught . . . to consider . . . the kinds of questions science can and cannot answer' (DfEE/QCA 1999: 37, 46) and, more, recently, 'that there are some questions that science cannot answer, and some that science cannot address' (DfEE/QCA 2006: 37). Nevertheless, science studies may prompt such questions. 'Why is there something rather than nothing?' is a question of great antiquity, which the noted scientist Stephen Hawking (1988: 174) has recently rephrased as 'Why does the universe go to all the bother of existing?' A debate in class over this question could constitute an awareness of that which is of ultimate value.

More recently has come an awareness of the apparent 'fine-tuning' of the universe for life. If the physical constants of nature were even minutely different – some estimates give a minuscule difference of one part in one followed by 60 noughts as significant – we should not be here. Does this mean the universe is planned and purposeful? The mystery does not disappear by pointing out that this fine balance may result from an inflationary model of the universe. That simply pushes the question back a stage further to 'Why did the early universe have the properties which gave rise to an inflationary period, which in turn gave rise to the "fine tuning"?' It is important to remember when teaching science that there is more than one type of explanation. A scientific explanation of the existence of the universe in terms of a hot Big Bang is compatible with a religious explanation in terms of a purposeful creator. Failure to recognize a plurality of explanations is perhaps the most serious and probably the most common philosophical error encountered in science teaching. However, such recognition provides an opportunity for a discussion on the variety of world views held by members of the class. Such acknowledgement of this diversity would again be addressing questions about ultimate value.

The first half of the twentieth century saw an elevation of the status of science to a level that could not be justified. Since science had been so successful in its rightful area of mapping the natural world, it was elevated by some philosophers to the position of the ultimate test of meaning, in a movement called logical positivism. Supposedly based on science, all statements had to be verified empirically if they were to be counted as meaningful and therefore possible candidates for truth. The system crumbled, however, because science itself contained assumptions, like the uniformity of nature, that could not be verified scientifically. Science as a subject does not have all the answers, but if the logical positivist position had been defensible it would have negated notions of transcendence.

Feelings of transcendence

The term 'spiritual' has come into fashion in education over recent years, used in a way that encompasses those who do not hold specific religious beliefs as well as those that do. Although, as Ofsted (1993a: 21f) has pointed out, ' "Spiritual" is not synonymous with "religious" ', religious beliefs do form a major component of the broader concept of spirituality. Religious beliefs have played a role in the development of modern science from the seventeenth century onwards, and studies of the interplay between these two disciplines have become a big industry worldwide in academia over the last few decades. True, some sections of the media persist in an outdated confrontational approach and give to a few voices a disproportionate amount of air time to back up the notion of conflict. But academic historians of science have found the 'warfare model' inadequate to describe a set of relationships that is much more positive and interesting. Even the folklore accounts of the Galileo affair and the Darwinian controversies have been weighed in the balance and found wanting. Geoffrey Cantor, Professor of History of Science at Leeds, has summed up a contemporary view of these episodes:

> Galileo can no longer be portrayed as the harbinger of truth and enlightenment who was pitted against reactionary priests ... his censure resulted partly from his mishandling of a sensitive diplomatic situation. The other paradigmatic conflict concerns the Darwinian theory of evolution and centres on the Huxley–Wilberforce confrontation in 1860. These opponents are now viewed as trading minor insults in the heat of debate and not as exemplifying the necessary conflict between science and religion.
>
> (Cantor 1991: 290)

Teaching science in the National Curriculum provides many natural opportunities for introducing topics such as these from the history of science when the work of Galileo and Darwin are taught. In parallel with such historical episodes, it is valuable to include certain philosophical points about science, such as the nature of explanation, reductionism, scientific laws, language and models as well as the presuppositions of science. It has largely been due to misunderstandings about points like these that the idea of a mismatch between science and spirituality has arisen. A detailed discussion of such points and some practical classroom suggestions can be found in Poole (1995, 1998) and Charis Science (2000). A further encouragement for the engagement of science with spirituality, albeit within the time constraints of a crowded curriculum, comes from the religious education community. A survey of two-thirds of the locally determined Agreed Syllabuses for Religious Education (Bausor and Poole 2002, 2003) showed that two-thirds of these contained entries on 'science-and-religion'. It was evident that more could be done and the appearance of the *Non-Statutory National Framework for Religious Education* in October 2004 set a good example by including substantial reference to the importance of treating this aspect of spirituality.

Concluding comments

For many teachers, the current climate of education, with its stress on academic attainment at the expense of a commitment to the development of the whole child, is a cause of deep concern. There is a real danger of the soul of education being smothered by bureaucracy and a range of political agendas. Despite such concerns, the fact remains that teachers have a fundamental responsibility to develop the spiritual lives of their pupils by enabling them to engage in an informed, sensitive and intelligent manner with questions about the ultimate meaning and purpose of life.

References

Bausor, J. and Poole, M.W. (2002) Science-and-religion in the agreed syllabuses – an investigation and some suggestions, *British Journal of Religious Education*, 25(1): 18–32.

Bausor, J. and Poole, M.W. (2003) Science education and religious education: possible links? *School Science Review*, 85(311): 117–24.

Cantor, G. (1991) *Michael Faraday, Sandemanian and Scientist*. Basingstoke: Macmillan.

Charis Science (2000) *Resources for Spiritual and Moral Development across the Curriculum*. Nottingham: The Stapleford Centre.

Copley, T. (2000) *Spiritual Development in the State School. A Perspective on Worship and Spirituality in the Education System of England and Wales*. Exeter: University of Exeter Press.

Department for Education (DfE) (1994) *Circular 1/94, Religious Education and Collective Worship*. London: HMSO.

Department for Education and Employment (DfEE) (1998) *Circular 4/98, Requirements for Courses of Initial Teacher Training*. London: HMSO.

Department for Education and Employment/Qualifications and Curriculum Authority (DfEE/QCA) (1999) *Science in the National Curriculum*. London: HMSO.

Department for Education and Employment/Qualifications and Curriculum Authority (DfEE/QCA) (2006) *Science: The National Curriculum for England*. London: HMSO.

Department for Education and Science (DES) (1988) *Education Reform Act*. London: HMSO.

Gold, A. and Evans, J. (1998) *Reflecting on School Management*. London: Falmer.

Gutting, G. (1994) *The Cambridge Companion to Foucault*. Cambridge: Cambridge University Press.

Hamilton, E. and Cairns, H. (eds) (1961) *Plato: The Collective Dialogues*. Princeton, NJ: Princeton University Press.

Hawking, S.W. (1988) *A Brief History of Time*. London: Bantam Press.

Locke, J. ([1693] 2000) *Some Thoughts Concerning Education*. Oxford: Clarendon Press.

Office for Standards in Education (Ofsted) (1993a) *Handbook for the Inspection of Schools: Part 2, Framework for the Inspection of Schools*. London: HMSO.

Office for Standards in Education (Ofsted) (1993b) *Handbook for the Inspection of Schools: Part 4, Guidance on the Inspection Schedule*. London: HMSO.

Poole, M.W. (1995) *Beliefs and Values in Science Education*. Buckingham: Open University Press.

Poole, M.W. (1998) *Teaching about Science and Religion: Opportunities within Science in the National Curriculum*. Abingdon: Culham College Institute.

Qualifications and Curriculum Authority/Department for Education and Skills (2004) *The Non-Statutory National Framework for Religious Education*. London: QCA.

Rousseau, J.J. ([1792] 1986) *Emile*. London: Dent.

School Curriculum and Assessment Authority (SCAA) (1995) *Spiritual and Moral Development. SCAA Discussion Papers No. 3*. London: SCAA.

Talbot, M. and Tate, N. (1997) Shared values in a pluralist society, in R. Smith and P. Standish (eds) *Teaching Right and Wrong: Moral Education in the Balance*. Stoke-on-Trent: Trentham Books.

Wright, A. (1998) *Spiritual Pedagogy. A Survey, Critique and Reconstruction of Contemporary Spiritual Education in England and Wales*. Abingdon: Culham College Institute.

Wright, A. (2000) *Spirituality and Education*. London: Falmer.

23

The importance of teachers and schools in health promotion

Peter Duncan

Sex and school dinners: what exactly *is* health promotion?

In February 2005, the celebrity chef, Jamie Oliver, appeared in the Channel Four television series, 'Jamie's School Dinners'. Featuring Kidbrooke School in the London Borough of Greenwich, Oliver's programme focused on the poor quality of food being served up in UK schools and the general lack of training and understanding in the area of nutrition. The series led to a petition of nearly 300,000 signatures being taken to 10 Downing Street and the then Education Secretary, Ruth Kelly, agreeing to a £220m increase in funding for school catering services. It was also central to the establishment of the 'watchdog' School Food Trust and provoked wholesale changes to menus and food choices in schools across the country (Plunkett 2005; Lawrence 2006).

Towards the end of the same year, a report from the Government's independent advisers on sexual health and teenage pregnancy recommended that detailed knowledge about sex should be included routinely in the education of all pupils. The report came in the wake of Britain continuing to maintain a Western European lead for teenage pregnancy rates, and rising levels of many sexually transmitted diseases among young people (Campbell 2005).

These separate stories of school dinners and sex represent a number of important things. First, they tell of the wide levels of interest in schools as places where 'good health', whatever that means, can be encouraged. Second, they signify that our interest in promoting the health of young people is often accompanied by high degrees of emotional fervour and debate. Third, they represent the complexity inherent in efforts at health promotion. We want young people to choose a healthy diet and be careful in their sexual behaviour, but how do we balance this with a desire that they should make the choices *they* want, and in the context of a wider world that, in some respects, is not much interested in people 'choosing health'?

Above all else, though, the stories raise the question, what exactly *is* health promotion and what can be done to promote health in schools? Should we be banning fizzy drinks and crisps, or engaging in dialogue with pupils about food choices? Should we be scaring young people into sexual abstinence with horror stories of disease and unwanted babies, or should we be supporting their emotional development so that they make the best decisions for themselves about their own sex lives and relationships? I think the answer to these questions lies in developing a careful understanding of the nature of health promotion; of why it's important for schools to commit themselves to the promotion of health; and what teachers can do in support of effective health promotion. This chapter tries to address these issues.

It all depends on what 'health' is . . .

If we want to move towards greater understanding of what needs to be done to promote health, it makes sense to suggest that we need a clear idea of the nature of 'health' itself. Achieving this clarity, though, will be problematic, because health is a contested concept (Katz *et al.* 2001; Seedhouse 2001). Different individuals, communities and societies are likely to hold separate views about the nature of health. What might be called the 'medical model' account, that is, health as 'the absence of disease', has historically been highly influential in shaping understanding, but has met with robust challenges, particularly over the last half-century or so. These challenges, often reinforced by empirical evidence, assert that health is (or ought to be) seen in much broader terms; as encompassing notions of positive well-being, and possessing emotional, social, mental and spiritual dimensions as well as the narrow physical one (World Health Organisation 1986).

Whatever our views about the nature of health, it seems clear that they will play a large part in moulding our perceptions of what influences and determines health, what needs to be done to promote it and who has responsibility for taking action. If someone believes that health is, say, the absence of disease, they may well consider that what determines an individual's health is access to good quality health care and disease prevention services. The purpose of health promotion then becomes the provision of expert-led advice on health care access and on the prevention of disease. If this advice was persuasive and offered from the 'top down', we might call it 'medical model' health promotion (Tones and Green 2004). On the other hand, if information was presented in a more even-handed and neutral way, we might consider this to be health promotion according to the 'educational model'. Then again, if we think that health has quite a lot to do with a capacity to function appropriately in our social context, then what determines it might be things like our levels of income, the quality of our family and other relationships, our environment and so on. The purpose of health promotion might now be to engage in sustaining or improving these sorts of things, either through work addressing social structures (health promotion according to a 'social change model') or through supporting people as they attempt to deal with them for themselves. We might call this latter 'empowerment model' health promotion (Tones and Green 2004).

It all depends on values . . .

Of course, it's not impossible that our conceptions of the nature of health and the purpose of health promotion will involve both disease prevention and a concern with social circumstance. This is quite reasonable, and an attempt to deal with 'health' by addressing issues in both respects would certainly be pragmatic and quite possibly worthwhile. But it's also important to recognize that the models above, and the subsequent approaches to health promotion that they suggest, are essentially rooted in *values*. If we believe, say, that health promotion is about the prevention of disease (the medical model), then we will place value on work and approaches that aim to reduce disease. We are also likely to value the knowledge of expert professionals who we think are best placed to direct individuals about what they need to do to avoid health-harming, disease-causing behaviours. We are much *less* likely to place value on the development of people as autonomous individuals who have the capacity to make up their own minds about whether they choose to avoid the behaviour that professionals deem to be health-harming. On the other hand, this would be *exactly* the kind of value important to the 'empowerment model' health promoter.

If this discussion about values sounds rather abstract and makes health promotion seem rather vague, there are two important points to be made. First, the essential place of values in understanding and going about the promotion of health makes it no different from any other aspect of the enterprise of schooling and education (Cribb and Gewirtz 2001). Second, depending on the values we hold, the ways in which we undertake health promotion might be very different. Imagine, for a moment, that there are two teachers in separate schools, both of whom have responsibility for co-ordinating health promotion. Both have also been asked by their respective heads to address the issue of smoking. Mr Green believes in 'medical model' health promotion and the values associated with this, while Ms White has a strong belief in the values of the 'empowerment model'. My assertion is that the separate values of these two teachers mean that they will want to plan and implement two quite different programmes for smoking prevention in their schools. Yet both of them would believe that they are engaging, in a worthwhile way, in 'health promotion'.

Why should we be concerned about health promotion?

If health promotion is as potentially disputed and contested an area as this, the question of why we should be concerned with it at all becomes pertinent. I want to suggest that there are three possible kinds of reasons.

Because we have to be concerned

Health promotion in the National Curriculum – what is referred to as Personal, Social and Health Education (PSHE) – is subject to non-statutory guidelines at Key Stages 3 and 4 (Qualifications and Curriculum Authority 2006). Sex education, which we might reasonably see as contributing to health promotion, is different again. Here, there is an obligation on schools to teach biological aspects of sex through science. Schools also have an obligation to teach about HIV/AIDS and other sexually transmitted infections. However, parents may request that pupils be excused from any aspect of sex education apart from that contained in the National Curriculum (Scriven 2001; Campbell 2005). The closely connected area of citizenship education is also a compulsory subject at these Key Stages.

All of this complexity contributes to a sense that education policy makers are both grappling with, and wary of, health promotion. It seems as if they recognize its importance but, at the same time, realize the potential for contention that it contains. This situation is perhaps no more than is to be expected, given the value-laden nature of the field. Overall, however, it is possible to suggest that the policy climate is gradually edging towards a position in which the promotion of health becomes a requirement, one way or another, placed on schools and teachers. Ofsted now expects, for example, that schools are able to demonstrate how they are contributing to the five national outcomes for children stipulated by *Every Child Matters* and the Children Act 2004:

- being healthy
- staying safe
- enjoying and achieving
- making a positive contribution
- economic well-being (Department of Health 2005).

It has been suggested that this inspection requirement can be closely connected to the purposes and outcomes of effective health promotion, particularly in the context of the National Healthy Schools Programme (Department of Health 2005). In short, there is more and more reason to believe that teachers *have* to be concerned with health promotion.

Because we want to be concerned

Arguably, though, an organizational and policy requirement to be concerned with the promotion of health is not the best reason for involvement. A sense of the value of health promotion also ought to be driving interest; the idea that, because of your identity as a teacher and your professional persona, you *want* to be concerned with it.

At one level, the promotion of health is important, professionally, to the teacher because healthier pupils and schools are likely to be more productive places of learning and teaching. There is strong evidence to support the connection between positive learning and the kind of environment created by and within schools committed to health promotion (Weare 2000).

This reason for the professional value of health promotion to teachers is important, but it is also rather instrumental. A more fundamental reason is that health promotion, or at least the version connected to notions of empowerment that I described earlier, aligns very closely with what many regard as the essential ideals of education.

Liberal notions of the aims of education involve, among other things, its attempting to foster not simply an individual's ability to function in society, but to develop in ways that are autonomous and independent (Schnack 2000). These are also the ideals of health promotion according to the empowerment model. We want to encourage the development of young people who have due regard for their health. We want to do so in ways that recognize them as individuals moving towards independence and autonomy. Indeed, for empowerment model health promotion, autonomy development is a fundamental aspect of the 'health' we are seeking to promote. Is it possible to see someone as properly 'healthy' if they are constrained and coerced at every turn in their daily lives? So the goal of health promotion in the empowerment model is analogous to the broad aims of liberal education. If, as a teacher, you are committed to the ideology and values of liberal education, part of this commitment should include an interest in empowerment-oriented health promotion. Some might even see (rightly in my view) liberal education itself as health promotion. Of course, none of this is to suggest that everyone in our society will subscribe to the particular ideal of liberal education.

Because being concerned makes sense

Carefully considered, the set of reasons I have just presented for being concerned about health promotion – revolving around policy requirements and professional values – come together to form the view that interest in this area is simple good sense. Encouraging development of the capacity to make appropriate health-related decisions will benefit pupils (Halstead and Reiss 2003). Engaging in activity that is (or at least ought to be) closely related to the ideals of liberal education itself will benefit teachers. It will do this, in part, through enhancing their senses of professional identity and the fundamental importance of their occupational task. This is perhaps especially important at a time when critique and criticism of the profession of teaching is relatively widespread in our society (Weare 2000). And the benefit of health promotion to pupils and teachers will naturally result in benefit to schools as institutions, with a key social role in promoting the health of future populations (Tones and Green 2004).

Perhaps the central questions, at this point, are these: can you, as someone becoming a teacher, agree with any or all of these kinds of reasons that I've given for being concerned with health promotion? Are there additional reasons you would want to draw on? And if it's the case that you're not able either to agree with my reasons or construct any of your own, why is this so?

The difficulty with empowerment

My account of the reasons for teachers being concerned with health promotion has revolved, in part, around it operating according to what I have called an empowerment model. It is true that there are good reasons for bringing this to the foreground in any discussion of the field. The model holds a prominent position in the writing of theorists (Ewles and Simnett 1995; Naidoo and Wills 2000; Tones and Green 2004). The powerful theoretical construction of the model has included claims that individuals who are genuinely empowered are far more likely to make healthy choices. Those who are held back by misinformation or by the health promoter's desire to control, are likely to adopt strategies of resistance, including forming or continuing with 'unhealthy' behaviours. In the context of efforts to promote health, then, empowerment is regarded as a practical necessity as well as a moral requirement (Tones and Green 2004: 2).

But this formulation of the importance of empowerment in health promotion also contains its essential difficulty. In imagining empowered individuals making 'healthy' choices, and others 'resisting health', empowerment health promoters are tacitly admitting that they have preferences about the choices people make (Lucas and Lloyd 2005). Would Ms White, in the example above, *really* be happy if the end result of all her hard work according to the empowerment model was that the number of pupils smoking in the school stayed the same, or even increased? The blunt truth might be that while their methods will be different, both Ms White and Mr Green (who is wedded to the medical model) actually have the same aim in mind, that is, they both want to see smoking levels reduced. The difficulty for Ms White lies in the fact that her efforts at empowerment might have that specific (although probably not explicit) aim. If they do, how can they be *genuinely* empowering?

The problem is compounded by the context in which school health promotion takes place. While we might possibly be able to imagine Ms White being genuinely disinterested in all outcomes except empowered pupils making independent choices, what about her headteacher? The head may well see rising levels of smoking as a poor indicator of the school's success in promoting health. This is particularly likely given the wider political context in which the Department for Education and Skills and the Department of Health have established or agreed national 'health' priorities, which include 'reducing young people's drug, alcohol and tobacco use' (Department of Health 2005: 3).

The reality for health promotion in schools (as well as in other settings) is that there are limits to empowerment. The limits are placed, in part, by the political nature and the political context of schools and education. Of course, this does not necessarily mean that teachers should abandon all efforts to work in ways that aim to be empowering. I have tried, so far, to emphasize the importance of the empowerment model. I have done so both because of its essential connection with the aims and purpose of wider liberal education, and because there is substantial truth in the idea that empowering people is more likely to result in health improvement (regardless of what we understand 'health' to be). But we need to recognize and understand both the limits and the possibilities contained within the idea of empowerment health promotion, and how these might play out in the context of schools and the practice of teaching. This is now the direction of my discussion.

Empowerment in context: healthy schools

The idea of schools as important settings in which health promotion takes place is not a new one. The genesis, however, of what might now be called 'The Healthy Schools Movement' can be traced back to a 1989 World Health Organisation (WHO) conference (Tones and Green 2004) and the publication of *The Healthy School* (Young and Williams 1989). The latter identified the three central components of the health promoting school:

- health promotion as taught through the formal curriculum (what some people would refer to as health education)
- school ethos and environment
- relationships between the school and the wider community in which it is located.

For a school to be regarded as health promoting there is a need for each of these components to operate in synergy with the others. So 'health' is not confined, for example, to an hour of teaching a week. Rather, curriculum opportunities are enhanced and fed by wider work (the development of appropriate school-wide policies related to health, say, or the building of community links).

This relatively holistic understanding of how schools might be able to promote health led, in the mid-1990s, to the establishment of a European Network of Health Promoting Schools (ENHPS). Detailed sets of criteria and specifications for action were developed and refined, which schools seeking to be recognized as 'health promoting' needed to meet. Criteria included, for example, the active promotion of the self-esteem of all pupils, and of the health and well-being of school staff (Beattie 2001).

In England and Wales, the concept of the health promoting school was taken up in part through the establishment of the National Healthy Schools Programme (NHSP). Schools were invited to work towards the achievement of 'Healthy School' status. Revised guidance issued in September 2005 clarified what schools were required to do in order to achieve such status:

Schools are asked to demonstrate evidence in [all of] the core themes *using a whole-school approach involving the whole school community*:

- personal, social and health education including sex and relationship education and drug education (including alcohol, tobacco and volatile substance abuse);
- healthy eating;
- physical activity; and
- emotional health and well-being (including bullying).

(Department of Health 2005: 4)

Government expectation is that by 2009, *every* school will be working towards achieving national 'Healthy School' status.

A number of key issues emerge when considering the potential for success (or otherwise) of schools that seek to become 'health promoting'. Given the emphasis of both ENHPS and Department of Health criteria on whole-school involvement, there is a clear need to encourage participation of all of the school community. As Tones and Green (2004) have pointed out, however, this participation can't be token. If all in the community are to commit to the ambitious objectives of a school aspiring to be health promoting, then everyone needs to be drawn into what Elliot-Kemp (1982) calls 'the circle of understanding'. Principles such as involvement and equity become fundamentally important in establishing and maintaining such a circle. There is also a need to try to ensure that the programme of work is sustainable, as far as possible, and, again, this is only likely to be the case if there is a groundswell of participation from the community concerned.

But while those managing schools might, in theory, agree with the sorts of principles that ought to lie at the heart of the health promoting school, commitment in practice could be altogether more difficult. A school can be regarded as, essentially, a hierarchical organization, depending for its existence and progress on particular kinds of power relationships, both within and outside the institution itself (Ball 2003). As I have already described, schools are also subject to conflicting policy demands, with 'health' often seeming to occupy an uncomfortable place in orders of priorities. Given that part of the school's context involves organizational hierarchy and policy conflict, how easy will it be to adhere to the principles that I have argued are needed to develop schools as health promoting, empowering environments? As one recent evaluation of the impact of the National Healthy School Standard found, more active participation of children and young people is essential if the future success of the programme is to be ensured (National Foundation for Educational Research/ Thomas Coram Research Unit 2004). The central question is one of how this can be achieved, given the nature of schools. To what extent can a school really empower its pupils to engage in issues related to their emotional and mental health, say, when its existence is premised on highly structured and organized power relationships?

Empowerment in context: health in the curriculum

The NHSP makes clear that health-related teaching in the curriculum is just one component of a wider and more holistic approach to health promotion in schools. However, the curriculum is such an important representation of schools' purpose and priorities that it is worth thinking specifically about the extent to which it might support the kind of health promotion according to the empowerment model for which I have been mainly arguing.

NHSP guidance contains clear criteria that schools need to meet with regard to the PSHE curriculum if they are to achieve 'Healthy School' status.

These include use of the National Curriculum framework to deliver a planned programme of PSHE, which is monitored and evaluated to ensure teaching and learning quality, and involves assessment of pupils' progress in line with Qualifications and Curriculum Authority (QCA) guidance (Department of Health 2005: 6).

At Key Stages 3 and 4 (as well as the earlier primary stages), there are three strands to the framework:

- developing confidence and responsibility and making the most of abilities
- developing a healthy, safer lifestyle
- developing good relationships and respecting the differences between people.

(Qualifications and Curriculum Authority 2006)

The clarity of both the NHSP guidance and the National Curriculum framework is certainly encouraging. Commentators have seen the framework as providing greater opportunity for consistency, coherence and progression in the area of PSHE than had perhaps previously been the case (Scriven 2001). Some have gone so far as to suggest that the PSHE framework, together with citizenship education, represent the beliefs and aims of the National Curriculum itself. In particular PSHE, allied with citizenship, can be connected to the belief that education is the route to individual well-being; and to the broad curriculum aim of promoting moral, social and cultural development (Bramall and White 2000; see also Chapter 22). The emphasis on understanding and skills development within the framework, rather than simply the acquisition of knowledge, seems especially important for those wedded to the idea of health promotion as empowerment. Surely one of our central purposes is to support the development of 'confidence and responsibility' within young people?

In the midst of all this positive talk, however, there is a need to offer, again, the reminder that the PSHE framework, in contrast to citizenship, is non-statutory (Qualifications and Curriculum Authority 2006). Once more, context might well place limits on health promotion. Schools and teachers will naturally allow more importance to those subjects that they are statutorily required to teach. Crucially, success in compulsory subjects such as English, mathematics and science (as measured through examination results) is frequently seen as the prime embodiment of individual schools' success – or otherwise. In a feverish climate of exam results and league tables, how easy will it be for teachers to commit themselves to a non-statutory, unexamined subject of considerable complexity?

We might consider that, to some degree, this circumstance is odd. On the one hand, PSHE is seen by some as an important representation within the curriculum of an education policy imperative related to self-development. Part of this representation might entail an orientation towards empowerment health promotion. On the other hand, much of the remaining message from policy makers, embodied within the bulk of the curriculum, is that young people (and those who teach them) need to be firmly pointed in certain ways if their development is to be effective in educational terms. Why is there this conflict?

The example of sex and relationships education (SRE) might help to answer this question. Sex education is the one aspect within the broad field of PSHE that is designated as a statutory requirement. At Key Stages 3 and 4 sex education is a compulsory subject. There are, however, limits to this compulsory nature. In the first place, parents can ask for their children to be excused from any aspects of sex education outside the National Curriculum (HMSO 1996). In effect, it is possible to divide SRE into *sex* education (biological, scientific and compulsory) and *relationships* education (emotional, cultural and vulnerable to the right of parental excuse). In the second place, the way in which this 'relationships' aspect of SRE should be taught is subject to restrictions. Students should be taught, among other things, 'about the nature and importance of marriage for family life and bringing up children' (Qualifications and Curriculum Authority 2006).

So SRE, as the single compulsory component of PSHE, is potentially constrained through both parental acceptance and governmental prescription. This constraint emerges as a result of conflicting values. For some, the value lies in forming and maintaining stable relationships, and promoting this should be the fundamental aim of SRE. Others might see value as lying in the development of questioning, autonomous young people who are able to make up their own minds about the kinds of relationships they have. This clash of values is rendered even more problematic by the real possibility that some people might well think that schools and teachers ought not to have any kind of role in teaching about relationships; this is a job to be conducted by parents, within families. These conflicting values lead, in turn, to separate views of the *aims* of SRE and *frameworks* within which it is conducted. Frameworks might range from believing that schools sex education should not occur at all, through to one founded on the belief that it is about promoting autonomy (Halstead and Reiss 2003).

If, as the example of SRE seems to demonstrate, values lie at the heart of how (and indeed whether) teaching about health is included in the curriculum, then there is a need to recognize that the value of empowerment is only one of a cluster of health-related values. Others holding different values and conceptions might well challenge this way of learning and teaching. And as thinking about SRE has shown, the minefield of values is compounded by policy and curriculum directives and guidelines, which somehow have to balance the separate perceptions of individuals, communities and societies about what kind of 'health' we should be promoting.

The value of health promotion

I began this chapter by raising the question of what exactly it is we are trying to do in promoting health. When schools and teachers think about food and food choice, say, or about sex and relationships, should they be trying to restrict what is considered 'unhealthy' or should they be attempting to encourage pupils to come to their own decisions about these things? I have tried to argue that, for both practical and moral reasons, schools and teachers should broadly be trying to do the latter. However, their capacity to do so may well be limited by policy and organizational structures that often seem to be much more interested in attempting the former. Where does this leave our discussion?

There are a number of things that it is important to emphasize to move forward the debate, and our wider development with regard to health promotion. We need to remind ourselves that 'health' is fundamentally important and a huge source of interest within society. So, given this, it is natural that schools and teachers have an essential role in promoting health to the young people with whom they work.

Ways of promoting health are based on values. Recognizing this is key to establishing what we want to do in promoting health – in determining our purpose and practice in the area. Recognition of the importance of values is also central to understanding how others might or will react to our health promotion work. And if we can understand and predict reactions, there seems to be a greater possibility of engaging in robust justification that might convince others about the worth of our approach. At the very least, understanding others' reactions and perspectives will help us to tailor our work so that it fulfils our own demands as well as others'; a 'win-win' situation is often possible.

And while compromise might sometimes (perhaps often) be required, we need to hold on to the essential importance of empowering as a goal of health promotion in schools; both because of its match with the values of liberal education; and because, plainly speaking, it's more likely to be effective. Schools and teachers have an essential role to play in promoting health. I hope you will take up the challenge of that role.

References

Ball, S. (2003) *The Micropolitics of the School*. London: Routledge.

Beattie, A. (2001) Health-promoting schools as learning organisations, in A. Scriven and J. Orme (eds) *Health Promotion: Professional Perspectives*. Basingstoke: Palgrave.

Bramall, S. and White, D.J. (2000) *Will the New National Curriculum Live up to its Aims?* Ringwood: Philosophy of Education Society of Great Britain.

Campbell, D. (2005) Sex lessons planned for all children, *Observer*, 4 December.

Cribb, A. and Gewirtz, S. (2001) Values and schooling, in J. Dillon and M. Maguire (eds) *Becoming a Teacher* (2nd edn). Buckingham: Open University Press.

Department of Health (2005) *National Healthy Schools Status: A Guide for Schools*. London: Department of Health.

Elliott-Kemp, J. (1982) Managing organisational change, in J. Anderson (ed.) *HEA Health Skills Project*. Leeds: CCDU.

Ewles, L. and Simnett, I. (1995) *Promoting Health* (3rd edn). Harrow: Scutari.

Halstead, J.M. and Reiss, M.J. (2003) *Values in Sex Education*. London: Routledge Falmer.

Her Majesty's Stationery Office (HMSO) (1996) *Education Act*. London: HMSO.

Katz, J., Peberdy, A. and Douglas, J. (2001) *Promoting Health: Knowledge and Practice* (2nd edn). Basingstoke: Palgrave.

Lawrence, F. (2006) Junk foods banned in schools from September, *Guardian*, 3 March.

Lucas, K. and Lloyd, B. (2005) *Health Promotion: Evidence and Experience*. London: Sage.

Naidoo, J. and Wills, J. (2000) *Health Promotion: Foundations for Practice* (2nd edn). London: Bailliere Tindall.

National Foundation for Educational Research/Thomas Coram Research Unit (2004) *Evaluation of the Impact of the National Healthy School Standard: Research Summary.* Slough: NFER.

Plunkett, J. (2005) Oliver reheats school food debate, *Guardian*, 26 October.

Qualifications and Curriculum Authority (QCA) (2006) National Curriculum Online. www.nc.uk.net (accessed 14 March).

Schnack, K. (2000) Action competence as a curriculum perspective, in B. Jensen, K. Schnack and V. Simovska (eds) *Critical Environmental and Health Education.* Copenhagen: Danish University of Education.

Scriven, A. (2001) The influence of government policy on the provision of health education in schools, in A. Scriven and J. Orme (eds) *Health Promotion: Professional Perspectives.* Basingstoke: Palgrave.

Seedhouse, D. (2001) *Health: The Foundations for Achievement* (2nd edn). Chichester: Wiley.

Tones, K. and Green, J. (2004) *Health Promotion: Planning and Strategies.* London: Sage.

Weare, K. (2000) *Promoting Mental, Emotional and Social Health: A Whole School Approach.* London: Routledge.

World Health Organisation (WHO) (1986) *Ottawa Charter for Health Promotion.* Ottawa: World Health Organisation.

Young, I. and Williams, T. (1989) *The Healthy School.* Edinburgh: Scottish Health Education Group.

Further reading

Department of Health (2005) *National Healthy Schools Status: A Guide for Schools.* London: Department of Health.

Lister-Sharp, D., Chapman, S., Stewart-Brown, S. and Sowden, A. (1999) Health Promoting Schools and Health Promotion in Schools: Two Systematic Reviews, *Health Technology Assessment*, 3(22): 1–207. Available at http://www.ncchta.org/execsumm/summ322.htm (accessed September 6, 2006).

Ryder, J. and Campbell, L. (1988) *Balancing Acts in Personal, Social and Health Education.* London: Routledge.

24

Education, the environment and sustainability

Justin Dillon

Introduction

It is a little known fact that we are in the Decade of Education for Sustainable Development. The Decade, which began in 2005, was proposed by the United Nations (UN) in 2002 (Resolution 57/254). The resolution was adopted by the UN General Assembly and UNESCO, the United Nations Educational, Scientific and Cultural Organisation, was designated as the lead agency responsible for the Decade's promotion (see, UNESCO 2006). As part of its contribution to the Decade, the Department for Education and Skills (DfES) published its Sustainable Development Action Plan under the title *Learning for the Future* in 2006. In this chapter, I examine the tensions and controversies around the term 'Education for Sustainable Development' (ESD) and why it is important that all teachers understand some of the many connections between education, the environment and sustainability.

The environment

Before we go any further, it is worth noting that the word 'environment' is itself contested. Writing in 1996, the Canadian researcher, Lucy Sauvé (1996), summarized different ways of conceptualizing the environment, and indicated how they were related (see Table 24.1). It should be evident from Sauvé's taxonomy how a science teacher, a geography teacher, a warden of an environmental education centre, and the head of education at a natural history museum might use quite different conceptualizations of the environment. These different views of the environment might well affect how they teach and what they teach.

Table 24.1 Conceptualizations of the environment (Sauvé 1996)

Environment as nature . . .	to be appreciated, respected, preserved: dualistic, Cartesian interpretation, humans are removed from nature.
Environment as a resource . . .	to be managed: this is our collective biophysical heritage and we must sustain it as it is deteriorating and wasting away. As, for example, in the Judeo-Christian view (Book of Genesis).
Environment as a problem . . .	to be solved: the biophysical environment, the life support system is threatened by pollution and degradation. We must learn to preserve its quality and restore it (problem-solving skills emphasized).
Environment as a place to live . . .	to know and learn about, to plan for, to take care of: day-to-day environment – characterized by its human, socio-cultural, technological and historical components.
Environment as the biosphere . . .	in which we all live together, in the future: 'Spaceship Earth' (Fuller) and Gaia (Lovelock) – self-regulating organism.
Environment as a community project . . .	in which to get involved (that is, a context that affords opportunities for working with others for the benefit of all).
Environment of a human collectivity . . .	a shared living place, political concern, the focus of critical analysis: solidarity, democracy and personal and collective involvement in order to participate in the evolution of the community.

So, for example, in *Our Common Future* (WCED 1987) which, as we will see below, is a seminal document in the history of education and the environment, the implicit conceptualization of the environment appears to be dualistic and Cartesian, that is, the environment is seen as a *global resource*, to be developed and managed for sustainable profit and as *nature*, to be revered and respected for the enjoyment and survival of human beings, thus:

> the environment does not exist as a sphere separate from human actions, ambitions and needs and attempts to defend it in isolation from human concerns have given the very word 'environment' a connotation of naivety in some political circles . . .
>
> (WCED 1987: 6)

There are many who see *Our Common Future* as a simplistic document that tries to be all things to all people. However, one of the positive elements of *Our Common Future* was that it recognized the links between development and the environment:

The environment is where we all live; and development is what we all do in attempting to improve our lot within that abode. The two are inseparable.

(WCED 1987: 6)

Now this is an important statement because it recognizes that focusing on the physical aspects of the environment without considering social issues such as health, employment, legislation and education is, at best, problematic and, at worst, intellectually bankrupt and morally indefensible (see, also, Dillon and Teamey 2002). In the next section, I will examine the key concepts of sustainability and sustainable development, pointing to some problems with the ways in which the terms are used and understood.

Sustainability and sustainable development

Opinions vary as to what is meant by sustainability or sustainable development. In general, though, the lack of agreement about the terms is glossed over, and policy makers make bold assertions without much by way of a caveat. So, for example, the UK Government's sustainable development strategy (DfES 2006: 4) aims 'to enable all people throughout the world to satisfy their basic needs and enjoy a better quality of life, without compromising the quality of life of future generations'. The policy contains five principles that underpin the UK's sustainable development policy. The principles provide clues as to how sustainable development is conceptualized by elements within the government. The five principles are:

- living within environmental limits – ensuring the natural resources needed for life are unimpaired and remain so in the future;
- ensuring a strong, healthy and just society – meeting diverse needs and creating opportunity for all;
- achieving a sustainable economy – with efficient resource use incentivized;
- using sound science responsibly – strong scientific evidence, taking into account scientific uncertainty and public attitudes and values; and
- promoting good governance – effective, participative systems of governance in all levels of society.

(DfES 2006: 4)

In essence, then, we can have our cake now as long as we ensure that there will be enough cake for future generations to eat. Although the principles are contentious and open to interpretation – just what is meant by 'effective' governance, for example? – it would be hard to argue that they are hugely undesirable. It would, however, be easier to argue that they are unachievable or that they do not address some of the key problems facing the world. The DfES sees the overall vision as one which is 'an innovation agenda, inviting us to rethink how we organise our lives and work so that we don't destroy our most precious resources' (2006: 4). Given that policy framework, how do teachers contribute to such laudable, far-reaching aims? What do you need to teach in order that 'all people throughout the world [are enabled] to satisfy their basic needs and [can] enjoy a better quality of life, without compromising the quality of life of future generations'?

In order to address questions such as those, the UK Government established a Sustainable Development Education Panel in 1998. One of the recommendations, in the Panel's first annual report, was that all children should have an entitlement to education for sustainable development (SDEP 1999). This entitlement was to be ensured through the requirements of the National Curriculum, the school inspection framework and through initial and in-service teacher training. The panel commented that:

> Education for sustainable development is not new. It has roots in environmental education, which has evolved since the 1960s, and in development education which first emerged in the 1970s, and also links with a number of related approaches to education which stress relevance to personal, social, economic and environmental change. In the past decade these approaches have increasingly found commonality under the label of 'education for sustainable development' and there is a strengthening consensus about the meaning and implications of this approach for education as a whole.
>
> (SDEP 1999: 28)

The idea that there is a 'strengthening consensus' is questionable. In 1998, the Panel commissioned a study to 'identify a coherent language for the education of Sustainable Development which is relevant to a wide range of bodies and individuals' (SDEP 2000). The authors of the study commented that: 'A "pure" or uniform understanding of Sustainable Development is unlikely to develop, given the necessarily diverse interests of different Influencers – meaning that different sectors (business, education, etc.] will approach it through different "gateways" ' (SDEP 2000). Partly because the language of sustainable development is so unfamiliar, perhaps, the report's authors also commented that:

> Broadly speaking, people are not able to make even the most rudimentary connections between their behaviours and those of businesses and nations on local and global societies, economics and environments.
>
> (SDEP 2000)

If there is a challenge for everyone involved in education, it is to enable people to see the connections and to appreciate how so many of our actions influence a network of individuals and communities around the world.

Some context

Even if it is difficult to appreciate fully the connections between our lives and those of others, it would be difficult not to be aware of the global nature of environmental problems. The impact of the environment on people's lives whether they be in New Orleans or Phuket, whether they be affected by storm or tsunami, is all too apparent. To what extent environmental catastrophes are caused by, or exaggerated by, human impact is not yet known but the 'strong scientific evidence' mentioned above points to the need for humans to do more to protect the environment. Doing more might mean imposing more rules and regulations, it might mean travelling by train not plane, or it might mean teaching other people not to make the mistakes of this and previous generations.

Concern about the environment grew rapidly around the middle of the last century and, although the topics of concern have changed, there is still wide public interest in issues such as global warming, climate change, air and water quality, the impact of development on communities and so on. In recent years, links between food, the environment and health have become more widely understood. Politicians and parents are concerned about immunizations, what children consume and about the amount of exercise that they get. The links between health, the environment and education are explored further in Chapter 23.

In the 1950s and 1960s, people became increasingly aware that scientific and technological advances sometimes came with undesirable side-effects. Rachel Carson's *Silent Spring*, which celebrated its fortieth anniversary in 2002, exposed the catastrophic effects of pesticide spraying in the USA and elsewhere (Carson 1962/1999). The book has rarely been out of print, although Carson was heavily criticized at the time of its publication by politicians, industrialists and the media (Dillon 2005).

In the 1970s and 1980s, a series of international conferences and declarations helped to focus the attention of environmentalists, educators and policy makers on the key environmental problems and how education might play a role in their solution. The United Nations Conference on the Human Environment in Stockholm in 1972 was a key event in the development of what became commonly known as environmental education (EE). There are many definitions and conceptualizations of environmental education and there are several reviews of the EE literature (see, for example, Hart and Nolan 1999; Rickinson 2001). The differences between environmental education and education for sustainable development are complex and it is beyond the scope of this chapter to do them justice. Suffice to say that it is impossible to talk about ESD without understanding that it has its roots in EE as well as in development education, as was mentioned earlier.

The publication of *Our Common Future* (WCED 1987) (also known as the Brundland Report) by the World Commission on Environment and Development, in 1987, led to the popularization of the definition of sustainable development as 'development that meets the needs of the present without compromising the ability of future generations to meet their own needs'. This conceptualization underpins much current thinking about sustainable development. Five years later, in 1992, The Rio Declaration from the World Conference on Environmental and Development (WCED or 'The Earth Summit') began by stating:

> Human beings are at the centre of concerns for sustainable development. They are entitled to a healthy and productive life in harmony with nature.
>
> (WCED 1992)

Education as the foundation of sustainable development was reaffirmed at the Johannesburg Summit, as was the commitment embodied in Chapter 36 of Agenda 21 of the Rio Summit, 1992. A decade later, at the

World Summit on Sustainable Development, the Johannesburg Declaration announced that world leaders were committed 'to build a humane, equitable and caring global society cognizant of the need for human dignity for all' (UNESCO 2006). In the same year, 2002, the United Nations proposed the Decade of ESD. The Decade can be seen as another attempt to get the environment and development into the school curriculum across the world.

Criticisms of sustainable development and ESD

Verbal felicity and practical logic

Sustainable development as a concept has its critics. Speaking at a conference in 2000, the *Guardian's* architecture correspondent Martin Pawley criticized the Brundland definition, and another simpler version which spoke of 'leaving the planet to the next generation in no worse state than that in which the present generation found it', as embodying 'a breathtakingly serious number of contradictions and flaws' (Pawley 2000). He added, 'What they gain in verbal felicity they lose in practical logic.' Pawley pointed out that both definitions were 'textbook examples of the political fudge' which combined opposing positions (sustainability and development) by proposing a third (sustainable development). Another critic, Sachs, argued that, 'sustainable development calls for the conservation of development, not for the conservation of nature' (1995: 343). This extract from *Our Common Future* hints at another of the tensions in the term sustainable development: 'What is needed is an era of new economic growth – growth that is forceful and at the same time socially and environmentally sustainable' (WCED 1987: 6). Easy to say but incomparably difficult to achieve. The Canadian environmental educator and philosopher Bob Jickling (2000) related the contradictions inherent in sustainable development to Orwell's 'double think' – that is, ordinary citizens become brainwashed into accepting contradictory meanings for a term. Sustainability is so hard to pin down that its utility becomes questionable. Terms such as sustainable development, Stables argues, are 'paradoxical compound policy slogans' (2001). This might not necessarily be a bad thing, argue Scott and Gough (2003), as long as teachers can use the debate about terms to educate students about the use of language in everyday life.

Education 'for' . . .

Critics of Education *for* Sustainable Development have not been reticent in their arguments. When Hopkins wrote that 'education should be able to cope with determining and implanting these broad guiding principles [of sustainability] at the heart of ESD [education for sustainable development]' (Hopkins 1998: 172), Jickling responded by arguing:

> When highlighted in this way, most educators find such statements a staggering misrepresentation of their task. Teachers understand that

sustainable development, and even sustainability, are normative concepts representing the views of only segments of our society. And, teachers know that their job is primarily to teach students how to think, not what to think.

(Jickling 2000: 469)

Jickling also expressed his concerns about the lack of educational philosophical analysis in environmental education and the use of education as a tool for the advancement of sustainable development: 'if education is trying to get people to think for themselves then education "for" anything is inconsistent and should be rejected' (Jickling 1992: 7). So, although there are many advocates of ESD, it has its critics. In the next section I will examine what an education about or for sustainability might involve.

What should people learn and how could they be taught?

Despite continued concern about the environment, both local and global, the low levels of public knowledge and understanding continue to worry environmentalists. In a relatively recent study, only three in ten people in a telephone survey in the USA recognized the term 'biodiversity' and could describe accurately what it meant (Belden *et al.* 2002) (On the positive side, the figure in 1996 had been two in ten.) Education about the environment is manifest in the curriculum in many countries. For example, in England, Key Stage 3 pupils should be taught 'about ways in which living things and the environment can be protected, and the importance of sustainable development' (QCA 2006).

Early ideas about what should be taught in ESD were relatively simplistic and general. So, for example, the UK Sustainable Development Education Panel's (SDEP) 1998 report recommended that:

- Schools [should] provide education for sustainable development, and [should] be making progress at implementing policies to become sustainable institutions.
- Pupils [should] be competent to practice sustainability at the end of compulsory schooling.
- Initial and continuing school and pre-school teacher training [should] integrate education for sustainable development.

UNESCO provides guidance on what ESD might look like, at least in terms of overall learning outcomes. UNESCO says that ESD is about learning to:

- respect, value and preserve the achievements of the past
- appreciate the wonders and the peoples of the Earth
- live in a world where all people have sufficient food for a healthy and productive life
- assess, care for and restore the state of our planet
- create and enjoy a better, safer, more just world
- be caring citizens who exercise their rights and responsibilities locally, nationally and globally.

Over a decade ago, Fettis and Ramsden argued that 'one of the best educational experiences is to have students conduct short research projects on topics directly relevant to or leading to sustainability' (1995: 89). Sustainability for them meant the:

> beneficial use of resources by minimum intervention or cyclical renewal to retain the *status quo* with the least practical waste of energy and pollution levels which do not lead to the long term detriment of the environment.
>
> (Fettis and Ramsden 1995: 84)

which they argued could be a universal definition of the term. On a similarly positive note, Rauch (2002) saw the environmental education and ESD as providing opportunities for schools to become thematic breeding grounds for innovation. In the UK, Huckle (2001) has suggested having 'healthy schools' for children as part of education for sustainability. Other writers have identified a broad range of outcomes for teaching about issues relating to sustainability beyond knowledge and understanding (see Rickinson *et al.* (2004) for a comprehensive review of the effects of outdoor learning).

One of the 'founding fathers' of environmental education, Bill Stapp (2000), who began the Global Rivers Environmental Education Network (GREEN), saw watershed and rivers as linking different interests and cultures together towards environmental problem solving. Hopkins and McKeown (1999), outlining what they describe as key steps towards sustainability, argued that 'students in programs that have been reoriented will also learn to practice a sustainable lifestyle by gaining skills tailored to the conditions of the community':

> For example, in a community that relies on wood for fuel, pupils may learn about sustainable harvesting, replanting and other silviculture techniques. In an area of shrinking water supply, pupils may learn to use new agricultural techniques and to plant crops that require less water. In affluent communities, pupils may be taught media literacy and awareness of the influence of advertisers in promoting a level of consumption that leads to increased resource use.
>
> (Hopkins and McKeown 1999: 25–6)

However, cautiously, they go on to note that:

> Messages such as vaccinate your children, boil drinking water, do not drive drunk, and do not take drugs are simple statements compared to the complex range of environmental, economic, and social issues that sustainable development encompasses. Success in sustainable development education will therefore take much longer and be more costly than simple-message public opinion campaigns.
>
> (1999: 27)

Although they pointed out that a range of bodies including governments, ministries of education, school districts are willing to adopt education for sustainable development, they added that 'no successful working models currently exist' (1999: 27).

In a later paper, Hopkins and McKeown (2001) describe innovative curriculum development in Toronto schools in the 1990s. Pedagogic strategies, such as residential fieldwork for all students and environmentally-friendly practices, such as the examination of chemicals used in cleaning schools, were instigated across a number of schools. Ironically, the development was not sustained – a change in the complexion of the local government resulted in the project's abandonment.

Later attempts to describe possible pedagogical approaches mixed older ideas of holism and interdisciplinarity with newer ideas such as participatory decision making. So, for example, according to UNESCO, ESD will aim to demonstrate the following features:

- Interdisciplinary and holistic: learning for sustainable development embedded in the whole curriculum, not as a separate subject.
- Values-driven: it is critical that the assumed norms – the shared values and principles underpinning sustainable development – are made explicit so that that can be examined, debated, tested and applied.
- Critical thinking and problem solving: leading to confidence in addressing the dilemmas and challenges of sustainable development.
- Multi-method: word, art, drama, debate, experience ... different pedagogies which model the processes. Teaching that is geared simply to passing on knowledge should be recast into an approach in which teachers and learners work together to acquire knowledge and play a role in shaping the environment of their educational institutions.
- Participatory decision-making: learners participate in decisions on how they are to learn.
- Applicability: the learning experiences offered are integrated in day-to-day personal and professional life.
- Locally relevant: addressing local as well as global issues, and using the language(s) which learners most commonly use. Concepts of sustainable development must be carefully expressed in other languages – languages and cultures say things differently, and each language has creative ways of expressing new concepts.

(UNESCO 2006)

In 2006, the DfES claimed that since 2003 it had 'pushed sustainable development significantly higher up the education agenda' (DfES 2006: 6). It pointed to a series of 'significant achievements':

- providing a richer and more enjoyable learning experience by encouraging schools to take learning outside with the Education Outside the Classroom Manifesto and Growing Schools;
- improving pupils' well-being with school transport and health initiatives, such as Travelling to School: an action plan, and the Healthy Living Blueprint;
- ensuring pupils gain knowledge about people and life in other countries through the international and citizenship work we have undertaken, creating and developing the Global Gateway and each year holding a successful International Education Week;
- making the school infrastructure more sustainable through the BREEAM [Building Research Establishment Environmental Assessment Method]

Schools environmental assessment method, which considers a wide range of environmental factors that are affected by the construction and operation of school buildings; and

• building greater awareness of sustainable development in the higher and further education sectors with the development and implementation of the sustainable development strategies of the Higher Education Funding Council for England and the Learning and Skills Council.

The Education Outside the Classroom Manifesto

In the light of the success of the Manifesto for Music, the Education and Skills Select Committee recommended that the government should publish an 'Education Outside the Classroom Manifesto'. The manifesto was announced by the DfES in 2005 and its draft vision states:

We believe every child and young person should experience the world outside the classroom as an integral part of their learning and development, complementing learning in the classroom. High quality education outside the classroom can stimulate and inspire; foster independence; aid personal and social development; and can often motivate reluctant learners. These experiences should be stimulating, safely managed and enjoyable, and contribute to meeting the needs of every child.

(Teachernet 2006a)

The manifesto is an attempt to ensure that all pupils have reasonable access to the outside environment. Opportunities to address sustainability through learning outdoors are plentiful and the Growing Schools website (Teachernet 2006b) provides a host of useful links.

Growing Schools

The Growing Schools programme aims to 'reconnect young people with their environment, in both urban and rural settings, through the National Curriculum' (Teachernet 2006b). Within three years of its beginning, more than 15,000 schools had registered their interest in the programme. Growing Schools focuses on food, farming and the countryside and on ensuring that pupils are given first-hand experience of the natural world around them and that outdoor learning activities are integrated into everyday teaching practices.

The Growing Schools website brings together a range of resources, projects and initiatives including the Eden Project's Growing for Life programme, the National School Fruit Scheme and the Five-a-day Programme. The 'Making the case' section of the website describes research into learning outdoors and discusses relevant education theories.

Learning in out-of-school contexts

In recent years there has been growing interest in the opportunities available for learning out of school whether it be in residential centres, museums or the school grounds (see, for example, Dillon *et al.* 2005). The curriculum on offer at such centres tends to match the National Curriculum. However, the range of teaching approaches used goes beyond what is the norm in schools. Minstead Study Centre in the New Forest is a well known example of an innovative residential centre. The centre aims to provide both environmental education and education for sustainable development during its courses, which normally last five days (Dillon and Reid, in press). The centre's ethos is to promote respect for all living things and to encourage children to work together:

> Developing personal responsibility and nurturing positive attitudes towards each other ranks high amongst the aims of the Centre. Such diversity allows us to reach a wider audience. We feel it is through such experiences that children are able to establish and understand their connection, influence and responsibilities towards the people, plants and animals of Planet Earth.
>
> (Minstead Study Centre website: www.wildwoodweb.co.uk/)

Concluding comments

I have tried to show that we are still struggling to understand whether education for sustainable development is more than a slogan and, if it is, how might it be enacted in schools and beyond. Underlying the debates about the validity of the terms 'sustainability' and 'sustainable development' there are bigger, more philosophical issues to do with what is the purpose of schooling – what or who is education for? In the end, I have to disagree with my Danish colleagues, Jensen and Schnack who, when describing environmental activities carried out by school students, wrote:

> it is not and cannot be the task of the school to solve the political problems of society. Its task is not to improve the world with the help of pupils' activities. These activities must be evaluated on the basis of their educational value and according to educational criteria [. . .] The crucial factor must be what students learn from participating in such activities . . .
>
> (Jensen and Schnack 1997)

Education is about change and teachers are change agents. If you believe that you can offer a value-free education, then I believe that you are mistaken. Whether education actually *will* make a difference to the public's view of the environment or will help us to stop destroying the environment, is another question. But I believe that we need to consider what contribution we are going to make to that goal in our lives as teachers. Whether you agree with the Sustainable Development Education Panel's analysis:

The term sustainable development is not well understood and is not 'user-friendly'. The real challenge is to make sustainable development relevant to the experience of people from all backgrounds and to engage them in making all aspects of their own lives and those of their community more sustainable.

(SDEP 2000)

or not, there is clearly a long way to go in whichever direction we decide to travel.

References

Belden, Russonello and Stewart (2002) *Americans and Biodiversity: New Perspectives in 2002*. Available at http://www.biodiversityproject.org/02toplines.PDF (accessed on May 1, 2006).

Carson, R. (1999) *Silent Spring*. Originally published in 1962. Penguin: London.

Department for Education and Skills (DfES) (2006) *Sustainable Development Action Plan, Learning for the Future*. London: HMSO.

Dillon, J. (2005) 'Silent Spring': Science, the environment and society, *School Science Review*, 86(316): 113–18.

Dillon, J., Morris, M., O'Donnell, L. *et al.* (2005) *Engaging and Learning with the Outdoors – The Final Report of the Outdoor Classroom in a Rural Context Action Research Project*. Slough: National Foundation for Educational Research.

Dillon, J. and Reid, A. (in press) Science, the environment and citizenship: teaching values at Minstead Study Centre, in D. Corrigan, J. Dillon and R. Gunstone (eds) *The Re-emergence of Values in the Science Curriculum*. Rotterdam: Sense Publishers.

Dillon, J., Rickinson, M., Teamey, K. *et al.* (2006) The value of outdoor learning: evidence from research in the UK and elsewhere, *School Science Review*, 87(320): 107–11.

Dillon, J. and Teamey, K. (2002) Reconceptualising environmental education – taking account of reality, *Canadian Journal of Science, Mathematics and Technology Education*, 2(4): 467–83.

Fettis, G.C. and Ramsden, M.J. (1995) Sustainability – what is it and how should it be taught? *ENTRÉE '95 Proceedings*, 81–90.

Hart, P. and Nolan, K. (1999) A critical analysis of research in environmental education, *Studies in Science Education*, 34: 1–69.

Hopkins, C. (1998) The content of education for sustainable development, in M.J. Scoullos (ed.) *Environment and Society: Education and Public Awareness for Sustainability; Proceedings of the Thessaloniki International Conference*. Paris: Unesco.

Hopkins, C. and McKeown, R. (1999) Education for Sustainable Development, *Forum for Applied Research and Public Policy*, 14(4): 25–8.

Hopkins, C. and McKeown, R. (2001) Education for sustainable development: past experience, present action and future prospects, *Educational Philosophy and Theory*, 33(2): 231–44.

Huckle, J. (2001) Primary education for sustainable development, *Primary Practice*, 29: 13–19.

Jensen, B.B. and Schnack, K. (1997) The Action competence approach in environmental education, *Environmental Education Research*, 3(2): 163–78.

Jickling, B. (1992) Why I don't want my children to be educated for sustainable development, *Journal of Environmental Education*, 23(4): 5–8.

Jickling, B. (2000) Education for sustainability: A seductive idea, but is it enough for my grandchildren? Available at http://www.ec.gc.ca/education/ee_jickling_e.htm (accessed on September 3, 2006).

Jickling, B. (2001) Environmental thought, the language of sustainability, and digital watches, *Environmental Education Research*, 7(2): 167–80.

Jickling, B. and Spork, H. (1998) Education for the environment: a critique, *Environmental Education Research*, 4(3): 309–27.

Pawley, D. (2000) Sustainability: a big word with little meaning, *Independent*, 11 July. Available at http://www.audacity.org/Resourcing%20the%20future.htm (accessed on May 1, 2006).

Rauch, F. (2002) The potential of education for sustainable development for reform in schools, *Environmental Education Research*, 8(1): 43–51.

Qualifications and Curriculum Authority (QCA) (2006) *Science KS1–4*. Available at http://www.qca.org.uk/1594.html (accessed on May 1, 2006).

Rickinson, M. (2001) Learners and learning in environmental education: a review of recent research evidence, *Environmental Education Research*, 7: 207–317.

Rickinson, M., Dillon, J., Teamey, K., Morris, M., Choi, M.Y., Sanders, D. and Benefield, P. (2004) *A Review of Research on Outdoor Learning*. Preston Montford: Field Studies Council.

Sauvé, L. (1996) Environmental education and sustainable development: A further appraisal, *Canadian Journal of Environmental Education*, 1: 7–33.

Scott, W.A.H. and Gough, S. (2003) Rethinking relationships between education and capacity-building: remodelling the learning process, *Applied Environmental Education and Communication*, 2(4): 213–20.

Stables, A.W.G. (2001) Who drew the sky? Conflicting assumptions in environmental education, *Educational Philosophy and Theory*, 33(2): 245–56.

Stapp, W.B. (2000) Watershed education for sustainable development, *Journal of Science Education and Technology*, 9(3): 183–97.

Sustainable Development Education Panel (SDEP) (1999) *First Annual Report*. Available at http://www.defra.gov.uk/environment/sustainable/educpanel/1998ar/05.htm (accessed on May 1, 2006).

Sustainable Development Education Panel (SDEP) (2000) *Towards a Language of Sustainable Development*. Available at http://www.defra.gov.uk/environment/sustainable/educpanel/language/index.htm (accessed on May 1, 2006).

Teachernet (2006a) *Education outside the Classroom Manifesto*. Available at http://www.teachernet.gov.uk/teachingandlearning/resourcematerials/museums/outsideclassroom/ (accessed on May 1, 2006).

Teachernet (2006b) *Welcome to Growing Schools*. Available at http://www.teachernet.gov.uk/growingschools/ (accessed on May 1, 2006).

United Nations Educational, Scientific and Cultural Organisation (UNESCO) (2006) Education for Sustainable Development. Available at: http://portal.unesco.org/education/en/ev.php-URL_ID=19648&URL_DO=DO_TOPIC&URL_SECTION=201.html (accessed on May 1, 2006).

World Commission on Environment and Development (WCED) (1987) *Our Common Future*. Oxford: Oxford University Press.

Further reading

Foster, J. (2001) Education as sustainability, *Environmental Education Research*, 7(2): 153–65.

McKeown, R and Hopkins, C. (2003) EE ≠ ESD: defusing the worry, *Environmental Education Research*, 9(1): 117–28.

Lucas, A.M. (1991) Environmental Education: what is it, for whom, for what purpose and how, in S. Keiny and U. Zoller (eds) *Conceptual Issues in Environmental Education*. New York: Peter Lang Publishing.

Sachs, W. (1995) Global ecology and the Shadow of development, in H. Huni and K. Tato (eds) *Deep Ecology for the Twenty-first Century*. Boston and London: Shambhala, 428–44.

Scott, W. and Gough, S. (2003) *Sustainable Development and Learning. Framing the Issues*. London: RoutledgeFalmer.

Stables, A.W.G. (1996) Reading the environment as text: literary theory and environmental education, *Environmental Education Research*, 2(2): 189–95.

25

Information and communications technologies

Ian Stevenson

In 1998, the UK Government launched its ambitious National Grid for Learning (NGfL), investing £700m in connecting schools via the NGfL, and £230m on training teachers and librarians in the use of Information and Communications Technologies (ICT). It established the British Educational Communication and Technology Agency (Becta) to oversee the Grid and develop content for teaching and learning. The combined initiatives were relaunched in 2003 as 'ICT in Schools', spending £510m in that one year alone. A range of other ICT initiatives have been introduced including a popular Laptops for Teachers scheme, Strategic Leadership in ICT for managers, Curriculum Online to provide evaluated content, Regional Broadband access for schools, and the Testbed Project in which schools in three diverse geographical areas have been equipped to very high levels and evaluated (Ofsted 2004). Large numbers of schools and colleges have introduced ICT as some part of their approach to teaching and learning (DfES 2004). Recent reviews show that there is great progress in the introduction of hardware such as computers, interactive boards, and other digital devices, but much slower embedding of ICT in the day-to-day practices of teachers and learners (Becta 2006).

Why is ICT so important in education that it warrants such a large investment? Hawkridge (1990) identified four main reasons which are still valid: ICT is a life skill since technology is an integral part of everyday life (social); ICT is part of the working world (vocational); ICT changes the way pupils are taught (pedagogic); and ICT changes the nature of schooling (catalytic). Introducing ICT into education has, and continues to have, a major impact on teachers and what they are expected to do (Preston 2004). Developing both personal and professional skills in using ICT are now a key part of initial teacher training, with the expectation that teachers will use technology as an integral part of their practice (Stevenson and Hassell 1994).

This chapter presents four ways that ICT is commonly used – as a support for teaching; as a tutor; as a tool; and as an environment – together with some examples and evidence from research to show in what ways they are effective. Learners' uses of ICT outside the classroom and their implications for learning are explored in the final part of the chapter.

ICT as support for teaching and learning

The most common use of ICT in education is to support teaching and learning. This approach integrates ICT into existing educational practices, ranging from teachers using presentation software with interactive whiteboards in face-to-face sessions, through to courses delivered completely on-line, often taken at a distance. Choice and control of the technology are determined by the needs of the curriculum, institutional policy and commitments, and the discretion of teachers (Scrimshaw 2004). Also known as Technologically Enhanced Learning, this broad approach usually takes the form of blended or on-line learning.

Blended learning

Blended learning uses a variety of technologies as part of established educational practices in achieving the learning objectives of a fixed curriculum. A range of on-line resources is used together with subject-specific and generic applications (for example, word processors, spreadsheets, databases) to help learners with particular curriculum topics. Degrees of blending can happen with ICT being used in classroom work as well as real-time chat and messaging (synchronous communication) or bulletin and discussion boards (asynchronous communication) activities to support face-to-face activities.

Snapshot 1 Nazi propaganda with Year 11 history class at a Technology College

The activity began with revision of previous work on Hitler, which consisted of two-and-a-half lessons on Nazi Germany, one lesson looking at chronology and one lesson looking at Hitler's background. In the first phase of this activity the teacher used an interactive whiteboard to recap on the main points, and introduced a paper-based activity to sort a randomly ordered timeline. Learners worked individually or in pairs on the task to highlight, summarize and classify, and report back their results for recording on the interactive whiteboard. Finally, the whiteboard was used to show propaganda posters, and the group worked together in directing a student scribe to highlight areas of impact on the posters. The teacher sign-posted key ideas, and later there was a plenary question-and-answer session to consolidate the activity. To follow up the session, there would be more analysis of Hitler's propaganda methods with groups of students choosing one method to research.

On-line learning

On-line learning covers a range of uses for communications technologies such as email and conferencing, together with resource delivery and assessment. Use is made of the Internet and other networks to provide flexibility and personalization so that teaching and learning is not constrained by time or place. Learners can choose where, when and how they learn, and teachers can make use of virtual spaces to engage with individuals or groups of learners either in real time or through discussion boards. Associated with this approach are Virtual Learning Environments (VLE), which combine content delivery and course management systems – such as electronic submission of work and assessment – with synchronous and asynchronous communication tools. Blogs, where teachers and learners can share their thoughts and ideas on-line, are being used to support classroom activities in different ways. Communications technologies offer excellent opportunities for MFL through pupils having email 'key pals', making presentations or accessing appropriate web pages and 'news feeds' in their target languages.

Snapshot 2 Using a Virtual Learning Environment in a mixed comprehensive

Mortwell School draws its pupil intake from a large area in a major city with below the national average in socio-economic terms and a range of ethnic minority backgrounds. There are at least 20 interactive whiteboards installed in several departments in the school, and most departments have access to 30 laptops. The school uses a VLE for revision and exam practice covering the main subjects taught at Key Stage 3 level, as well as most GCSE subjects. Pupils work on activities in school and then continue at home using a password protected, dial-in system, submitting their work either for automatic assessment or for teachers to view and comment. The system keeps records of pupils' progress, and how often they log in. It is popular with both pupils and parents, who can track progress together.

ICT and attainment

Starting with the first ImpaCT study (Watson *et al.* 1993), evidence has accumulated to show how using ICT can positively affect attainment in, for example, literacy and numeracy (Moseley and Higgins 1999). ImpaCT2 (Becta 2002) is the most recent large-scale study to examine the connection between using ICT and attainment. Commissioned by the DfES, it evaluated the gains associated with the introduction of the NGfL, and aimed to identify the factors that contribute to raising attainment with ICT. It took place between 1999 and 2002, involved 60 schools in England, and was organized into three strands. Strand One analysed the statistical relationship between the effective implementation of ICT and standards of performance in national tests and at GCSE. Strand Two examined how pupils use ICT, particularly out of school, and what they gain from this experience, while Strand Three explored the nature of teaching and learning using ICT in a variety of settings, focusing on pupils, teachers and managers.

Strand One's approach was to measure attainment in terms of pupils' relative gains in their formal examination scores when compared with those predicted for pupils with a similar profile but no ICT experience. The gains were set against the amount of time spent using ICT, and showed a variety of positive results across different Key Stages and subjects. There was also variation in the outcomes which did not display a consistent pattern, and raised a number of questions about the relationship between attainment and ICT (Stevenson 2004).

More recently, a smaller study tried to access the impact of using interactive whiteboards (IWB) on pupil attainment in Year 6 mathematics, English and science (Higgins *et al.* 2005). By comparing Key Stage 2 test results in mathematics and science with pupils of similar profile who had not been taught using IWB, the research team concluded that there was no consistent pattern. Although the IWB pilot schools showed a small but statistically significant improvement in mathematics and science Key Stage scores during the first year (2003), there was no difference in 2004. Following this up with a more detailed analysis using a comparison group of schools from each of the LEAs used in the study showed a similar picture. Low-achieving pupils showed some improvement in English with the overall impact being greatest on writing, but there was no difference in the ways that boys and girls performed.

A recent subject-by-subject review of the relationship between ICT and attainment concludes that there is a positive effect from specific uses of ICT on pupils' attainment in almost all the National Curriculum subjects (Cox and Abbott 2004). The most substantial positive outcomes are in mathematics, science and English at all Key Stages. However, there is a strong relationship between the ways in which ICT has been used and the resulting attainment outcomes, suggesting that the crucial components in the use of ICT within education are teachers, and the degree to which ICT is embedded in their approaches to teaching and learning.

ICT as tutor

Using computers as 'teaching machines' is an idea that has been around for over 40 years. Based on ideas from behaviourism and artificial intelligence research, these tutorial applications aim to adapt to a learner's development by matching their responses to an 'ideal' learner model. At their heart is a very detailed breakdown of a specific knowledge domain which forms the basis for a range of tutoring strategies selected on the basis of learner's responses to questions.

Integrated learning systems (ILS) are the most common form of this approach to an adaptive testing model found in schools and colleges (Underwood and Brown 1997). They consist of three main elements:

- curriculum content organized according to a specific model of the knowledge to be learnt, together with a range of tutorial, practice and assessment modules based on that domain model
- a pupil recording system that maintains information on pupils' levels of achievement against the 'ideal' learner model
- a management system which interprets pupils' responses in relation to an ideal 'learner model', automatically updates records based on individual responses, selects curriculum pathways based on learners' responses, and constructs an appropriate sequencing of learning modules.

The systems are interactive and give feedback to pupils and teachers, with the direction and selection of learning determined by the management system, and the pace through the modules controlled by the learner. Figure 25.1 shows the interactions between these elements, and is the basis for most adaptive testing approaches.

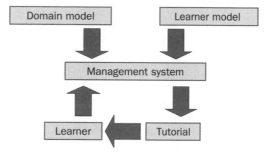

Figure 25.1 Structure of an integrated learning system. The management system constructs pathways using the domain model by comparing learners' responses to an 'ideal learner' model.

Thinking of the computer as a tutor is highly attractive, but current implementations lack the intelligence of human teachers to select and adopt strategies in real time according to specific needs of individuals. Their main use is for developing skills in mathematics, science and languages, and they are often used with pupils with special needs.

Snapshot 3 Revising times tables with a lower band Year 7 in a mixed ability comprehensive

The lesson starter was an oral revision, solving problems using the 6-times table in whole group with extensions to the 7 and 8-times tables. For the main section of the lesson groups of six pupils went to a computer suite with a teaching assistant to use an ILS, with the pupils each having their own work project. Most pupils were at a similar level, and the remainder of the class worked on problems using addition, subtraction and spatial reasoning. Five groups had 15 minutes using the computers, and the computer-generated work allowed individual pupils to access interactive activities, with support and feedback. Assessment was available automatically for pupils and teacher, to help planning and provide a sense of progression. As a plenary, the class reviewed their tables.

Between 1994 and 1998 there were three studies on the impact of ILS on pupils' attainment in secondary schools (Becta 1998). Reviewing the studies Wood *et al.* (1999) concluded that outcomes ranged from 'statistically significant, positive and educationally worthwhile effects' for the first study, through 'relatively neutral findings' in the second study, to the third study in which 'it was difficult to find anything but an apparently negative effect on achievement' (p. 91). Although the three parts of the evaluation used different methods, a large study undertaken in the third part of the evaluation used a similar approach to ImpaCT2 Strand One. It compared the examination scores of pupils who had used ILS for varying amounts of time with students of a similar academic and socio-economic profile, but with no ILS experience. The ILS study showed that the gains were negative across subject and age range.

Following up these studies by classroom observations, Wood *et al.* (1999) point to the importance of considering the relationship between an 'ICT system', learners and teachers, and by implication its designers (Squires and McDougal 1994). ILS are designed to be used by individuals in well-defined circumstances. By contrast, Wood *et al.* found that ILS were used in a variety of ways, including some not recommended by the designers. They found that teachers' training and attitudes to ICT played vital roles in an ILS's effectiveness, and they also noted a considerable mismatch between the format of assessment in ILS (mainly multiple choice) and those found in public examinations. Wood *et al.* (1999) concluded that an ILS's impact on pupil learning needed to be examined in the context of how the technology was integrated into actual classroom practices over an extended period of time.

ICT as problem-solving tool

Describing ICT as a tool is one of the most common ways of talking and thinking about digital technology in everyday life, suggesting both usefulness and availability. Two senses of this metaphor are usually associated with ICT. On one hand, ICT is a neutral tool (Somekh 1997) rather like a pencil or pen, simply available to do a range of jobs and chosen according to what has to be achieved – a tool to work with. On the other hand, ICT is a 'mindtool' (Jonassen 2006) that amplifies and extends thinking and problem solving – a tool to think with.

The English and Welsh ICT National Curriculum is based on the idea of digital technologies as problem-solving tools, structured by the System Life Cycle, illustrated in Figure 25.2.

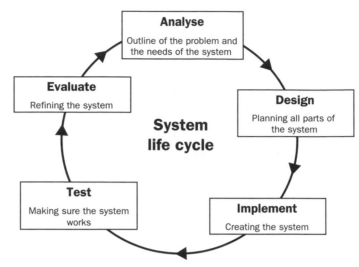

Figure 25.2   System Life Cycle (DfES 2006)

The System Life Cycle has the following stages:

- analysis of a problem
- designing a solution
- implementing the solution in a practical situation
- testing to check that the solution works
- evaluating the outcomes in light of the original problem.

In the English and Welsh ICT National Curriculum, 'fitness for purpose' is the main criterion for evaluating ICT-based solutions, and learners have to access their own solution by comparing what they intended with what they achieved in practice. This process helps learners to be self-critical and enables them to access other people's solutions, although they do not have a choice, by and large, about which problems they should solve.

ICT-based modelling illustrates the instrumental and cognitive aspects of 'ICT as tool' both as part of a subject and across the curriculum. Mathematics and science are the most obvious subjects where ICT-based modelling can be used since they both rely heavily on making or using models for their content. Learners can explore existing models to develop their understand of mathematical or scientific ideas by asking 'what if' questions, and extending models by adding new elements in the light of their experience. By building and using their own ICT-based models, learners can express their understanding of, for example, mathematical and scientific concepts (Bliss 1994). Besides design and technology other subjects using ICT-based modelling include geography and business studies, and there are opportunities for cross-curricular work, often around topics or themes.

Snapshot 4 Year 9 mixed-ability pupils working on the topic of insulation

The classroom was laid out with benches/tables around the room for group work, with half of the class working on experiments and the other half building computer models, before changing over. Experimental work involved investigating how heated water lost its heat with different forms of insulation around its container. Using *Model Builder*, a dynamic modelling application, pupils worked in groups of two or three to build up a model of the inputs (heat gains) and outputs (heat losses) to the heat balance of a house. Once they were happy with the model, they had to find out what happened to the heat balance over time and then investigate how much effect altering the variables would have. The pupils had been introduced to the software prior to the session, and were able to complete the practical experiment without much help. The class teacher, with some support from another teacher during the lesson, spent most of the time helping those on the computer. Support was of two types: helping with the use of the program; and posing questions to make the pupils think about the content of their model. The pupils wrote up both the experiment and the computer-based work using word processing facilities, and stored the report and models in their personal work area on the network.

GCSE ICT exam results are one of the main ways of assessing the outcomes of this approach. Using the System Design Cycle is both an integral part of ICT as a curriculum subject and its assessment criteria. Ofsted (2004) report that the greatest improvements in ICT capability is due to it being taught and assessed as a subject within the National Curriculum. A recent development in assessing ICT as a problem-solving tool is the Key Stage 3 on-screen tests that are being piloted for introduction in 2008 (QCA 2006b). The tests are set and assessed within a closed and secure on-screen system that makes use of a specially developed suite of generic applications for pupils to use. The applications are similar to those which pupils normally use, but focus on functionality that pupils would be expected to know: (for example, word processor, spreadsheet, email, file manager, web browser, database, presentation and control). Unlike the first approach above but in common with the second, the tests make ICT an integral part of the assessment process. However, unlike both the first and second approaches (that is, as a support for teaching and as a tutor), ICT is also an integral part of the pupils' learning of the subject.

ICT as environment

A central claim for ICT is that it allows learners to follow their own interests and build their own understandings. Inspired by Piagetian views of learning as an active, adaptive and constructive process, this use draws on the idea of ICT as a collection of tools and resources that can be used flexibly by learners, either on their own or with others. Simulations, games, web browsing and searching, and programming languages all place control with learners, who decide how and what they choose to focus on.

A classic example of this approach is Papert's Turtle Geometry which aimed at enabling young children to use powerful computers, using the turtle as an 'object to think with' (Papert 1980). He introduced the idea of a microworld as a simplified slice of reality which could be actively explored, extended or which learners could build for themselves. More recently he has identified six dimensions that draw out the sense in which a micro-world contains a model of a knowledge domain, a set of tools for learning, and a theory of cognitive development (Papert 2002).

Qualitative research into ICT as an environment and its relationship to conceptual and personal development has been going on for 25 years. As Cox and Abbott (2004) point out in their review, there is substantial evidence from small, focused studies which indicates that specific uses of ICT aid pupil's learning. These include the use of simulations and modelling in science and mathematics, and the use of word processing in English. Personal factors such the development of self-confidence, motivation, autonomy and collaboration are also linked to this use of ICT (Crook 1994). However, these are areas of attainment that are not recognized by formal assessment, but have been identified as ones to which ICT makes a contribution.

Snapshot 5 Designing personal databases with Year 11 in a mixed-ability PSHE group

As part of a PSHE programme, the group was introduced to pro-gramming using MITSI, a form of the programming language Prolog. A database in Prolog consists of facts about a topic, and a set of rules for generating new facts from those given. Starting with a prepared data-base based on family relationships in a well known BBC soap, the group extended it by adding more characters as facts or creating new relationships, such who was dating, who was cheating on who, and who was pregnant. Once the students discovered that they could add any-thing (within reason), they became very creative, and followed their own interests with the soap. The next task was to make a database on a topic of the pupils' own choosing. Phil was not very talkative and found programming quite difficult, but asked if he could create a database about films which were his real interest. He turned up to the next session with his notebook and proceeded to enter information with great intensity, and spent several hours of his own time working on the database. When it came to presentations, Phil demonstrated his, by now, sophisticated and large database in a confident and articu-late way, having mastered a number of advanced programming techniques.

Two difficulties exist in evaluating attainment based on this approach to using ICT. First, it can lead to learners developing knowledge, under-standings and skills in areas that are not covered by the school curriculum. Very early on in the development of ICT there was a debate about the relevance of this approach to learning, in a period when there was a move away from so-called 'child-centred' strategies towards teacher-centred and whole-class approaches. As a result seeing ICT as an environment in the sense being used here became unfashionable and it disappeared from classrooms (Noss and Hoyles 1996). With the Government's strategy document *Harnessing Technology; Transforming Learning and Children's Services* (DfES 2005), there is a swing back to learner-centred approaches in ICT. A second issue is the relationship between ICT and formats of assessment since the school curriculum is predominantly based around 'paper and pencil' technologies, which do not fit easily with digital media. A fundamental separation of the medium of learning – in this case ICT – from the methods of assessment (for example, handwritten sit-down exams) means that the role of digital technology becomes ambiguous. One possible solution is a greater use of e-portfolios in which learners can collect, manage and share their work in a digital form, and ICT becomes an integral part of both learning and assessment (QCA 2006a; Ridgeway 2004). E-portfolios are currently being piloted, and reflect a commitment to using the flexibility that ICT offers in fostering personalization and inclusion.

ICT in the home

An emerging theme since 1998 is the recognition that learners have a rich experience of ICT outside of classrooms and schools, which has an impact on their work and attainment. Significant factors include access to ICT at home, playing games, use of mobile technologies and person-to-person contact including chat, messaging and music exchange. Childrens' and young adults' experiences of ICT in the home are varied both in terms of types and extent. Several factors are present in the domestic uses of 'computers', which relate to children's education, parental needs and entertainment. Increased Internet access and use, together with more sophisticated equipment than is found in school settings, lead to children mixing educational activities with entertainment (Becta 2002; Valentine *et al.* 2005). The *ScreenPlay* Project (Sutherland *et al.* 2000) identified specific differences between school and home, which are summarized in Table 25.1 taken from the final report (Furlong *et al.* 2000).

Table 25.1 Differences between home and school uses of ICT (*Screenplay* Project, Furlong *et al.* 2000)

At home	At school
Young person chooses activity	Teacher chooses activity
Time for exploration	Insufficient time for exploration
Learning is incidental	Learning is the purpose
Expertise is celebrated	Expertise not recognized/rejected
Extensive social and artefactual resources	Limited resources
Depth model	Breadth model

They conclude that, in terms of control and use of resources, home use can lead to 'deep' learning. If this is the case, then disjunction between home and school experiences seems to suggest that they do not interact, and may even be antithetical. However, the increase in confidence, autonomy and motivation with digital technology which may emerge through this personal use does have some influence on children's activities in classroom.

Game playing, far from being an activity undertaken by 'lone' males, is actually the focus for a range of social interactions. With the convergence of digital, print and communications media, communities form around games and gaming, with their own social structures. Expertise in specific games confers status and power on individuals who induct and support new members of groups that coalesce around gaming activities (Williamson and Facer 2003). Developing expertise in playing games and the associated uses of technology has the potential for influencing attainment, albeit in subtle and diverse ways. Attempts to harness this experience of game playing for educational purposes is an important contemporary area of investigation, particularly with commercial simulations such as *SimCity*, *Civilisation* and *The Sims* (MacFarlane *et al.* 2002; Sefton-Green 2004). Sharing music also has a number of important social facets. One's status is expressed through the amount of hard-drive space or bandwidth that one makes available for others to share music. Working on the principle of a 'gift economy', trust and status are built through demonstrations of generosity or 'citizenship' by sharing music files freely (Ebare 2004).

Over the past few years there has been a rise in the use of and access to mobile phones, chat and email, suggesting that children are making greater use of the communications possibilities offered by digital technologies. Recent work by Ito (2003) explores how mobile technologies are used by Japanese teenagers to subvert adult controls, while de Zengotita (2005) focuses on their role in mediating adolescent identity. A number of projects have been set up to try and use the mobile technologies to include young adults who are disengaged with formal education. More worrying for formal education is the uncritical access to a range of on-line sites and resources, which conflict with the formal curriculum and lie outside of adult control.

Concluding comments

How far the current ways of using ICT in schools matches the supposed rationales for its use is an open question. Although the principal use of ICT is currently to support existing forms of teaching, it will be a long time before it can be used to replace teachers, which is how Hawkridge's catalytic rationale is sometimes interpreted. What the research on teacher's integration of ICT into teaching and learning does indicate is that this is a process of adapting and reconfiguring technology, designed mainly for non-educational purposes, to suit a non-digital curriculum (Squires 1999; Cox and Webb 2004). Learners need to be given the opportunities that ICT offers to work in ways that suit them, and as the research on out-of-school ICT uses indicate, they are already highly sophisticated users of digital technologies. Digital technologies are a permanent feature of our lives, and will play an increasingly significant role in education. ICT provides a lens on current educational practices, and prompts us to ask whether the knowledge, understanding and skills that are being developed and assessed by the present 'pencil' curriculum are appropriate for a digitally mediated 21st century world? Whatever the answer to this question, it promises to be an interesting journey.

References

British Educational Communication and Technology Agency (Becta) (1998) *Integrated Learning Systems. UK Evaluation Report.* Coventry: Becta.

British Educational Communication and Technology Agency (Becta) (2002) *ImpaCT2: The Impact of Information and Communication Technologies on Pupil Learning and Attainment.* Coventry: Becta. Available at http://partners.becta.org.uk/index.php?section=rh&rid=11218.

British Educational Communication and Technology Agency (Becta) (2006) *The Becta Review 2006.* Coventry: Becta. Available at www.becta.org.uk.

Bliss, J. (1994) From mental models to modelling, in H. Mellar, J. Bliss, R. Boohan and C. Tompsett (eds) *Learning with Artificial Worlds: Computer-Based Modelling in the Curriculum.* London: Falmer Press.

Cox, M. and Abbott, C. (eds) (2004) *ICT and Attainment – a Review of the Research Literature. Full Report.* Coventry/London: Becta/DfES. Available at http://www.becta.org.uk/research/research.cfm?section=1&id=3119.

Cox, M. and Webb, M. (2004) *An Investigation of the Research Evidence Relating to ICT Pedagogy. A Report to the DfES.* Coventry: British Educational Communication and Technology Agency. Available at http://www.becta.org.uk/research/research.cfm?section=1&id=3119.

Crook, C. (1994) *Computers and the Collaborative Experience of Learning.* London. Routledge.

Department for Education and Skills (DfES) (2004) *Information and Communication Technology in Schools in England. (Provisional).* Office of National Statistics. London: Department for Education and Skills. Available at www.dfes.gov.uk/rsgateway/DB/SFR.

Department for Education and Skills (DfES) (2005) *Harnessing Technology; Transforming Learning and Children's Services.* London: Department for Education and Skills. Available at http://www.dfes.gov.uk/publications/e-strategy/.

Department for Education and Skills (DfES) (2006) *Key Stage 3 Strategy.* London: Department for Education and Skills. Available at www.standards.dfes.gov.uk/key stage3/subjects/ict/.

Ebare, S. (2004) Digital music and subculture: sharing files sharing style, *First Monday*, 9(2) (e-journal). Available at http://firstmonday.org/issues/issue9_2/ebare/index.html.

Furlong, J., Sutherland, R. and Furlong, R. (2000) *Screen-play: an Exploratory Study of Children in 'Techno-popular' Culture. Full Report of Research Activities and Results.* Award R000237298. Report to ESRC. Swindon: Economic and Social Research Council. Available at www.esrc.ac.uk.

Hawkridge, D. (1990) Who needs computers in schools, and why? *Computers and Education*, 15: 1–6.

Higgins, S., Falzon, C., Hall, I., Moseley, D., Smith, F., Smith, H. and Wall, K. (2005) *Embedding ICT In The Literacy And Numeracy Strategies. Final Report*. University of Newcastle upon Tyne. Centre for Learning and Teaching, School of Education, Communication and Language Sciences. Available at www.becta.org.uk/page_documents/research/univ_newcastle_evaluation_whiteboards.pdf.

Ito, M. (2003) Mobile phones, Japanese youth, and the re-placement of social, in R. Ling and P. Pedersen (eds) *Mobile Communications: Re-negotiation of the Social Sphere*. Available at http://www.itofisher.com/mito/archives/mobileyouth.pdf.

Jonassen, D.H. (2006) *Modelling with Technology: Mindtools for Conceptual Change*. Columbus, OH: Merill/Prentice Hall.

McFarlane A., Sparrowhawk, A. and Heald, Y. (2002) *Report on the Educational Use of Games: an Exploration by TEEM of the Contribution Which Games can Make to the Education Process*. Teem: Cambridge. Available at www.teem.org.uk/publications/teem_gamesined_full.pdf.

Moseley, D. and Higgins, S. (1999) *Ways Forward with ICT: Effective Pedagogy using Information and Communications Technology for Literacy and Numeracy in Primary Schools*. Newcastle: University of Newcastle. Available at http://www.leeds.ac.uk/educol/documents/00001369.htm.

Noss, R. and Hoyles, C. (1996) *Windows on Mathematical Meanings*. Dordrecht: Kluwer Press.

Office for Standards in Education (Ofsted) (2004) *ICT in Schools. The Impact of Government Initiatives Five Years On*. London: Office for Standards in Education. Available at http://www.ofsted.gov.uk/publications/index.cfm?fuseaction=pubs.summary&id=3652.

Papert, S. (1980) *Mindstorms. Children, Computers and Powerful Ideas*. Brighton. Harvester Press.

Papert, S. (2002) The Turtle's long slow trip: macro-eudological perspectives on microworlds, *Journal of Educational Computing Research*, 27(1–2): 7–27.

Preston, C. (2004) *Teachers' and Trainers' Perspectives: Researching the Outcomes of the New Opportunities Fund (NOF) ICT Teacher Training*. Oxford: MirandaNet. Available at http://www.mirandanet.ac.uk/tta/.

Qualifications and Curriculum Authority (QCA) (2006a) *QCA's e-assessment vision*. London. Qualifications and Curriculum Authority. Available at http://www.qca.org.uk/7192.html.

Qualifications and Curriculum Authority (QCA) (2006b) *Onscreen KS3 ICT testing. QCA Testing*. London: Qualifications and Curriculum Authority. Available at www.ks3ictpilot.com.

Ridgeway, J. (2004) *Literature Review of E-assessment. A Report for NESTA Futurelab*. Bristol: NESTA Futurelab. Available at http://www.nestafuturelab.org/research/reviews/10_01.htm.

Scrimshaw, P. (2004) *Enabling Teachers To Make Successful Use Of ICT*. Coventry: Becta. Available at http://www.becta.org.uk/research/research.cfm?section=1&id=3310.

Sefton-Green, J. (2004) *Literature Review in Informal Learning with Technology Outside School Report 7: Nesta Futurelab Series A Report for NESTA Futurelab*. Bristol: NESTA Futurelab. Available at http://www.nestafuturelab.org/research/lit_reviews.htm.

Somekh, B. (1997) Classroom Investigations. Exploring and evaluating how IT can support Learning, in B. Somekh and N. Davis (eds) *Using Information Technology Effectively in Teaching and Learning*. London: Routledge.

Squires, D. (1999) Educational Software and Learning: Subversive Use and Volatile Design. *Proceedings of the 32nd Hawaii International Conference on System Sciences*. Available at http://csdl2.computer.org/comp/proceedings/hicss/1999/0001/01/00011079.PDF.

Squires, D. and McDougal, A. (1994) *Choosing and Using Educational Software: A Teachers' Guide*. London: Falmer Press.

Stevenson, I.J. (2004) *Measures for Assessing the Impact of ICT use on Attainment. Report for DfES*. Coventry: Becta. Available at http://www.becta.org.uk/research/research.cfm?section=1&id=3119.

Stevenson, I.J. and Hassell, D. (1994) Modelling and teacher change, in H. Mellar, J. Bliss, R. Boohan and C. Tompsett (eds) *Learning with Artificial Worlds: Computer-Based Modelling in the Curriculum*. London: The Falmer Press.

Sutherland, R., Facer, K., Furlong, R. and Furlong, J. (2000) A new environment for education? The computer in the home, *Computers and Education*, 34: 195–212.

Underwood, J.D.M. and Brown, J. (eds) (1997) *Integrated Learning Systems: Potential into Practice*. Oxford: Heinemann.

Valentine, G., Marsh, J. and Pattie, C. (2005) *Children and Young People's Home Use of ICT for Educational Purposes: The Impact on Attainment at Key Stages 1–4*. Research Report RR672. London: Department for Education and Skills. Available at www.dfespublications.gov.uk.

Watson, D., Cox, M. and Johnson, D. (1993). *Impact: The Report. An Evaluation of the Impact of Information Technology on Children's Achievements in Primary and Secondary Schools*. London: DfES and King's College London.

Williamson, B. and Facer, K. (2003) *More Than 'Just A Game': The Implications For Schools Of Children's Computer Games Communities. NESTA Futurelab*. Bristol: NESTA Futurelab. Available at http://www.nestafuturelab.org/research/draft/02draft01.htm.

Wood, D., Underwood, J. and Avis, P. (1999) Integrated systems in the classroom, *Computers and Education*, 33: 91–108.

de Zengotita, T. (2005), *Mediated: How The Media Shapes Your World And The Way You Live In It*. London: Bloomsbury Publishing.

Useful websites

British Educational Communication and Technology Agency www.becta.org.uk
Department for Education and Skills Standards www.standards.dfes.gov.uk
Office for Standards in Education www.ofsted.gov.uk
Qualifications and Curriculum Authority www.qca.org.uk
National Curriculum on-line www.nc.uk.net

26

14–19 education and the great divide

Alex Manning

Introduction

The intention of this chapter is to explore the specific issues related to education for 14–19-year-olds in the UK. Historically, ideas about educational provision have changed and evolved, as has been highlighted in previous chapters. However, arguably none have been in such a state of flux as those in 14–19 education. The courses students follow and the exams they sit have changed and will continue to change. In fact, the only guarantee is that the age range is static. The 14–19 education you received is highly unlikely to be the same as you will be teaching now and it is similarly doubtful that it will remain unchanged throughout your time in the profession.

A historical perspective

Prior to 1944, the education system was somewhat makeshift, in fact the concept of secondary education was not suggested until 1926.

> Primary education should be regarded as ending at about the age of 11+. At that age a second stage, which for the moment may be given the colourless name 'post-primary' should begin; and this stage which, for many pupils would end at 16+, for some at 18 or 19, but for the majority at 14+ or 15+, should be envisaged so far as possible as a single whole.
>
> (The Hadow Report 1926)

A range of sponsors supported different schools, education was not available for all and, since it was a drain on financial resources, secondary education remained a luxury, mostly for the middle classes. Very few working-class children received a formal education beyond the age of 12. However, in 1944, the tripartite system was introduced, comprising of grammar, technical and secondary modern schools. The three tiers of school were state run and the intention was to assign students to one of the three school types which were deemed to best suit them and their needs. The decision as to which school children were sent was based on the results of the 11-plus examination.

The tiers can be thought of as a pyramid (though this representation was not publicized), with grammar schools at the top and secondary moderns at the bottom, in terms of prestige. Grammar schools 'catered for the top twenty per cent of the top ability age range' (Gill and Johnson, 2001: 274). Owing to limited funding, there were very few technical schools and, consequently, about 70 per cent of the school population was consigned to secondary modern schools. Sanderson (1994) provides a detailed overview of technical schools, and their decline, for most of the twentieth century, while Taylor (1963) offers a comprehensive account of the secondary modern school.

The Labour Party had been in favour of the comprehensive system since the late 1950s and after gradual implementation, the tripartite system was replaced with the comprehensive school system. Approximately 164 grammar schools still remain. Although specialist schools, city academies and city technology colleges have been introduced over the years, they can be seen as developments of the comprehensive ideal rather than a full-blooded return to selection for all.

In terms of changes in the 14–19 setting more specifically, from the late 1960s onwards, this phase has been characterized by almost constant restructuring and reforming. Wright and Oancea (2005) present 'A Chronology' of policies from 1976 to the present day for the Nuffield 14–19 Review. They themselves claim to have only considered the 'key proposals, and may not reflect the complexity of some documents and programmes' (Wright and Oancea 2005: 1). Despite this, in tabular form only, they manage to fill more than 40 pages of their review with policies which have impacted on 14–19 education.

Both the academic and vocational pathways have experienced a series of qualification reforms. In the academic route, there has been the Certificate of Secondary Education (CSE), and the General Certificate of Education (GCE) Ordinary and Advanced level. Whilst A levels currently remain, albeit with the new AS/A2 separation, the CSE and O level were replaced by the General Certificate of Secondary Education (GCSE). New vocational courses have also been introduced.

Gill and Johnson (2001) highlight the relative success of the Technical and Vocational Education Initiative (TVEI), in providing money for schools to design and implement 'a heavily technologically orientated curriculum for 14–16-year-old pupils' (Gill and Johnson 2001: 275). Vocational qualifications organized by the Business and Technology Education Council (BTEC) and City and Guilds courses were introduced in many sixth forms but were very specific: 'what schools needed was something more generalized' (Gill and Johnson 2001: 276). Given the wide array of courses available, the National Council for Vocational Qualifications (NCVQ) was set up to provide uniformity within vocational education but also to address the divide between vocational and academic education (Gill and Johnson 2001). This was a steep challenge, hence the development of the National Vocational Qualification (NVQ) and General National Vocational Qualification (GNVQ). These new vocational qualifications had nominal equivalence to the established academic qualifications. An advanced GNVQ being equivalent to two GCE A levels; an intermediate GNVQ, four GCSEs grade A–C. NVQs had five levels, level 2 (craft) can be compared with intermediate GNVQ and level 3 (technician supervisor) with advanced GNVQ (Smithers and Robinson 1993).

> It should be noted, however, that any equivalence here between NVQs, GNVQs and academic qualifications can only be regarded as a *claim* or an assertion which has yet to be substantiated. NVQs are not normally regarded as being equivalent to GCSE or A level by colleges and universities, and GNVQs have still to be empirically tested and evaluated.
>
> (Hyland 1994: 8)

The account above shows how vocational education has evolved; all these initiatives have been in response to the dissolution of the technical school. However, such courses have become heavily school-based. This has become known as 'weakly' vocational; vocational learning in school is very different from that in the workplace with respect to such resources as staff and equipment. Stanton (2004) describes 'weak' vocational learning as one end of the spectrum because although:

> it raises awareness of the world of work, and uses examples taken from it, it does not necessarily require staff with experience of the relevant sector, or equipment that is up to modern industrial or commercial standards.
>
> (Stanton 2004: 3)

Conversely, the 'strong' vocational learning is situated at the opposite end of spectrum:

> Vocational education that justifies the description of being 'strongly vocational' requires staff who not only have up-to-date experience of the relevant vocational sector, but the ability themselves to perform to modern occupational standards. The facilities – in the form of such things as motor vehicle workshops, training restaurants and in-college beauty salons – need to be of industrial standard.
>
> (Stanton 2004: 4)

Apprenticeships should be mentioned here as an example of an attempt at strong vocational learning: 'Apprenticeships of the past were *demand* rather than *supply-led*. Employers decided when and if they needed apprentices' (Fuller and Unwin 2003: 9). Young people were trained in the workplace and usually gained employment in their chosen profession. However:

in 1994, the then Conservative Government introduced the Modern Apprenticeship for 16–24-year-olds as an attempt to increase the stock of young people trained to intermediate (or technician) level. Apprenticeship numbers had been declining since the mid-1960s.

(Stanton 2004: 6)

The adjective 'modern' indicated these apprenticeships were unlike those of the past; they covered a wider range of occupations. Modern Apprenticeships were intended to improve the education offered by youth training schemes: 'many were treated as cheap labour, did not achieve any qualifications, and were sacked as soon as their traineeship ended' (Stanton 2004: 7). To achieve this goal, responsibilities for the new scheme were transferred from the government to National Training Organizations (NTOs). There are a number of issues which have arisen; there are huge variations in pay, length of training, provision of training and qualifications offered. Fuller and Unwin (2003) assert that the employers are broadly accountable for the limited success of the scheme, with their lack of experience, low skill requirement and inadequate sense of ownership of the Modern Apprentice routes.

The issues

Constant change in the 14–19 setting, particularly in the area of vocationalism, has resulted in a number of key issues, discussed below.

Definitions

As was mentioned above, the tripartite system ultimately became a two-tier system. We now talk of academic and vocational education. However, defining these terms is problematic. Pring (in press) points out that *Roget's Thesaurus* associates academic with 'irrelevant' and the *Oxford English Dictionary* adds 'cold' and 'unpractical'.

> What school would be proud of its academic reputation where that means it produces lots of pupils who are unpractical, cold and merely logical.

(Pring in press)

Pring notes that vocational can mean 'answering a call' or related to a particular job or career. Pring goes on to suggest that these definitions are weak and therefore unhelpful and confusing as 'Law is regarded as an academic subject and yet it is clearly geared to the preparation of Lawyers' (Pring in press). Pring continues by looking at the level of abstraction and intention associated with each term. However, we need to establish an understanding in order to move on. Academic education is mostly concerned with acquisition of theoretical knowledge in certain subjects while vocational education is mainly concerned with preparing an individual for work and concentrates on practical concerns.

Divisions

In defining the terms 'academic' and 'vocational' we have made them distinct, however, the distinction within education is much more divisive.

> In the UK high quality learning and its associated benefits are best ensured through the types of what is commonly termed as formal academic education. What is termed as vocational education comes a poor second and in some cases shares third place with those who appear to have benefited little from the many millions that are put into the provision of formal educational opportunities of any kind.
>
> (Halliday in press)

It is commonly perceived that vocational courses have become less desirable as the years have gone by:

> it is clear that the A-Level route is the preferred and most sought after route by large numbers of students. Few middle or aspirant middle-class parents will be satisfied with any other routes.
>
> (Tomlinson 1997: 6)

Hayward (2004) explores the decline of vocational learning particularly in the work-based setting. In the late 1980s and the 1990s, there was a rapid increase in participation rates in 16–19 education and training, but over the past decade these rates have remained virtually constant. However, as Hayward points out, participation rates are highest for 16-year-olds, and they decrease as the age of the participants increases. He describes this as a 'progressive loss of learners between the ages of 16 and 19 resulting in a medium participation system with a high rate of attrition' (Hayward 2004: 6). This change in participation has the consequence that, 'as the size of the age cohort declined, institutions could not afford to be as selective if they were to maintain their student numbers and the associated levels of funding' (Hayward 2004: 8). A greater proportion of young people now choose to stay in full time education rather than follow work-based training routes. Hayward (2004: 16) believes schools offer 'weak vocational learning which serves its clients and the economy poorly'.

Aims, values and purpose

Pring (1995) claims that, all too often, we discuss economic aims rather than educational values; for example, our 'need' for an educated workforce, in order to compete with economic rivals. He suggests it is somewhat short-sighted to educate to our current needs as this does not take into account possible future changes in our market, and it also restricts the number who are educated to a particular level. In an earlier work, Pring (1995) discusses a hierarchy of values that exist within the educational setting; for some it is 'the pursuit of knowledge for its own sake and the training of useful know how for others' (Pring 1995: 134). He prompts the questions: Why are some thought to be more educated than others? Why is an often narrow scope associated with intellectual excellence while a broader landscape is not seen to afford the development of the intellect?

Fragmentation

Teachers' views of 14–19 education, as Sally Tomlinson (1997) points out, have rarely been sought despite it being those professionals who teach and assess within the system. Tomlinson asked teachers about curriculum content, assessment and organization in the 14–19 setting. They reported being unhappy with the divide between academic and vocational education and reported they would prefer a more unified system:

> By and large the teachers were not in favour of dividing pupils up into those who 'can do' academic work and those suited to the vocational – although they admit that the divide had such a strong tradition in English schooling that it is difficult to overcome.
>
> (Tomlinson 1997: 81)

Having considered some of the enduring tensions in 14–19 education provision in England, I now wish to look at the current position and at where new policy proposals might be taking us. I shall consider the *Nuffield Review of 14–19 Education*, and the independent information which has been gleaned through the review. Additionally I will look at *The Tomlinson Report*, which was commissioned by the government, and at some of the papers published after the report was made public.

The Nuffield review of 14–19 education and training

The Nuffield Foundation commissioned a three-year review of 14–19 education and training. The review began in October 2003 and was intended to be independent and comprehensive, providing evidence-based recommendations for policy and practice. In the first year alone, 23 papers were commissioned covering the background to the 14–19 area. These and many other useful resources can be found on the review's website (www.nuffield14–19review.org.uk). The review's premise was that:

> there is a need to think afresh about education and training and about how it is organised to determine what would be appropriate and beneficial both for the young people themselves and for the economic and social world they are entering.
>
> (Hayward *et al.* 2004: 18)

The review draws attention to a number of areas mentioned above, such as participation rates and the polarization between vocational and academic education. However, the review refers to other issues. The first is that young people's decisions, and the factors influencing them, are not only complex but also poorly understood, particularly those related to 'the disengaged' (that is, disaffected young people) (but see Ball *et al.* 2000). The second is that the quality of work-based and work-related learning is variable. Thirdly, partnerships between learning agencies are fragmented due to their competitive ethos; the partnerships need to be more coherent and the role and responsibility of employers need to be more evident in the

14–19 debate. As the review states, 'there is too much discontinuity of policy and too many abortive attempts to reform qualifications' (Nuffield 2004: 54). The review notes that relevant statistical evidence is patchy and it is therefore difficult to see generalized patterns.

In the light of these initial findings, key questions were set to focus the next year of the review team's work. The analysis and findings published in 2005 fit into three strands; aims, learning and curriculum; understanding the dynamics of the system; and the institutional dimension.

Given that the directorate of the review includes a number academics quoted in this chapter, including Richard Pring, Geoff Hayward and Ewart Keep, it is hardly surprising that their views and agendas feature in the review. One point made in the review was the necessity to involve the learners in decisions about this crucial phase and their teachers in the development of the curriculum. The review recognized that pedagogy needs to change; curriculum development alone is 'pointless' (Hayward et al. 2005: 52). The review also comments that the assessment driven system is impacting on worthwhile learning. The new diplomas, which we shall consider later, are discussed in relation to the haste with which they have been introduced. Incentives were suggested to address the participation rates. Finally, the point was made that the effect of 'piecemeal policies' is short-sighted and fails to learn from previous legislation.

The Nuffield Foundation independent review identified key issues in the 14–19 debate. What is difficult to understand is why policies are being changed by government at such a rate rendering it impossible for the findings of the review to inform policy. Keep (in press) discusses the central control role of government:

> The resulting shift has been characterized by a process of delocalization, centralization and nationalization, whereby the English education system moved over a period of 15 years from being the least to the most centrally-controlled system in the world.
>
> (Keep, in press)

Recent government policies and reports

In October 2004, the 'Working Group on 14–19 Reform' published its final report ('The Tomlinson Report'), chaired by Mike Tomlinson. The working group was set up by ministers to advise on the reform of curriculum and assessment arrangements for 14–19-year-olds. Tomlinson stated from the outset that:

> it is our view that the status quo is not an option. Nor do we believe further piecemeal changes are desirable. Too many young people leave education lacking basic and personal skills; our vocational provision is too fragmented.
>
> (Working Group on 14–19 Reform 2004: 1)

The recommendations of the lengthy report refer to a new framework of 'core' and 'main' learning. 'Core' learning would include the necessary basic generic skills and it should include an 'extended project'; 'main' learning would be selected by the learners. The report also proposed that 'programmes should be certified by diplomas available at the first four levels of the National Qualifications Framework' (Working Group on 14–19 Reform 2004: 6) Therefore 'successful completion of a programme at a given level should lead to the award of a diploma recognising achievement across the whole programme' (Working Group on 14–19 Reform 2004: 7). The intention of the diploma framework was to be transparent, easily understood and to improve vocational provision.

Ministers, having received the detailed advice they requested, then responded with the 14–19 Education and Skills White Paper, in a matter of months, in February 2005. On the surface it would seem that many of the working group's suggestions had been adopted, with slight tinkering with respect to numbers of available levels and lines; however, closer consideration revealed a different story. The proposals in the White Paper are less student-centred and the framework for qualifications is less unified than anticipated. Hodgson and Spours (2005) explore this lack of cohesion in policy development. Their main criticism is the need for a more unified approach to the 14–19 phase, as is the case in much of the reform in other European countries. They believe unification in vocational qualifications across the European Union will 'bring to an end a political era of upper secondary education dominated by conservative ideology and to open up a new and progressive era of system expansion based on inclusion and collaboration' (Hodgson and Spours 2005: 3). They discuss how the policy process is affected by the political space. The 'opened up political space' following the Tomlinson Report was closed down by the upcoming general election and changes of key ministers, with a:

> White Paper Drafted behind closed doors [. . .] the 14–19 White Paper with its political compromises reminds us of the temporary nature of political space in the English system and the limits of government radicalisation of policy.
>
> (Hodgson and Spours 2005: 6)

Let us finally turn our attention to the implementation of the White Paper (DfEE 2005a) and to where 14–19 education might be heading. An 'Implementation Plan' was presented in December 2005 (DfEE 2005b), and is currently (at the time of writing) going through Parliament as a Bill. In line with recommendations from the Tomlinson report, implementation will be carried out over ten years. Fundamentally, there will be two types of diplomas; 'general' and 'specialized.' The general diploma will be awarded to those achieving five A*–C grade GCSEs, including English and maths, and specialized diplomas will be employer-designed. There will also be a 'functional skills qualification' to be incorporated into specialized diplomas. There will be 14 specialized diplomas, developed by Diploma Development Partnerships (DDPs) and led by the relevant Skills Sector Councils (SSCs). The Qualifications and Curriculum Authority (QCA) will set the standards and accredit the diplomas. The first five specialized diplomas will be ready for teaching in 2008, the next five in 2009 and the final four in 2010. The underlying aim is to raise the participation rate of 17-year-olds from 75 per cent to 90 per cent by 2015.

Keep (2005) highlights some key absences in 14–19 policy debates, in line with those of Fuller and Unwin (2003), with regard to employers and the labour market. Keep comments that previously employers 'have proved unwilling or unable (perhaps sometimes both) to deliver the goods' (Keep 2005: 536). Keep relates his ideas to the new diplomas, noting it is unclear how much consultation there has been between the DfES and SSCs with regard to employers' willingness to engage with the Government's agenda. Given that the employers' role is crucial, their lack of support will surely affect the success of the diplomas. Keep goes on to consider how the inconsistency between the skill demand and the skills provided by vocational education might make the diplomas ineffective. The final point worth considering is the employer opinions of qualifications:

> only 22% of employers said they took qualifications into account 'a lot' when recruiting young people [. . .] with a small number of exceptions, employers place relatively little emphasis on qualifications or specific technical skills or experience when talking about things they look for in potential new recruits.
>
> (Keep 2005: 541)

Keep suggests that 'softer' social attributes, which are often not considered to be certifiable, such as interpersonal skills, are becoming more necessary in the workforce. The Award Scheme Development and Accreditation Network (ASDAN) does aim to certify such skills but, as yet, this is not widely available. Additionally, low-level vocational qualifications, below level 3, are not associated with better financial rewards in salaries: 'Unfortunately, the government's obsessive love affair is not a passion necessarily shared by employers to anything like the same extent' (Keep 2005: 543).

Overall, in terms of curriculum and certification, there appears to be very little change in the *status quo* with regard to the General Diploma, other than greater focus on basic skill development. It would appear then that this 'new' curriculum has been set up on the basis of a divided system from the start, and, in many ways, it appears to replicate many of the issues explored earlier in the chapter in relation to the academic/vocational divide.

One issue that emerges from any review of education and training for the 14–19 age group is that it has always been, and continues to be, a classed and gendered provision (Ball *et al.*, 2000). Many middle-class students have tended to progress though the academic 'gold-standard' route of A-level work. Their career goals have, in the main, been related to some form of higher education and professional work. In contrast, the routes for working-class male and female students have more frequently been circumscribed by stereotypical outcomes in post-compulsory education and training. Working-class young people have been more likely to move out of, and away from, schools where they may well have perceived themselves as 'less successful', towards some form of (almost compulsory) vocational training in FE institutions (Archer and Yamashita 2003). I say 'compulsory' because social welfare benefits are no longer available to most young people aged 16 and this significantly reduces their options.

Simultaneously, a group of young people, mainly those who have done least well in formal schooling, have drifted away from any post-compulsory education and training, working perhaps in the 'black economy'. New Labour has been particularly concerned with this group, which might involve as many as 20 per cent of the national cohort, and have implemented policies designed to support and keep them in the education and training system. New Labour have been concerned that this group might be at risk of longer term social exclusion as a result of their less successful schooling, lack of skills and lack of certification (Ecclestone 2005). One policy imperative has been the development of the Education Maintenance Allowance (EMA) (HERO 2006) that 'pays' students to stay in postcompulsory education and training. Another set of policies lie in the diploma courses that are intended to attract and retain the 'disaffected' 14–19-year-old students, and thereby contribute towards New Labour's 'knowledge economy' and 'learning society'.

Concluding comments

The new vocational diplomas are expected to achieve 'parity of esteem' with academic routes. If this is to have any serious meaning in terms of choice of route and labour market outcomes one aspect of this parity must be some narrowing of the gap in the individual rates of return between academic and vocational qualifications. This in turn means that employers must come to value vocational qualifications more highly, favour them more strongly in recruitment and selection decisions and be willing to pay a significant wage premium to those who possess them [. . .] a very large mountain to climb [. . .] unless and until employers change [. . .] the proposed diplomas will fail.

(Keep 2005: 544)

As Keep notes, there appears to be very little change in the overarching approach to 14–19 education. The introduction of the new diplomas will no doubt cause much upheaval, especially for teachers. Teachers will be required to rewrite schemes of work, yet again; align schemes with a new curriculum; retrain to be able to effectively provide the new framework; liaise with a number of external agencies; and prepare students for new courses and assessments. There will also be a degree of competition between establishments to attract young people to complete these new courses.

I would like to think that this latest initiative will bring progressive change to 14–19 education. However, the seemingly constant revisions to policy have had negligible impact on the archaic divide between academic and vocational education. If every child really matters, then we should have an educational system which does not set up segregating social pathways, as 14–19 education has been doing for so long.

References

Archer, L. and Hiromi Yamashita, H. (2003) 'Knowing their limits'? Identities, inequalities and inner city school leavers' post-16 aspirations, *Journal of Education Policy*, 18(1): 53–69.

Ball, S.J., Maguire, M. and Macrae, S. (2000) *Choice, Pathways and Transitions Post 16: New Youth, New Economies in the Global City.* London: Routledge/Falmer.

Department for Education and Skills (DfES) (2005a) *14–19 Education and Skills Summary.* London: Department for Education and Skills.

Department for Education and Skills (DfES) (2005b) *14–19 Education and Skills: Implementation Plan.* London: Department for Education and Skills.

Ecclestone, K. (2005) *Understanding Assessment and Qualifications in Post-compulsory Education and Training: Principles, Politics and Practice.* Leicester: NIACE.

Fuller, A. and Unwin, L. (1998) Reconceptualising apprenticeship: exploring the relationship between work and learning, *Journal of Vocational Education and Training,* 50(2): 153–73.

Fuller, A. and Unwin, L. (2003) Creating a 'Modern Apprenticeship': a critique of the UK's multi-sector, social inclusion approach, *Journal of Education and Work,* 16(1): 5–25.

Gill, P. and Johnson, S. (2001) 14–19 Education: broadening the curriculum, in J. Dillon and M. Maguire (eds) *Becoming a Teacher: Issues in Secondary Teaching.* Buckingham: Open University Press.

Halliday, J. (in press) Social Justice and Vocational Education, in L. Clarke and C. Winch (eds) *Vocational Education in an International Context; Historical and Philosophical Dimensions.* London: Routledge Taylor & Francis.

Hayward, G. (2004) Vocationalism and the decline of vocational learning in England. Vocational and Business Education and Training in Europe: Qualifications and the World of Work. *Berufs- und Wirtschaftpädagogik,* 7 www.bwpat.de/7eu/.

Hayward, G., Hodgson, A., Johnson, J. *et al.* (2004) *The Nuffield Review of 14–19 Education and Training. Annual Report 2003–04.* London: Nuffield Foundation.

Hayward, G., Hodgson, A., Johnson, J. *et al.* (2005) *The Nuffield Review of 14–19 Education and Training. Annual Report 2004–05.* London: Nuffield Foundation.

Higher Education and research Opportunities (HERO) (2006) Educational Maintenance Allowances. Available at: http://www.support4learning.org.uk/money/financial_support_for_further_education_students/education_maintenance_allowance.cfm (accessed on September 3, 2006).

Hodgson, A. and Spours, K. (2005) *14–19 Education and Training in England: A Historical and System Approach to Policy Analysis.* Discussion Paper 8 for Seminar on Policy Learning in 14–19 Education. www.nuffield14–19review.org.uk.

Hyland, T. (1993) Competence, knowledge and education, *Journal of Philosophy of Education,* 27(1): 57–68.

Hyland, T. (1994) *Competence, Education and NVQs: Dissenting Perspectives.* London: Cassell Education.

Hyland, T. (1997) Reconsidering competence, *Journal of Philosophy of Education,* 31(3): 491–503.

Keep, E. (2005) Reflections on the curious absence of employers, labour market incentives and labour market regulation in English 14–19 policy: first signs of a change of direction? *Journal of Educational Policy,* 20(5): 533–53.

Keep, E. (in press) The multiple paradoxes of state power in the English education and training system, in L. Clarke and C. Winch (eds) *Vocational Education in an International Context; Historical and Philosophical Dimensions.* London: Routledge Taylor & Francis.

Oancea, A. and Hayward, G. (2004) *Patterns of Participation and Attainment 14–19.* Briefing paper for Nuffield Foundation Review of 14–19 Education and Training. www.nuffield14–19review.org.uk.

Pring, R. (1995) *Closing the Gap: Liberal Education and Vocational Preparation.* London: Hodder & Stoughton Educational.

Pring, R. (in press) 14–19 and Lifelong Learning: Distinguishing between Academic and Vocational Learning, in L. Clarke and C. Winch (eds) *Vocational Education in an*

International Context; Historical and Philosophical Dimensions. London: Routledge Taylor & Francis.

Sanderson, M. (1994) *The Missing Stratum: Technical School Education in England 1900–1990s.* London: The Athlone Press.

Smithers, A. and Robinson, P. (1993) *Changes Colleges: Further Education in the Market Place.* London: Council for Industry in and Higher Education.

Stanton, G. (2004) *The organisation of full-time 14–19 provision in the state sector. Nuffield Review of 14–19 Education and Training. Working Paper 13.* London: Nuffield Foundation. www.nuffield14–19review.org.uk.

Taylor, W. (1963) *The Secondary Modern School.* London: Faber and Faber.

The Hadow Report (1926) *The Education of the Adolescent.* London: HM Stationery Office. http://www.dg.dial.pipex.com/documents/hadow/2603.shtml.

Tomlinson, S. (ed.) (1997) *Education 14–19 Critical Perspectives.* London: The Athlone Press.

Working Group on 14–19 Reform (2004) *14–19 Curriculum and Qualification Reform: Final Report.* London: Department for Education and Skills.

Wright, S. (2005) *Young People's Decision Making in 14–19 Education and Training: a Review of the Literature.* Briefing paper for Nuffield Foundation Review of 14–19 Education and Training. www.nuffield14–19review.org.uk.

Wright, S. and Oancea, A. (2005) *Policies for 14–19 Education and Training in England, 1976 to the present day: A Chronology.* Briefing paper for Nuffield Foundation Review of 14–19 Education and Training. www.nuffield14–19review.org.uk.

27

Beyond the subject curriculum: the form tutor's role

Jane Jones

Your mental image of yourself teaching probably involves you explaining key elements of your subject. However, you will spend a significant amount of time in school doing something for which you may have had little preparation and which opens up innumerable opportunities to frustrate and fulfil. Government policy means that schools can be pressed to deliver national policies on such diverse matters as teenage pregnancy, the respect agenda, healthy eating, etc.; it is frequently the form tutor who has to manage this response. Almost certainly, you will be involved as a form tutor within months of starting to teach. With the pressures on young people seemingly increasing with each generation, you will play a major part in the lives of large numbers of pupils in ways in which it is hard to imagine now. This chapter is an attempt to help you to prepare for the challenges that lie ahead beyond your role as subject teacher in your school.

The work of the form tutor cuts across subject specialisms and emphasizes study and coping strategies as well as personal, vocational and life skills, creating a multidimensional role (Startup 2003). Thus, the form tutor needs to provide support and act as first port of call and a guide – in short, be available on a daily basis to provide stability for the pupils. Consequently, the role of the form tutor, which is currently undergoing changes, is challenging, unique and rewarding.

The character and ethos of a school are, according to Tattum, determined by 'decisions about the curriculum, the allocation of resources, the grouping of pupils and the arrangements made for guidance and welfare' (1988: 158). While government policy and funding largely determine factors such as school resources and the content of the curriculum, pupil grouping, student welfare and personal guidance, under the guise and auspices of the pastoral system, still remain within the decision-making processes of individual schools and teachers. Partly in response to teachers' legitimate complaints, over many years, about administrative overload (but mainly as a response to a DfES commissioned report (Smithers and Robinson 2003) on continuing high rates of wastage from the teaching profession), the government published, in 2003, *Raising Standards and Tackling Workload: A National Agreement* (DfES 2003), which brought in a process referred to as 'workforce remodelling'. This initiative was designed to ensure some non-contact time for all teachers and to shift many of their administrative functions, as well as some aspects of the former tutor role, to support staff and to non-teaching staff (Cooper 2005). These members of staff may be referred to as pastoral assistants, behaviour managers or student development leaders, amongst other things.

The agreement was followed by the introduction, in January 2006, of teaching and learning allowances (TLRs). The agreement required all management allowances to be replaced by TLRs by September 2008 with new job descriptions to be agreed with the relevant staff. Since allowances can only be given for teaching and learning responsibilities, with which the existing concept of pastoral support sits uneasily, traditional pastoral posts of responsibility can no longer be remunerated and even the term 'pastoral' is falling out of use. Bottery and Wright (2000) found that, in a large number of secondary schools, the pressure of targets, performance management and the focus on delivering the National Curriculum meant that wider aspects of being an extended professional, for example, in the tutor role, were being displaced (Bottery and Wright 2000). Such a shift, potentially threatening jobs, and also challenging a core belief of many teachers in the pastoral role, has met with some opposition.

Schools have been directed to introduce the changes, and have implemented them in diverse ways. Many are structuring their organizational and pastoral support in ways that reflect the school's strategic awareness, priorities and its culture. The form tutor's role is, doubtless, in transition from the traditional role to something quite different, involving liaising with a team of support staff and using more electronic means to deal with administration and monitoring, thus providing the tutor with the best overview regarding the progress and general development of pupils. Even with a diffusion of the role and ongoing substantial changes that you, as a new tutor have to be aware of, the role is one that remains vital to the well-being of pupils and central to that of being a teacher.

The tutor within the school system

There are over 4500 secondary schools in England and, within each one, the headteacher faces the demanding task of organizing the pupils, staff and other resources to produce an effective learning environment. During the setting up of the comprehensive system in the 1950s and 1960s, considerable thought was given to developing an organizational system in which individual pupils would feel valued, noticed and encouraged in their learning. Some schools – but not many state schools – set up vertical systems, in which three or four pupils from each year group were placed in the same tutor group, resulting in a mixed-age group somewhat akin to a (very large) family, where younger pupils could rely on the help and support of older pupils, as well as on their tutor. In return, older pupils took care of the younger ones in the tutor group, which assisted the development of their social and life skills. However, while the vertical system provided a strong integrating system to support individual pupils, it also created problems, particularly administrative ones.

During research in a Kent school, in 2006, which was about to change from a year (horizontal) group system to a vertical system (Jones 2006), pupils in a Year 7 class stated that they would prefer to be in a form of their own age because that was how they made friends. Their tutor's view was that the group dynamics were crucial in a vertical system, and that the mix of pupils needed to be arranged very carefully. She also stressed that continuity of tutoring was important, as pupils needed time to develop their confidence and to share their feelings, a factor also emphasized by Hornby *et al.* (2003).

By far the most common arrangement found in schools is the horizontal system, in which tutor groups contain pupils from only one year group, which is the system normally found in primary schools (with the form tutor replacing the class teacher). Such a system, with pastoral leaders working with a group of form tutors, creates a pastoral management structure which may, or may not, integrate well with the academic system of heads of department and subject teachers. Whilst this structure brings stability, some Year 10 pupils, for example, in the school mentioned above, reflected that it was 'unfair if you are stuck with a tutor you don't get on with'.

There are, of course, exceptions to the rule, and some schools have combined horizontal and vertical systems with pupils belonging both to a house *and* a year group. In these schools, the year group is the main organizational division, with the house system bolted-on for activities such as competitive sports. It is, however, a focus on making provision for personal growth and achievement rather than the particular type of system that is the key to success (Standish *et al.* 2006).

Learning to be an effective form tutor

A form tutor is the one person, probably in conjunction with a pastoral assistant, who has daily contact with a group of pupils, monitoring their general well-being and possessing an exclusive overview of their progress across all subjects. Just 'being there' is an important factor, providing pupils with what might be the only point of security in the case of pupils with chaotic home lives. When a pupil mistakenly calls a tutor 'Mum' or 'Dad', it can be a powerful reminder of how few adults actually talk *with* rather than *at* their children.

Your own education, in terms of school studies and degree work, may not have prepared you for the variety of routine and not-so-routine tasks that a form tutor may face. Discussing the death of a friend or relative of a pupil, monitoring a target or explaining notices, might well constitute the daily 'pastoral agenda' of a form tutor – all within a very brief time slot. The range of issues raised in those few minutes may be greater than in the rest of your day in school. Admitting to not knowing the right answer may work in lessons, but pupils expect their tutor to follow up the issues they discuss with her or him.

Pupils in a form may come from very different backgrounds to yourself, may hold very different attitudes and may have faced a range of emotional experiences that you may never encounter, except through them. The lives of some pupils may be so fraught with problems that you may wonder how they manage to cope. Trying to empathize without direct experience is challenging, and cannot be learnt quickly. Learning to be a good form tutor may be more demanding than learning to be a teacher of your subject. The role is a highly skilled one, requiring a range of personal qualities, skills and attitudes. One headteacher interviewed by Jones (Jones 2006) described a 'good tutor' as 'one who knows the pupils well, is highly structured and organised, and that includes the fun bits like the end of term parties, sets boundaries so the pupils are clear and well informed, and is fair'.

Observing experienced tutors, taking part in target setting and reviewing sessions, attending parents' evenings, talking to colleagues about your concerns, listening to pupils and hearing their views and keeping up-to-date with official documentation with regard to pastoral concerns – and developing your own experiences – will help you to become an effective tutor. To learn effectively, however, needs commitment on your part, as well as access to the right information. The DfES website is a priority for researching and keeping up-to-date with the constant stream of government initiatives. A key document in this respect is the influential DfES (2004) report, *Every Child Matters*, an all-embracing initiative concerned with the well-being of children from birth to the age of 19. It also provides you with guidelines, case studies and other practical advice to help you acquire the knowledge and skills that will enable you to undertake what is expected of a form tutor as effectively as possible.

Tutor knowledge and skills

In addition to invaluable experience in the classroom, there are many publications and other resources available on PHSE,[1] for example, Best's review of research in the pastoral domain (see further reading) can be used to develop your knowledge and skills in this role. Relevant publications, for example, *The Journal of Beliefs and Values*, contain articles on issues such as sexuality and bereavement, and *Pastoral Care in Education* is a particularly rich resource for tutors. In this journal, you find discussions about topics such as work planners, careers education, citizenship, bereavement courses,

[1] Many schools now deliver citizenship as part of the pastoral, health and social education programme (PHSE). Accordingly, more schools now refer to what they call the PHSCE curriculum.

the development of study skills, personal development, behaviour management, and bullying. The latter has become, in recent years, a considerable social problem in various areas of life and in schools in particular, and there is no shortage of literature on the topic (for example, Sullivan 2005).

Evidence, collected over many years, and in many countries, shows that bullying is usually a much bigger problem than most teachers realize. A pupil who claims to have been bullied must always be taken seriously and a pupil asking for help needs time and reassurance, even if it is not immediately available. This gives a potent message, first to those pupils who are bullied and, even more importantly, to would-be bullies who may be deterred by visible, decisive and speedy action by form tutors. Schools are required to have an anti-bullying policy and the form tutor needs to be familiar with this and with the associated procedures. Furthermore, as a form tutor you are not alone for you will invariably have recourse to the support of experienced colleagues. As long as bullying is endemic to school life, many pupils will experience unhappiness as a result of incidents generated by the school culture. They need to be made aware that the form tutor is the one named person to whom they can turn and who will be fully informed. With sensitive issues, counselling skills are needed and the form tutor, who is categorically not a counsellor, may well have to act as counsellor at times in situations where individual pupils need personal responses. As King (1999: 4) writes:

> The emphasis now is on equipping teachers with basic counselling skills: not training them as counsellors or to work as counsellors, but helping teachers perform their 'pastoral' work more effectively, and enabling them to recognize problems which need referring on to a specialist or a specialist agency.

Pellitteri *et al.* (2006) call this 'emotionally intelligent school counseling'. Such basic skills, King (1999: 4) suggests, would involve 'listening skills, the skills of empathetic understanding, responding skills and a clear awareness of boundary limits'. Some schools have experimented successfully with peer counselling whereby older pupils are trained to listen to and to provide support for younger pupils.[2] Keeping an eye on the education press can alert you to strategies that others have used successfully to deal with what, for you, might seem an intractable problem.

During the 1960s and 1970s, some schools were able to appoint counsellors, but their numbers declined as budgets were tightened in the decades that followed. Counselling pupils will normally be part of the form tutor role, but lack of time and expertise will mean that many issues will, by necessity and perhaps to the benefit of a greater number of pupils, be explored within the tutor group context. The task here is to create a

---

[2] The Workforce Remodelling Agreement's teaching and learning allowances (TLRs) can only be awarded for teaching and learning responsibilities. At time of writing, schools are still wrestling with this regulatory change. Many are starting to appoint behaviour managers/counsellors to manage behaviour issues and attendance problems. The cost of employing these non-teaching personnel is cheaper than paying a teacher for non-contact time to undertake this work. Thus, the traditional binary role of the pastoral team, academic mentoring and behaviour management, is being divided up and reallocated. These sorts of changes will influence and shape pastoral work in the future.

supportive environment and to nurture support through activities such as role play, drama, debate and discussion. One-to-one counselling, with all the time implications involved, should still be the right of pupils, particularly those for whom the form tutor is the only caring adult that they encounter on a daily basis.

Responsibilities and problems take up a fair share of the tutoring time available, but there are humorous moments to be shared within the form group and many occasions when you will be uplifted by their spontaneity, their acts of generosity and by the care that they show for each other. Tutors should also celebrate the full range of achievements of their pupils, sometimes with due pomp and circumstance if certificates are to be awarded, for example, or a quiet word of praise to an individual pupil in another situation. Many pupils tend to dislike being praised in front of their peers – possibly because they are embarrassed or because there is more status in receiving a reprimand. However, good behaviour and good work benefit from reinforcement through appropriate praise.

The negative self-image that results from inadequate feedback about a pupil's ability can manifest itself when it is time to write self-assessments, for example, for a record or statement of achievement, or student portfolio. Pupils are notoriously lacking in confidence when it comes to identifying their strengths and achievements, which are often considerable. It is the form tutor who, as the teacher with an overview of a pupil's progress across all subjects, can coax these strengths out, thereby helping pupils to increase their self-esteem and construct a more positive, more accurate self-image and self-assessment. Following the 'remodelling of the workforce' initiative, monitoring and assessment to focus on individual pupil requirements and learning needs are becoming, increasingly, the key function of the role of the form tutor, as more of the traditional pastoral aspects are devolved to support staff.

Monitoring and assessing

The integration of electronic communication into the everyday life of schools facilitates collecting the tracking data relating to registration, and the recording and monitoring of progress. Once a crucial function of the form tutor, with schools now obliged to report their attendance rates, filling in the register and 'chasing up' absences have become key tasks of the school central administration using appropriate technological support systems. Essentially, the form tutor's role in relation to attendance consists of a single act of entering pupils' presence and absence electronically. One system found in schools is Bromcom, which uses codes for reasons for absence when these have been evidenced by parents or carers (for example, M = medical). Given the greater efficiency of electronic registration, paper registers are rapidly being replaced, at least in secondary schools, and some schools have initiated self-registration, using swipe cards, for their post-16 students. The information is instantaneously available to the school administration, where the designated attendance manager pursues unaccounted absences by phone or email. The attendance manager also enters reasons for absence which have been notified to the school by phone or email.

Schools have facilitated communication with parents by setting up telephone numbers offering a menu that allows parents to report lateness or absence by voicemail rather than handwritten note. A pupil's presence/absence and the reason is therefore available centrally to the form tutor and other staff who teach the pupil. A *bona fide* appointment is an 'authorized absence', although many schools are restricting such absences in the school day and expressly forbid their pupils to go on holiday in term time. From a school's point of view, the absence of even one or two pupils can affect the national test results or, indeed, GCSE percentages. In addition to the 'record book' or 'homework diary' used to monitor and to communicate with parents and guardians, schools have started to use email as a mode of communication with parents. Teachers can now use their laptops to communicate using email between year teams as well as between members of a department and receive whole-staff communication rather than putting up notices in the staff room (which has the added benefit of increasing pupils' privacy: only those who need to know are given personal information about pupils). Technological advances can, thus, assist tutors in identifying irregular attendance patterns and acting quickly in response to this and other behaviours of concern that contribute to pupil unhappiness and underachievement. As with any continuous monitoring, these methods help to identify problems sooner rather than later, allowing for solutions to be negotiated, targets set and achievements recognized and rewarded.

In addition to information on attendance, you will, in your role as form tutor, receive assessments made by colleagues of other subjects on your tutees' learning. Based on this information, and taking the 'whole' pupil into consideration, you will need to work out with the pupil, parents and colleagues an individualized learning plan. The importance of the personalized learning agenda in developing teachers' leadership and mentoring capability, with a view to creating and supporting student autonomy, self-assessment and a sense of pupils' responsibility for their own learning, has been highlighted in the National College for School Leadership's (2005) paper *Leading Personalised Learning in Schools: Helping Individuals Grow*.

Many schools have moved away from the end-of-year summative report and now build in progress reviews, on a one-to-one basis, in tutorial time, in accordance with the widespread adoption of formative practices in classrooms (part of an assessment for learning framework discussed in Chapter 17). This system is more likely to be targeted at older pupils, who may have GCSE support tutorials (Year 10 is a major transition time for pupils who may be launched into a different pace and style of learning and may quickly come to grief without support), but in an increasing number of schools, academic tracking and support starts in Year 7. In fact, target setting and progress reviews are now well established in most schools with proper timetabled slots that enable pupils to have, what one tutor called, 'private quality time for all, not just those seen to be in trouble and singled out' (Jones 2006). Whilst the focus of the system is on academic progress, this tutor also commented that 'it is the form tutor who, alone, sees how personal issues impact on learning' (Jones 2006).

Typically targets will relate academic matters (for example, spelling in English or developing revision strategies), social concerns (for example, lateness or a lack of organization) and extra-curricular activities (after school contributions or interests and responsibilities outside of school). Each pupil will then specify, 'How I am going to achieve this target'. The review provides an opportunity for the pupil to consider 'How am I doing?', and to set new targets. Increasingly, schools organize tutorial days, an arrangement by which the timetable is suspended on particular days so that pupils and their parents can attend interviews with the form tutor to discuss any concerns, as well as progress across their subjects and target setting.

Personal, health, social and citizenship education

The concept of spiritual, moral, social and cultural (SMSC) education, which underpins the National Curriculum, emphasizes the need for a whole-school approach to the drawing up and delivery of a pastoral curriculum (Best 2000). All dimensions of a school, and the curriculum as a whole, contribute to the personal and social development of the pupils in some way. Nonetheless, pastoral programmes will be clearly identifiable in most schools, and many topics, issues, activities and outcomes will be considered best handled by form tutors, as part of a tutorial programme. The tutor's role, which up to now may appear sometimes reactive and random, becomes coherent within the whole-school personal, health, social and citizenship education (PHSCE) structure. In the best systems observed by Ofsted, teams of tutors worked alongside a pastoral leader/student development manager on a range of issues related to personal development relevant to each age group. This strategy often results in a pastoral curriculum built on the identification of issues deemed relevant to a particular age range. Thus a Year 7 group may undertake an induction programme and focus on transition; Year 9 may focus on 'options'; and Year 11 may look at study skills or careers. A spiralling model, whereby themes are constantly revisited (but in different degrees and in different ways) optimizes learning opportunities and deepens understanding of the issues. Crucially, the success of the PHSCE programmes depends, to a large extent, on a school's commitment to them. Effective PHSCE delivery requires:

- an adequate time allocation
- ownership of materials (participation by staff in their creation)
- variety of inputs (outside speakers, videos, debates, etc.)
- managerial support.

Unfortunately, you will find that all these factors are not always available, and for historical and financial reasons, the programmes are typically delivered by form tutors as an 'add on' to their subject. Schools with a more strategic awareness of the purpose of TLRs, are devising more effective and imaginative ways of delivering PHSCE; for example, timetabling whole days for teaching the programmes and developing the expertise of a team of selected form tutors to teach them, enabling them to show the initiative and creativity that they invariably demonstrate in their subject teaching. In such cases, tutors can seek to develop tutorial skills that can enhance the learning environment for all the pupils, and enable them to take advantage, on a daily basis, of all that the school offers. In the longer term, tutors help pupils to feel that they are an integrated and important part of classroom and school life and to develop the skills and understanding needed to live confident, healthy and independent lives.

Whole-school worship and moral education

The majority of schools have experienced some difficulty in responding to the legal requirement for a collective act of worship, although as Gill (2000: 110) asserts: 'Most schools claim to make a regular provision for their pupils which, taken over a year, incorporate a broadly religious dimension.' The provision might include whole-school assemblies, tutor and year group assemblies, and opportunities for individual silent reflection. In county primary, denominational and independent schools, Gill found that assemblies were considered an opportunity for the pupils 'to encounter the possibility of religious commitment' (Gill 2000: 109). In some schools, notably denominational ones, teachers were able to demonstrate, and share, their faith, while in others teachers experienced a personal dilemma, as Gill (2000: 110) explains:

> in the conflict they experience between their desire to be seen by pupils to uphold the law in respect of a religious activity in which they feel unable to participate, while retaining their standing with pupils as individuals of personal and professional integrity.

It will be important for you to assert your beliefs and to recognize your own personal dilemmas, but also to resolve and accommodate these within the culture and ethos of the school in which you have chosen to work. At the very least, you will be expected to accompany pupils to assemblies, support them in form assemblies, and undertake whatever tasks are required of you in that aspect of tutor time that comprises the collective act of worship.

Gill discovered a more fulsome acceptance by teachers of a responsibility to contribute, generally, to the moral development of the pupils. This aspect of the teachers' role, for example, took place in PHSCE or form time, and focused on social interactions and the application of moral principles, such as justice and respect, and the discouragement of prejudice, bullying and racism. According to Gill, the teachers sometimes organized structured debates, while on other occasions, spontaneous discussion arose as a result of 'critical incidents' in school.

Marland and Rogers suggest that the tutor's role is to identify issues and prompt group discussion, enabling pupils not just to arrive at decisions, but to focus on how to arrive at decisions. They argue that:

> The process of tutoring is empowering the tutee, but with the giving of

self-power must go the development of the ability to be sensitive and appropriately generous. Morality and ethics are at the heart of tutoring.

(Marland and Rogers 1997: 26)

In my own research with adolescent girls (Jones 2006), many said that they liked the opportunity to gather in a larger group, especially if pupils were presenting an assembly, or if they had a special visitor, or if the focus of an assembly was an issue of concern and interest to them. Likewise, they enjoyed debates on similar themes in PHSCE, especially where they had an opportunity to air their views (and for these not to be scorned by tutors), and to be listened to with seriousness and respect. Gill, in her research, found that 'what young people value most is sincerity and relevance' (Gill 2000: 114). Pupils had strong feelings about apparent injustices and the problems of modern society, and were greatly moved by natural catastrophes and other disasters, possessing an instinctive desire to want to help. As Gill suggests: 'Contemporary issues, current affairs and a wider discussion about the problems which confront the young in an imperfect world should receive a much greater emphasis' (Gill 2000: 115). She echoes Marland and Rogers' suggestion for the need to create opportunities for pupil participation and involvement in the exploration of such issues. You, as form tutor, have a role in helping to create such opportunities within the whole-school spiritual, moral, social and cultural (SMSC) development framework and in helping the pupils to relate these concerns to their own lives.

Pupils' perceptions

The pastoral system, as part of your new school's ethos and culture, provides a framework for initiating and sustaining shared perspectives of individual pupils. In secondary school, pupils are frequently taught by ten, or more, teachers and may be perceived differently by each one. This atomistic approach does little to help them to create a sense of identity as learners and as participants in the school system. The form tutor's role within the system is to mediate between the teachers, parents and learners. By presenting a more complete picture of the pupils in a class to its teachers, you may ensure that future interactions take place in an informed and stable environment – neither marred nor exaggerated by uncharacteristic episodes or behaviours.

To do so, it is useful to know how the organization, in this case the school, is perceived by the individual, that is the pupils, since this perception is, as Handy and Aitken (1988) point out, one of the most important factors in organizational theory. To investigate this issue, I undertook a small-scale survey in a large, mixed London comprehensive in 1995 (Jones 1995) and again in 2006 (Jones 2006) in a school in Kent, and found remarkably similar and consistent results in terms of the pupils' perceptions of the form tutor role. In each case, 40 pupils across years 7–11 were asked:

- What do you think a form tutor is for?
- What makes a good form tutor?

The 1995 cohort of pupils had very clear ideas, and gave responses that were remarkable in their uniformity. The responses to the first question focused primarily on the pastoral support role, evidenced by comments such as 'to look after you', 'to see how you're doing' and 'to help you solve your problems'. Some aspects of organization and administration were identified, such as 'to take the register', 'to watch punctuality' and 'to help the kids during fire drills'. Most surprising of all, was the fact that almost every response given made reference to what the pupils saw as a central disciplinary function of the tutor role, expressed in a variety of ways: 'to teach you to behave', 'to stop us from talking and getting into trouble' and, more graphically, 'to stop us from getting up and ranging around and to stop fights'. The 2006 cohort made similar comments, although they distinguished between the 'talking about problems' role of the pastoral assistants and the monitoring role of their form tutors: 'she checks our homework diaries, talks about progress, gives out notices'. They were quite clear that their first point of contact was always the form tutor.

Responses to the second question exemplified and validated these comments, with the pupils suggesting the following qualities as essential for a 'good' form tutor:

- someone who listens
- [someone who has] a sense of humour
- [someone who is] helpful and understanding
- [someone who is] strict and having the ability to keep order.

Typical responses were: 'She talks to people a lot and listens and she's good fun'; 'He's funny and he helps his tutor group and he's good at keeping order' and 'He's funny, but strict but he makes you laugh when he's strict.'

You can carry out a similar piece of research to find out and verify the expectations your pupils have of you as their tutor. The results from the research I undertook reflect two very basic pupil needs: first individual care and support, and, second, the need for the teacher to maintain orderliness within the peer group. This conclusion concurs with Delamont's enduring assertion that the 'main strength of a teacher's position is that, in general, pupils want her to teach and keep them in order' (1983: 90). While the demands the pupils put on teachers may seem simple, the means of providing for their needs remains a challenging and diversified task in the case of the form tutor. Sizing up pupils is a continuous and evolving task for you, as form tutor, as you will be in a unique position – perceiving pupils in a holistic manner, mapping their strengths and weaknesses, and recognizing their successes and needs. With this perspective in mind, the form tutor fosters and supports the classroom interactions to assist pupil learning and development.

Concluding comments

The form tutor's role then, in conjunction with pastoral team colleagues, is to cohere all aspects of the pastoral and academic curricula. The tutor is, accordingly, 'the integrative centre for the school's whole curriculum' (Marland and Rogers 1997: 6). Research such as that by Weare (2005), shows that schools that focus on this aspect of their work with young people, actually enhance pupil attainment. These schools are also aware of changes and developments and, after critical analysis, integrate these into their work. Currently, there is an upsurge of interest in emotional intelligence and literacy, and helping youngsters to be happy and confident through enhancing their self-understanding, their capacity to understand others and their ability to manage and reduce conflict and stress. The role of the tutor is going through an exciting renaissance, and an important task for experienced and new form tutors, like yourself, is to consider how you can elaborate the developmental and creative potential of this role and the special contribution you can make in each of your tutees' personal development.[3] It is a role that, though challenging and changing, is immensely rewarding, and a good form tutor, who adheres to being firm, friendly and fair, is rarely forgotten.

References

Best, R. (ed.) (2000) *Education for Spiritual, Moral, Social and Cultural Development.* London: Continuum.

Bottery, M. and Wright, N. (2000) *Teachers and the State.* London: Routledge.

Clarke, P. (2000) *Target Setting.* London: RoutledgeFalmer.

Cooper, V. (2005) *Support Staff in Schools: Promoting the Emotional and Social Development of Children and Young People.* London: National Children's Bureau.

Delamont, S. (1983) *Interaction in the Classroom.* London: Methuen.

Department for Education and Skills (DfES) (2003) *Raising Standards and Tackling Workload: A National Agreement.* Available at http://www.remodelling.org/remodelling/nationalagreement.aspx (accessed on September 5, 2006).

Department for Education and Skills (DfES) (2004) *Every Child Matters: Change for Children.* London: DfES.

Gill, J. (2000) The act of collective worship, in R. Best (ed.) *Education for Spiritual, Moral, Social and Cultural Development.* London: Continuum.

Handy, C.B. and Aitken, R. (1988) *Understanding Schools as Organizations.* London: Penguin.

Her Majesty's Stationery Office (HMSO) (2002) *A Time for Standards.* London: The Stationery Office.

Her Majesty's Stationery Office (HMSO) (2004) *The Children Act.* London: The Stationery Office.

Hornby, G., Hall, C. and Hall, E. (2003) (eds) *Counselling Pupils in School: Skills and Strategies for Teachers.* London: RoutledgeFalmer.

Jones, J. (1995) *What Makes a Good Form Tutor?* King's College London: unpublished paper.

[3] The form tutor's role is currently undergoing substantial changes, as outlined above. Some of the traditional duties, such as collecting money and analysing attendance figures, have already been passed to non-teaching members of the school staff such as the attendance manager. In the future, it may be that the work of the teacher will become more like that of her other European colleagues, where form tutors and heads of year are unknown. At time of writing, it is too early to know what the longer-term impact of changes in the TLRs will be for this area of work in school. There is a transition underway, from the more traditional role, to a different model whose details are yet unclear.

Jones, J. (2006) *Student Perceptions of In-school Tutoring and Mentoring*. King's College London: unpublished paper.

King, G. (1999) *Counselling Skills for Teachers. Talking Matters*. Buckingham: Open University Press.

Marland, M. and Rogers, R. (1997) *The Art of the Tutor. Developing Your Role in the Secondary School*. London: David Fulton.

National College for School Leadership (NCSL) (2005) *Leading Personalised Learning: Helping Individuals Grow*. Nottingham: NCSL.

Pellitteri, J., Stern, R., Shelton, C. and Muller-Ackerman, B. (eds) (2006) *Emotionally Intelligent School Counseling*. Mahwah, NJ: Lawrence Erlbaum.

Smithers, A. and Robinson, P. (2003) *Factors Affecting Teachers' Decisions to Leave the Profession*. Nottingham: DfES.

Standish, P., Smeyers, P. and Smith, R. (2006) (eds) *The Therapy of Education: Philosophy, Happiness and Personal Growth*. Basingstoke: Palgrave Macmillan.

Startup, I. (2003) *Running Your Tutor Group*. London: Continuum.

Sullivan, K. (2005) *Bullying: How to Spot it and How to Stop it; A Guide for Parents and Teachers*. London: Rodale.

Tattum, D. (1988) Control and welfare: towards a theory of constructive discipline in schools, in R. Dale, R. Fergusson and A. Robinson (eds) *Frameworks for Teaching*. London: Hodder & Stoughton.

Weare, K. (2005) *Improving Learning Through Emotional Literacy*. London: Paul Chapman.

Further reading

Bullock, K. and Wilkeley, F. (2004) *Whose Learning? The Role of the Personal Tutor*. Maidenhead: Open University Press.

Burgess, R.G. (1988) House staff and departmental staff, in R. Dale, R. Fergusson and A. Robinson (eds) *Frameworks for Teaching*. London: Hodder & Stoughton.

Hamblin, D. (1993) *Tutor as Counsellor*. Oxford: Basil Blackwell.

Pring, R. (1984) *Personal and Social Education in the Curriculum*. London: Hodder & Stoughton.

Qualifications and Curriculum Authority (QCA) (1997) *The Promotion of Pupils' Spiritual, Moral and Cultural Development: Draft Guidance for Pilot Work*. London: QCA.

Tindall, J.A. (1994) *Peer Programs: An In-Depth Look at Peer Helping, Planning, Implementation and Administration*. Bristol, PA: Accelerated Learning. Available at: http://www.bera.ac.uk/pdfs/BEST-PastoralCare&PSE.pdf (accessed on September 5, 2006).

28

What's next? CPD and the whole school

Philip Adey

Continuing to learn

Rosenholtz (1989) made an extensive study of schools in Tennessee. Some were well set up with well-qualified teachers, while others were in difficult areas where it was hard to recruit staff, and these often resorted (illegally) to employing unqualified individuals. Rosenholtz distinguished schools which she described as 'learning enriched', where there was a positive attitude to curriculum change and new learning methods, from 'learning impoverished' schools where teachers basically went through the motions of transmitting set textbook material to the students. She asked hundreds of teachers an apparently simple question: 'How long did it take you to learn to teach?' (You might pause to consider how long you think it will take you to master the art of being an excellent teacher and, if you are brave, you might try asking the same question of a few teachers in your practice schools.)

What Rosenholtz discovered was that in the impoverished schools teachers tended to answer something like 'Oh two or three years' while those in the learning enriched schools gave a completely different sort of answer. They would be far more likely to say, 'Oh I'm still learning' or 'You've never learned it all', however long they had been teaching. You should not find this depressing, it is the sign of professional activity (see Chapter 2 for a full account of what it means to be a professional). Teaching is not simply a skill which can be mastered in a finite period of time; it is a complex professional art which you will continue to develop throughout your teaching career. And that is one of the things that makes it so engaging.

Continuing Professional Development, (CPD) should be just that, a process of professional development which continues throughout your teaching career. Here are some of the types of CPD in which you may engage:

- learning specific skills, such as use of the interactive whiteboard
- updating your subject knowledge and making it part of your teaching repertoire
- developing your general teaching methods or introducing new ones, such as questioning skills, behaviour management, or teaching for high-level thinking
- preparing you for increased responsibilities, for example, a course for new heads of department.

Of these, only the first is a relatively simple matter of acquiring new skills which you will readily master with adequate practice. All of the others will require some conceptual development and possibly even belief changes on your part. They will inevitably take time and, if effective, will lead to changes in your practice and to changes in your students, such as better learning, better thinking, or better behaviour. Such changes are not earned lightly and in this chapter I will explore some of the key indicators of *effective* professional development and try to offer some sort of 'buyer's guide' to help you judge when professional development is worth pursuing and when it is not.

Drivers of professional development

Your development as a professional has parallels with the ways in which your students develop understanding of your subject area, but it also has unique features. Professional development involves *conceptual change*, and this is of the same type as the conceptual change you are trying to engender in your students. It also requires *reflection on practice* and this may have a parallel in your students' learning, if you are in the habit of encouraging them to be metacognitive (for example, asking them to think back to how they learned something, or what mistakes they made and how they corrected them). Finally, your professional development requires you to practise new skills so that they become intuitive, and this is rather particular to the development of professional skills. This section will consider each of these 'drivers' in turn.

Conceptual change

Borko and Puttnam (1995) put a cognitive-psychological perspective on professional development in which change in practice is associated with changes in the inner mental workings of teachers and their constructions of new understandings of the process of learning. An example of approaching professional development in the context of conceptual change is provided by Mevarech (1995) who discusses the role of teachers' prior conceptions of the nature of learning and describes the U-shaped learning curve which they encounter when trying to replace one skill, and the epistemology on which it is based, with another. Bell and Gilbert (1996) also approach the professional development of teachers from a constructivist perspective, showing how teachers need to interrogate their own current constructs of teaching and learning before they are ready to re-construct new beliefs. The value of this conceptualization of teacher change is that it can draw on the extensive parallel literature on conceptual change and attitude change in students. It leads us to focus on teachers' prior conceptions and to recognize that you are unlikely to make significant changes in practice unless you face up to and, if necessary, challenge your current deep-rooted beliefs about the nature of knowledge transmission. It indicates that such change is likely to be a slow and difficult process, and that real change in practice will not arise from short programmes of instruction, especially when those programmes take place in a centre removed from your own classroom.

In focusing on the need to tackle fundamental concepts and attitudes, I am not necessarily prescribing that this is the first thing that must happen before change in teaching practice can occur. Indeed Guskey (1986) has argued persuasively that changes in teachers' beliefs and attitudes may well follow the change in perceived student responses which come about from changed teaching practice. Nevertheless, whether they are a precursor or a consequence, such deep-seated changes are necessary for permanent effects on teacher practice.

Reflection on practice

The idea of the teacher as a reflective practitioner has had a long and respectable history in the literature. For example, Baird et al. (1991) have shown the central role that reflection – both on classroom practice and on the phenomena of teaching and learning – has in the pedagogical development process of both pre-service student teachers and experienced teachers on in-service courses. More recently, Cooper and Boyd (1999) have described a scheme of peer- and group-oriented reflection on practice developed amongst teachers in a New York City school district which provided a systemic self-help strategy for the long-term maintenance of innovative methods in classrooms.

Reflection may be achieved through diaries or other forms of logs, or orally at 'feedback' sessions with colleagues and course leaders. You benefit from such feedback sessions through putting your experiences and associated feelings, both positive and negative, into words and discussing them with peers.

Intuitive knowledge in teaching practice

It is now well accepted that expert practitioners possess a complex personal knowledge base which they draw upon intuitively. This knowledge base is acquired through training and experience but individuals may not always be able to articulate why they do what they do (Atkinson and Claxton 2000; McMahon 2000).

In discussing the intuitive nature of much of the procedural knowledge of teaching, it is important not to confuse the ideas of 'intuitive' and 'instinctive'. The latter implies something in-built, perhaps a personality factor over which no normal professional development course could be expected to have much influence. 'Intuitive', on the other hand, implies a behaviour which occurs without explicit cognition at the moment at which it arises. The basis of the behaviour remains in the unconscious. The term 'implicit knowledge' is used for this type of unconscious understanding which gives rise to intuitive behaviour (Tomlinson 1998). Intuition is how, as teachers, we react almost instantaneously to situations as they arise in the complex social environment of the classroom. It would be impossible to proceed through every classroom moment entirely on the basis of rational and conscious decision making or problem solving. The 'professional' response in such situations depends much on intuition, a process well described by Brown and Coles (2000). The important point here is that this intuitive behaviour is based on our implicit knowledge, and that knowledge is based on previous situations and on the constructs we have built on such experience but not necessarily externalized or made conscious.

Such implicit knowledge may be an influence for good or for ill in the direction it proposes for action. Implicit knowledge can be derived from working in a traditional context rooted in an authoritarian view of teacher–student relationships and based on a simple transmission epistemology. On the other hand, it may be derived from a combination of a personal philosophy of guided democracy with some experience of the process of constructivism, and the observation of colleagues who have shown how all students can be encouraged to contribute to the construction of their own understandings. This relates to the 'professional' strand in Bell and Gilbert's (1996) three-part model of the professional development of science teachers.

These three strands of thought on the nature of professional development (concept change, reflection and intuition) are not alternatives. On the contrary, they intertwine and feed into one another. What is an effective way of inducing a process of conceptual change? Why, to encourage reflection. And what is the basis of the intuitive knowledge which guides action? It is the underlying conceptions and attitudes of the individual. Guided reflection assists the process of conceptual change, and conceptual change re-structures the intuitive knowledge upon which teaching practice rests. In his seminal work on professional development, Schön (1987) shows how reflection is an essential part of the process by which teachers incorporate the perceived needs of a situation within their own system of beliefs, and this is all part of the development of their 'professional artistry'. This is a good description of practice arising from implicit understandings.

The practicalities of effective professional development

Recently, colleagues and I (Adey *et al.* 2004) were able to undertake a comprehensive study of the factors which make for effective professional development, where we interpreted 'effective' rather stringently, as professional development which has a real effect on teachers and on their students. The factors which determine whether a professional development programme is effective or ineffective fall into two broad categories: those internal to the school (such as school ethos, the senior management, and the attitudes of teachers) and those which are more to do with the professional development programme itself (such as its duration, intensity, quality and subject matter). Altogether the factors can be grouped as two school-level factors, and two professional development programme level factors. We will deal with the latter first and rather briefly (as you have less direct control over them) and then attend more closely to the internal school factors which determine the effectiveness of professional development.

Effective professional development programmes

What is being introduced?

Firstly, the material or method being introduced by the professional development must itself have proven value. Fullan and Stiegelbauer (1991) emphasize the pointlessness of organizing professional development for an innovation which is not itself worthwhile or of established quality. They attribute failure of the post-Sputnik reforms in science education in the USA to the fact that the innovations were driven by politicians and had not been established as educationally sound. In selecting a professional development experience from those on offer, ask yourself: Does the innovation being introduced have any sound theoretical foundation? Is any good evidence offered for the effectiveness of the innovation? As an example, a professional development programme introducing the idea of 'learning styles' (visual, auditory, kinaesthetic) may be fun, may be well presented, and may appear plausible but you will not find many psychologists who give any credence to the validity of learning styles, nor will you find any evidence (in peer reviewed academic journals) for the efficacy of labelling children with a supposed learning style (Adey *et al.* 1999; Coffield *et al.* 2004).

How is it being introduced?

Secondly, the quality and quantity of the professional development programme matters. The one-shot, in-service education and training (INSET) day is universally recognized as a complete waste of time for bringing about any real change in teaching practice or student learning, but how many 'shots' are needed to be effective? Fullan and Stiegelbauer (1991, Chapter 4) think that two years is a minimum for real change to occur and Joyce and Weil (1986) believe that a new pedagogic skill requires 30 hours of practice before it becomes intuitive. Our own experience of running cognitive acceleration programmes (see Adey *et al.* 2004) for the last 15 years suggests that although there can be some trade-off between the intensity and the longevity of a programme, the general guidelines of two years/30 hours are sound. This estimate of a minimum requirement is entirely consistent with the notion that real change in practice requires conceptual change in the teacher, and conceptual change is well known to be slow. The building of new skills into intuitive practice must require plenty of practice aided by opportunities for reflection. It is more for the professional development designers and school senior management than it is for a newly qualified teacher to consider how these difficult-sounding requirements can be met, but you should at least be aware of the potential problem.

As for the quality of presentations on professional development courses, nothing is less convincing or more ironic than a formal lecture on the benefits of constructivist teaching. It seems obvious that a teacher is unlikely to be encouraged to use active methods in the classroom by a monologue delivered from the front of the room. This seems so obvious that it would hardly seem worth writing, had we not ourselves frequently experienced such mis-matches between message and delivery method. So, yes, I will spell it out: if you want to promote teachers' use of cognitive conflict, then present your teacher audience with some cognitive conflict at their own level. If you want to encourage teachers to promote social construction in their classrooms, the professional development course should have activities for teachers which can only be solved by collaboration with colleagues.

Finally, a professional development programme which fails to reach into the classroom will fail. There must be some mechanism by which, as you try new methods in your own classroom, you can enlist a critical friend to observe your efforts and provide coaching. From a meta-analysis of nearly 200 studies of the effect of professional development, Joyce and Showers (1988) concluded that of all the features which are normally incorporated into professional development programmes, it was coaching which proved to be an essential ingredient when the outcome measurement was student change. Coaching in innovative teaching methods can be provided by peers, by senior colleagues, by the professional development tutors, or by local authority advisers, and it may be managed using video recordings. But it must, emphatically, be distinguished from appraisal or inspection. Coaching is a friendly, supportive, and non-judgemental process.

An effective environment

Collegiality

Notwithstanding the main focus of this book on the teacher her- or himself, it is clear from the literature and from experience that teachers are rarely if ever able to make real changes in their pedagogy unless the school environment in which they find themselves is, at the very least, tolerant of innovation. My colleague Nicki Landau produced some very deep case studies of teachers engaged in long-term professional development programmes (Chapter 8 of Adey *et al.* 2004). She looked into the situations of teachers whose attitudes to change were either positive or negative, working in schools whose ethos was either supportive or unsupportive of change. Obviously not much can be expected of a negative teacher in an unsupportive school, while the positive teacher in a supportive environment must fly. The interesting cases were the other two combinations and they tell us a lot about the nature of a 'supportive school ethos'. It turns out that there are two main aspects to this: one is the presence or absence of collegial support and the opportunity to share experiences informally but frequently; and the other is more related to the extent to which innovation is embedded in the management structure of the school.

Stoll and Fink (1996) list collegiality as one of ten features of a positive school culture (which include also shared goals and responsibility for success, continuous improvement, lifelong learning, risk taking, support, mutual respect, openness, celebration and humour), but under collegiality they note that:

> this much used but complex concept involves mutual sharing and assistance, an orientation towards the school as a whole, and is spontaneous, voluntary, development-oriented, unscheduled, and unpredictable.
>
> (Stoll and Fink 1996: 93–4)

Teachers who are trying to change their practice find it extremely difficult to be 'different' from their colleagues in the same school. Schools which are most successful in taking on an innovation are ones in which there was much communication between teachers in the department about the new methods. No one individual, however well-motivated and energised, can maintain a new method of teaching if she or he feels isolated. McLaughlin (1994: 33) quoted by Fullan (1995) reported that:

> as we looked across our sites at teachers who report a high sense of efficacy, who feel successful with today's students, we noticed that while these teachers differ along a number of dimensions . . . all shared this one characteristic: membership in some kind of strong professional community.

Just what this collegiality looks like on the ground can be described on a scale from teachers having virtually no professional conversations with one another, through informal chats about the innovation in the corridor or over coffee, to the situation where one or two members of a department have responsibility for overseeing the implementation, and can act as sounding-boards for the others as they try out novel approaches. Better again is the addition of regularly scheduled meetings devoted to assessing progress in implementing the innovation, and best of all is some form of peer-coaching. Units of collegiality within schools form subcultures which may be productive (as in the case of a department that happily shares both professional and social experiences) or may be 'Balkan' (Stoll and Fink 1996), a carping and disruptive influence.

Senior management

Critical to establishing a school ethos supportive of change and development is the senior management team (SMT). Joyce *et al.* (1999) place much emphasis on the necessity of effective leadership for the implementation of any educational innovation, as do Fullan (2001); Mortimore *et al.* (1988) and most other writers on the subject of effective schools. There are two particular aspects where the headteacher's role is necessary, without which professional development is unlikely to be effective. The first is in recognizing the time required for in-school professional development, and the second is in building the innovation into the structure of school, or at least of the department. These correspond roughly to two of the key features which Fullan and Stiegelbauer (1991) report as essential if an innovation is to become institutionalized: the commitment of the headteacher and the incorporation of structural changes into school and classroom policy. Let us consider each of these in turn.

All of the strategies described in the last section for maximizing productive collegiality depend critically on recognition by managers in the school – typically the headteacher and the head of department – that investment in time for sharing amongst teachers is at least as important as is time for in-service training provided by outsiders. I have, from time to time, been quite surprised to find that a headteacher who is prepared to find a significant sum of money for a professional development programme then baulks at creating the time for teachers to meet together to share experiences and to develop their practice collaboratively within the department. This occasional headteacher seems to act as if paying the money was all that was required for magic to follow. The best professional development programme in the world will have no deep-seated effect on practice if there is no active support mechanism for teachers introducing new methods, to ensure that the hard work involved in high-quality teaching is recognized, and to establish methods of sharing practice.

The second aspect, a common factor in failing and struggling schools, is the absence of any structural sustainability built into the school. It is the responsibility of senior management in the school to provide systems which ensure that a method or approach that has been introduced and which is still considered positively is actually maintained. Practical signals that an innovation has been adopted into the structure include requests from the headteacher for updates on the implementation, attention by management to timetabling requirements, and the inclusion of the innovation in departmental policy documents and development plans. Without the establishment of such sustaining structures, efforts put into in-service work are in danger of being lost when one or two key teachers leave the school.

Concluding comments

As you progress through your career over, with luck, 30 or even 40 years from beginning teacher to NQT, accruing new responsibilities in the pastoral and subject areas, then increasingly demanding management posts, possibly back into academia, or into local authority advisory roles, or out to curriculum projects, or through union activity, or straight through the school system to headteacher of increasingly demanding schools, at every step you will be meeting new challenges. You will need to acquire new skills and new understandings, learn to see things from new perspectives, occasionally even to change camps as from poacher to gamekeeper. At every step, grab what opportunities arise for professional development. Some of it will be inspiring, some of it adequate, and some of it rubbish. As a rough guide to finding your way through the maze of professional development on offer, ask these questions (all based on principles summarized in this chapter, and spelled out in Adey *et al.* (2004):

- Will there be an opportunity to share the professional development experience with others, or is it likely to remain an individual personal experience? If the latter, beware.
- Looking at what a professional development programme offers, ask about theoretical bases, whether the programme shows any evidence of effect on students, and whether the teachers who are to use it find the materials accessible and relevant.
- Find out whatever you can about the quality of delivery. Look for active workshop approaches.
- Does the programme claim to lead to changes in students' achievement, motivation, or other characteristics on the basis of a short one-off intensive course? If so, be sceptical. Effective programmes should provide for follow-up which explores implementation and actually assists you in trying new methods in your own classroom.
- Look to your school: are senior managers prepared to make any structural changes to the timetable and/or to school and department development plans to maximize the chance of an innovation becoming a long-lived feature of the school? If not, you may be wasting your time.

And as you progress through your career, and find yourself in a position where you are allocating CPD funds within a school, bear in mind the difficulties of managing effective (as opposed to stylish) professional development for yourself and colleagues. It may be better to distribute the funds 'unfairly' across departments in order to concentrate funds where they have a chance to be effective than to be 'fair' in the distribution of one-day INSETs, not one of which will have any effect at all on classroom practice.

No, you will not have got it all sorted out in a couple of years' time. If you are fortunate you will continue to learn and develop more complex subject knowledge, pastoral understanding, and management capabilities throughout your career. That's a pretty exciting prospect.

References

Adey, P., Fairbrother, R. and Wiliam, D. (1999) *A Review of Research on Learning Strategies and learning styles*. London: King's College.

Adey, P., Hewitt, G., Hewitt, J. and Landau, N. (2004) *The Professional Development of Teachers: Practice and Theory*. Dordrecht: Kluwer Academic.

Atkinson, T. and Claxton, G. (eds) (2000) *The Intuitive Practitioner. On the Value of Not Always Knowing What One is Doing*. Buckingham: Open University Press.

Baird, J.R., Fensham, P.J., Gunstone, R.F. and White, R.T. (1991) The importance of reflection in improving science teaching and learning, *Journal of Research in Science Teaching*, 28(2), 163–82.

Bell, B. and Gilbert, J. (1996) *Teacher Development: A Model for Science Education*. London: Falmer.

Borko, H. and Puttnam, R.T. (1995) Expanding a teacher's knowledge base: a cognitive psychological perspective on professional development, in T.R. Guskey and M. Hubermann (eds) *Professional Development in Education: New Paradigms and Practices*. New York: Teachers College Press.

Brown, L. and Coles, A. (2000) Complex decision making in the classroom: the teacher as an intuitive practitioner, in T. Atkinson and G. Glaxton (eds) *The Intuitive Practitioner. On the Value of Not Always Knowing What One is Doing*. Buckingham: Open University Press.

Coffield, F., Moseley, D., Hall, E. and Ecclestone, K. (2004) *Learning Styles and Pedagogy in Post-16 Learning*. London: Learning and Skills Research Centre.

Cooper, C. and Boyd, J. (1999) Creating sustained professional growth through collaborative reflection, in C.M. Brody and N. Davidson (eds) *Professional Development for Cooperative Learning*. Albany: State University of New York Press.

Fullan, M. (1995) The limits and potential of professional development, in T.R. Guskey and M. Habermann (eds) *Professional Development in Education: New Paradigms and Practises*. New York: Teachers College Press.

Fullan, M. (2001) *Leading in a Culture of Change*. San Francisco: Jossey-Bass.

Fullan, M.G. and Stiegelbauer, S. (1991) *The New Meaning of Educational Change*. London: Cassell.

Guskey, T.R. (1986) Staff development and the process of teacher change, *Educational Researcher*, 15(5), 5–12.

Joyce, B., Calhoun, E. and Hopkins, D. (1999) *The New Structure of School Improvement*. Buckingham: Open University Press.

Joyce, B. and Showers, B. (1988) *Student Achievement through Staff Development* (1st edn). New York: Longman.

Joyce, B. and Weil, M. (1986) *Models of Teaching* (3rd edn). Englewood Cliffs: Prentice Hall.

McLaughlin, M. (1994) Strategic sites for teachers professional development, in P. Grimmett and J. Neufeld (eds) *Teacher Development and the Struggle for Authenticity: Professional Growth and Restructuring in a Context of Change*. New York: Teachers College Press.

McMahon, A. (2000) The development of professional intuition, in T. Atkinson and G. Glaxton (eds) *The Intuitive Practitioner. On the Value of Not Always Knowing What One is Doing*. Buckingham: Open University Press.

Mevarech, Z.E. (1995) Teachers' paths on the way to and from the professional development forum, in M. Hubermann (ed.) *Professional Development in Education: New Paradigms and Practises*. New York: Teachers' College Press.

Mortimore, P., Sammons, P., Ecob, R., Stoll, L. and Lewis, D. (1988) *School Matters: The Junior Years*. Salisbury: Open Books.

Rosenholtz, S.J. (1989) *Teachers' Workplace: The Social Organization of Schools*. New York: Longman.

Schön, D.A. (1987) *Educating the Reflective Practitioner*. San Francisco: Jossey-Bass.

Stoll, L. and Fink, D. (1996) *Changing Our Schools: Linking School Effectiveness and School Improvement*. Buckingham: Open University Press.

Tomlinson, P. (1998) *Implicit Learning and Teacher Preparation: Potential Implications of Recent Theory and Research*. Brighton: British Psychological Society Annual Conference.

Index